*The Transformation
of Criminal Justice*

Studies in Legal History

Published by the
University of North Carolina Press
in association with the
American Society for Legal History

Editor
Thomas A. Green

Allen Steinberg

The Transformation
of Criminal Justice
Philadelphia,
1800–1880

The University of North Carolina Press

Chapel Hill and London

For Susan and Zachary

© 1989 The University of North Carolina Press
All rights reserved
Manufactured in the United States of America

The paper in this book meets the guidelines for
permanence and durability of the Committee
on Production Guidelines for Book Longevity
of the Council on Library Resources.

Library of Congress Cataloging-in-Publication Data
Steinberg, Allen.
    The transformation of criminal justice, Philadelphia,
1800–1880 / by Allen Steinberg.
        p.   cm. — (Studies in legal history)
    Bibliography: p.
    Includes index.
    ISBN 0-8078-1844-5 (alk. paper)
    1. Criminal justice, Administration of—Penn-
sylvania—Philadelphia—History—19th century. 2. Private
prosecutors—Pennsylvania—Philadelphia—History—19th
century. I. Title. II. Series.
HV9956.P45S74   1989
364'.9748—dc19   89-5485
                            CIP

93 92 91 90 89   5 4 3 2 1

Contents

Tables

Preface

This book began a long time ago. As a teenager growing up in a lower-middle-class suburb, I was struck by the difference between the ideals about law we were taught in school and the realities of law in daily life. In the classroom, our teachers talked at length about democracy and consent, the manner in which the people chose their leaders, and how the laws they made served and protected us all. But outside the schoolhouse people expressed mostly contempt for their leaders, few participated in politics or government in a meaningful way, and for many of my friends, the law was something to be feared and avoided. Our relationship with most of its representatives was antagonistic, even hostile.

The tension between the commitment to, and respect for, law and the disregard of law in favor of competing values is a recurrent and intensifying theme in modern American life. Sadly, by the end of the Reagan era, disregard and contempt of the law seems to have reached even the highest levels of the state. The role of law in everyday life is, like other things, something that has changed over the course of the United States' two centuries, and it is worth asking whether its hold on the nation has always been this tenuous.

Although a study of primarily obscure people and minor crimes in one city in the nineteenth century, this book concerns the origins of the alienation, antagonism, and disrespect for law that is a prominent part of the relationship between the citizenry and the modern American state. The book has been taking shape for over a decade, and many people have contributed along the way. My parents, William and Beatrice Steinberg, have offered constant support and encouragement. David Rothman suggested the original topic and directed the research from which it is derived. During my years at Columbia University, I also benefited from the guidance of James Shenton, Eric McKitrick, and especially Eric Foner, who gave the manuscript an extremely useful and critical reading.

At various stages of my work, a number of friends and colleagues read parts of it. Jeannie Attie, Elizabeth Blackmar, and Joshua Brown provided me with helpful criticism and conversation. My good friends Michael Merrill and Leonard Wallock have watched this project develop from its inception, encouraged me to take it where I believed it should go, and have continuously offered me indispensable enthusiasm and skepticism, for which I am especially grateful.

Of all the benefits of studying the history of Philadelphia, none has been greater than my exposure to the people I met there. Theodore Hershberg, at the Philadelphia Social History Project, helped see me through the early stages of research. I especially want to thank Eudice Glassberg, Bruce Laurie, John Modell, Mark Stern, and Henry Williams. Of all the scholars I met through the Philadelphia Social History Project, my most enduring personal and intellectual debt is to Michael B. Katz and Michael Frisch. Their searching and creative minds, enthusiasm, and support have been invaluable to me. Without their help this book would be a far less thing than it is.

Later, I was fortunate enough to spend two years at the Philadelphia Center for Early American Studies, where I benefited from an association with an extremely able collection of faculty, students, and research fellows from the University of Pennsylvania and neighboring institutions. I am especially grateful to Richard Dunn, Richard Beeman, and Michael Zuckerman for the opportunity to work at the Philadelphia Center for Early American Studies and to share my ideas with them and other center participants. Susan Davis, Elizabeth Fisher, John Murrin, and Steven Rosswurm all contributed to my revision of the manuscript. Still others in Philadelphia also helped. Walter Licht and Mark Haller deserve thanks, and I am ever grateful to Roger Lane, whose passion for social history, good humor, criticism, and support made a major contribution to this book and my ability to endure the trial of writing it. Finally, much appreciation is due Ward Childs and his staff at the Philadelphia City Archives, the staff of the Historical Society of Pennsylvania, and the staff of the Library Company of Philadelphia.

Eric Monkkonen has been a valuable supporter and critic of my work for a long time. Others in the nebulous world of criminal justice history who have offered advice and support along the way are Douglas Hay, David R. Johnson, Peter Linebaugh, Craig Little, and Wilbur Miller.

During the latter stages of work on the manuscript I have benefited from the assistance of several colleagues at Harvard University and elsewhere. David Herbert Donald gave a complete draft a penetrating and extremely helpful reading. Shannon Stimson shared her thoughts on the development of early American law and jurisprudence. Amy Bridges, Alan Brinkley, Judith Coffin, and Joel Perlmann all also helped. In recent years I have been especially buoyed by the friendship and wisdom of William Forbath. My editor in the Studies in Legal History series, Thomas A. Green, has been enormously enthusiastic, intelligent, and helpful. At the very end, Edward Ayres offered extremely constructive criticism. Thanks to his help, this is a much better book than it would have been.

Susan Schechter encountered this book when she first encountered me, and through the years since, she has been unwavering in her support and confidence in it and in me, even as her skeptical mind and passion for truth has forced me to discard more ideas and passages than I care to remember. She has shared the good times and helped see me through the bad times. Her commitment to change and social justice has always helped me to keep the writing of books in the proper perspective, and with the arrival of Zachary Schechter-Steinberg two years ago, she has also helped me realize life's most astonishing joys.

A. S.

Brookline, Mass.
July 1988

Introduction: The Greatest Luxury of All

His curiosity piqued by a recent grand jury's description of "horrible and immoral" conditions in south Philadelphia and neighboring Southwark and Moyamensing, *Evening Bulletin* reporter Casper Sounder recruited a guide and set out early in 1853 to investigate first-hand what he would call the "mysteries and miseries" of Philadelphia. He found densely packed "streets, scores of alleys and courts almost without number," home to thousands of "poor wretches" living in "hovels which are not fit to be the abiding places of swine." Many of the residents—both men and women—were habitual drunkards, their children distressingly "pale, sickly, and emaciated." Even worse, the neighborhood seemed to be growing, a "cancerous sore . . . (threatening) to infect and poison adjacent comparatively healthy portions" of the city.

Besides begging and petty theft, the most "popular vocation" among these desperately poor people was "ragging and boning." Little more than scavenging, it consisted of a tour that could last for a week or more and take the "collector" over an area of up to six square miles. Afterwards, the collector returned "to his old haunts," sold "his stock-in-trade," and enjoyed several days of "high revelry," which included drinking, dancing, gambling, and other popular pleasures. But there was an additional activity that seemed utterly out of place. "The greatest luxury of all in which the 'flush' Ragger and Boner indulges," Sounder explained, "is litigation—the law must be brought to bear upon somebody; actions and cross-actions for defamation, and assault and battery—the suits often encouraged by unscrupulous magistrates—are freely entered into, until between the rum sellers and the alderman, and the dance house, the poor shorn dupe starts forth on another collecting tour, without a cent of capital in his pocket."[1]

These were mysteries indeed. How could criminal litigation be the "greatest luxury" for Philadelphia's poor on those few occasions when they came upon some cash? How was it that the law was "brought to bear" upon citizens not by policemen or state officials but by each other? Could this have been as important a part of popular culture as Sounder implied?

In fact, the criminal law did have a central place in the everyday social life of mid-nineteenth-century Philadelphia. Private prosecution—one citizen taking another to court without the intervention of the police—was the basis of law enforcement in Philadelphia and an anchor of its legal culture, and this had been so since colonial times. By 1836, city recorder and noted American jurist John Bouvier was convinced that "among the evils which our fellow citizens suffer, particularly among the poorer classes, is the spirit of litigation. . . . Having no property about which to quarrel, too many . . . come into [criminal] court for redress."[2] Well past mid-century, private prosecution remained popular among a broad spectrum of ordinary Philadelphians. Familiar and frequent, it was rooted in a complex political and legal structure that linked political parties, courthouses, saloons and other centers of popular culture, real crime and dangerous disorder, and ordinary disputes and transgressions of everyday life.

Through the process of private prosecution, the criminal courts of Philadelphia developed a distinctive set of practices and a culture that was remarkably resilient in the face of constant official hostility and massive social change. Based on the English common law, criminal prosecution was shaped less by a need to combat crime than by community needs for third-party dispute resolution.[3] In Philadelphia's criminal courts, it produced a process of prosecution that was, like other aspects of early national politics and government, popular, particularistic, and extremely locally based. It was also flexible, subject to exploitation, and often, relative to the formal law, quite corrupt. This book describes and analyzes this way of conducting criminal justice and its demise, or at least the major turning point leading to its disappearance—the destruction of Philadelphia's traditional minor judiciary.

The transformation of the state is one of the most prominent themes of nineteenth-century American history. For the most part, it is a story of the expansion and increasing complexity of government and of the professionalization and decreasing popular character of politics. Whether one looks at the rise of administrative capacities and the conduct of presidential elections on the national level or at the development of the police and the battles between machines and municipal reformers on the local level, the story is similar. The point is that the United States moved from a society that was scarcely governed to one in which, by century's end, government regularly touched the daily lives of the people.[4]

An ancillary point is that, to the extent that American society *was* governed through much of the nineteenth century, it was governed locally and by the courts. The usual assumption is that this kind of government was remote from the people, but if criminal prosecution in Philadelphia was at all typical, local and court-centered government was not necessarily remote. Rather, it was easily accessible and close to the everyday affairs of ordinary people. The frequency of litigation and, probably, the popularity of partisan politics were expressions of this, and both were the result of the distinctive quality of local, court-centered government. Unlike the later administrative and policy-making state, the early nineteenth-century local state was reactive, particularistic, and extremely informal. There was no better example of this than the conduct of criminal justice.[5]

Late in the nineteenth century, reformers, professionals, experts, and visionaries attempted to fashion a more efficient, accountable, and, some believed, democratic process of urban government, and in so doing, they ushered in the modern state. But the consequence of late-century urban reform was, of course, an inefficient, bureaucratic, corrupt, and less democratic state. This was in part the result of the efforts of reformers, but it was also the result of the continuing influence of established leaders and habits. Powerful local politicians and traditions could not prevent change, but they did limit its possibilities. Through direct resistance to reform and the maintenance of control over the processes of government, local politicians helped determine the shape of the new urban state. The story of the transformation of criminal justice in Philadelphia is a prime example of how this was so.

Changes elsewhere no doubt took place somewhat differently, but the implication of this study is that the late-nineteenth-century city was not so much governed more as governed differently than before. The two broadest aims of this book are: first, to identify the difference and explain its greatest consequence, the gradual disempowerment of ordinary citizens; and second, to examine the process of change and show how the new relationship grew, ironically, out of the old. This study begins by examining how the system of private prosecution worked, how it adapted to massive social change, and how it continued to dominate the culture of criminal justice even after the establishment of the police; in short, how deeply private prosecution was a part of both the popular life and political culture of the city. It also shows how the efforts by judges and grand jurors to change it repeatedly failed, mostly because of the political, legal, and structural power of the minor judiciary. The book next explains how state prosecution originated within the world of private prosecution, and then how, through the struggles between old authorities and new reformers, a criminal justice system, anchored by the the police and the public prosecutor, replaced the one based on private prosecution. Private citizen-litigants saw the patrolman, the bureaucracy, and crime control measures take the place of the alderman, the courthouse, and dispute resolution. Simultaneously, they saw the legal and political culture change as more discretion and power gravitated to city-wide officials and professionals and less to local leaders and ordinary citizens.

The decline of private prosecution was at least as much a result of external assault as it was the consequence of internal faults. It was susceptible to a broad elite reformer attack upon popular culture, political parties, and the particularistic structure of city government precisely because it was so intimately and fundamentally a part of all three. The transformation of criminal justice was in this way at the center of the social and political reform that swept across the United States in the nineteenth century. Concerned in part with sharpening the boundaries between the various features of urban life, reformers produced (if not in the way they intended) a more precisely and narrowly defined (if institutionally more elaborate) "public" sphere. In so doing, they fundamentally changed the authority relationships and social processes of which this sphere was comprised.[6]

If this book is in a broad sense about the transformation of the state, it is at heart an examination of the relationship between law and popular life. Its core is a history of the process of criminal prosecution, framed not by the history of any of the components of the criminal justice system but by the relationships through which criminal prosecution was conducted. For the citizenry, criminal justice institutions may come and go, but the need to interact with the state in order to invoke the authority of the law remains. The collision of this popular need and the process of institutional innovation provides much of the dynamic for the story, but it is always guided by the notion that criminal law is not simply a "coercive instrument to punish crime" but also a way of ruling, important to both the rulers and the ruled, that is shaped alike by the architects, officers, and users of institutions.[7] As Douglas Hay has noted, the "root of the legitimacy of the law" is found at the intersection of the experiences of the poor, working, or "dangerous" classes and "the interpretations of the judiciary and the police."[8]

If there is an institutional focus to this study, it is the courts. Courts assume an active citizenry, a contest between juridically equal parties mobilized on their own behalf.[9] Although—or perhaps because—the courts were the first agents of criminal justice, they have been neglected by scholars in favor of police and prisons, innovations that assumed not active citizens but rather submission to the coercive authority of the state. Indeed, much of criminal justice history consists of analyses of the increase of the authority of these institutions, surely an important story for historians seeking to grapple with the institutional state of the late twentieth century. Nonetheless, this focus has too often prevented historians from adequately examining criminal justice within its larger legal, political, and social contexts. More importantly, it has prevented them from fully grasping the significance of the transformation of criminal justice.[10]

Private prosecution and the minor judiciary, the two fundamentals of this study, require clarification at the outset. Private prosecution refers to the system by which private citizens brought criminal cases to the attention of court officials, initiated the process of prosecution, and retained considerable control over the ultimate disposition of cases—especially when compared with the two main executive authorities of criminal justice, the police and the public prosecutor. The minor judiciary is the generic term for the officials to whom these private cases were brought and in whose offices the criminal justice process began. Together with the private litigants, the minor judiciary exercised most of the discretion over the processing and disposition of criminal cases under private prosecution. The minor judiciary were known in Philadelphia as justices of the peace, magistrates, and, mostly, aldermen. I refer to them usually as either aldermen or the minor judiciary and occasionally as justice or magistrate when the context warrants. But in all cases the meaning is the same.

Private prosecution and the minor judiciary were firmly rooted in Philadelphia's colonial past. Both were examples of the creative American adaptation of the English common law. By the seventeenth century, private prosecution was a fundamental part of English common law. Most criminal cases in England proceeded under the control of a private prosecutor, usually a relatively elite person, and often through a private society established for that purpose. Justices of the peace were the most important authorities in this process.[11] Although hardly a democratic precedent, English private prosecution found its way into Pennsylvania in a form that helped legitimate third-party dispute resolution without the use of lawyers. William Penn and the settlers of Pennsylvania established a judiciary that merged the Quaker tradition of arbitration with the larger English tradition of the justice of the peace. Upon taking possession of the colony in 1682, Penn commissioned six justices of the peace, and though their numbers fluctuated, they remained the chief functionaries of local government in the province. In Philadelphia they were called aldermen, and in addition to their duties as justices, they sat on a special criminal court for the city and had legislative responsibilities. Though they were generally propertied and enfranchised members of the Philadelphia corporation, the people who appeared before them generally regarded them as neighbors and "plain people."

Pennsylvania Chief Justice William Tilghman explained the subsequent development of the American common law in 1813: "Every country has its Common Law. Ours is composed partly of the Common Law of England and partly of our own usages. When our ancestors emigrated from England, they took with them such of the English principles as were convenient for the situation in which they were about to place themselves. . . . By degrees, as circumstances demanded, we adopted the English usages, or substituted others better suited to our wants, till at length before the time of the Revolution we had formed a system of our own."[12]

All colonies had complex hierarchies of courts which bottomed out with "the early and widespread adoption of the justice of the peace . . . almost on a neighborhood basis." This brought "justice close to each man's door" and set a precedent for meeting the "increase in the volume and complexity of judicial business by sheer multiplication of judges and courts." It also meant that "no other branch of government more directly affected the day-to-day lives of Americans than the judiciary" in the colonial period.[13]

Justices of the peace presided over courts "closest to the life of many people," the places "set up to handle the small disputes of the average man."[14] There was nothing mysterious or intimidating about these courts. Justices were rarely learned in the law. Usually they were men of modest means. Always they were familiar local faces, and since there were no formal qualifications for office, its incumbents could and often did rotate frequently. In the context of a system of laws closely attuned to local custom—during these "dark ages" of American law, there were virtually no written reports of cases or law books—this was conducive to the widespread lay use of the law. Hector St. John Crèvecoeur proclaimed proudly that "the value of our laws and the spirit of freedom . . . often tends to make us litigious." A more recent observer noted more plainly that colonists were "of a querulous nature, quick to argue, quick to threaten each other, and quick to file lawsuits."[15]

Affinity for the law did not, however, mean love of lawyers. Precisely because the popularity of the law was dependent on its familiarity, lawyers were often considered dangerous. In part an inheritance of the English distrust of lawyers as designing manipulators of the common law, American resentment was rooted in a fear that lawyers could use artifice and technicality to make the law a tool of oppression and domination. Colonists preferred plain dispute resolution without potential for chicanery. Pennsylvania was "a happy country" because "they have no lawyers. Everyone is to tell his own case, or some friend for him."[16]

This was in part because early Pennsylvanians, as they established their courts, also created a parallel system of arbitrators, or "common peace-makers," to whom people could bring minor disputes for legal settlement. Arbitration was a direct extension of the internal dispute resolution process of the Quaker meeting, and while it was not imposed on non-Quakers, it helped encourage litigation and establish the Pennsylvanians' reputation for filing lawsuits. So did the Philadelphia courts' arbitration-like practices, such as the taking of a surety that would be forfeited if a proscribed act was committed. "Peace bonds" could be issued by a justice upon the complaint of any citizen without the necessity of a formal criminal prosecution.

Similar procedures were typical in most other colonies. In North Carolina, justices of the peace were "the most important law enforcement officer(s) in each county." Justices were also of central importance in New York, where they "were, on the whole, an ignorant lot" who were prone to the abuse of power. They had summary power over the bulk of minor criminal cases, which were often dismissed because of the unwillingness of prosecuting parties to complete the process. In Massachusetts, most criminal cases were commenced by the state in name only; they "were in reality contests between subjects rather than contests between government and subject." Justices also had wide-ranging jurisdiction over criminal matters in Connecticut, and in Virginia the early establishment of public prosecutors was a direct response to the power of private citizens to abort prosecutions.[17]

The eighteenth-century town in which private prosecution and the minor judiciary became rooted was quite unlike the nineteenth-century city in which they would flourish. The pace of economic life in colonial Philadelphia was decidedly leisurely in contrast to what was to come. Even in this most urban of American areas, agriculture remained a major activity and the foundation of the export trade. Most people worked as individuals or in a family group, most merchants had to conduct all aspects of their business from financing to retailing, and most people "used part of their houses as places of business."[18] Custom regulated wages and prices as much as supply and demand, and there was still a great deal of involuntary labor of bound servants and slaves.[19] Artisans in the many thriving trades comprised the largest part of the city's population. They depended on merchants for business, lived and worked in close proximity to the merchants, and generally accepted merchant leadership. But artisans also regarded their own values and life-style—which emphasized control over their own time, literary and scientific pursuits, respect for the private property that was the result of visible labor, and exaltation of the "independence" of the small-producing master craftsmen—as the foundation of civic virtue.[20]

Deference ruled political relationships. Merchants and educated gentlemen were the recognized civic leaders, but master craftsmen considered themselves spokesmen for their journeymen and apprentices and probably exercised political rights even when unable to meet the laxly enforced property qualification. Disenfranchised "lower" orders—journeymen, apprentices, laborers, immigrants, servants, and slaves—also adopted deferential attitudes toward the merchant elite and accepted the artisans' political leadership. The political participation of the disenfranchised consisted of "constitutional" crowd activity that either enforced customary rights or furthered the ends of some designing member of the ruling elite. The ruling elite saw themselves as just that, the paternalistic leaders of society, moving easily from their business concerns to political meetings and on to the organization and oversight of charitable activities upon which many of the "lower" orders depended in slack times.[21]

Although there was a distinct subculture of drink and violent sport among the "lower" orders of Philadelphia, and no small amount of chronic street disorder accompanying it, crime was not a major concern in colonial Philadelphia. Taverns were often noisy and offensive to some, and a small night watch was established in 1751, but the prosecution of crime was not a major municipal preoccupation. Elected aldermen and judges of the mayor's and quarter sessions courts heard the predominantly minor charges of theft, assault, and disorderly conduct and imposed the typical sentences—fines, whippings, stocks, banishment, and, on rare occasions, imprisonment. The political monopoly of the elite members of the Philadelphia Corporation and restricted suffrage kept these officials in a properly paternalistic relationship to the litigants who came before them. The fee system for engaging in legal procedures both reinforced this relationship and regulated popular access to the courts. Still, aldermen were probably the least elite of the city's public officials, their doors were open to anyone, and by the late colonial period, the courts were already public entertainments that bore the stamp of popular life.[22]

Finally, a word on the choice of locale. Although the undoubted possessor of great charms and no little intrinsic fascination, Philadelphia became the site for this book because of the extremely local level of research required to execute an intensive case study. The weaknesses of the literature on criminal courts convinced me that a city rather than a larger political jurisdiction was the appropriate unit for study, especially given my interest in the effects of that quintessential urban institution, the police, on the criminal justice process. I chose Philadelphia because a good institutional history of its police and a study of early nineteenth-century Pennsylvania criminal law were already available, providing a context for the research; the city was, during the 1970s, a site of much exciting and varied research in social history; the local archives contained an unusually complete set of criminal court and prison records for the years before 1880; and, most importantly, what material there was on criminal justice in eighteenth- and early nineteenth-century Philadelphia suggested that there would be something there for me to find.

Part I The Duality of Criminal Justice

1. *Courtrooms and Cases*

In 1836, when Philadelphia's "penny press" began publishing daily accounts of the city's criminal courts, reporters came face-to-face with one of the court's most enduring features. "The moment the doors are opened, the standing corps of soaplocks and loafers rush in, and . . . appropriate to themselves in an unceremonious manner all the seats inside of the bar, so that when the attorneys, reporters and parties really interested in the proceedings of the court come in, they are compelled to stand and gaze on." One day in 1839, when some fifty prisoners entered a room designed to hold twelve, defendants and grand jurors became inextricably intermingled. The judge and constables lost all sense of who was who and in the confusion one of the prisoners escaped. His absence was not discovered until the next day. In a hearing to discover who was responsible, Judge Robert Conrad could find no one to blame.[1]

Nearly thirty years later, the reporters were different but the court's circumstances were much the same. "The hundreds of loafers who make the Quarter Sessions their place of daily resort" regularly forced witnesses into the square outside, regardless of the weather. This group, "equally divided between males and females, blacks and whites," included at least fifty who were in attendance daily. "The most disgusting details of a case are not sufficient to make them vacate their places."[2]

Despite the enormous changes that took place in the process of criminal prosecution between 1800 and 1875, a number of things remained constant. Crowded and unruly courtrooms were perhaps the most obvious of them, and they are important to understand if one is to comprehend the transformation of criminal justice.

The Urban Setting

One of the constant features of life in general in nineteenth-century Philadelphia was, of course, change, both rapid and uneven. The constants in criminal justice, including the persistence of private prosecution, seem all the more remarkable for this, but the character of social change also contributed to the persistence of old habits.

Between 1800 and 1875, urban Philadelphia grew from 67,000 people concentrated in a two-square-mile city and two adjoining districts to a massive metropolis of 800,000, encompassing the entire 129 square miles of Philadelphia County. A population of mostly native-born people of English and German descent (with a smattering of blacks) became a melting pot comprised in half by recent Irish and German immigrants and their children. The commercial and household manufacturing town had become an industrial city with prominent iron, textile, railroad, and shipbuilding industries; a kaleidoscopic variety of workplaces; and a huge population of skilled and semiskilled workers. By 1875, railroads, trolley cars, factories, sweatshops, mansions, tenements, shanties, and characteristic row houses had fashioned a teeming urban landscape out of the compact walking city of 1800.[3]

The most startling changes occurred by mid-century. Consolidation in 1854, which put under one government the forty distinct political units that had until then comprised Philadelphia County, was an overdue recognition that Philadelphia had ceased to be a "green-country town" and had become a "sprawling port and mill city" of roughly one-half million people, perhaps the fourth largest in the world.[4] At the end of the colonial period, the line between public and private remained blurred, and the paternalism and mutuality of preindustrial life was very much alive.[5] Although urban Philadelphia (including Southwark and Northern Liberties) in 1800 was still the largest city in the United States, and although the area of dense settlement was expanding, farms, parks, and country gardens were still only a short walk from the center of town. Capitalist development during the revolutionary period had yet to eclipse many features of the household economy.[6] On the whole, for example, a journeyman could still "look forward to setting up his own shop (and) earning a modest income as an independent producer." Bankers and merchants still preferred safe traditional investments in land and shipping, dampening their entrepreneurial and manufacturing spirit.[7]

It was not long, however, before Philadelphia businessmen became more adventurous. The embargo of 1808 was a major boon to manufacturing. The growth of New York City and the noises being made about road and canal construction worried merchants and commercial leaders, who began to enlarge Philadelphia's coastal shipping trade and initiate their own internal improvement projects.[8] Between 1815 and 1835, Pennsylvania, with Philadelphia as its hub, constructed over 3,000 miles of roads and 900 miles of canals, and then, by 1852, 900 miles of railroad track.[9]

The transportation revolution turned Philadelphia into the economic center of the Delaware Valley and eastern Pennsylvania, expanding the oppor-

tunities for growth in commerce and manufacturing. Not only did this acceler-
ate the process of capitalist development, but it also swelled the city's population. Even before massive immigration, the demand for cheap manufacturing
labor spurred rural-urban migration. Philadelphia's population grew to over
250,000 in 1840, on its way to doubling between 1825 and 1854. The densely
settled area expanded rapidly westward after 1820, and the population of
the nearby suburban districts—Southwark, Northern Liberties, Kensington,
Moyamensing, Manayunk, and Spring Gardens—soon outstripped Philadelphia's.[10] By the 1840s, the suburban districts were manufacturing centers and
the home of many newly arrived wage earners, now increasingly immigrants.
Only 10 percent of the work force in 1836, German and Irish immigrants
comprised nearly 40 percent by 1850. They settled in great numbers in most
areas and accounted for 30 percent of the city's population by 1860, over half
including their children.[11]

Philadelphia's occupational structure also became extremely complex,
reflecting the old trades of the manufacturing town as much as the industrial
city looming on the horizon. Old crafts, such as carpenter, shoemaker, tailor,
and weaver, still abounded. The largest single occupational category remained
that preindustrial catchall, the common laborer. At the same time, entirely new
major occupational groups appeared, the middle-class clerk and the working-
class factory operative, while the traditional prospects of artisanship were
disappearing. Work settings were similarly complex. Over half of Philadelphia's work force toiled in places with fifty or more employees in 1850. But
the majority of firms still had fewer than five workers, and over half of the
operatives in the largest textile, clothing, and shoe concerns were actually
outworkers, those who toiled in small places, usually their homes.[12]

Despite the variety of settings, the vast majority of workers were now
simply wage laborers, quite unlike the artisans of even the recent past. Most
were either unskilled or employees of firms with twenty or more laborers and a
significantly subdivided work process. Artisanal working conditions prevailed
in only a few trades and among some of the most vulnerable and impoverished
workers, such as the largely immigrant hand-loom weavers. The tenuousness
of their artisanal status was only heightened by the unregulated, speculative,
and cyclical manner in which early American capitalism developed. During
the 1837 depression, for example, some two thousand small masters, still
seeking to maintain artisanal shops with a few journeymen, were "reduced
. . . to journeymen . . . working for large [manu]factories," never to return to
the status of independent craftsman.[13]

Never again would the city see an era of such rapid, tumultuous, and extensive social change. Population kept increasing, the process of urban sprawl throughout the county continued, and the city embarked on the Industrial Age, but by the time of consolidation, the fundamental features of capitalist big-city life had been stamped upon Philadelphia.[14] Yet this was not an unambiguously modern city but rather a bewildering hybrid of tradition and innovation, farm and factory, splendor and squalor, development and decline. This was as true of the city spatially as it was socially. Philadelphia's famous grid street network had by 1850 become an extended agglomeration of "shacks, shanties, and back-alley two-room houses for the poor; three-room row houses, or three rooms in multi-family row houses for the skilled workingman; and six to eight room row houses and flats for middle class managers, prosperous shopkeepers, professionals, and downtown businessmen." Although the city had its fashionable areas—in the western part of the central city and several of the newer surrounding communities—and an overwhelmingly commercial downtown, it was not characterized by great segregation. The shoddy homes of the poor "proliferated to the saturation point" in the 1850's throughout central Philadelphia.[15]

As a result of the city's spatial integration, social classes remained in close contact. Even many of the professionals and businessmen who lived in the most fashionable areas commuted daily to the downtown wards. Especially in the central city and surrounding manufacturing districts, people who engaged in a vast array of pursuits closely intermingled, including, of course, those with no place of work and nowhere to call home. Poverty and squalor were very much a part of everyday life at mid-century, even among people who were regularly employed, and were, like everything else, distributed widely throughout the city.[16]

Such a complex and uneven process of social change allowed old habits to die slowly during the nineteenth century, only adding to the bewildering and disorderly quality of social life. The most basic enduring feature of criminal justice was simply the popularity of the criminal law and the large number of people who, in one capacity or another, passed through the criminal courts.

The Character of the Courtrooms

The spatial and social density of life in Philadelphia produced the circumstances in which ordinary people came to depend—and prey—upon one another. All facets of popular life in Philadelphia created the propensity toward litigation: poverty, the stress of bewildering social change, family tensions, ethnic and racial prejudice and rivalry, the boisterousness of the streets and saloons—in short, the everyday affairs of ordinary people living in crowded conditions in, or on the edge of, poverty. The resolution of their quarrels and spats, and their attempts to take advantage of one another or to avenge injustices, took them regularly to court. The popular character of both the local alderman's office and the more imposing courts of record never subsided.

By 1854 there were over fifty aldermen in the city, each presiding over a neighborhood office to which residents flocked with civil and criminal business. The most important alderman was the mayor, who presided over the central police station downtown. Until 1826 he was chosen from among those men who were already aldermen; afterwards, the popularly elected mayor became one by virtue of his office. In 1840, all of the aldermen became elected officials, assuring their close ties to partisan politics.[17]

Criminal justice was completely decentralized. The alderman's office was a community center in every ward, the point of origin for all court business as well as the headquarters of a prominent neighborhood politician. The mayor acted as alderman for the more weighty crimes that tended to cluster in the central business district and for the many cases of drunkeness and disorderly conduct that comprised the bulk of the arrests made by the paltry pre-1850 police and watch. But the majority of criminal prosecutions originated throughout Philadelphia County in the local offices of the neighborhood alderman.

All day long, every day, residents of a ward streamed in and out of the alderman's office, bringing him a variety of civil and criminal business ranging from marriage to murder. Constables attached to the aldermen waited for an opportunity to serve a summons or an arrest warrant. People eager to serve as someone's bail loitered about looking for business. Notorious lawyers, "the *vermin* of the profession," also frequented the offices in pursuit of clients. On a typical day in 1848, one alderman heard six assault and battery cases, three larceny cases, three breach of ordinance cases, one firecracker case, one fast driving case, and one case of throwing torpedoes on the stage of the Arch Street Theatre. He committed three boys to the house of refuge; issued two landlords' warrants of eviction, two private notices, and eight summonses; and had one man examined for life insurance and one operated on for ophthalmia. He also conducted one marriage ceremony.[18]

Spectators also attended, especially at the offices of the committing magistrates who heard the cases brought by policemen. Monday morning hearings generally attracted the largest crowds, with the prisoners' dock full of a weekend's worth of vagrants, drunks, and other assorted miscreants. "The office of Mayor, as usual on Monday, was yesterday morning crowded with individuals, most of whom, we are glad to say . . . were spectators, mere lookers on in Venice, and only interested in the disposition which His Honor would make of those . . . who for 'doing nothing' were arraigned before him."[19]

Sometimes the rush of spectators to the magistrate's office became a crush of spectators. "As soon as the door opened, the pushing and crowding to get into the office was immense, not unlike some of the scenes witnessed at sales of Bank stock some six or eight years ago." By the 1840s spectators became such a nuisance that the mayor moved the opening of court back from nine to seven in the morning and then instituted Sunday hearings, hoping to reduce the typical tumult of Monday mornings.[20]

Such ploys never succeeded. People did not simply attend hearings at the magistrates' offices; they actively followed them. Spectators knew when a good show was expected. For a case involving a young girl "of superior personal charms," the office was "thronged—some fun was evidently anticipated." The crowd that reminded the court reporter of eager stock speculators was awaiting the hearing of sixteen "attractive Ladies and Gentlemen" arrested the night before at a "disreputable dance house." Special occasions—election days, Christmas, and Independence Day—regularly attracted crowds because they were unusually disorderly. The arrest of a notable person, a complex case continued to the following day, or one involving a new or newly enforced law also attracted large audiences. During the temperance fever of 1854, the police began prosecuting persons for selling liquor on Sundays. On the first day of hearings, the mayor's office was filled with spectators, but they were disappointed; only two defendants attended.[21]

They were not often disappointed, however; the magistrate's office was like a grand, free popular theater, with friends and neighbors as the performers. This was, of course, an era of popular theater in America, no less so in Philadelphia than elsewhere. The Arch Street and Chestnut Street theaters were major stops for touring actors and companies, and as elsewhere the theaters were frequented by people of all classes and races. In fact, dominated by the rowdy and unruly behavior of the lower classes, they resembled a twentieth-century sporting event more than a theatrical performance—the virtual institutionalization of "the guilty third tier" reserved for blacks and prostitutes; the incessant chattering of voices, munching of peanuts, and spitting of tobacco; and the regular expression of audience opinion by cheering, booing, hissing, and throwing objects toward the stage. Critics constantly complained of the tyranny that popular taste held over theatrical offerings. People attended the theater as much for the social as the dramatic pleasures, whether in search of illicit sex, simple conviviality, or the opportunity to show off. On holidays, the performance became "almost superfluous" to the socializing that made the theater such a popular mecca.[22]

This extremely popular character of the theater meant that the content of drama often had great meaning for ordinary people, that the line between art and life was often quite thin. Dramatic, if unscripted, representations of life, the "theatre of the streets," were prominent parts of the frequent demonstrations and parades in which all of Philadelphia's people participated.[23] Court proceedings provided an even better parallel to the theater, with their real-life drama and obliteration of the line between audience and actor. Indeed, they could be quite entertaining, even instructive, and like Victorian theater could offer a melange of harshness, humor, and sentimentality. On a busy day the mayor might hear fifty cases, and there were sure to be several good shows among them.[24] Drunks were especially amusing. Sometimes it was all the mayor could do to maintain "the dignity of his station," such as when "jolly" old Samuel Curry had the spectators in "convulsive, ill-suppressed merriment" by winking, smiling, and silently paying his fine while the watchman stood before the mayor presenting evidence he believed Samuel would contest. On another occasion, Clarissa Davis was sentenced to prison in lieu of paying a fine. She admitted being drunk but then lectured those in the office, asserting her right to be on the streets and angrily concluding that "woman's liberty is a malicious mockery . . . while tyrant man rules, women must suffer." While immigrants amused the audience with their versions of the English language, they sometimes raised disturbing objections. "Vat for kind of liberty dat be, ven me no can drink what I like, as much as I like?" wondered a French immigrant fined for drunkenness in 1842.[25]

Comedy sometimes gave way to farce at these hearings. The huge crowd that turned out for the appearance of Colonel John Cole, charged with insulting several merchants, heard the colonel ramble on about the right of free speech and foreign affairs, and declare himself "an independent candidate (but for what he did not state) and intended to continue so until he died." Even serious drama might take the stage. A "heavy and robust" black man was found in another's home, and the frightened residents chased, subdued, and arrested him. Moments before the mayor was to commit the man to prison, his mother appeared "who in a very sensible and affecting strain, satisfied the Mayor that he was laboring under temporary mental derangement [and] was at present under medical care." She took her son home.

The mayor sometimes used cases to instruct citizens, especially regarding parents' responsibility to discipline their children or to indenture them only to respectable masters. Prisoners could also be seen bowing in humility before the magistrate, asking forgiveness or leniency, swearing never again to run afoul of the law. On the rarest of occasions, an alderman might even have a chance to pronounce on a matter of law and public policy, such as when Alderman James Mitchell dismissed a suit brought by temperance advocates against Sunday liquor vendors.[26]

The mayor's and committing magistrate's offices were central scenes of popular culture and public life. The more typical alderman's office was a much simpler affair, nothing more than a small room with a desk, located near the alderman's home or shop. It was rarely a magnet for spectators and journalists but regularly one for litigants. The courts of record, the more august halls of justice where legally trained judges presided over jury trials, were much more like the mayor's office than the local alderman's or the civil courts.

Criminal cases were returned to the courts of record as soon as an alderman determined that further action was warranted. According to the official process, with the defendant in jail or on bail, the case went first to a grand jury for consideration and, if they issued an indictment, to trial. Until 1838 there was one criminal court for Philadelphia city and another for the rest of the county. The mayor's court served the city, and its bench was comprised of a rotating group of city aldermen. With its abolition, aldermen ceased presiding over any court of record. The court of quarter sessions soon became the criminal court for the entire county, its judges the same men who sat on the court of common pleas for civil matters. When they took the bench in the quarter sessions though, they looked out at a courtroom that retained the familiar flavor of the alderman's office.

Even more so than in the mayor's office, crowds of spectators treated criminal trials as popular entertainment. "The Criminal Court appears to have the powers of a magnet—everybody seems to be attracted to it," observed a court reporter in 1839. Even on slow days, with only a handful of cases on the docket, spectators flocked to court. Sometimes they practically stormed the gates.[27] People came for the entertainment of routine cases, which served "no purpose other than to amuse the spectators." But, as with the minor courts, they also followed the calendar and turned out in greatest numbers for cases of special interest. At a forgery trial of two well-to-do bankers, the courtroom was "not only crowded, but crammed." The audience followed the proceedings intently, and when sentence was pronounced, they broke into "a general stamping of feet."[28]

Throughout the century this pattern continued. Spectators, "rude people, lovers of these disgusting exhibitions . . . crowd [the court]room, not those whom the city compels to be there," noted a reporter in 1859.[29] Particular cases also continued to attract large and varied audiences. An 1866 controversy over the enforcement of Sunday drinking laws drew widespread attention, for example, and crowded the courtroom "with members of the bar, clergymen, temperance men and women, tavern keepers and other citizens manifesting the general interest which pervades the community on the temperance question."[30]

Certain groups attended court out of a sense of collective identity and security. Blacks sometimes rallied around each other when one of them faced a criminal trial. Though he probably exaggerated, Mayor Isaac Roach chastised a black defendant in 1839, "Whenever one of your color is brought up on any charge, the whole colored population is immediately interested, raise an excitement and crowd into the courts to see that judge and jury render justice." Subject more than any other Philadelphians to the arbitrary power of criminal justice authorities, blacks sometimes responded by attempting to exercise as much control as possible over the criminal justice process. Crowding courtrooms was one way of doing this, and as with most other aspects of criminal justice, it differed in degree, but not in kind, from the behavior of whites.[31]

Not only was the court generally very crowded, but it was also generally quite unruly, even disorderly. Business was often conducted rapidly. Defendants, prosecutors, and witnesses were shuttled in and out of the room, pleading and testifying, in trials that sometimes lasted only a few minutes. Court officers were in constant motion, ushering parties about, escorting prisoners to the lockup, and quieting noisy spectators. A reporter referred to this typical scene as a "whirlpool." Even when cases did not proceed so rapidly, the excitement did not necessarily abate since the delays were generally caused by the heated debates and "corkscrew arguments" of the attorneys, who, like actors and politicians in this age of oratory, could themselves be popular attractions.[32]

Rapid turnover meant that the courtroom was always crowded with witnesses and parties. In 1843, in order to handle a crush of tippling-house cases, the judges impaneled two juries, one on either side of the courtroom, and the deputy attorney general shuttled back and forth presenting cases to each. For breach of the peace cases, which were heard by the judge alone, the mostly poor defendants were transported together from prison to court, crowding the defendant's area with many "miserable outcasts, . . . wretched inebriates and . . . unfortunate victims of poverty." Eventually these cases became so numerous that, rather than crowd the courtroom with this motley assembly, the judges instead went to the prison and heard them there. Even without any special cases, the number and behavior of defendants might draw notice. One Saturday in 1848, some sixty prisoners received sentence, including a sixteen-year-old girl, who burst into contemptuous laughter while the judge pronounced her fate.[33]

Laughter was not uncommon in the chambers of the criminal courts. Judge Edward King perhaps laughed too much. Considered by some the "best judge that ever occupied [the criminal] bench" during his tenure in the thirties and forties, he was also criticized for a "want of gravity," which included joking and familiar conversation with persons gathered in the courtroom. His protégé, Judge William D. Kelley, also adopted King's familiar style. In contrast, Judge Robert T. Conrad was criticized for being excessively stern. "The court room may be in convulsions at the development of some laughable occurrence, but he invariably knocks on the bench with his penknife and cries 'order!'" One hilarious incident occurred during Reuben Allen's trial for assault on a police officer. While Reuben was testifying, a constable brought a box of fresh apples into the court. As all the officers "fell to scrambling for the apples as if no more were to be had till next year's crop," Reuben escaped. The red-faced constables then scrambled after the prisoner, who was captured a few blocks away.[34]

Even during routine proceedings, the behavior of spectators was much like that of theater audiences. After 1860, partly because of the "daily and hourly" chattering of the spectators, it became "impossible, at the best of times, to maintain entire order in the Quarter Sessions." Conversations raged about politics, cases under trial, the weather, "all subjects, no matter how lofty or how insignificant." Try as he might, the crier's efforts to silence the courtroom were in vain, there being "no timid ones among [the spectators] to quail at his appeal." Adding to the disorder were the antics of attorneys, whose vituperative exchanges included pranks and occasional rushes to the bench to consult with the judge or a client.[35]

The problem of overcrowding and unruliness in the courtroom was exacerbated by the poor facilities provided by the county for the courts. Located on one floor of the Old Congress Hall on the corner of Sixth and Chestnut streets in Independence Square and after 1867 in a "very plain brick building" just to its south, the court facilities were repeatedly an object of criticism. None of the rooms was large enough to accommodate the judge, jury, parties, witnesses, attorneys, reporters, and spectators who regularly attended. Depending on the size of the crowd, the court might have to move from room to room during the day. Witnesses had to wait in the lobby and then negotiate a maze of bodies, legs, and feet to reach the witness stand. When many defendants were present, they would overflow into the public areas and force other principals into the hall. Juries had difficulty finding rooms in which they could meet or wait when forced to leave the courtroom. So poorly ventilated as to be "beyond the power of man to improve," the rooms became intolerably hot in the summer. Jurors and others forced to attend became ill and the court often had to adjourn until temperatures moderated. Judge Kelley complained of ruefully sitting on the bench and staring out at the sunshine, eager to escape "this vile place."[36] The death of Judge Oswald Thompson in 1866 was widely attributed to overwork and the "miserable character of the Court accommodations." One newspaper editorialized that "every man who has been a party, a witness, a juryman, or even a spectator of the proceedings . . . must remember with infinite loathing the vile atmosphere, the scant accommodations, the utter absence of ordinary decencies or comforts."[37]

As a result of these conditions, some believed that respect for the law was demeaned. People sometimes refused to prosecute simply because they did not want to go to the disagreeable courtroom: "The miserable dens and holes into which our Courts are now forced to shrink, are certainly of a character to excite any feeling but respect. . . . The consequence is that all order is lost. The crowd is huddled into one confused and chaotic mass and no energy on the part of the Court can secure order and quietude. . . . Noise, confusion, levity and contempt prevail."[38]

Judges of the courts of record tried in several ways to establish control over their courtrooms. When the court of quarter sessions reacquired criminal jurisdiction in 1843 it was saddled with old, inadequate rooms but with a confident new group of judges. In his opening remarks, Judge Edward King established strict policies to maintain courtroom order. All persons would be kept out of the officer's part of the room so that the cases could be tried without disturbance. The judge ordered extra constables placed throughout the room to keep people out of areas in which they did not belong and remove the disorderly from the court. However, the judges' efforts were typically ineffective. By 1848 the rooms were still so overcrowded that parties could not even get inside for trials in which they were participants. Ventilation was so bad that people became ill even during the winter. Only after Judge Thompson's death did the county make a new courtroom available. Until then, the cost-conscious

opposition suggested that a cheaper alternative was simply to exclude spectators. A new courtroom was ready for use in March 1867, but the crowds
remained, and the frequent need for double sessions kept the old rooms in
almost constant use.[39]

The physical circumstances of criminal court gave it the unmistakable
aura of the people whose cases filled its dockets. Crowded, noisy, dirty, and
unhealthy, the court was hardly an awe-inspiring place. Rather, to Philadelphia's largely poor and working-class criminal litigants, it seemed familiar,
not too different from their homes and neighborhoods or the alderman's office
in which their cases were initiated. Familiarity, in turn, encouraged the same
unrestrained behavior that characterized people's daily lives at home. As in the
streets and at other popular events, the limits of acceptable public behavior
were being tested and defined for a distinct "public sphere" still in formation.
The effort of the judges to control their courtrooms was part of this, and so, we
shall see, was the effort of jurists and reformers to restrain and replace private
prosecution.

Criminal Cases and the Duality of Criminal Justice

Ordinarily, we classify criminal cases in terms of the nature and severity of the alleged crime, as a serious assault or a petty theft. This is also, of
course, the manner in which the law categorizes them, so our thinking tends to
correspond to the categories in which they are presented to us. This is probably
all to the good when considering criminal acts, whether one wants to avoid,
punish, or analyze them. It has a serious drawback, however, when one is
interested mainly in criminal justice, because activities other than crime are
involved. The most important are those that comprise the process of accusing,
prosecuting, and sometimes punishing people for criminal acts. Like rates and
types of crime, the process of criminal justice changed over time, but court
and prison records provide no categories in which one can measure it. So, in
order to tell the story of the transformation of the process of criminal prosecution, one must look within, and beyond, the formal categories of crime to find
other means of differentiating cases.

Thinking about a duality of criminal justice—about the balance between the popular use and the terrors of the criminal law—is one way of doing
this. The fundamental difference between types of criminal cases from this
perspective is, most simply, who controls the process of prosecution, who has
the greatest discretion at its key moments. Like all classification schemes, this
one obscures several important differences, but according to it two basic types

of cases were present in nineteenth-century Philadelphia, private prosecutions and state prosecutions. Early in the century, private cases were overwhelmingly dominant, but as the decades passed state prosecution became ever more prominent.

Private prosecution allowed citizens to mobilize the criminal law on their own behalf in matters that ranged from trivial to abusive to legitimate. Their ready access to, and easy manipulation of, the criminal law was made possible by the city's aldermen and justices, who were motivated by the profitability of the fee system, and this set the tone for the whole of criminal justice. However, though the relationship between aldermen and litigants was the most important factor in criminal justice, it was never the only one. Many other officials inhabited the higher rungs of the criminal justice ladder— prosecuting attorneys, grand jurors, judges, even the governor—and they all played major roles when criminal cases moved beyond their initial stages in the alderman's office. During the initial stages, the major additional players were the city's bewildering (until 1854) array of police officers and prison officials. All of these state officials established relatively independent relationships with the minor judiciary and the citizen-litigants. As their power and discretion gradually increased, the differences between private and state prosecution became increasingly clear.

The process of change was anything but simple, however. As the century progressed, aldermen and justices realized that they could reap an ever greater bonanza from the arrests made by the ever larger and more sophisticated police force. If private prosecution meant that for every complaint there was a defendant who was subject to at least harassment and often imprisonment, then the police's broad powers of arrest made possible an even wider field for manipulation of the law, imprisonment, and profit by the minor judiciary.

Perhaps the major development in criminal justice during the fifties was the manner in which the police inserted themselves into the already well-established system of private prosecution, forging a relationship with the minor judiciary which broadened the power of the latter while it increased the vulnerability of Philadelphians to state-initiated prosecution. Paradoxically though, because this increased the power of the aldermen, it simultaneously encouraged the persistence of private prosecution, which remained a source of profit for the magistrates and which the citizenry had no reason at all to abandon. So, instead of replacing it, police and state prosecution flourished alongside private prosecution for over two decades.

The Volume of Cases

Many people saw the inside of an alderman's office as a party to a criminal case. Because the process was so informal, the offices so widely scattered, and the aldermen such poor record keepers, it was impossible for anyone even to estimate the precise number. As all students of crime and justice well know, there is always a "dark figure" representing crimes that go unreported and contacts between the criminal justice system and the citizenry that go unrecorded. Even so, contemporaries offered considerable suggestive and some direct evidence of the great number of criminal prosecutions initiated in aldermen's offices in nineteenth-century Philadelphia.[40]

Probably the most compelling suggestive evidence comes from the commonplace recognition of the major role criminal litigation played in everyday life, reflected in comments like those of Caspar Sounder and numerous other observers, critics, and reformers of criminal justice. Reports of cases repeatedly emphasized the readiness with which ordinary people used the criminal courts. "The colored people love the law" began one report of a transaction among blacks which involved an underpaid fortune teller and led to six separate assault and battery cases. A criminal court judge in 1839 chided a man for bringing an assault and battery prosecution, calling the use of the law, inaccurately but suggestively, "the course of women and children." A newspaper court reporter marveled in 1848 at how "the miserable outcasts of society" race to the alderman's office over their petty quarrels, "each endeavoring to . . . have their opponents arrested before they were taken into custody themselves" and, in so doing, "expend . . . the greatest portion of the money that falls by accident within their grasp."[41] After the professional police became part of the process in 1854, the number of cases increased, and general sensitivity to widespread criminal prosecution only deepened.

Documents that simply recorded the events in the aldermen's offices were less ubiquitous. The closer one gets to the alderman's office, the rarer the document. As one moves further away from primary justice, records become more abundant, but they include only a fraction of the cases originated before the aldermen. Aldermen were under no obligation to keep regular and complete records, and even if they had been, the informality of the process would necessarily cast doubt on their ability and inclination to do so.

From time to time, observers tried to assess the number of cases heard by aldermen. One alderman was reported as having heard 195 cases during a three-month period in 1839, another as averaging 2,000 annually during the 1830s.[42] Also, at least a few aldermen did keep docket books, however incompletely. William Milnor was one of the fifteen Philadelphia city alder-men during the 1820s, and he kept at least one docket book covering the period from April 1823 to December 1829. In it he recorded not only the criminal cases he heard but also the marriages he conducted and the apprentices he indentured in his Dock Street office. Of these, 522 were criminal cases, or roughly 100 a year. Alderman J. B. Kenney kept a docket covering almost two years, from April 1845 to February 1847. Most of the cases he dealt with were street ordinance violations, but there were also 88 criminal cases. Coachmaker Amos Gregg was an alderman and sometime police magistrate from Frank-ford, a suburban district incorporated with the rest of Philadelphia County into the city in 1854. Gregg began recording criminal cases in a docket late that year, and he continued intermittently until 1878. When he stopped, there were only 327 entries, but it is illustrative of aldermanic record keeping that the entries break off abruptly in the middle of 1856, resume with only scattered cases in 1861, stop again in 1867, and conclude with cases heard by an unknown magistrate from 1874 to 1878.[43]

Clearly, it is difficult to draw conclusions about the volume of cases from observers or from the aldermen themselves. More complete records were kept by other criminal justice institutions, but each set suffers in its own way from being removed from the scene of primary justice. The recorded event that was closest to the alderman's office was a police arrest. The great majority of arrests probably resulted in at least an alderman's hearing, but in this era of private citizen prosecution, a police arrest was not a necessary component of the criminal justice process and could, indeed, be a consequence—even the only consequence—of a hearing before an alderman. Furthermore, arrests were probably of secondary quantitative importance before 1850. There are no police-generated arrest records at all before then, and Aldermen Milnor and Kenney made no notation of police involvement in any of the cases they recorded before 1850. However, Alderman Gregg noted police involvement in 45 percent of the cases he recorded after 1854, and if this is at all representa-tive, the number of cases heard by aldermen after 1850 was very large. For the seven months bridging November 1850 and July 1851, Philadelphia's first real police force made 7,076 arrests. Beginning in 1855, the consolidated city's permanent police force made many more, over 38,000 during the first year, as many as 43,000 in 1866, and never under 21,000 a year. Together with perhaps a roughly equal number of privately prosecuted cases, this must have meant that aldermen were kept exceedingly busy, both before and after 1850.

The number of cases returned to the courts of record increased in spurts between 1800 and 1876, roughly doubling between 1800 and 1815, again between 1836 and 1850, 1850 and 1860, and from the end of the war to 1876. These are, however, a poor index of the number of cases aldermen heard, because aldermen could and did dismiss or otherwise resolve a large and unknown number of cases without ever sending them on to the court. For example, among the indictable offenses—cases that could have been sent forward to a grand jury—recorded by Alderman Milnor, 65 percent were completely resolved in his office. Later in the century, Alderman Gregg completely resolved 41 percent of the indictable offenses he recorded. Yet another alderman was said to have settled 149 of 170 cases during a three-month period in 1839. But not all aldermen were alike. The fee system by which they were paid—which provided aldermen with greater rewards the further along the process a case went—gave them an incentive to return cases to court, and some apparently responded. Alderman Kenney, for example, resolved only 31 percent of the indictable offenses brought to him during the mid-forties.[44] Whatever the overall pattern, court cases represented only a fraction of the indictable offenses brought to the aldermen and were far fewer than the number of arrests. Still, as we have seen, 5,000 to 8,000 annual cases, typical of the post–Civil War years, were a major load for the court.

One of the most regular features of criminal prosecution was imprisonment, both before and after conviction, both legal and not. Imprisonment was useful for all of the parties involved in criminal cases. For a private prosecutor, it was a very powerful lever to use against a foe; for a policeman, an effective way to establish his authority; and for an alderman, a form of legitimate punishment and an unparalleled instrument of extortion. But for the prison officials it was a major headache, which caused overcrowding and, in their view, unwarranted suffering. For this reason, the prison inspectors also became important in the process of primary justice by releasing prisoners and frequently, wittingly or not, thwarting the designs of those responsible for the commitment.

Prison inspectors kept the most regular records, duly noting each commitment to, and discharge from, the "untried" department of the prison. This included everyone detained for whatever reason before trial and those committed after a conviction by an aldermen or justice for such minor offenses as drunkenness or disorderly conduct. These figures also undoubtedly represented only a minority of the cases brought before the aldermen. Alderman Milnor committed only 31 percent of the defendants recorded in his docket to prison; Alderman Kenney, only 4 percent; and Alderman Gregg, 24 percent.[45] Nevertheless, this net captured some cases that escaped all others since many cases that resulted in a prison commitment involved neither the police nor the higher courts. Prison commitments numbered roughly 4,000 or 5,000 per year before 1850, then increased rapidly to nearly 11,000 in 1851 and over 21,000 in 1860, finally settling at between 15,000 and 20,000 a year after the war.

Clearly, then, each set of figures provides only a fraction of the number of cases heard by Philadelphia's aldermen each year. Because these records also overlap to an undetermined extent, even basing estimates on them is a hazardous enterprise. If we assume that commitments represent one-quarter to one-third of all the cases, then the total number for the first postpolice year, 1855, would range between 42,510 and 56,680 among a population of about 500,000. Roughly 45 percent of the cases Amos Gregg heard involved police arrests. This would lead to an estimate of 86,000 cases for the same year. Court returns might represent anywhere from 4,600 to almost 25,000 indictable offenses for 1854. These estimates are, of course, based only on scattered newspaper comment, three alderman's dockets, and the unlikely assumption that there were no unrecorded cases. Still they do nothing but support the impression of observers that the number was very large, that criminal prosecution was a regular feature of everyday life, and that it remained so throughout the period.[46]

The Variety of Cases

The most fundamental distinctions among criminal cases were based on the severity of the charge, and they were of two kinds. The first was the difference between nonindictable and indictable offenses, the former being cases over which alderman and justices had complete summary jurisdiction, the latter those that required a grand jury hearing and possible jury trial. Then, within the latter group, there was the familiar distinction between misdemeanors and felonies. Though these categories seem to disregard entirely the distinction between private and state prosecution, there was a correspondence. Nonindictable offenses—primarily drunkeness, disorderly conduct, and vagrancy—were most often state-initiated. Indictable offenses—mostly assault and battery or petty larceny—were usually private prosecutions.

Before the professionalization of the police, nonindictable offenses were probably only a minority of the cases heard by aldermen. Afterwards, they were undoubtedly the majority. This difference is illustrated by the examples of William Milnor and J. B. Kenney, typical prepolice neighborhood aldermen, and Amos Gregg, who was a committing magistrate at the 23rd Ward police station after 1854. Between 1823 and 1829, only 7 of the 273 cases (1.3 percent) recorded by Milnor, and between 1845 and 1847, only 11 of the 88 cases (12.5 percent) recorded by Kenney were nonindictable. In contrast, 43 percent of the cases in Amos Gregg's docket were in this group.[47]

Cases initiated by police arrests became the largest part of the minor judiciary's criminal case load only after the police expansion of 1850 and city consolidation of 1854. Yet the character of arrests probably did not change much after this date. The part-time and untrained pre-1850 police force was ill-equipped to do much more than apprehend the drunk and disorderly, and this remained the primary task of the professional police after mid-century. Nonindictable offenses became a majority of all prison commitments in 1838 and remained so, peaking at about 70 percent, during the late 1850s.[48] Among prison commitments for minor offenses, drunkenness comprised 21 percent of the total through 1854 and 22 percent afterwards; all forms of disorderly conduct, 57 and 60 percent; vagrancy, 22 and 17 percent. Arrest patterns after 1850 were similar to these commitment patterns. Of the roughly 27,000 arrests made by the police between 1850 and 1854, 81 percent were for drunkenness and disorderly conduct. The pattern remained remarkably similar thereafter as the number of annual arrests skyrocketed. Drunkenness ranged between one-quarter and one-third of all arrests; disorderly conduct, between one-third and one-half; and vagrancy, between 2 and 7 percent of all arrests. Arrest patterns before 1855 were probably much the same, with perhaps a somewhat higher proportion of drunks.

Nonindictable offenses were primarily brought to the aldermen's attention after a police arrest. Such charges could also be initiated by a private citizen, and sometimes they were. This is illustrated by the unequal distribution of minor offenses among the county's aldermen and justices. Before 1855 the mayor was nominal head of the various small police forces that served the city, and when a drunk or vagrant was arrested, the officer brought him or her to the mayor for a hearing. Over half of all commitments for drunkenness between 1815 and 1836, and nearly one-third of those for vagrancy, were made by the mayor. Another quarter of the vagrancy commitments were made by one alderman. Of the 2,793 cases heard by the mayor of Philadelphia in 1848, 37 percent were for drunkenness, 11 percent for disorderly conduct, 7 percent vagrancy, 7 percent larceny, and 21 percent for "minor breaches of law and city ordinances." From October 1850 to October 1851, after the police force was expanded, the mayor heard 6,974 cases. Just over half, more than the entire number of cases heard by the mayor for all charges in 1848, were for drunkenness. Another 21 percent were for disorderly conduct. Vagrancy accounted for 8 percent of the cases, and larceny and assault and battery, 5 percent each.[49]

Before 1854 there were significant differences between the criminal business of the mayor and that of the aldermen, even those who were also committing magistrates in the suburban districts. Two-thirds of the drunkenness commitments, two-fifths of the vagrancy commitments, and one-quarter of the disorderly conduct commitments between 1838 and 1854 were made by the mayor. No alderman even approached these proportions for these charges. After the expansion of the police and the number of committing magistrates in 1854, this pattern naturally became markedly less pronounced but did not disappear. Nonindictable offenses continued to be more concentrated among a few aldermen than were indictable offenses. One alderman committed 15 percent of the drunks; another nearly 10 percent of the drunks; another, 9 percent of the vagrants; and yet another, 9 percent of those charged with breach of the peace.

One minor offense, however, was exceptional. Both before and after 1854, charges of disorderly conduct were much more widely distributed among the aldermen than were the other minor offenses. Between 1815 and 1836, only 21 percent of the commitments for this charge were made by the mayor, and this percentage increased only slightly (to 26 percent) from 1838 to 1854, despite a large increase in the number of arrests for disorderly conduct during those years. The distribution pattern for this charge resembled indictable offenses more closely than did the other minor offenses, suggesting that it was often privately initiated. Disorderly conduct was a vague and complicated category, blending the features of both private and police prosecutions, and its frequent use signified its fruitfulness as a source of manipulation for aldermen, policemen, and private citizens alike.

Indictable offenses probably comprised the majority of cases heard by ordinary aldermen. Over three-quarters of William Milnor's cases during the 1820s and 88 percent of J. B. Kenney's during the 1840s were indictable offenses. Amos Gregg, despite the fact that he was a part-time committing magistrate between 1854 and 1878, still heard mostly—56 percent of his cases—indictable offenses.[50]

Just as the records of prison commitments suggest an increasing percentage of minor offenses over time, they imply a decreasing percentage of indictable offenses, but this is easily misconstrued. Prison commitments represent only a fraction of all cases and perhaps a smaller fraction of indictable than nonindictable offenses. The complex and informal manner in which private prosecutions—surely the majority of indictable cases—were handled will make this clear, but even the docket books suggest it. Kenney committed only two of seventy-seven people charged with indictable offenses. Milnor and Gregg committed one-quarter of those charged with indictable offenses (these and all prison commitments made by aldermen for indictable offenses were pretrial commitments, generally in lieu of bail). Assault and battery, the most common indictable offense and the one most likely to be privately prosecuted, resulted in commitment even less frequently. Milnor committed only 10 percent of those charged with assault and battery, Gregg, only 21 percent.[51] So the decreasing percentage of assault and battery commitments— 16 percent from 1815 to 1836, 14 percent from 1838 to 1854, and 10 percent between 1855 and 1874—does not necessarily indicate that indictable offenses and private prosecutions were in any sense decreasing, nor even that they had ceased to comprise the majority of the criminal business presented to the aldermen.[52]

Assault and battery was the most frequent indictable offense and larceny second. The former comprised the absolute majority of all cases heard by Milnor—52 percent—while larceny was a distant second, only 13 percent. Kenney heard 38 percent assault or assault and battery cases, with larceny third at 11 percent. Gregg's cases later in the century were strikingly similar. Even with the rise in minor offenses, assault and battery made up 25 percent of his cases and larceny 12 percent.[53] Accused thieves were more frequently committed to prison than those charged with assault—85 percent of those charged compared to 10 percent for Milnor, 38 percent to 21 percent for Gregg. Therefore, larceny commitments (17 percent of the total) actually exceeded assault and battery commitments from 1815 to 1836, they were only slightly lower (11 percent) between 1838 and 1854, and they were virtually equal (9 percent) from 1855 to 1874.[54] The remaining roughly one-third of the indictable offenses consisted mostly of liquor, gambling, and morals offenses. Felonious personal and property crimes were rare. There were, for example, no such cases recorded by William Milnor, two by J. B. Kenney, and only fourteen by Amos Gregg over a twenty-five-year period. Only 3 percent of the prison commitments for the entire period were for serious crimes.[55]

The cases that were returned to the courts of record were, except in extraordinary circumstances, indictable offenses and, therefore, mostly private prosecutions, especially before 1850. Larceny and assault and battery comprised the vast majority of court cases, accounting for roughly 70 percent of all cases recorded in court dockets. The remaining 30 percent, roughly half liquor prosecutions and half serious crime, were often state prosecutions, especially after 1850.

The most striking difference between indictable and nonindictable offenses was their distribution among the aldermen. Unlike minor offenses, indictable offenses were distributed widely and relatively evenly among the aldermen and justices. Between 1815 and 1836, no alderman made more than 11 percent of the assault and battery commitments, and the mayor made only 6 percent. Neither the mayor nor any other magistrate made more than 8 percent of the assault and battery commitments between 1838 and 1854 or more than 6 percent from 1855 to 1874. Larceny patterns were similar, if somewhat less extreme. From 1815 to 1854, the mayor made 19 percent of the larceny commitments and no other magistrate more than 5 percent; between 1854 and 1874, no alderman made more than 8 percent.[56]

So some charges, generally minor offenses, were heavily concentrated among the mayor and committing magistrates, and others, mostly indictable offenses, were more widely distributed among the aldermen and justices. Criminal cases fell into two groups: minor cases such as drunkenness and vagrancy, initiated typically by a police arrest and heard primarily by the mayor or another committing magistrate; and indictable but often petty offenses such as assault and battery, initiated typically by private citizens, heard in relatively equal numbers by many aldermen and justices, and subject to a return to the courts of record. Some important cases escaped this strict classification. Larceny, though an indictable offense, sometimes involved the police; disorderly conduct, though a minor offense, was often privately prosecuted.

The minor judiciary had original jurisdiction over all criminal cases. This fact obscured the difference between police cases and private prosecutions. At their core, the two groups embodied distinct, and in some ways, contradictory concepts of criminal justice. The former represented the power of the state to suppress crime and disorder; the latter represented the power of the citizenry to invoke the criminal law voluntarily as they saw fit. This was the duality of the criminal justice process for the citizens of Philadelphia.

This duality distinguished criminal cases, but it was also present in all of them. Throughout the period, the traditions and practices of private prosecution dominated the culture of criminal justice in Philadelphia, influencing police cases and placing a popular and unruly stamp on the courtrooms. In every case, however, this was in part offset by the coercive power of the state, especially the terror of imprisonment, the specter looming behind even the flimsiest of private cases, reminding everyone that criminal prosecution was truly a serious matter.

Part II The World of Private Prosecution

2. The Aldermen and Primary Justice

August 1863 was a typically hot and atypically tiresome wartime summer month. Shut away for several weeks in the fetid quarter sessions courtroom, the grand jurors lost their patience and began quarreling with each other, the district attorney, and the judges. The issue was whether the aldermen or the private parties were more to blame for the flood of exasperatingly petty cases with which the jurors were presented, preventing them from escaping the oppressive atmosphere of Independence Square. Although they had little use for either group, most of the two dozen grand jurors were inclined to blame the aldermen, believing that they had the power to keep cases out of court. So spirited was the discussion that, when the grand jurors issued their written presentment, they included their complaints. In one passage, replete with Dickensian images, the foreman provided illustrations that "will serve for as many hundreds":

> Mrs. Fightall's little boy Mike, aged 4, pushes Mrs. Fireup's little girl Sally, aged 5, into the gutter, for not giving him any of her peanuts, in doing which Sallies clothes were soiled, whereupon Mrs. Fireup rushes to Alderman Graball, who, upon the receipt of $1, forthwith issues a warrant upon the oath of the mother, who did not see the circumstances, but has only heard the child say so, as she knows the little puss would not tell an untruth. Mrs. Fightall is arrested, arraigned and required to give bail at once, failing to find which, it is suggested that he, Mr. Graball, can prevail upon Mr. Alwaysdry to go her bail, provided she brings a cross-action, which will compel Mrs. Fireup to either withdraw her suit or settle the case, all of which will cost her but $1, which she pays over, and *these two cases are finally submitted for the consideration of 24 citizens*, and these two neighbors of long standing are made inveterate foes, whereas, by one kind word from the magistrate, their friendship might have been the more firmly cemented.
>
> Biddy McGab, in washing her pave, lets some water run over the side of Chloe Curlwool, who, in consequence, calls Biddy pretty hard names, not relishing which, Biddy, in turn, gives Chloe a push with her mop, and she under an impulse of a moment hastes off to Squire Niggerfip, the "culled pussen's frien'" and procures a warrant at half

price, rather than lose the job, on which Biddy is arrested, taken to his office, and in default of bail or a *satisfactory consideration*, she is sent to Moyamensing, the disgrace of which, induces her friends to "come down" handsomely for her liberation to this apostle of justice.[1]

Focusing on the women, children, and blacks who were overrepresented in the wartime city, the foreman was complaining about the simple fact that the criminal law was so frequently used by all kinds of people for all sorts of reasons.[2] Although characteristically hostile and condescending, the 1863 grand jury pinpointed the key relationship in criminal justice, the one between aldermen and the private parties to criminal cases. It was, of course, futile by then to debate which party was more "to blame" for the torrent of criminal litigation because, as in all long-standing relationships, a balance had been struck which met the needs of both and assured its continuation. Private litigants had access to the law as a formidable element in the resolution of personal disputes and grievances. Aldermen and justices received a considerable bounty in legal and illegal fees, gained a certain status in their communities and, sometimes, created the foundation of a promising political career.

During the first half of the nineteenth century, private prosecution dominated criminal justice in Philadelphia. Every criminal prosecution was initiated before an alderman or justice of the peace, and most criminal prosecutions were initiated by private citizens. Though the "spirit of litigation" was, as observers hinted, manifest mainly "among the poorer classes," private prosecutions involved a wide variety of circumstances and were initiated by citizens from all walks of life. Through the exercise of fee-system based relations with neighborhood magistrates, prosecutors secured the intervention of the criminal law in virtually any kind of personal circumstance they chose. The same system also allowed them, with a cloak of legitimacy, to employ informal means with which to limit the law's impact on their affairs and to maintain, with the aldermen, most of the discretion within the process of criminal justice. Primary justice touched more people than any other part of the process. As the point of initial contact between the citizenry and the criminal law, it necessarily involved a great deal of discretion and informality. Given the extreme localism of early nineteenth-century government and politics, the relationships established in the aldermen's offices became the most influential ones in criminal justice.

The aldermen assumed the duties of the city's justices of the peace when Philadelphia was reincorporated in 1789. Fifteen aldermen, one of whom would be elected mayor, were appointed in 1789 to seven-year terms Two of them sat as judges on the mayor's court, which had been reestablished by the new charter, and three others sat on the aldermen's court, a special civil court for disputes under £10.[3] As the years passed, the number of aldermen steadily increased and suburban aldermen and justices came more and more to resemble their urban counterparts.

Aldermen exercised a broad criminal jurisdiction. "Every criminal offence is presumed to be within the scope of their authority to inquire into, take bail, or commit the accused."[4] Without a jury, aldermen could convict persons accused of drunkenness, vagrancy, or disorderly conduct and impose fines or prison terms. Alternatively, they could hold an offender to bail with the provision that he or she not repeat the misdeed. In indictable misdemeanors and felonies, the alderman or justice heard the testimony of the prosecutor and, if persuaded that a crime had occurred, returned the case to a court of record for trial. He then either held the accused to bail or committed him or her to prison to await trial. Whenever an alderman returned a case to the court, made a commitment to prison, or held someone to bail, he was compensated by fees paid by the parties to the case.[5]

Litigation, other legal business, and entertainment all combined to give at least the appearance that these "biggest fish" had "a genuine interest in the well-being of their neighbors."[6] If this appearance helped to encourage ready use of the criminal law, it was only reinforced by the aldermen's own social origins, which were not too different from those of their neighbors and constituents. Most were members of an emerging "new" middle class, and many had backgrounds as workers. Joshua Raybold began as a baker, then became a constable before becoming an alderman. John Allison was a conveyancer and board of health clerk before becoming justice of the peace. Alderman Andrew Hooten was first a cabinetmaker, then deputy keeper of the convict department of the Arch Street Prison. Joseph Shermer was a master shoemaker. Others were members of fire companies. One, William McMullin, became the city's most powerful Democratic boss of the Civil War era. Half were real-property owners; half of these owned property valued at over $500. The majority of aldermen and justices were men firmly rooted in their communities and probably familiar to their neighbors by virtue of their backgrounds as artisans, merchants, service providers, and public servants.[7]

Even the exceptions prove the rule. The most notable alderman early in the century, if not the most typical, was John Binns. The polemical publisher of the anti-Jackson *Democratic Press*, Binns found his newspaper fortunes declining when the Jacksonians triumphed in Pennsylvania, so he turned his energies to his position as an alderman, to which he was appointed in 1822 by one of his political beneficiaries, Governor Joseph Heister. His most notable

Table 2.1 Occupations of 82 Philadelphia Aldermen and Justices, 1812–1854

	Number	Percentage
Craftsmen and other skilled workers	27	32.9
Service providers and shopkeepers	19	23.2
Government employees	14	17.1
Professionals	8	9.8
Attorneys	7	8.5
Other	7	8.5

SOURCE: Philadelphia County Prison Daily Occurrence Dockets and City of Philadelphia Directories.
NOTE: The names of all aldermen and justices committing people to prison were recorded and traced in the directories. The specific occupations among the craftsmen were baker, boot- and shoemaker, potter, printer, chairmaker, iron monger, silver plater, wood corder, and gilder. Among the service providers were tavern-keeper, conveyancer, shop-keeper, grocer, trader, merchant, and apothecary. Government employees included superintendant of roads, constable, board of health clerk, flour inspector, collector of taxes, keeper of the prison, inspector of customs, prothonotary of the county court, and clerk of the quarter sessions. The professionals included three teachers and a physician. Others included a gentleman, a publisher, and a sea captain.

accomplishments were exposing bakers' frauds and compiling two handbooks, *Binns' Justice* and *Binns' Daily Companion*, which became the standard reference works for aldermen and justices throughout Pennsylvania.[8] Binns became a model of the honest, responsible alderman, a servant of the public interest in the eighteenth-century tradition of the elite magistrate—a man of means or talent administering laws disinterestedly, identified wholly with the law and the corporation of the city. By 1820, however, most aldermen and justices no longer resembled Binns. For most, returns from the office were an important part of their living. An exception to this two decades later, a wealthy loom boss and land speculator, Alderman Hugh Clark was unusually unpopular. During the 1844 Kensington riots, his home was burned to the ground.

The alderman's office was a lower- and working-class world, and the aldermen themselves looked for the most part like the "natural superiors" of that world, men who provided the political voice of the working class in municipal affairs, the "payrollers, lawyers, publicans, and other shopkeepers, who were deeply involved in the daily lives of working people and had often risen from their ranks, but who enjoyed sufficient income, control over their own working time, and social connections to be able to participate actively in party and governmental affairs."[9]

Private Prosecutions before Consolidation

Even though private prosecutions did not always make up the majority of criminal cases, the relationship of parties to private cases and the minor judiciary was the dominant one in criminal justice. The largely informal practices that were typical of this relationship determined the disposition of private cases in the aldermen's offices and became the expected mode of criminal procedure among most of the parties to criminal cases at all levels. As a result police cases were often handled informally by magistrates, usually according to the expectations of the arrested person. Similarly, parties to cases that proceeded into the courts of record expected continued informality there.

When a person wanted to initiate a criminal prosecution, he or she went off to the nearest alderman's office, complained, and usually secured a warrant for the arrest of the accused. After the alderman's constable escorted the defendant to the office, the alderman conducted a formal hearing, and the process was underway. Most often, private prosecutors charged their adversaries with assault and battery, larceny, or some form of disorderly conduct. Well before 1850, aldermen and litigants established patterns of case disposition that would last through most of the century. Most criminal cases were fully disposed of by the alderman, even though this was often contrary to formal criminal procedure.[10] For example, William Milnor completely disposed of 66 percent of the criminal cases recorded in his docket book between 1823 and 1829 and 70 percent of the assault and battery cases. This meant that only 34 percent of the cases brought to Milnor's office were returned to the courts of record for further action, and only 31 percent of the defendants were committed to prison to await it. Other alderman went more by the book. J. B. Kenney disposed of only 18 percent of his assault and battery cases.[11]

Even when an alderman returned a case to the criminal court, it was not necessarily heard there, and this was one reason that aldermen and private prosecution tended to annoy court officials. A return and prison commitment did not mean that the alderman was finished with the case as, most of the time, he should have been. This was partly the result of the law itself. In response to complaints from the court about an intolerable number of assault cases, the legislature, in 1806, permitted aldermen and justices to settle assault and battery cases in their offices and still receive a 25 cent fee. The settlement law reduced the number of assault cases that went to trial, but it also encouraged aldermen to accept assault and battery—and probably other—cases and settle them informally. So, through 1854, 82 percent of the people committed to prison for assault and battery or other minor personal crimes were released from prison by the magistrate who made the original commitment, after an average stay of eleven days. The corresponding figures for larceny were 37 percent and twenty days; for disorderly conduct, 30 percent and nine days; and for breach of the peace, an increasingly popular form of a disorderly conduct commitment among aldermen, 53 percent and ten days. Though these figures are the best direct evidence supporting contemporary claims that aldermen used imprisonment for extortionate purposes or to further the designs of malicious private prosecutors, the legitimacy of at least assault and battery settlements suggests that they may just as well reflect a less sinister pattern of informal dispute resolution. Either way, they mean that aldermen resolved a large number of the cases that they had officially sent elsewhere.

As the settlement law indicated, prominent Philadelphians had mixed feelings about private prosecution. Jurists often advised aldermen not to encourage trivial and malicious litigation. John Binns made the point in his handbook, *Binns' Justice*, "It . . . becomes the justices . . . to prevent the name of the Commonwealth from being used as an engine to gratify private malice, rather than as an instrument to promote the peace and dignity of the Commonwealth. They should discourage all criminal prosecutions of a trivial nature. The magistrate, who, from selfish considerations, encourages the angry and revengeful passions, is a nuisance in his neighborhood."[12]

Just as frequently, aldermen were encouraged to take all cases seriously. Richard Vaux, the respected attorney and recorder of the city, equated the prosecutor's right to press his case with the defendant's right to the presumption of innocence. "This is old-fashioned law and old-fashioned justice," Vaux asserted.[13] The *Public Ledger*, a leading critic of aldermen, defended private prosecution even for trivial assaults. Claiming that "trivial" usually meant an altercation in which the prosecutor chose not to retaliate physically, the *Ledger* insisted that such persons should be praised and their complaints taken seriously. "It is plain that in point of morality, and for the preservation of the peace of society, it is better to vindicate the cause of the innocent without the fight than with it. It is better to encourage a reliance on the laws. . . ." So whether aldermen went Milnor's route or Kenney's, they were bound to hear conflicting opinions about what they were doing.[14]

Aldermen received such inconsistent advice because the actual practice of private prosecution was so complicated. Malicious prosecutions were difficult to identify. Ordinary Philadelphians made no strict distinction between the use of the law and other methods of dispute resolution. Thus people regularly initiated criminal prosecutions even when they retaliated physically. On one inclement Wednesday in 1840 "the wimmen" of Southwark "were even more tremendous than usual—such hard works, hard looks, and harder blows, mixed up with an assortment of face scratching, and hair pulling, and other like attentions, were scarcely ever known before. In . . . the course of a few hours . . . Alderman Manderfield had, on different suits, some twenty or thirty of the 'dear creatures' before him."[15]

It is extremely difficult to describe precisely the kinds of people who ordinarily were involved in private prosecution. Women accounted for nearly one-third of prison commitments for assault and battery, minor personal crimes, and larceny. They were also about 20 percent of all criminal court defendants. Blacks comprised over 40 percent of all criminal court defendants from 1823 to 1825. This is consistent with the strong impression of court observers that blacks and women were frequent participants in private prosecution.[16]

Detailed descriptive information was kept only for imprisoned convicts. Imprisoned thieves were, of course, an unrepresentative sample, but observers suggested, and the convict descriptions confirm, that they were not too different from other parties to criminal cases. Convicts were overwhelmingly manual laborers, many of them unskilled, and they were disproportionately black.

Between 1843 and 1851, 29 percent of first-time convicts, 44 percent of recidivists, and 34 percent of all convicts were black. Another 10 percent were categorized as mulatto. Women convicts were even more frequently black: 44 percent of first-time offenders and 62 percent of recidivist women were black; 14 and 15 percent of each group were mulatto.[17] No wonder so many blacks turned out when one of their number stood trial.

Private cases set the tone for all of criminal justice in part because they were at first the most numerous, but also because they tended to be the "higher" indictable crimes, the complete prosecution of which required the full negotiation of the judicial process. Private cases were more serious and complicated than typical minor police cases and, in theory at least, required greater legal sophistication to adjudicate. Even among legally trained judges, this bred a respect for private criminal prosecution as a foundation stone of the legal culture. Private prosecutions were cloaked in the solemn and majestic robes of the law, robes that private prosecutors and aldermen alike had good reason to want to don.

If its legal stature draped private prosecution with awe and respectability, the actual informality of primary justice kept it within everyone's reach. This lent legitimacy to even the most mean-spirited and trivial cases and at the same time demystified even the most deserving. The combination encouraged litigation, and since litigation lined the magistrates' pockets, they did all they could to maintain the balance. There was also, of course, a double edge to criminal prosecution for the citizens involved in it. Defendants were subject to imprisonment, and all parties were responsible for financial expenses that could be quite burdensome. But defendants could also wield some power in a system of justice, which was often little more than arbitration by fee, and at any time could themselves assume the role of prosecutor.

Assault and Other Nonproperty Cases

According to most observers of primary justice, "the spirit of litigation" in Philadelphia was especially pronounced "in cases of assault and battery."[18] Not only were charges of assault and other similar personal crimes the most common private prosecutions, but they also exhibited most of the characteristic features of this form of criminal justice. All sorts of commonplace incidents resulted in assault and battery prosecutions. Jane Collins, keeper of a "genteel boarding house," charged Ellen Carey with assaulting one of the residents of her establishment. Mrs. Carey claimed that the individual in question was in the habit of ridiculing her husband, a poor "soap fat and hickory ash" gatherer, and she simply wanted to put a stop to it. The alderman held Ellen to keep the peace. Two German men, dissolving their partnership in a small hog-butchering business, disagreed over the division of property and took to pelting each other with dishcloths and sausages. One of them charged the other with assault and battery.[19]

Since they could legally arbitrate an assault case for a fee, aldermen rarely simply discharged the entire matter, a major reason for the popularity of the criminal law. When a case was refused, it was not because the case was unusually trivial, but because the poor people involved, often women and blacks, could not afford the magistrate's fees or because the prosecutor could present absolutely no evidence that an offense had taken place. When women quarreled over their children, for example, aldermen sometimes refused the case, claiming a desire to save the county the costs of a private spat but also probably recognizing that neither party had the cash to pay a fee. A black woman brought Spring Garden Alderman Scott a complaint against two other women for assault and battery on a fourth woman who shared her house. The alderman refused to take the case, advising her not to "go to law for trifles" and to spend her money instead on wood and food. She discarded the advice and went off to find a "more pliable magistrate." Even when a case was discharged, a prosecutor was not without recourse to the law. There was no limit to the number of aldermen or justices to whom a person might bring a criminal charge. If one refused a case, it could be taken to another and another, until it was accepted. If a prosecutor was determined, he or she could almost never fail to institute a case.

Rejected prosecutions were exceptional, but they were also remarkable examples of the kinds of disputes that people expected a criminal prosecution would resolve. Consider Jerry Medicks, a Moyamensing weaver, who took Biddy Burton to the alderman for assault and battery in 1843. "Now I'll get justice," declared Jerry, accusing her of stealing his blanket and pawning it to buy drink. The perplexed alderman demanded a consistent charge, whereupon Jerry accused the woman of refusing to leave him alone and pleaded with the alderman to force her to turn her amorous attentions elsewhere. The alderman dismissed them both, but Jerry returned an hour later claiming this time that Biddy had stolen and pawned his shuttle! Then there was Issachar Dingy, a black, who also sought out an alderman after a spat. "Master Bos, Sam Allen has kicked and cuff'd me," announced Issachar, placing the altercation at a Water Street eating house the night before. However, his only witness, a mutual friend known as Coaley Sable, claimed he had his mouth "full of wittles" at the time and saw nothing. Issachar reminded his friend that he did not eat with his eyes, but Coaley insisted that the charge was a "dirty, nasty, nonsensish trick" and left the office. Sometimes the tables were turned on a prosecutor. Moses Blumenthal brought Patrick Cummiskey to Alderman Elkington, but all the witnesses corroborated Patrick's story that Moses had induced Patrick into his clothing store and forcibly detained him there hoping to persuade Patrick to buy a coat. Patrick refused and forced his way out, whereupon the charge was brought. The outcome was a discharge for Patrick and $300 bail for Moses.[20]

Though thwarted in their attempts to invoke the criminal law in commonplace incidents, these people demonstrated that the use of the criminal law was commonplace indeed. This determination to control their personal affairs by invoking the law continued throughout the process of primary justice. Private prosecutors almost always attempted to exercise as much discretion over the process as possible. They might ask that leniency be shown to the accused. Though Alexander McClain had beaten Jonathan Williams's wife, Williams requested that McClain only be bound to keep the peace, "not wishing to do the man any harm as he had a family." The alderman obliged.

Defendants likewise sought to control the process, and the best way for them to do so was to become prosecutors themselves. They did this by instituting cross-bills, in which an accused person retaliated by pressing the same charge against the original prosecutor. Lewis Conrad's squirrel was attacked by Benjamin Morris's dog. Conrad kicked the dog, Morris kicked Conrad, and "a regular scraping took place." Morris accused Conrad before Alderman Binns, and Conrad brought Morris before Alderman Mitchell. "The dog and squirrel came off without harm, and have thus far avoided lawsuits," added the reporter. The typical scenario was summarized by a court reporter in 1848:

> Two men charged each other before different aldermen with assault and batteries. The case of one was heard when defendant No. 1 was committed in default of giving bail. In the custody of the constable he desired to go before the other alderman and have a swear against plaintiff No. 1, which was acceded to, and the result that plaintiff No. 2 had plaintiff No. 1, and now defendant No. 2, committed, and both were taken down to prison. All parties in these cases had their satisfaction, the aldermen and constables coming in for their shares—each plaintiff having paid the costs.[21]

Prosecutors, and even defendants if they chose to become prosecutors, had great success in gaining satisfaction from aldermen and justices and great latitude in determining how the magistrate would treat the accused. The commonplace substance of the cases did not detract from the seriousness of the process. Much of the time, people used the criminal law in their private affairs in order to combat a perceived injustice or to assert basic rights they felt were being violated.

There was no better example of this than battered wives. Women regularly brought charges against men for assault. Over one-quarter of the assault and battery cases heard by Alderman Kenney were brought by women against men. Kenney also recorded four cases specifically as wife abuse, one brought by the couple's son. Sometimes charges were brought by friends or neighbors of the woman.[22] Depending on the frequency and severity of the beatings, the alderman's action might range from commitment, in lieu of high bail, to a small bond to keep the peace or simply a reprimand. John Sarch was able to make "a pretty good defense" to a charge brought by his wife and was discharged with only a warning. Most often, however, the batterer was punished in some manner. George Ausby, a silver plater, had "unquestionably" been beating his wife Eliza for years. He was committed in lieu of $300 to keep the peace. Most accused men suffered a similar fate, but Thomas Rose escaped it. Bound in only $100, he made the bail and returned home. Most of the time, batterers were held on bail to keep the peace. In fact, all four of the men brought before Alderman Kenney for wife abuse were held on bail to keep the peace. Two of Kenney's six assault and battery cases (of a total of thirty-three) that resulted in bail to keep the peace were wife abuse cases. Assaults of this kind were also more likely than others to be settled or discharged at some point, at least among the cases of the rather straight-laced Alderman Kenney. In only two of eighty-eight cases did he record a discharge after taking bail, and both were wife abuse cases. Also, the only assault and battery case settled in his office was an assault by a man upon a woman. In extremely severe cases, the batterer was charged with a more heinous offense. For a beating that rendered a woman bedridden, Alderman Eneu held her husband in $1,000 bail for assault and battery with intent to kill.[23]

Because the magistrates were so receptive to assault and battery prosecutions, battered wives had somewhere to go to exert some control over men who exceeded their authority in the home. Yet battered women also tried to avoid having their husbands sent to prison and to have cases discharged. They were, in short, able to use the law as a tool in their struggle to define the power dynamic of the family, to challenge the legitimacy of violence as an element of that dynamic.

In a variety of ways, husbands sometimes resisted. One way was simply by being more violent. Some men attacked neighbors who tried to intervene, which often prompted the neighbors to bring complaints. Men attacked the constable sent to bring them to the hearing; sometimes they even attacked the alderman when they arrived at his office. Another form of resistance was to use the same law against their wives. For example, James Hughes was brought before Alderman Griscom for badly beating his wife. A few days before, just after the assault, he had complained to Alderman Mitchell that she had beaten him, for which she was committed in default of bail. However, several neighbors came to her aid, procured her release, and prosecuted Hughes, who then was himself committed.[24]

Probably the greater part of private prosecution stemmed from relatively honest attempts to resolve ordinary disputes. But at least some prosecutors were more manipulative, according to those they accused. John Corbett was charged by a man who lived in the same house with beating his wife. Corbett claimed that he was innocent and had, in fact, been put out of his own house by this man and another, both his tenants, who had instituted this action in order to avoid paying the rent for that week. If this was so, the tactic was successful; Corbett was held in $300 bail.[25]

Citizens even prosecuted officers of the law for assault and battery. This was further evidence of the popularity of private prosecution and a variation of the practice of instituting cross-bills. Typically these cases involved constables or watchmen who were accused of being drunk or using excessive force while making arrests. A particularly complex example occurred when Constable Ratcliff brought a Southwark man, Charles Smith, before Alderman McCall on a disorderly house charge. The next day Smith charged Ratcliff before Alderman Johnson for eavesdropping on Smith's home. Then Ratcliff charged Johnson's constable, named McGinnis, who had arrested him, for assault and battery before Alderman McCall. Finally, McCall and Ratcliff were charged before Johnson for "conspiracy to falsely charge and arrest Constable McGinnis."[26]

Private prosecutions for personal offenses other than assault and battery were also very common. Domestic disputes that stopped short of assault often found their way into court. Henry Blake's wife prosecuted him for refusing to come to bed and making too much noise, preventing her from sleeping. He was bound over to come to bed when called. In another case, John Fort was sent to prison on a complaint lodged by his mother whose furnishings he would destroy whenever he was drunk, which was often.[27]

The use of offensive or threatening language also prompted cases. George Mundy was brought before the mayor for cursing the city councils, but the mayor ruled that there was nothing illegal in that. A man prosecuted Fanny Lewis before Alderman Bryant for threatening his property. "May it please your honor, I appeal to you, whether this prosecution can be sustained, as the prosecutor has no property, nor never had." Fanny was committed nonetheless. Threats could be a serious matter, however. In 1843 Rebecca James appeared before Alderman Kenney, terrified of William Stevenson. "I am in danger of my life—afraid he will kill me—he said if he could not kill me he would make me remember—I am afraid to go out of the door." Stevenson was held in $150 bail to keep the peace.[28]

Other sexual and marital matters also moved people to use the criminal law. These were not public morals prosecutions but rather private prosecutions prompted by personal feelings of injury. Parents of young women prosecuted men for seduction; husbands prosecuted their wives' paramours for adultery; wives prosecuted husbands for desertion. A Southwark man charged a fortune teller with conspiracy for beguiling his wife into believing that for a fee information could be provided about his infidelities.[29] As we have seen, even disorderly conduct was often privately prosecuted. According to the court, these cases exhibited "only a litigious disposition on the part of those who commenced them." One such case heard by Alderman Kenney charged four men with "disturbing the public peace by assembling with others in Little Pine St. nightly and using profane language and disturbing . . . neighbors by noise." Kenney held each man in $200 to stay on good behavior.[30]

Because the criminal law was so accessible and pliable, it was often used to influence the outcome of a private squabble. Any pair of citizens in a relationship that was potentially antagonistic might resort to the criminal law should the antagonism materialize. So, for example, landlords and tenants often brought charges against one another. Usually landlords prosecuted tenants for disorderly behavior or keeping a disorderly house. Often both parties were poor. Ann Golding was one such landlord, a woman forced to take any tenants she could find. As a result, she had "considerable trouble" with them and was "under the necessity of bringing them every couple of weeks to the Mayor, to have them regulated." Though the mayor punished the tenants on this occasion in 1838, he warned Mrs. Golding to "be more particular in the choice of her tenants; otherwise, he would have nothing to do with her cases." Generally the landlords' wishes were granted. Mrs. Ann Gulden had an especially valid complaint. One of her tenants repeatedly ran after her with a bucket of water, intending to give her a "shower." Mrs. Gulden succeeded in getting this tenant committed for thirty days. Evictions prompted the rare instances in which tenants prosecuted landlords, either for assault and battery or destruction of property attendant to a forcible eviction. In these cases, the landlord was usually bound over, but the eviction was upheld.[31]

Similarly, gamblers initiated criminal prosecutions in order to recover a debt or loss. Alderman Elkington held both parties in an 1851 lottery case to bail, in order to prevent a private settlement between the prosecutor and defendant before trial. Unsuccessful gamblers simply wanted to recoup some of their losses by forcing their creditors to buy off the prosecution. Sometimes defendants then instituted suits of their own for conspiracy to extort money. The threat of imprisonment was usually enough to persuade a gambler that his luck had run out. Cases of this kind were good examples of the effective use of cross-prosecution, a tactic also used by others, such as fire companies accused by rivals in riots and disturbances. Cross-bills neatly prevented any company from prosecuting another and thereby taking their disputes off the streets.[32] In gambling and fire riot cases most private prosecutors were not interested in convictions or even punishment. Instead, they sought the restitution of a desired balance in a private relationship. Because of this characteristic of private prosecution, it was not a form of law enforcement well suited to the suppression of popular activities.

Liquor prosecutions were rarely privately initiated; those that were, were either exceptional attempts at suppression by temperance societies or typical efforts by individuals to use the law to solve a private problem. In 1844 the Young Men's Temperance Society brought a charge against a public house for operating on Sunday, in violation of a previously unenforced colonial statute. The alderman dismissed this suit on a technicality. The more common practice of bringing charges against liquor dealers for selling to intoxicated persons or minors, usually pressed by angry wives and mothers, began only in 1854 after new legislation was passed. Gambling charges were sometimes related to liquor charges since gambling often occurred in taverns. One Moyamensing innkeeper was charged by three men for allowing patrons to bet on shuffleboard games. He was fined and held for keeping an unlicensed tippling house.[33]

Assault and battery and other nonproperty cases comprised the bulk of private prosecutions and demonstrated better than any others the easy accessibility of primary justice and the extent to which private prosecutors could manipulate and control the process. They were by no means, however, the only kinds of private cases. Property crime was also frequently privately prosecuted.

Property Cases

Though the legal requirement that property cases be fully prosecuted probably dissuaded some people from initiating them, they were still very common. Like other private cases, property prosecutions were generally petty. Larceny was the typical charge. Thomas Kenyon stole $7 worth of items from Thomas Bailey, John Baker took a coil of rope, John Wilson pilfered eight fowls. They also generally involved people already known to one another, for example, masters and servants. Lucy Davis, a black employee of a Mrs. Freeman, was charged by the lady with stealing a carpet that had been left in Lucy's care. Gamblers also prosecuted each other for small thefts that allegedly occurred in the course of gaming. When the magistrate discovered the nature of the case, he generally ignored the larceny charge and held everyone involved for gambling.[34]

Most property cases occurred among friends and acquaintances and stemmed from all sorts of circumstances. William McAvoy accused Margaret and Daniel Shannon, Irish immigrants all, of stealing $5, but Mrs. Shannon claimed she was merely taking back $5 that McAvoy had taken from her friend Peg, who was sleeping in the Shannons' house when McAvoy dropped off some laundry. They were all bound over. One Reverend Fred Bagans, connected with a small Northern Liberties German congregation, convinced Mrs. Catherine Burr that he was an angel. He was thus able to entice her into his bed and, in the process, suggested to her that Mr. Burr was the devil. Accordingly, it would be a service to the Creator for her to take his money and give it to the Reverend. After he wrested a tidy sum from the Burrs, they brought charges against the Reverend Bagans, who was held in $400 bail. A white man, John Miller, charged two blacks with stealing his money. During Miller's testimony, however, it was revealed that the three were friends and had been drinking together at a Fourth Street oyster cellar. They had gotten drunk and Miller lost his money. According to the magistrate, his charge could not be upheld because he was intoxicated at the time of the alleged theft. All three were, nevertheless, held in $200 bail for disorderly conduct.[35]

Cases like these were no different from the typical personal case; they just happened to be about property. There were, however, some people who appeared to be professional criminals who were charged by private prosecutors. Two young men who had committed a series of thefts from the tavern and boarding house of Mrs. M. Duncan on Market Street were seized by the proprietor and several friends as they were hiding under beds in one of the rooms. They were taken to the magistrate and committed. Fredrick Faustenberg, a jewelry thief, was finally captured by William Patten, owner of a small shop from which Faustenberg had taken some gold spectacles. He too was committed by the mayor.[36]

Larceny cases, in general, differed from personal cases because of the prosecutors' more earnest desire (or legal responsibility) to procure a criminal sanction. Nevertheless, possibilities for flexibility existed in these cases just as in others. When three boys were charged before a Manayunk magistrate for the theft of iron, the anonymous prosecutor allowed the magistrate to release the boys with a stern warning about the possibility of a commitment to the house of refuge. Property cases were also subject to forms of manipulation uncommon to personal prosecutions. As one would expect, property case defendants had greater leverage than other defendants; they frequently had the means with which to influence the magistrate. For example, in 1840 three black men were charged by a tavernkeeper with passing a counterfeit note. They were committed by the alderman and taken to prison by the constable. "Soon however he returned, and after some conversation with the alderman, the men were discharged upon paying a certain amount of costs, say $5.50."[37] Though the formal substance, and some of the informal methods, differed, there was really little that distinguished primary justice in property cases from other private prosecutions.

Private Prosecution after Consolidation

Although police cases came to quantitatively dominate criminal justice after 1854, private prosecution continued to thrive. The new police did not interfere directly with the old structure of neighborhood aldermen's offices. Their appearance on the streets did not, in itself, lead people to take their disputes to an officer rather than to the alderman as they had been doing.[38] Observers of private prosecution were, if anything, more explicit about its prevalence and peculiarities than ever before. Typical prosecutors according to one judge were "of a class that think all personal redress lie[s] in an appeal to the magistrate, and a trifling quarrel in a neighborhood frequently leads to . . . a foot race to see which shall first enter complaint before a magistrate."[39] Aldermanic behavior did not change much either. Between 1855 and 1874, the committing magistrate released 80 percent of those imprisoned for assault and battery after an average stay of only nine days and an even higher percentage of those committed for other minor personal and property crimes.[40]

Similarly, aldermen continued their lax habits of returning cases to the quarter sessions. Alderman Gregg returned fewer than 60 percent of the indictable offenses initiated in his office to the quarter sessions after 1854. In February 1855, over fifty persons were in prison awaiting trial for whom no returns had been made. In March 1855 a man accused of seriously stabbing another was released on bail and able to escape trial because no return was made for two months. By the middle of November, there were still "at least fifty" in prison awaiting a return. In October 1857, Judge Oswald Thompson threatened to take action against the defaulting magistrates, declaring his astonishment at the fact that the prisoners in these matters "have been forgotten in prison for a time longer, in many cases, than a just sentence for the offenses would have extended." The problems did not disappear, however. In 1862 Thompson again threatened to punish the aldermen and complained that delays in making returns severely slowed the court's work. Aldermen were called into court by Judge Brewster in 1869 to explain why they failed to make returns; grand juries complained of the problem into the 1870s.[41]

Looking to discredit the process, critics after 1854 emphasized the large number of malicious assault and battery prosecutions. They were, however, no more common in the court reports than they had been before. Still, the increasing scrutiny under which primary justice was placed led some observers to concentrate on the most abhorrent forms of popular manipulation of the criminal law. "Perhaps the most painful, because the most unrighteous, of this kind of suits, are those in which a quarrelsome drunkard, having beaten his wife, proceeds at once to the magistrate and charges her, on oath, with assault and battery, or with assault and threats, and the poor woman comes down to the prison with her head bruised, her eyes blackened, and her whole frame bearing marks of outrageous injury inflicted by her . . . husband."[42]

Most private assault and battery cases remained neither malicious nor obviously serious but were, as reporters frequently noted, simply disputes among neighbors, friends, co-workers, and acquaintances.[43] They still often resulted in burdensome penalties—even acquittal occasionally left one or both of the parties saddled with the court costs, which sometimes led to imprisonment for default. Yet litigation flourished. Cases developed out of perceived insults, competition among business rivals, youth gang activities, revenge, arguments in saloons, long-standing quarrels, the treatment of students by teachers, unnecessary noise, drunken sprees, and disputes about pets. Parties were as old as eighty-nine years, as young as eight; at least one was blind. And for all those cases that the reporters chose to describe, there were many more disregarded as trivial incidents of no public interest.[44]

The content of larceny cases also continued to be astonishingly mundane. Other cases reflected how deeply the criminal law still was incorporated into everyday community life. People went to aldermen in order to swear off drinking, force spouses to return home, or determine how to get rid of disagreeable tenants, all of which, in the words of a reporter, gave "but a sorry exemplification of the dignity which should surround the Seat of Justice."[45]

Liquor and gambling prosecutions now received special notice because the new police had such difficulty in prosecuting people for these popular recreations. Reformers and court officials occasionally urged private citizens to prosecute, but it was hardly possible for private prosecutors to effectively enforce laws that were so unpopular that even the police could not do so. Popular control of private prosecution was particularly glaring in, for example, gambling cases, because the police were often unwilling to make arrests and most potential witnesses were uncooperative. The rare private case brought against a gambling proprietor received much praise until it became clear that, as before, most were attempts to extort money or get revenge for prior losses.[46]

Liquor cases were a bit more complex. New laws that permitted the prosecution of persons selling to minors or the intoxicated were recommended by court officials to citizens, especially women, as a tool to discipline their men and prevent physical abuse. From time to time, such prosecutions took place. More controversy surrounded enforcement of the city's license law and Sunday law. Grand jurors commented several times during the late 1850s that the new license laws were so widely disregarded that constables could not return all violators and urged private citizens to bring cases. Honest prosecutors were difficult to find; most were well-known "public informers" who brought cases only to extort money and pursued prosecutions only against those who would not or could not pay. Juries looked skeptically at the testimony of such prosecutors, and convictions were rare. License law cases would have to rest largely with the constabulary, despite the urgings of the court.[47]

Sunday drinking laws were also virtually impossible to enforce. By the Civil War era, Sunday drinking, especially by immigrants, had become an open and popular recreation. Unwilling to lose popularity, both Mayor Alexander Henry and Mayor Morton McMichael rebuffed petitions by clergymen and temperance advocates asking them to have the police enforce the law. Using dubious legal reasoning, the two men decided it was illegal and unconstitutional for the police to do so. They urged private citizens to take action instead, but people rarely did. When one man did prosecute in March 1872, the alderman's office was besieged by hundreds of people, shouting "kill him" at the prosecutor, throwing stones, and keeping the man a virtual prisoner in the office until after nightfall. Politicians and private citizens knew what they were doing when they refused to enforce this law.[48]

Private prosecution remained entrenched after the creation of the professional police because it was so deeply rooted in the city's legal and popular culture. The relationship of the many litigious Philadelphians to the minor judiciary was the most important one in the administration of the criminal law because primary justice worked for those using it. Prison was a terrifying place in nineteenth-century Philadelphia, and the very real threat or brief experience of confinement there might well have tamed a violent husband, quieted an annoying neighbor, gotten revenge for a petty assault, or even, perhaps, gained a measure of deserved justice.

There was much more than this, however, to primary justice. The symmetry of private prosecution under the fee system—the ease with which a citizen could move from the role of defendant to prosecutor—and the ability of private litigants to manipulate the process and control its consequences resulted in a special kind of incorporation of the citizenry into this pervasive part of the nineteenth-century state. Private prosecution's signal characteristic was the citizenry's invoking the public power of the criminal law, taking positive action to influence their affairs. Even by 1874, criminal justice in Philadelphia was not primarily distinguished by police-initiated, negative state action designed to control population groups, despite the appearance at mid-century of a police force capable of doing this. Though the police introduced this new mode of criminal law enforcement to the city, the system continued to be characterized by individuals asserting their rights, both substantively regarding their relations with other individuals and procedurally regarding their ability to mobilize the law. The criminal law was there to be used, accessible both to "men with great respect for the law seeking to use it, or men with no respect for the law seeking to exploit it."[49] In either case, it was a source of individual power with state backing that was employed by one citizen against another, not a source of state power that was extended over the citizenry in general by an external (even if democratically chosen) authority. The minor judiciary of Philadelphia mediated the disputes, transgressions, and disorders of popular life among the county's residents, but they did so in a specific way, which corresponded to a system of law enforcement in which the authority of, and respect for, the criminal law was dependent upon its voluntary popular use.

Primary justice was at the center of this system, but there was also another level of criminal courts. Only a small percentage of the cases heard by aldermen and justices found their way into the courts of record, but these tended to be disproportionately private prosecutions. The threat that a private prosecutor would pursue a case beyond the alderman's office was a major element of the effectiveness of criminal prosecution, and many prosecutors carried through with it, extending the popular penchant for the manipulation and informal resolution of criminal cases into the higher courts. The domination of the trial courts by private prosecutions was a major reason that they, more than any other cases, defined the era. For a full sense of the process of private prosecution, we must follow indictable offenses into the courts of record.

3. The Courts of Record

By the summer of 1860, the professional police had been on the job for six years, some of the immediate resistance to them had quieted down, and it might have been reasonable to assume that their legitimacy as the city's primary law enforcement agency had gained acceptance. Yet in commenting about his beat, the *Public Ledger*'s court reporter remained amazed that "people . . . will go to law about matters of no moment whatever." Even at decade's end, after the tumult and disruption of the Civil War, judges were still complaining that, rather than relying on the police, people were retaining old habits: "it would hardly be believed that the criminal law is resorted to every day in hundreds of cases without any justification, yet this is literally true."[1]

The courts of record were continually confronted with cases that court officials believed were only cluttering their calendars. Private prosecutors, despite having to negotiate a more complex legal process, still frequently took cases into the trial courts. Though they could not control the process as fully as they had during a case's primary stages, prosecutors nonetheless wielded considerable influence over the proceedings in the courts of record. Manipulation of the criminal law by the parties to cases resulted in extremes in every possible direction. One court reporter, for example, was struck by how much court space and time was wasted by the demands of prosecutors that their cases be heard. The parties, "hard working people," managed "to secure sufficient money to fee counsel and to prosecute or defend, and the result is a trial of unnecessary length." Private prosecutors attended court daily, accompanied by their families, waiting sometimes weeks to have their cases called. To the reporter, some of these cases were "meritorious . . . but they are very few."[2]

Equally as common, however, was precisely the opposite—the failure of prosecutors to follow through with their cases. Grand juries constantly dismissed cases because of the "unwillingness of persons to prosecute." The jurors thought there were several reasons for this. Often, they claimed, prosecutors simply wanted cases to go no further, "considering they have given their victim sufficient trouble and annoyance without bringing any to themselves." At other times, prosecutors did not realize the case would be sent to a grand jury. Wanting simply to order someone to keep the peace, they were astonished to learn that, when the magistrate declared the defendant "bound over," he meant bound over for trial.[3]

Yet other prosecutors pursued their cases to the grand jury, but often the inquest was obliged to dismiss them because the charges were "wholly unfounded" and the testimony "nothing short of absolute perjury." Still others presented the jury with enough evidence to procure a true bill but never appeared for the trial.[4] Some, of course, did take their cases all the way to a jury trial, but this also failed to satisfy most grand juries. "Nearly the whole time of the Quarter Sessions is occupied with the trial of parties charged with assault and battery, arising out of disputes among neighbors, or disputes between females about children. The assault and battery generally turns out to consist in pushing or throwing water, or some such silly annoyance."[5]

Judges and jurors were unhappy with whatever took place in the criminal courts because they had so little control over the process of prosecution. Private litigants and the minor judiciary exercised almost all of the discretion over criminal cases, despite best efforts of those in ostensible control of the process. Though the trial courts were completely separate from, and totally superior to, courts of primary justice, in practice their officers were often subordinated to the aldermen and private parties to criminal cases. Control over the initial stages of a case gave aldermen and private prosecutors the power to sustain their influence. More importantly, before the "higher" court could exercise any authority, the law had already been used in a meaningful way by one citizen against another.

Although complaining officials sometimes made it seem as though annoying private prosecutions were the only matters that occupied the court's time, this was not the fact. Just as there was a duality in criminal justice generally, so there were two kinds of cases in the courts of record. Scattered among the relatively minor prosecutions were a smaller number of serious attempts to punish crime formally, cases that were supported by court officials as well as the prosecutor. Some of these, of course, involved rather major crimes, and as time went on, the state initiated more and more of them. Most of the time, however, these cases too were private prosecutions, in most particulars no different from the first type of cases.

The problems this complex case load presented prompted a day-to-day struggle between court officials, on the one hand, and private litigants and the minor judiciary, on the other, over seemingly simple matters of criminal procedure such as whether to prosecute, when to hear a case, whether and when to discontinue a case, and what to consider in arriving at a sentence.

However, because procedural questions had so much to do with the real consequences of the criminal justice process, and because they were so entwined with the prior authority of the minor judiciary, procedures also involved substantive matters. The most important of these were which acts deserved the criminal sanction of the state, when and under what conditions, and how extensive that sanction should be. A paramount issue was whether the legal process should be employed at all, as it often was, when the object was not necessarily to obtain a criminal sanction. Another was who should be ultimately responsible for administering the law, determining its penalties, and therefore deciding what the role of the criminal law should be in everyday life. These were live questions throughout most of the nineteenth century in Philadelphia because of the dominance of private prosecutions among the cases of the criminal courts.

Case Disposition

The judicial process in the courts of record began when a magistrate detained or released a defendant on bail pending a trial. He was then required to send the case to the court's prosecuting attorney, who would present it to the grand jury. At this moment, the alderman or justice's jurisdiction over the individual officially ceased.

According to the formal process, the grand jury, comprised of twenty-four randomly chosen taxpayers, first heard evidence presented by the prosecutor and supporting witnesses. If they felt that the charge was without merit, the inquest "ignored" or dismissed the case, but when they were satisfied that the case deserved to be tried, the grand jury returned a "true bill" of indictment against the defendant. If the accused did not then plead guilty, a trial soon took place. Sentencing by the judge followed a conviction either immediately, a few days later, or took place at the end of the term.[6] Most cases, of course, completed only a part of this formal process.

Until 1836 criminal jurisdiction in Philadelphia was divided between the mayor's court for the city and the quarter sessions for the rest of Philadelphia County. Created by the 1789 Act of Incorporation, the exclusively criminal mayor's court was composed of the mayor or recorder of the city and at least three aldermen.[7] The quarter sessions court, which heard criminal cases arising from the suburban districts and many noncriminal matters from the entire county, was presided over by two judges of the county court of common pleas, appointed by the governor for good behavior. A defendant in the mayor's court could request a transfer to the quarter sessions. Each court held sessions four times each year. Unlike aldermen, quarter sessions judges were paid an annual salary; like aldermen, they were not yet necessarily learned in the law.[8] After the mayor's court was abolished in 1837, the county experimented with two other exclusively criminal courts before criminal jurisdiction for the entire county was returned to the quarter sessions in 1844, where it remained until 1875.

The division of criminal jurisdiction between the quarter sessions and the mayor's court was characteristic of the extreme localism of politics and government in the early nineteenth century. Private prosecution thrived on this same localism, which was one reason for its becoming entrenched in the criminal justice process during the first half of the century. By 1830 the features of case disposition characteristic of nineteenth-century private prosecution were present in both courts, and they only intensified afterwards.

The most important and enduring effects of private prosecution on the courts were a low conviction rate and a high proportion of cases that never reached a verdict at all. Overall, from 1820 to 1874, only 22 percent of all cases that were returned to the criminal courts ended in a conviction. This ratio decreased as time went on. One-third of the cases that entered the courts between 1820 and 1838 resulted in a conviction, and about one-quarter between 1844 and 1854. Over 40 percent of the cases that entered the courts between 1820 and 1838 failed to reach a verdict, and this proportion increased to 53 percent between 1844 and 1854.[9] Between 1854 and 1874 this matter became even more extreme. The conviction rate fell to only 17 percent, and 62 percent of all cases never reached a verdict. As a result, after 1854 court officials regularly lamented the ratio of convictions to cases—537 to 4,928 in 1866, 555 to 5,861 in 1867, 599 to 5,396 in 1860, and 555 to 5,067 in 1870.[10]

This pattern reflects the influence of private prosecution more clearly when considered by charge. Three-quarters of the cases heard by courts of record were relatively minor personal and property disputes. Overall, personal cases and property cases each comprised roughly 42 percent of criminal cases. Assault and battery and other minor scrapes accounted for over 90 percent of personal cases or 39 percent of all cases. Larceny and other minor property crimes made up about five-sixths of property cases or 35 percent of all cases. Although some assault and battery cases were sincere attempts to punish crime and some larceny cases were manipulative private prosecutions, the difference in case disposition between the two reflects the fact that assault and battery cases were usually private prosecutions for which the full process of prosecution and punishment were of minor importance, and larceny and other property cases were more often serious attempts to punish crime formally.

Assault and battery, which was almost always privately prosecuted, had much lower conviction rates and much higher dismissal rates than larceny, and both tendencies increased over time. In 1859 the *Ledger*'s court reporter was amazed that, during the August session, only 51 of 308 assault and battery bills resulted in convictions, but this was actually a bit above average. Conviction rates for personal crimes were lower than those for property crime primarily because of the high percentage that never reached a conclusion, in part a consequence of the fact that these cases could be legally settled by the minor judiciary. Overall, 67 percent of assault and battery cases failed even to reach the plea stage compared to "only" 48 percent of larceny and minor property cases. When cases did proceed to a formal conclusion, assault defendants were almost as likely as larceny defendants to be convicted. Overall, 48 percent of larceny defendants and 40 percent of assault and battery defendants who went to trial wound up being convicted, and before 1854 assault defendants were actually more likely to be convicted.

The peculiarity of this pattern for typical minor criminal cases stands out when they are compared to more serious cases. Major property and personal crime comprised only about 10 percent of all cases, but their proportion was increasing and their disposition pattern was clearly different, especially before the police became more involved in the process in 1854. Grand juries dismissed significantly fewer serious cases. Only 27 percent of serious personal and 40 percent of serious property cases failed to reach a verdict. If the very seriousness of these charges made prosecutors more intent on going to trial and court officials more willing to support them, it also made jurors somewhat more reluctant to bring convictions. Only 35 percent of serious property case trials ended in conviction, markedly less than among minor property cases, and the percentage for serious personal cases was virtually identical to that for assault and battery.

Something unique was occurring among ordinary minor criminal cases, especially among minor personal cases, that distinguished them from more serious criminal prosecutions. One should not, however, make too much of the difference between personal and property cases since the influence of private prosecution was strong among both groups. Even though property cases slightly outnumbered personal cases between 1844 and 1854, for example, the court's conviction rate kept falling.[11] The especially sharp decrease in the conviction rate after 1854 was in part a result of a relative increase in assault and battery cases, but it was also a result of a steadily decreasing conviction rate for larceny and all property crime. Private prosecutions, then, were a consistently prominent proportion of both personal and property cases and, among both, were more likely to be incompletely prosecuted as time went on.

The vast majority of people formally punished by the courts were convicted of property crimes. For example, between 1841 and 1864, fully 81 percent of the convicts in the county prison were convicted of larceny. Another 10 percent were imprisoned for other property crimes. Property offenders were also, therefore, far more likely than other convicts to be imprisoned. Imprisonment rates at all times were much higher for larceny and other property crimes than for assault and battery, which only rarely resulted in a prison term after conviction.[12]

These distinctions also help explain the differences in case disposition between the two criminal courts before 1838. Assault and battery comprised 35 percent of the mayor's court cases and 45 percent of the quarter sessions cases; larceny and minor property cases, 40 and 25 percent respectively. Higher conviction rates and imprisonment rates were characteristic of the mayor's court, which had a larger percentage of larceny cases. Property crime was concentrated in the central city and thus came under the mayor's court's jurisdiction.[13] We might also assume that this was where most of the repeat offenders and serious criminals were to be be found. The city proper was a very small area, with by far the most effective police force for the time. The consequence was a relatively high conviction rate for the relatively more serious problem of theft in the central city.

In contrast, the quarter sessions had jurisdiction over the remainder of Philadelphia County. Typical private prosecutions, the most difficult cases on which to gain a conviction, probably prevailed among this court's cases, with far fewer frequent offenders and far less familiarity between judges and litigants. The result was a higher proportion of personal cases and a lower conviction rate.

Despite the difference between the two courts, it is important to remember that, even for larceny in the mayor's court, only 56 percent of the accused were convicted, and this was the highest the conviction rate would be in any court until after 1874. In fact, by the 1830s, the conviction rate was already falling, while the rate of ignored and undisposed cases was rising. Generally over 40 percent through 1830, the mayor's court conviction rate was almost always below this afterwards, and its ignored and nondisposed rate regularly exceeded 40 percent. In the quarter sessions, this pattern was even more extreme.

Convicts subject to the discretion of the bench also faced the seeming arbitrariness of judges' sentencing decisions, a factor that only added to the

Table 3.1 Average Sentence by Judge (in months)

	Judge			
	Campbell	Parsons	Kelley	King
Committee (1848–51)	8.0	17.0	12.1	13.9
Sample (1844–54)	8.0	15.1	10.6	11.8

SOURCE: *Report on the County Prison* (1851), p. 21; Quarter Sessions Dockets.

difference between the typical private prosecution and the typical conviction for property crime. Sentences varied among different charges and even varied widely among similar kinds of thefts, but there is no reason to believe that any one judge heard a greater proportion of any kind of crime than any other judge. Mean sentences also roughly corresponded to the severity of the offense, and they were also somewhat higher for recidivists, but here too there should have been no great difference among the judges.

Yet the differences in sentences meted out by judges were enormous. A committee investigating the county prison in 1851 was "forcibly struck" by the inequality of sentences and suggested that the discrepancy was based on the personal differences of the judges. Most likely, these differences were rooted in politics and the judge's familiarity with everyday life in Philadelphia. The most lenient judges, James Campbell and William Kelley, were men of modest backgrounds who were closely associated with the Philadelphia Democratic party. Edward King was a much older Democrat and less involved in local politics, and Anson Parsons, a conservative lawyer who meted out by far the toughest punishment, was not even from Philadelphia. The committee published a table based on all convictions in the quarter sessions from December 1848 to September 1851, and the differences among the judges presented in this report conform closely to the differences derived from our quarter sessions sample beginning in 1844.[14]

No other single factor—race, sex, age, ethnicity, or occupation—made such a difference in sentence length.[15] This pattern persisted past 1854. Defendants convicted of similar petty thefts continued to receive widely differing sentences, and the differences in mean sentence among judges remained as great as it had been before 1854.[16] Judge Joseph Allison's average sentence was 12.5 months, Judge Oswald Thompson's 7.6, Judge James Ludlow's 13.5, Judge William Pierce's 6.3, and Judge F. Carrol Brewster's 4.3.[17] Once convicted, a defendant was at the mercy of the court, his or her fate determined in large part by the chance factor of which judge presided. The convict's vulnerability was a pervasive aspect of the everyday experience of the courts of record, second only to the ubiquity of private prosecution.

Private Prosecutions: Personal Cases

Personal cases set the tone for a court process dominated by the informal methods of the private parties and minor judiciary. The overwhelming majority of these cases were for minor assault or assault and battery, most of which were either ignored by the grand jury or only partially pursued by the parties.

Many things occurred inside the courtroom in addition to the routine process of indictment, plea, trial, and verdict. Accustomed to getting what they wanted from the aldermen, people believed that they could similarly control the disposition of their causes in the court of record. The major obstacle to this was the grand jury, which regularly ignored many assault and battery cases because of the failure of prosecutors to attend the hearing, the private settling of the matter by the parties, or the inadequacy of the evidence presented.

Each term grand jury presentments featured at least a passing remark about the large number of assault and battery cases that grand jurors were compelled to ignore. Sometimes, however, these cases drew greater attention. Judge Campbell specifically instructed the grand jurors for the March 1847 term to inquire carefully into the motives of assault and battery prosecutors, to ignore all trivial cases, and to place the costs on the prosecutors in cases that had "been brought with the design of unlawfully injuring the defendants." In response the jurors dismissed assault and battery cases at so great a rate— twelve of the first twenty-eight bills placed before them—that the *Public Ledger* wondered whether the jurors might be going too far. Just a few years earlier, the same newspaper had praised grand jurors for dismissing assault and battery bills, calling the policy "as it should be . . . perhaps no more effectual course could be adopted to keep out of court such trifling cases as have heretofore been chargeable upon the time of the court . . . without benefit to anyone, and in most cases brought only to gratify a personal pique."[18]

Perhaps the change in attitude resulted from exasperation with the persistent pace of the private prosecution of assault and battery. For, though ignoring cases surely was the court's best means of frustrating prosecutors, it was a limited one. At no time did the pace of private assault and battery prosecution slacken significantly. Grand jurors were hampered by the fact that they entered the process only after an alderman or justice had already accepted the case and in many instances detained the accused. The prosecutor had already received satisfaction—for some, sufficient satisfaction. This was undoubtedly the reason that some private prosecutors never appeared before the inquest, and it severely hampered the ability of grand juries to discourage the private use of the criminal law.

Adding to the court's frustration, though, was the fact that the further along the process went, the weaker its power of resistance became. If the grand jury returned a true bill in an assault and battery case, then the power of the private parties to determine the process of adjudication actually expanded. One reason for this was simply, as Judge F. Carrol Brewster remarked in 1868, that there were so many "returns of petty and malicious accusations as true bills." This problem received continuing attention, but little could be done except to urge grand jurors to ignore ever more cases.[19] Most of the cases that the grand jury did not ignore ended in pretrial settlements or acquittals. In privately settled cases, prosecutors got their satisfaction from the accused outside the courtroom, perhaps never having intended to go through with a trial. Regardless, private settlements continually troubled the court. On one occasion, "a circumstance perhaps unexampled in criminal litigation," a cross-bill was settled by the parties right in the courtroom, in the presence of the judge and jury. Pretrial settlements also occurred simply because the prosecutor felt that the matter had gone on long enough.[20]

It was also not unusual for acquittals to result from the failure of the parties to appear for the trial. By 1858 judges regularly urged grand jurors to dismiss cases because "true bills are found, the witnesses do not come to the court, and cannot be found on the trial." This circumstance became a regular feature of each court session. By 1862 the court reporter remarked that at every term, the court faced "the same difficulty to secure the attendance of witnesses. . . . It seldom happens that prosecutor and defendant are in court on the same day, and the consequence is, that the Court is compelled to assemble day after day . . . with scarcely enough business to keep them in session one hour."[21]

Sometimes the accused was prepared for trial but not the prosecutor. Prosecutors may have had weak cases against unpliable defendants and, fearing the probable burden of the costs, just disappeared; or they may have felt that the object of their prosecution had been accomplished and there was no need to continue. Most of these cases came up at the end of a term, in cases of defendants released on bail. The typical response of the court was not a postponement but a summary acquittal on instructions from the judge. By the

1860s the court began issuing subpoenas for the prosecutors and witnesses and announcing that defendants would be acquitted if there was no response. So many cases of this sort had accumulated through delays that, by the 1870s, the judges called special sessions for processing them. If a prosecutor failed to appear, the judge simply declared an acquittal. Often the court disposed of so many cases in this manner—twenty-five of thirty-three one day in January 1871, sixteen of thirty-six two weeks later, ten of sixteen on a September 1872 afternoon—that the reporter declared that it was nearly "impossible to get a case before the jury in the Quarter Sessions."[22]

In most such instances, jurors placed the court costs on the absent prosecutor. It was, however, unlikely that the prosecutor would be found and forced to pay. When Samuel Douglas was brought in to pay costs for a case he had abandoned, he was indignant. "People are not always ready to poney up the dust," he told Judge Joseph Doran when questioned about his failure to appear for trial, "I would rather go to prison than pay." Nevertheless, he ultimately paid and returned home.[23]

Douglas was an exception. Most of the prosecutors and defendants who only partially pursued cases used the criminal law without rebuke; how often they achieved their private ends must, of course, remain a mystery. More than a few defendants suffered from a brief pretrial confinement or having to raise bail. Many a prosecutor must have felt that this was sufficient revenge for a petty assault, many defendants must have felt sufficiently persuaded by this to accede to a prosecutor's demands in return for dropping the case. Other prosecutors must have rejoiced over exacting so much punishment on so flimsy a case and decided not to push their luck any further.

Many prosecutors did show up for trials, however, and these cases did not necessarily have more substance than those that had been discontinued. Over half of the minority of assault and battery cases that actually went to trial ended in acquittal. Though many private prosecutors were honestly seeking a conviction for a wrong they felt they had genuinely suffered, others had motives as ulterior as those of prosecutors who had dropped cases. Because cases that went to trial received greater press coverage, it is possible to examine more closely the motives of private prosecutors in them. Most acquittals occurred in cases that arose from disputes between the parties over mutual friends or property. Juries acquitted defendants because the assaults were minor and the charges seemed like attempts by disgruntled private prosecutors to resolve disputes in their favor. Many cases that never went to trial may well have had similar origins.

Examples of these cases abound. A dispute between two children over toys prompted the mother of one to bring charges against the other child. The jury seriously considered placing the costs in this case on Alderman Cloud, who accepted the prosecution. Nancy Smith lost $10 she had paid to a self-proclaimed sorceress for a cure that did not work. The two women came to blows when Nancy demanded her money back, and the sorceress instituted a prosecution for assault and battery. Paul Hess was prosecuted for an assault and battery on his wife Rachel by his father-in-law, who had never approved of the marriage. Rachel claimed that he was kinder to her than she was to him and would live with Paul in spite of her father's efforts to separate them. The costs were placed on the prosecutor, and both men were held in bond to keep the peace in order to prevent their animosity from precipitating some actual violence.[24]

Many cross-prosecutions for assault and battery found their way into court. Judges from time to time instructed grand jurors to look closely for cross-bills since they were not returned together and to dismiss as many as possible. These cases were sometimes completely without substance and were among the best examples of assault and battery prosecutions that were designed only to influence private affairs or simply gain revenge. Juries generally acquitted both parties and placed the costs on the prosecutors, a penalty as severe as a dual conviction would have brought. The difference, of course, was that the parties were punished, sometimes imprisoned, not for breaking the law but for using it.[25]

There were, of course, assault and battery cases in which prosecutors sought and won conviction for real offenses. Although a minority of assault and battery prosecutions, these cases also reflected the peculiarities of a system of private prosecution, the most notable being the infrequent use of the guilty plea. One-fifth of the people convicted of assault and battery pleaded guilty, but this represented only 8 percent of those who entered a plea. One reason for this was that the imprisonment rate for persons who pleaded guilty to assault or assault and battery was actually slightly higher than it was for the convicted. Sentences, however, were lower. Some people being seriously prosecuted probably took advantage of the opportunity to plead guilty if they expected a conviction, but most assault and battery defendants were able to avoid trial by other means. No systematic pattern of pleading guilty developed because the few serious cases were no burden to the court, and the minor cases that were a burden were usually resolved before the plea or trial stage was reached.[26]

Convictions, no less than in other cases, exhibited the extraordinary extent of popular involvement in criminal justice. The parties took many of these cases quite seriously and frustrated the court in their own way. Cases in which both parties had some financial resources moved slowly because the parties tended to engage private counsel to argue their cases. One court reporter remarked with typical disdain, "It is a curious fact that the less merit there is in a case of this kind, the more time is consumed in its trial, as learned counsel are engaged on both sides, and are expected to earn their fee by extended speeches." The court was able to complete only a few of these trials each day.[27]

Cases of this type became more frequent after 1860 as the use of lawyers became more common, but many cases were vigorously pursued before then. In 1839 a case had to be postponed because there was no room in court for the over fifty witnesses appearing for the defendant alone![28] The court reporter claimed that similar situations arose "almost every month." Usually, however, court reporters simply stated the verdict and the small penalty given to the convicted defendant without comment. Sometimes, though, the judge expressed his exasperation. When a defendant convicted of striking another man with a newspaper appealed for a new trial, Judge Campbell, a politician familiar with the rough and tumble world of the saloon and firehouse, was appalled. He dismissed the motion with the suggestion that both parties "had no courage" and resorted "to the course taken by children and old women, to look for protection to the law."[29]

A beleaguered and streetwise judge might have wished that only children and old women used the law, but, in fact, all kinds of people did. In general, the substance of assault and battery cases that resulted in convictions did not differ from those with other outcomes. Assaults that resulted in convictions included everything from pushing and shoving to attacks with deadly intent which resulted in serious injury. There were simple, perfunctory trials and trials of great length that captured the attention of the public. Minor cases involved such events as a man running his omnibus into another's cart or a quarrel among potato vendors. William Stevenson and Thomas Williams, two porters, could not agree on who was to carry a passenger's bags and removed to the rear of the depot to settle the dispute. Williams prosecuted and Stevenson was fined $2. Two sailors got into a scuffle near the docks over some borrowed tobacco and a knife. One was bed-ridden for five weeks as a result. He prosecuted and his adversary was confined to prison for three months. Occasionally cross-prosecutions resulted in dual convictions. In 1837 two men, Buckley and Korgill, prosecuted each other. Each man was fined one cent, but because Buckley could not pay, he went to prison.[30]

A large number of cases even involved law officers, both as prosecutors and defendants. Generally, the assault occurred in the course of the officer's carrying out or refusing to carry out an official duty. After the police expansion of 1850, these charges sometimes had political overtones since police appointments depended on political connections. If a prosecutor could prove his case, juries did not balk at convicting policemen, but one had to be sure. When Charles Knorr interfered with officer Edward Bozorth's attempt to arrest a woman, a fight ensued and each man prosecuted the other. Neither could offer much proof of the other's guilt, yet Bozorth was acquitted and Knorr convicted.[31]

Policemen and aldermen did not hesitate to prosecute citizens who assaulted them either. In 1838 Alderman Augustus Tarr prosecuted five men who he claimed assaulted him as he was trying to quell a disturbance at a tavern. Judge Parsons sentenced two men who were convicted of assaulting police officers in June 1848 to prison terms of one and two months respectively, severe sentences for minor assaults. One day in 1848, James McCort entered the office of powerful Kensington Alderman Hugh Clark and asked for a writ against his brother-in-law. Clark refused, stating a desire to discourage litigation among relatives, and in his anger (and probably surprise as well), McCort struck the alderman. After the defendant was convicted, Clark asked the judge to impose only a light sentence, explaining that he had prosecuted only to make the point that he should not be interfered with while performing his duties. Clark surely also recognized that his office was worthwhile only insofar as he "took care" of his constituents. His point made, he now had to do something for McCort. The judge imposed a $1 fine, responding approvingly to Clark for doing just what ordinary private prosecutors did with such annoying frequency: prosecuting someone to make a point, not to obtain legal punishment.[32] In general, though, the officers' standing as prosecutor or defendant in these cases was no different than that of any private citizen, and the citizenry's readiness to prosecute officers spoke simultaneously to their resistance to the idea of police arrests and preference for private prosecution.

Requests for leniency by prosecutors were not made only by aldermen with reputations to protect. Prosecutors sometimes felt that a conviction was all they desired and asked that the defendant not be forced to suffer in prison. In these cases, a $1 fine was the typical sentence. When Ann McMullen prosecuted her brother John for assault and battery in 1843, she appealed "in his favor" after conviction, and John was fined only one cent. Defense attorneys also requested leniency, and if a defendant could prove mitigating circumstances, the judge might impose only a small fine.

The private prosecutors who probably best captured the essence of the practice were battered wives. Among those cases in the court sample in which the gender of the victim was noted, 27 percent were assaults by men upon women. Just as these women were among the most active users of aldermanic justice, those among them who pursued their complaints into the courts of record remained intent on determining their disposition. Many of these cases were probably serious or repeat offenses, since in most instances a woman could have requested a peace bond from the alderman and avoided a court appearance altogether. These women, though, wanted more, often a conviction. Although over half of these cases were ignored, 73 percent of the cases that were not ended in convictions. Because of their economic dependency, most women wanted only to scare their husbands not to put them in prison. Pleas for leniency seem to have been part of the routine in cases of assaults upon wives. Without such a request, a judge was likely to sentence a man to a month in prison for the first offense and a longer period if the violence was repeated. With it, the man almost always left court with a warning, one that was no doubt reinforced by the occasional imprisonment of other batterers. Prison terms were common for convicted wife beaters whose wives were willing to see it happen. The criminal justice process beginning with the alderman and ending in the courts of record was a prime instrument in battered women's struggle to tame their husbands. This was probably the clearest example of the usefulness of the criminal law to a relatively powerless group, and of the extensive ability prosecutors had to determine how much of the law they would use.[33]

Minor violations of public order were similar to assault cases. Sometimes the result of incidents that must have seemed insignificant to outsiders, they were further evidence of how readily aldermen accepted criminal prosecutions. The conviction rate for order cases was about 18 percent, the same as for assault and battery. Roughly one-third of those going to trial were convicted, but 53 percent of the cases never reached the plea stage. Roughly half of those convicted received prison sentences, usually for the more serious offenses since the average term was a rather hefty 6.6 months.

Some of these cases were based on only the flimsiest of substance. Margaret Ross's landlord prosecuted her for leaving candles burning too late at night, causing him to fear that she would burn the house down. The alderman actually imprisoned Margaret but Judge Campbell had her released while "strongly express[ing] his contempt for the impudence and tyranny of the fellow." In 1839 an old man entered the court from prison on a charge of "further hearing." When asked what the charge against him was, the man replied "two dollars, may it please your honor." The judge remarked that indeed this was the only charge according to the alderman's record and asked the man what he was accused of. "Playing with the girls, your honor, on a Sunday." The spectators broke into laughter as the judge discharged the case.[34]

These people were defendants in what were known as "prison cases." For the most part, aldermen imprisoned them for assault, disorderly conduct, or some other minor offense, sometimes without a specific charge and for an unspecified period. Such commitments were of dubious legality, and they were often the cause of great over-crowding in the untried department of the prison. The defendants in these cases were almost always poor and without legal representation. Poverty was a major component of many of the cases, notably more common in the wake of the panics of 1837 and 1857. They proceeded in court much faster than bail cases. Defendants were crowded into the prisoners' dock each morning, "blacks and whites, young and old . . . packed together indiscriminately . . . a most motley appearance." First the prosecutor and perhaps some witnesses told their story. The defendant then had an opportunity to answer the charge; generally the response was either silence or a tale of woe, and the case was rapidly dispatched. Twenty-seven cases were completed by three o'clock one day in August 1860, twenty-eight on another day in February. On most days, the average was closer to ten. Reporters claimed that convictions were more numerous than among bail cases, but there is only scattered evidence to support this. In the June 1859 session, forty-nine of sixty-nine prison case defendants were reported as being convicted, but for the most part, reporters described only those prison cases that they thought were unusually interesting. Attendance problems also plagued these cases. "As usual at the commencement of the session, but few witnesses were present . . . and thus a number of cases had to be postponed," remarked the court reporter in 1858.[35] Generally, the judges simply discharged them. Sometimes they did question the defendants and received as responses the tragic stories of poverty and illness in the nineteenth-century city. One poor, ill, homeless old woman begged the judge in 1849 to let her stay in prison through the winter because she had nowhere else to go. He obliged.[36]

After the Civil War, the volume of prison cases caused delays. In 1866 the backlog of cases had become, according to one observer, a "manifest injustice to those committed to prison for trifling offenses, and who have a right to a speedy trial." A seasoned observer explained that the district attorney could not, because of "the immense amount of business," schedule all cases right away, so he picked only "the case which startles most by its criminality," leaving the imprisoned defendant in a less serious case to wait behind bars. By January 1867, the untried were waiting as long as four and six months for trial.

Judges and grand jurors were urging the court to work faster to assure these people speedy trials, and one of the first special sessions called that year was prompted by the need to "relieve the prison of the large number of cases returned."[37]

Another group of cases that closely resembled assaults was private prosecution for sexual transgressions—bigamy, seduction, adultery, fornication, and bastardy. These cases were responsible for most of the 24 percent of morals cases that resulted in a conviction. Half of them reached the plea stage, and half of these ended in convictions. Most of the convicts were sentenced to prison terms that averaged 6.4 months. No one in the sample was fined, but judges routinely required men guilty of bastardy to post bond and pay a monthly sum for support of the child. Grand jurors ignored only 11 percent of these cases and almost never placed the court costs on the prosecutor. Though sexual and family crimes were neither a major preoccupation of the courts nor an arena of public prosecution, court officers still took their responsibility as moral guardians seriously enough to support these cases more vigorously than most others. Private prosecutors, usually women, were also perhaps more determined to get a conviction and invoke the full power of the law in these cases.[38]

The punishing power of the court was a major feature only of private prosecutions for serious personal crimes. In 1839 a doctor was fined $100 for an assault on a colleague who had been having a love affair with his sister. A decade later, Judge Kelley, announcing his determination to punish severely all those who used deadly weapons, sentenced William Suttle to seventeen months for a knife attack on William Taylor. Judge Allison sentenced a fire company member to eighteen months for a serious assault in 1852. Defendants convicted of even more serious personal crimes regularly tried to appeal for leniency, but rarely did they succeed, partly because of minimum sentences determined by the legislature. Two men tried to talk Judge Thompson into leniency in an 1853 manslaughter case, but the judge sentenced one man to two years, the other to three.[39]

Serious assaults were, however, exceptions among the personal crimes entering Philadelphia's courts of record during these years. The vast majority were privately prosecuted assault and battery cases, rarely the authors of serious injury but often a serious matter for the participants. The largest single group of cases in the courts of record, assaults were also the cases over which the private parties maintained the greatest control. Very low conviction rates and high rates of cases being ignored by grand jurors or abandoned by prosecutors reflected a criminal justice process easily negotiated by the public and dependent upon community-based definitions of crime. This had received initial official sanction by the minor judiciary. Neither judges nor grand jurors had the power to prevent its extension into the higher courts, despite their displeasure. Popular determination of criminal justice was nowhere better expressed than in assault cases, those cases that occupied the largest portion of the court's calendar.

Private Prosecutions: Property Cases

Property cases were those that involved persons illegally or dishonestly acquiring or using objects of value. Larceny was by far the most common property crime, but the category also included burglary, robbery, forgery, receiving stolen goods, extortion, receiving goods under false pretenses, counterfeiting, and passing counterfeit currency. The formal punishing power of the law was more evident among these cases, which had less legal room for informal settlement and, therefore, higher conviction and imprisonment rates than personal cases. Yet there was a paradox here. As property cases grew in relative numbers, they also began to assume characteristics of personal cases—their conviction and imprisonment rates fell. As a result, even the relative increase in these cases, those with the highest conviction rates, did not reverse the overall decreasing conviction rates; indeed, they contributed to it. Here also litigants were not infrequently able to exercise control over the proceedings. Even among these cases, there were abundant examples of citizen use and manipulation of the criminal law. Private initiative and judicial power met face-to-face in petty larceny cases.

Most larceny cases were probably privately initiated. Grand juries considered petty larcenies second only to assault and batteries as privately prosecuted nuisances.[40] Even if a victim went first to the police, he or she had to report a theft that had already occurred. The officers' role was simply to arrest and bring the accused before the alderman. From then the case was in the hands of the victim. Because larceny was a felony, the prosecutor was obliged to press the charge fully; unlike assault and battery, the parties could make no legal settlement before the trial.[41]

Minor larceny trials were usually short. Each side presented a few witnesses, attorneys made brief remarks, and the jury often rendered a verdict without leaving their box. The property involved in these cases—money was rarely stolen—like that in the cases aldermen heard, was generally simple, useful, and cheap. In 1854 a grand jury criticized the aldermen and private prosecutors for submitting such petty larceny cases as the theft of one egg, valued at one cent.[42] The jurors ignored this case, but accepted many others that were not much more serious.[43]

Despite the similarity of most petty thefts, convicts received inconsistent sentences. On the same day in March 1842, one judge sentenced men convicted of thefts of 50 cents and $1 worth of goods to eight months each, one woman to one year for a $2 theft, and another woman to just one month for a $4 theft. In May 1840, a judge sentenced Charles Lee to six months for the theft of a $15 coat, two black brothers to twenty-nine months each for an $11 theft of shoes, and Edward Green to three years for stealing $3 worth of handsaws. Substantially larger values brought sentences of over a year. Andrew Liman stole thirty-six $1 breastpins and was sentenced to one month for each pin.[44]

Nevertheless, parties to larceny cases still retained some control over them. The first area of control was, of course, the decision to take the case into the criminal court. The volume of cases suggests that many persons chose to prosecute over very small thefts and that often the prosecutor and defendant knew each other. Employers were quick to prosecute servants suspected of theft. Peter Gilbert confessed to horse thievery after he tried to sell a horse given to him by a farmer to deliver to a stable. Mary Balentine stole $70 from her employer, who caught her with the money and called the police. By the time the police arrived, Mary had eaten the evidence, but she was convicted anyway. Servants were not always convicted, however. Jane Wolbert's employer charged her with the theft of silver spoons, claiming that the items had been lost and that Jane had behaved suspiciously after their absence was discovered. Alderman Thompson issued a warrant for the woman's arrest, but since the spoons were never found she was acquitted.[45]

Acquittals offered examples of the various ways private prosecutors used the law in property cases. Just over half of all larceny trials resulted in acquittals. Many private prosecutors obviously decided, or felt forced, to go to trial on charges they had either fabricated or could not prove. In 1846 public prosecutor William A. Stokes requested an acquittal for John Felton, charged with stealing a load of manure, calling the case "the greatest outrage that had come under his notice for some time past." When a judge or prosecuting attorney referred to a case as an outrage, he usually meant that it was a private prosecution that in his opinion should never have been initiated. In many such cases, people found the criminal justice process exceedingly pliable. Washington Richmond was released on a writ of habeas corpus after Manayunk Alderman Moses Miller committed him for the larceny of clothes belonging to his brother. Richmond's son was residing with his brother, and in a dispute over the custody of the child, Richmond took the boy back. He was prosecuted for stealing the clothing that the child was wearing! In granting the release, Judge Joseph Allison remarked that the only person who deserved imprisonment in the matter was the alderman. In 1844 Charles Simes charged Elijah Sparks with stealing a wagon. Simes had given the wagon to Sparks, a tavernkeeper, with instructions to find a buyer. Sparks took this to be a license to sell and went off to Wilmington to find a purchaser. Simes believed Sparks had decided to treat the wagon as his own, pursued him into Delaware, apprehended him with a pistol, and brought him before Alderman Erety, who entered the larceny charge. Quarter sessions judge Campbell was incensed at what he called a "civil case run mad" and ordered the jury to acquit Sparks. The jury was then immediately presented with an assault and battery bill entered by Sparks against Simes. Sparks could produce no evidence of a beating, however. Simes was acquitted, and the jury, believing that Sparks deserved some measure of condemnation for the whole affair, saddled him with the costs.[46]

Most acquittals occurred simply because the prosecutor could not link the defendant to the crime or because the defendant could prove that the property was acquired honestly.[47] Acquittals could result from all sorts of circumstances. Sarah Kimball and Ebenezer Woodward were acquitted in separate cases in 1840 because the indictments described the stolen property as belonging to a married woman. It was legally impossible for married women to own property at this time, so the defendants were acquitted on the defective indictment. A man who was falsely accused of stealing his own trunk was acquitted in 1844 after having pleaded guilty mistakenly, thinking he was admitting only to having possession of the trunk. Fortunately an attorney present in the courtroom intervened and advised the man to change his plea. In the case's aftermath, the court reporter wondered in how many similar cases "innocent, ignorant victims have been immolated in this court by the indecent haste with which they have been hurried, from the prison to the dock, and through the mere forms of a jury trial, to a felon's cell."[48]

This last case illustrates how vulnerable to punishment a citizen was when in the role of defendant, but this was, in part, offset by the ability of every citizen to adopt the role of private prosecutor. As in personal cases, prosecutors sometimes expressed sensitivity to the vulnerability of defendants by seeking neither a conviction nor imprisonment. Required to pursue a case, some larceny prosecutors expressed reluctance even when the accused was clearly guilty. Nicholas Fulmer charged Simon Wilson, a poor black man of good character, with stealing an old mare that Wilson believed Fulmer had offered to anyone who would take her away. After instituting proceedings,

Fulmer realized that Wilson was acting under an honest misapprehension and expressed his regret to the court. The judge insisted on imposing the minimum sentence for horse stealing of one year on Wilson but reassured both men that he would request a pardon after two or three months. John Phelan, an elderly man with six children who stole a saw and plane while drunk, was convicted despite the private prosecutor's statement that he appeared in court only because he was required by law to do so. Judge Joel R. Jones told the private prosecutor not to fret, that bringing prosecutions was the only way to deter crime. However, he sentenced Phelan to just one month in prison.[49]

Cases in which the defendant pleaded guilty to larceny made up a unique and instructive group. Guilty pleas occurred in nearly 10 percent of larceny and minor property cases, more than in any other group. It made more sense for a larceny defendant to plead guilty than for any other accused person. Nearly half of those who went to trial were convicted, and those confessing received shorter prison terms than those tried and convicted. Thus, 18 percent of the larceny defendants against whom true bills were found chose to plead guilty, with a noticeable increase after the unification of the courts. The increase can most likely be attributed to the clear preference in sentencing for those who pleaded guilty after 1838, a preference that did not exist earlier. Though conviction rates were higher in the earlier period, there was no sentencing advantage to pleading guilty, so defendants took their chances. Between 1844 and 1854, though, the average sentence for a defendant who confessed was less than half that of other convicts. Once an advantage existed, even though chances of acquittal increased, more defendants chose the sentencing break. Although this advantage nearly disappeared after 1854, the guilty plea rate remained constant.[50]

The practice of pleading guilty was, nevertheless, by no means widespread. Less than one-third of those guilty of larceny confessed. In order to consider pleading guilty, defendants had to be faced with both a relatively high likelihood of conviction and a clear advantage in sentencing. When this was not the case, defendants had less incentive to plead guilty and did so in smaller numbers. For example, because only 35 percent of serious property defendants who went to trial were convicted, and a guilty plea brought no likelihood of a lenient sentence, only 10 percent of serious property defendants against whom a true bill was found pleaded guilty. Similarly, minor property offenders had little incentive to enter a guilty plea. Of these defendants, 37 percent were convicted if the case went to trial, and sentences were generally light. So, even though persons pleading guilty received markedly lower sentences and were more likely to avoid a prison term altogether, only 11 percent of the minor property crime defendants against whom a true bill was found pleaded guilty, just slightly more than among serious offenders.

Another reason that the practice remained limited was the judges' arbitrariness in sentencing practices, which also affected defendants who pleaded guilty to larceny. Most of the time, as the dockets indicated, these defendants received milder punishment. James Benton pleaded guilty and received two months, low even for a 40 cent theft, and John McLaughlin served thirty days for stealing a shirt. In a particularly clear case of leniency, Samuel Andrews was sentenced to only three months imprisonment after pleading guilty in 1848 to the theft of a $75 watch.[51]

However, many individuals who pleaded guilty received sentences similar to, or even higher than, those given others convicted of the same crime. Charles Lee was sentenced to eighteen months for stealing a $28 frock coat in 1840. On the same day, Henry Miller also received eighteen months after confessing to a $6 theft. On one day in 1848, Judge King gave Joseph Meredith two years for stealing "a quantity of pickeled fish," gave William Alexander three years for taking "a quantity of mackerel," and gave John Funk three years for the theft of a "quantity of curled hair." A guilty plea was no guarantee of a light sentence; on a given day a judge could be considerably harsher than usual.[52]

Probably the most important reason that the practice was not more common was that there was no administrative need. While defendants in some instances had the incentive of a milder sentence, plea bargaining was not a part of the system. In part this was because the prosecuting attorney was not yet a powerful figure in the court process, but, more significantly, the court did not need to adopt plea bargaining to process cases without their reaching a trial. Private prosecution and the ease with which grand jurors and private parties could discontinue cases already accomplished this. So the practice of pleading guilty remained infrequent and unsystematic, its likelihood and benefits varying from case to case.

Property offenses, more than any others, displayed the duality of the criminal justice process in the courts of record. Prosecutors had less freedom to abandon cases, and a relatively large number of cases went to trial and resulted in convictions. By refusing to sanction informal settlement, lawmakers declared that the state's interest in achieving convictions was stronger here than elsewhere. As a result, some prosecutors were forced to pursue cases fully, and other potential prosecutors were dissuaded from initiating cases in the first place. Thus more property defendants were sentenced to prison terms than all others combined; more confessed their guilt than did any others. The power of the bench, a power that must have appeared arbitrary at times to the forlorn defendant, was nowhere greater.

Yet the harshness and arbitrariness of the court in property cases were tempered by judicial mercy and a degree of popular control. Many cases were petty; the pattern of private prosecution on charges of dubious legality was present here as well, though to a lesser extent than elsewhere. Although convicts were treated more harshly than in assault cases, prison terms were still fairly short, averaging less than a year. Prosecuting attorneys, juries, and judges displayed leniency in response to both the requests of prosecutors and the pleas of defendants. Even among property cases, conviction rates were falling, and 48 percent of the cases entering the courts never reached a plea, despite the fact that the parties could not legally settle out of court.

One might have expected that increasing levels of property crime would have led to increasing conviction rates on the assumption that property cases were more "serious" crimes in which the state and propertied classes had a greater interest in securing convictions, but falling conviction rates belie this assumption. They are more plausibly explained if we understand the expansion of cases to be as much a result of increased private prosecution—with all its possibilities for popular manipulation—as a result of increased state determination to punish thieves. Nevertheless, property crime, always a felony, was taken most seriously by the courts, and the penetration of popular justice and the alderman-litigant relationship was less extensive here than elsewhere. The punitive power of the state in the criminal courts was most strongly expressed in the processing of property cases, but even here it was limited by the influence of private prosecution.

Private prosecution gave citizens the power, in practice, to define crime. Because the minor judiciary let them do so, almost anything that annoyed or irritated a person could be treated as a crime, for whatever motives a prosecutor might have. Private prosecutions fell into two broad groups. Some cases were seriously and fully pursued, others only partially pursued. Within both of these groups, some cases were instituted with the honest intention of attaining some measure of justice, others with ulterior or malicious motives. There were substantial numbers of all types of cases. The determination of what acts would provide grounds for a criminal charge was made among the participants in the communities where the acts took place. Aldermen provided people with the freedom to police themselves, to determine when the law should be invoked and, often, how far the criminal justice process should continue, even though in an imperfect and sometimes exploitative way.

Moreover, this process had an important positive function. Most of the time, people used the criminal courts and exacted from the law some measure of satisfaction or vindication without having the case go to a jury trial. By 1850 in session almost continuously, this was no small matter for the courts. They could not possibly have tried all of the cases returned by the magistrates. Despite the endless complaints by court officials about its drastic deficiencies, this system at least encouraged people to find redress in the law without impossibly overburdening the system.

The central point is that, at bottom, the criminal court was dominated by the very people the criminal law was supposed to control. Convictions were difficult to achieve under the best of circumstances, nearly impossible in others. The ordinary people of Philadelphia extensively used a system that could also be so oppressive to them because its oppressive features were balanced by the peoples' ability to control much of the course of the criminal justice process. Popular initiation and discretion were the distinctive features of private prosecution, rooted in the offices of the minor judiciary where it began, and remained the most important aspect of the process even in the courts of record. Whether it be to intimidate a friend or neighbor, resolve a private dispute, extort money or other favors, prevent a prosecution against oneself, express feelings of outrage and revenge, protect oneself from another, or simply to pursue and attain a measure of legal justice, an enormous number of nineteenth-century Philadelphians used the criminal courts, and, as we shall see, no one could stop them.

4. *The Weakness of Court Officials*

On a day in 1853, an event occurred that was unusual even for the court of quarter sessions. A man who was accused of assault and battery waited for his case to be called. As he surveyed the courtroom, he recognized several of the faces in the crowd, witnesses to the alleged assault who he assumed were present to testify against him. When the district attorney called the case, the defendant approached the bench but the prosecutor failed to appear. There was certainly nothing unusual about this, one of the common occurrences that so annoyed judges and other court officials, but what happened next was surely out of the ordinary. Intimidated by the presence of witnesses, unsure of what was about to happen next, and unaccompanied by counsel, the defendant confessed. Judge Oswald Thompson saw an opportunity to provide everyone with a lesson in how the criminal law ought to operate, and he took it. Portending a position that would be adopted frequently by the bench in the years to come, he declared that he was concerned only with the "outrage to the public" not with the "private wrong," and so, despite the absence of the prosecutor, he sentenced the man to six months.[1]

This distinction was a key element in the transition from a criminal justice process controlled by private citizens and aldermen to one controlled by salaried state officials. Thompson's comment suggested that jurists were becoming aware by mid-century of a divergence between the interests of the state and those of the citizenry regarding the accessibility and usefulness of criminal justice. Most judges, like Thompson, conceived of this as a distinction between private and public and saw themselves as responsible to the latter, but this was, at best, a partial truth. It really represented two competing forms of public administration: one that had been evolving for over half a century and drew an indistinct line between the public and the private, and another that made the distinction much more sharply and depended upon a more proactive state to enforce it.

Though by 1853, the latter was still not the dominant belief among jurists, Thompson was able to articulate it so clearly, in part, because of the court's decades of frustration in trying to control the process of criminal prosecution. Private prosecutors had less control over the courts of record than over primary justice, but this was little comfort to court officials. From their perspective, the process of prosecution was often out of control. Almost continuously after 1800, judges and other court officials attempted to limit the influence of aldermen and the private parties over criminal cases. Each time, however, the power of the alderman-litigant relationship reasserted itself.

The tide of litigation was never stemmed. The complex relationship between private citizens and the minor judiciary was an intractable obstacle to the realization of the judges' and jurors' ideal of how the courts of record should operate. In the end, they had to make the best of a situation in which their power to adjudicate and punish was only an adjunct to the dominant mode of criminal justice. As a result, officials became increasingly aware of their weaknesses and, gradually, more capable of conceptualizing a different kind of "public."

The Public Prosecutor

One of the major reasons for the weakness of the court officials was the limited power of the public prosecutor. Most discretion was exercised by the magistrates and private parties, some by the grand and petit juries, and little by anyone else. As late as the mid-1860s, for example, jurists agreed that, despite their importance on the streets, the police had no role in ordinary criminal procedure.

More importantly, the same was basically true for the district attorney. In an 1863 outline of criminal procedure, Judge Joseph Allison did not mention the police and gave no discretionary role to the district attorney in the "usual and ordinary mode of procedure." He explicitly called "extraordinary" those times when the public prosecutor "by virtue of his office, without a previous binding over or commitment of the accused, prefers an indictment before a Grand Jury."[2]

Statutes defining the duties of deputy attorney general, as the public prosecutor was known until 1850, never included a responsibility to conduct all criminal prosecutions in the name of the state. They required only that he not "refuse or neglect to institute any suit on behalf of the commonwealth [or] use requisite diligence in prosecuting any business that has been or may be confided to him by law." Proposed penal codes retained the colonial-era requirements that a private prosecutor's name be included on all indictments and that, if no person declared himself the prosecutor, the court could investigate to determine who was. According to legal treatises, excessive private prosecution should be limited by grand juries and, more so, by "the justices of the peace to whom the complaint is made in the first instance."[3]

Attorneys general and their deputies plainly did not conduct all criminal prosecutions, and most jurists believed that this was proper. Richard Vaux, in a 1844 report on some of the cases for which he held a primary hearing, noted that he submitted returns of cases "to the Attorney General or person prosecuting the pleas of the commonwealth." A few years earlier, George Chambers appealed for an independent judiciary, in part because it would be a protection for the citizen against state-influenced prosecution. Even if "the government be the prosecutor, [or] official influence be brought in aid of the prosecution," an independent judiciary would assist the citizen to emerge unhurt from the ordeal of "persecution."[4]

The uncertain role of the prosecuting attorney was in keeping with the limited role of lawyers in criminal prosecution in general. Prominent attorney David Paul Brown's memoirs often refer to criminal cases that were conducted by private counsel. A major concern of his was to advise lawyers to abandon prosecutions if they discovered that they were dishonest and, as a rule, not to prosecute a capital charge—"never take blood money." Brown implied that capital offenses and other "great public wrongs" should be conducted by the public prosecutor, but even in these relatively rare events, this was not always the case. Brown himself was one of two private attorneys who assisted in prosecuting a riot case in 1825. Philadelphia's deputy attorney general explained to Attorney General John M. Read that he had not participated in an important 1846 riot case because "it has long been the practice in such cases to allow the officers of the district in which the disturbance occurred to hire private counsel to conduct the case."

Most cases, however, proceeded without an attorney's participation, and it was not necessarily to a prosecutor's advantage to have one. Popular hostility to lawyers peaked during the judicial controversies of the early nineteenth century when the influential Jeffersonian publisher William Duane led a fight against the "abuses upon which they thrive [and] the tyranny they display in courts." Brown, in an 1818 speech to a jury, tried to defuse what he called "the prejudice too generally entertained by jurors . . . that whatever may be the force or quality of the arguments of counsel, they are still entitled to but little weight, inasmuch as they are the offspring of the pocket, not the heart."[5]

The best evidence of the public prosecutor's limited role in criminal prosecution was the controversy precipitated by attempts to increase it. Early in 1841, the *Public Ledger*, concerned about the frequent settling and dropping of cases, reminded readers that this could only be done by the attorney general or his deputies under specific conditions set by law, one of the few powers specifically given to public prosecutors by statute. Then the editors went further, making the extraordinary assertion that the private prosecutor was a mere witness in a criminal case. All criminal cases were "at every period of the proceeding, from its inception to its conclusion . . . under the sole direction and . . . exclusive control of the attorney general or his deputies." However, when the prosecuting attorney acted later that year to assume "the right of conducting and concluding the prosecution" in all cases, the same editors were sure this was *not* what they had in mind. In fact, it was "an evil of no uncommon magnitude in the administration of justice." In most petty cases, "the only test which can be triumphantly applied is the fact that the prosecutor carries on the matter with his own funds . . . by . . . procuring witnesses and counsel." If conducted by the public prosecutor, jurors would be unduly prejudiced because the case would appear to have the sanction of the state. The public officer's duty "does not require him to espouse the cause of everyone who happens to obtrude himself upon the attention of a criminal court." Rather, he should prosecute only those "whose offenses are more especially aimed at the well-being of society." The public prosecutor should not allow people to drop cases, but neither should he act as their advocate.[6]

The discretion of the private parties in criminal cases was not checked by the public prosecutor. Instead, the public prosecutor in most cases adopted a stance of passive neutrality. He was essentially a clerk, organizing the court calendar and presenting cases to grand and petit juries. Most of the time, he was either superseded by a private attorney or simply let the private prosecutor and his witnesses take the stand and state their case. Like aldermen dependent on fees, the public prosecutor had a built-in incentive to channel all cases to the grand jury and beyond, leaving others to dismiss them. Because his fees were paid by the county from the court costs rather than by the private prosecutor, he had no incentive to prefer one case over another. His power to drop a case was severely restricted to extraordinary instances of malicious prosecution and a few misdemeanors with the parties' consent. When the legislature sought in 1832 to restrain aldermen from making prison commitments without sending returns to court, they called upon the deputy attorney general but still gave him no discretion. He was simply to present all such cases to the court on a monthly basis for the judge to act upon.

So, when the public prosecutor did act in a discretionary way, it provoked comment. Sometimes the response might be an outraged public complaint, like the one in 1841 that blamed the deputy attorney general for increasing crime. It seems he had either refused or neglected to present a private prosecutor's case to a grand jury, and he delayed so long that the man did not have the time to hire a private attorney to present the case instead. At other times, the public prosecutor's exercise of discretion brought revealing praise. When Deputy Attorney General William Stokes began to advise jurors to acquit defendants in particular cases in 1846, the court reporter commended him for his "quasi-judicial" behavior, but it was still a far cry from that of the modern public prosecutor. Stokes brought cases to trial, and then told the jury that the defendant was innocent.[7]

In 1850 the office of district attorney was established in Philadelphia to replace that of the attorney general. The prosecutor's official duties now were to "sign all bills of indictment, and conduct in court all criminal or other prosecutions in the name of the commonwealth, or when the state is a party." In practice, however, his duties remained much as they were before. There were several reasons for this. An 1859 grand jury that recommended that private citizens keep discretion over whether to pursue cases points to one reason. Why, they asked, did the district attorney present all cases to them when the majority of cases had to be ignored? For the fees, they concluded. Even a dismissed bill netted the district attorney $1.50.

The fee system effectively negated the district attorney's ability to assume any real discretion over criminal cases. Moreover, the district attorney was now an elected official, linking him closely to the aldermen and the city's political parties. So, despite the prosecuting attorney's heightened status, practical considerations minimized his control and bolstered the persistence of private prosecution.[8] In most cases, the prosecuting attorney's effect on the criminal justice process remained slight. The events of 26 September 1844 were still apt to be repeated. On that day, the prosecuting attorney prepared to present eleven assault and battery cases to the court, "but the parties . . . settled their difficulties the moment they found it was intended to present them to a jury," leaving the court without any business to conduct. No prosecuting attorney could have such an impact on the proceedings in court.[9]

Efforts at Control

Although before 1838 the courts were not really overburdened with cases, judges were still sensitive to what they considered time wasted on private prosecutions. As a result, they rebuked aldermen and justices for their willingness to accept criminal prosecutions for trivial matters, incidents long past, or disputes that really required civil adjudication. An 1827 report on the criminal code, written in part by quarter sessions judge Edward King, supported putting limits on prosecutions for misdemeanors because "the cause of the prosecution is but its ostensible object, its real one being a spirit of malice and uncharitableness . . . under which the guilty man becomes often more injured than he, who was originally aggrieved."[10]

As the number of cases—and especially the number of ignored and undisposed cases—increased after 1830, complaints from judges and grand jurors became more frequent. Each term the grand jury reported on the number of cases they ignored. The percentage of ignored cases varied from term to term but was never under 21 percent. Often the number was much higher. In the October 1849 term, 200 of 395 cases, 51 percent, were ignored. Over 45 percent were ignored in January 1838, November 1847, April 1850, April 1852, and November 1853.

Judge King's 1827 remarks surely represented the consensus among criminal justice officials throughout the century that too many cases were inspired by malice and greed. But the judges also knew that, as long as the criminal justice system continued to rely on the private initiative of citizens to bring cases to the courts, there was no way to control the numbers of cases or to enforce a definition of what constituted a legitimate prosecution.

Instead, they tried to induce justices "if possible, to prevent the case[s] from entering any further into legal channels."[11] One way to do this, stressed in the handbooks used by the magistrates, was for aldermen simply to refuse or to settle cases. As we have seen, however, the law allowing aldermen to settle assault and battery cases was probably counterproductive. A solution to the court's problems that assumed the system's reliance upon private prosecution, this law only strengthened the ties between aldermen and litigants. While it no doubt kept some assault cases out of the court and discouraged some people from instituting property prosecutions, this was probably offset by the number of cases encouraged by the prospect of informal settlement and the strengthened alderman-citizen relationship.

A more effective strategy was to increase the power of the courts of record to limit private prosecution by permitting jurors, both grand and petit, to act against private prosecutors. In 1804 Pennsylvania judges complained to the legislature that petty criminal prosecutions were keeping them from attending to more important civil matters. As a result, the legislature gave juries the power to place the court costs on the prosecutor in misdemeanor cases that resulted in acquittal, and it gave grand jurors the power to do the same in misdemeanors that they ignored. An 1808 court decision allowed jurors to charge prosecutors with the court costs even if the case was substantively sound but the indictment technically defective.[12]

The placing of costs on prosecutors became the major weapon in the court's struggle to check petty prosecutions. Most of the time, it was used in cases of assault and battery. This and the justices' settlement law clearly indicate that the courts felt most burdened by petty assaults; these two laws also demonstrated the jurists' reluctance to discourage prosecutions for property crime or to tamper with the ordinary mode of criminal prosecution.

Juries immediately began using the costs law. Overall, prosecutors were assessed costs in 7 percent of all mayor's court cases and 8 percent of all quarter sessions cases through 1838. Juries used this power much more frequently as conviction rates declined. After 1815 they placed costs on prosecutors in over 8 percent of mayor's court cases and over 10 percent of quarter sessions cases. Well over 90 percent of these cases were assault and battery, including probably a majority of all ignored assault and battery cases.

After the courts were unified, juries stepped up the practice of placing costs on prosecutors. As a result of increases in the percentage of ignored cases, the percentage of cases in which the jurors placed costs on the prosecutors rose to 13 percent from 11 percent between 1820 and 1838. The increase occurred in both personal and property cases but especially in assault and battery cases.[13] Juries saddled prosecutors with the court costs in two-thirds of all ignored assault and battery cases and a majority of all ignored personal cases, accounting for 85 percent of the instances in which they did so. In only 8 percent of ignored property cases did jurors place the costs on prosecutors.

The use of the power to put costs on prosecutors was virtually the exclusive province of the grand jurors. Petit jurors probably assumed that, if the grand jury thought a case worthy of being tried, it could not be too frivolous and should not be discouraged so that the precarious balance between deterring and encouraging prosecution would be maintained. But jurors could not maintain this balance to their liking. Whatever positive impact the costs law might have had was short-lived. After 1820 there was a clear decline in the percentage of assault and battery cases, but the percentage soon recovered, and these cases continued to be the bane of court officials.

Critics simply had no alternative to the control of the minor judiciary over the initiation of criminal prosecutions or the fee system and private prosecution as the main means of enforcing the criminal law. The dilemma posed by this situation was reflected in the continuing ambivalence of judges where private prosecution was concerned, which may itself have occasionally dissuaded grand jurors from using the costs law more vigorously. For example, in an 1836 charge to a mayor's court grand jury, Recorder Bouvier made extensive remarks about petty criminal cases. Although he recognized that assault and battery cases sometimes operated as a "valve" that allowed for the venting of "bad passions," he still believed that such cases were "too numerous" and "ought to be discouraged."[14]

Bouvier explicitly accused the poor of being responsible for petty litigation and implied that, if they had not been poor, they would have been like other Americans who brought civil actions against one another. Instead they initiated criminal cases involving themselves, the only objects of value they possessed. This interpretation placed private criminal prosecution in a better light by tying it to a celebrated American custom. Bouvier stressed that the aldermen and justices had a special relationship to people of "scanty or moderate means," whose "spirit of litigation" provided aldermen with the prime opportunity for corruption, but, unlike many other critics, Bouvier exonerated aldermen from responsibility for excessive litigation. He correctly stressed that, if parties refused to settle an assault and battery case, the alderman had no choice but to hold the accused to bail or, more likely, commit him or her to prison.

> I have reason to believe that perhaps not one out of four or five cases of this kind is returned to this court, and the remainder are settled by the benevolent and praiseworthy interference of the city magistrates. I know some mistaken notions are entertained that the magistrates in the city encourage this litigation, but I think these opinions unfounded, and are the result of ignorance of facts and a too ready disposition to cast blame on the ministers of the law, instead of placing it on the obstinate litigants, where it ought in justice to rest.

As in other charges, Bouvier recommended use of the costs law as the "remedy" for excessive litigation. However, he recognized that, in dealing with the poor, this too was of only limited use. To place the costs on a propertyless prosecutor simply meant that another poor person would be sent to prison, increasing both the burden of overcrowding and the cost to the county, which would have to pay for both the prosecution and the prosecutor's upkeep in prison.[15]

Bouvier was not alone in expressing support for private prosecution. Even during the midst of the riotous violence of the 1840s, judges insisted on the viability and indispensability of vigorous private prosecution. In a September 1845 charge, Judge Anson V. Parsons, a stern critic of aldermen, reminded the jurors that no standing army existed to guard the lives and property of the citizenry. "The majesty of the law is the mighty bulwark to which each one looks for support against any invasion of his rights; on this sustaining force all must rely, or civil society is sunk in anarchy." No one expressed more clearly the central role of the criminal law in the prepolice era; no one better evinced the ambivalence of the court regarding the legal culture of private prosecution.[16]

Some judges, nevertheless, tried to exercise what direct control they could. Many prison cases for minor order offenses never went through the typical court process leading to a jury trial. As disorder of all types increased in Philadelphia in the wake of the economic hard times of the early 1840s, the judges became more interested in suppressing it. Especially in breach of the peace cases, the judges assumed the summary jurisdiction usually exercised by aldermen and justices, but they were not primarily interested in discouraging these cases. Judges believed that order cases, like vagrancy and drunkenness prosecutions, were a useful means of restraining the offensive minor public disorder of the poor and working classes. The problem was that the informal methods used by the minor judiciary in minor order cases resulted all too often in the excessive punishment of some people and the insufficient punishment of others. Believing that the minor judiciary was failing to produce the results that justice and public decorum demanded, the judges sought to replace the authority of the aldermen with their own.

Led by the determined Judge Anson V. Parsons, the court assumed summary jurisdiction over many prison cases in 1846. This would allow the court to easily review all cases, release people unjustly imprisoned, and punish regular offenders more severely than an alderman would have done. Parsons announced the new policy at the start of the July 1846 term when he ruled that aldermen had the power to commit people to prison for breach of the peace only until the next term of the court and were required to return all of these cases to the court. The judge ordered the prison keepers to cease discharging persons who were committed by aldermen in default of bail or for disorderly conduct or vagrancy unless directed to do so by the court. Parsons specifically extended the order to cover disorderly conduct and vagrancy as well as breach of the peace in order to stop the aldermen from discharging prisoners before the expiration of their legal thirty-day sentence. The grand jury that term called this "one of the most important reforms the county has ever experienced."[17]

Nevertheless, considerable confusion regarding these cases persisted. None of them ever appeared in a quarter sessions docket book before or after 1846. Disorderly conduct remained a charge for which no one was ever given a thirty-day sentence, despite the statutory requirement that this be done. The prison keepers continued to record each commitment as the work of the alderman who heard the case originally, so it is impossible to know in any but an impressionistic way how the court of quarter sessions disposed of these cases. The average time served in prison did not increase appreciably for any of these charges; in fact, it began to decrease for disorderly conduct in 1846 and for breach of the peace in 1848. The only marked effect of the new policy recorded in the prison dockets was an exceedingly high percentage of breach of the peace commitments for the year 1846. In that year, 32 percent of all prison commitments were for breach of the peace, much higher than any previous year and not to be approached again until 1870.[18]

In any event, with an announcement of their "intention to inquire into the facts which led to the committal in each of these cases," the court began on 9 July to hear over 150 breach of the peace and vagrancy cases returned by the prison keepers. Throughout the month, many of these minor offenders apparently received a dose of justice harsher than any they had previously encountered. "Some were discharged, but a number were committed as vagrants, and ordered to give bail to be of good behavior for one year. This is equivalent to an imprisonment for that length of time, and the way most of them were astonished at the action of the Court was amusing." The judges believed that this policy would keep these people imprisoned "until thoroughly cured of their disorderly propensities, and not to be turned out upon the community at the whim and caprice of an alderman."[19]

This became the typical action of the court during the first year following the change in policy. On each day set aside for the hearing of breach of the peace cases, the defendants' dock was "thronged with prisoners of both sexes and different complexions, from the pale Caucasian to the ebony Ethiopian . . . the miserable outcast, the wretched inebriate, and the unfortunate victim of poverty." By July 1847, the court maintained that "many of these poor wretches being perfect outlaws, existing beyond the pale of moral society . . . will be compelled to remain in prison for a year at least" and then, after "the salutary treatment of the prison," allowed to return. Citing the diminution in cases from 144 in July 1846 to 30 in July 1847, Parsons declared the new system "advantageous" and expressed "a determination to sustain it, in the hope that . . . this kind of summary justice will make the law a terror."[20]

For one of the first times, faced with increasing public disorder and the troubling practices of the minor judiciary, a judge articulated the idea that law enforcement should be controlled by independent state institutions and directed at specific troublesome parts of the population. The logic of this ad hoc reasoning, however, demanded that the courts be an adjunct of an independent police force. This would soon turn Parsons and other judges into supporters of police reform, but for the time being, without one, any new policy to deal with minor offenses was doomed because case initiation remained firmly within the minor judiciary-citizen relationship.

The fall in the number of breach of the peace cases in 1847 was partly the result of the artificially inflated total of 1846. After 1850 the percentage recovered to near the typical pre-1846 level, in part because of the expansion of the police force and the resultant increase in the number of arrests for minor offenses, but there was no return of the earlier enthusiasm. Court reports ceased commenting on the salutary effect of the new policy. More typical was a report emphasizing how judges "tempered justice with as much mercy as the circumstances would allow." Certainly some persons were still held to bail, at least until 1850, but after the first year, it was no longer paid much attention. By 1851 a prisoner needed only to "promise reformation" to be "discharged with a word of caution."[21]

In fact the familiar complaints about the informal relations of primary justice resurfaced almost immediately regarding the quarter sessions' newest group of cases. As early as November 1846, a grand jury believed that most breach of the peace cases

> exhibit[ed] only a litigious disposition on the part of those who commenced them. . . . In two or three instances, the case arose from the mere quarrels of busy women, which the Court settled by holding both parties to bail to keep the peace, and dividing the responsibility of paying the costs between them. Several confident and valorous ladies, who were glorying in the prospect of sending their female neighbor to prison, or of putting her to the trouble of securing bail, were somewhat astonished to have themselves unexpectedly placed in the same predicament.[22]

By the early 1850s, prosecutors were commonly failing to attend breach of the peace trials, and aldermen were failing to send in returns, much like the situation before 1846. Prisoners were discharged, the cases dropped, and the court was again helpless to restrain what judges and jurors called the "improper motives" of prosecutors and the greed of the aldermen. In one 1848 case, a woman prisoner was confronted with no witnesses and no alderman's return. She claimed that Alderman McGarry, one of the most active magistrates in the county, committed her twice on an assault charge for having interfered to prevent a child from being beaten. She could pay the costs for her release only once and had to remain in prison until her day in court.[23]

The fact that an assault commitment wound up as a breach of the peace case with no record showed how pliable the law was for a determined private prosecutor and how seriously someone could suffer, but it startled no one. In just two years, officials and reporters stopped expecting the court to be able to regulate minor order cases. Breach of the peace had become a catch-all category that included vagrants, the disorderly poor, and ordinary victims of the excesses of private prosecution. When a private prosecutor abandoned a case or a magistrate failed to file a return, a defendant could find himself or herself languishing in prison and included among the breach of the peace cases, regardless of the crime originally alleged.

After the 1850 police expansion, the number of minor order cases reached unprecedented heights. The judges retained jurisdiction over them, but because there were now so many, the judges began to travel to the prison to hear the cases, which required neither jurors nor attorneys, rather than have the prisoners travel to court. Judge Campbell heard thirty such cases one day in May 1850. Judge Allison heard one hundred on an afternoon in 1852 and tacitly admitted the decline of the idea that public hearings of breach of the peace cases would serve as an example and terror. The winter of 1852 had been harsh, causing much "poverty and crime incident to a season of great pecuniary suffering and physical deprivation among a certain class of the community." No longer was the judge certain that meaningful punishment would reform the idle and vicious. No longer did he commend the regular sight of the degraded vagrants and disorderly alcoholics trooping into court as a useful corrective for a popular inclination toward licentiousness. Breach of the peace cases had themselves become nuisances, too numerous to safely handle in the public courtroom. Instead they were kept hidden in prison, "to prevent exhibitions of human depravity, loathsome to the eye and to some extent demoralizing in their effects."[24]

The judges' efforts to take command of minor order cases demonstrated the limits of their attempts to reform the criminal justice process as long as the minor judiciary remained central to that process. Any criminal justice solution to the problem of the disorderly poor required wholesale changes in the structure and concept of the criminal justice system. Although jurists sometimes articulated such ideas, they were still too wedded to traditional legal culture to embrace them wholeheartedly and were, in any case, powerless to implement such changes. Instead the jurists relinquished the idea of making the law a terror and chose to keep the victims of poverty hidden.[25]

Citizens were never dissuaded from bringing private prosecutions. Before the establishment of the police, the authority of the law was dependent on its voluntary use by the citizenry, centered primarily in the offices of the city's minor judiciary. Among these magistrates and the private citizens who frequented their offices, respect for the law was intertwined with the informal methods they favored. Judges recognized this, just as they recognized what they believed to be the excesses of private prosecution, and found themselves trapped by their ambivalence and relative powerlessness. Thus, by mid-century, private prosecution had become central to the city's system of criminal law enforcement, so entrenched that it would prove difficult to dislodge even after the police became an independent and formidable presence.

Despite the repeated conflicts between court officials, on the one hand, and private parties and the minor judiciary, on the other, this was a distinctive and coherent system of criminal justice, based on a voluntary popular participation in which virtually everyone believed. To be sure, it had flaws. The internal contradictions of this system weighed most heavily on judges, jurors, and, especially, the victims of private malice or magisterial excess. The weakness of the tools available to court officials and their relatively late arrival in the process, the need to process cases without jury trials, the dependence on private voluntarism for cases, and the belief in the legitimacy of the system prevented judges and jurors from being able to limit the power of the private parties and minor judiciary. In the last analysis, because private prosecution and the exercise of the criminal law began in the communities and the minor judiciary's offices, the citizenry and the minor judiciary maintained the primary control over criminal justice.

5. *Politics and Private Prosecution, 1800–1850*

"People have not much sympathy for Aldermen; the very name is associated with something lazy and fat." So began a story, in a July 1836 issue of the *Public Ledger*, of an incident involving Southwark Alderman Henry Manderfield. One night a watchman, summoned to a disorderly tavern, found Manderfield and several friends in the thick of a brawl. He ordered everyone to disperse, but Manderfield refused, "proclaiming himself superior to the watch." The officer prosecuted Manderfield for resisting his order and found a magistrate willing to hold the alderman in $500 bail. The paper reported feelings of "universal odium" toward Manderfield and widespread "joy at his degradation." It also offered the following description of the typical alderman:

> How To Make An Alderman—we must take a fellow who can neither read nor write . . . who understands the republic's English so well as to disregard all the artificial nonsense of grammar; who thinks sobriety the mere cant of interested hypocrites, and . . . gets drunk daily . . . who understands thoroughly the laws which he is called to administer, and can therefore give promptly, and without hesitation, a license to every pot companion to violate them at pleasure; who thinks that keepers of gambling houses cannot pay their rent unless permitted to carry on their trade unmolested.[1]

Rather than withering away as the city grew during the first half of the nineteenth century, private prosecution adapted to changes in the composition of the city's population, to new relations of social and economic life, and to the change of the leaders of local government from paternalistic elites to clubhouse politicians. One of the most important reasons for the increasing vitality of private prosecution was the ease with which it fit into Philadelphia's emerging informal structure of urban ward politics and patronage. As a result, popular democracy joined private prosecution as the foundation of the formidable link between the people of Philadelphia and their neighborhood politicians. So, as critics of urban politics became increasingly active—especially after the democratic reforms of the 1830s—they came increasingly to associate private prosecution with the alleged corruption of city government in general.

Public controversy over the criminal courts before 1850 had three distinct phases, more or less corresponding to the critics' increasing awareness of the relationship between politics and prosecution. During the first, which lasted through the 1830s, critics identified the magistracy and private prosecution as the lynchpins of criminal justice. Although they tinkered with the courts and prisons, the legal presumption and structural importance of private prosecution prevented critics from effecting any significant change. The second phase erupted in 1840 around the first aldermanic election of the century, the event that cemented the ties between the minor judiciary and the city's ward-based political parties. The third phase, a reaction to the obvious connection between party politics and local government during the 1840s, saw the emergence of the first, futile attempts to challenge the power of the politicians. Despite the failure of these early municipal reformers, they helped set the stage for those who would follow.

Legal and Prison Reform, 1800–1838

Criticism of the criminal courts was abundant before 1840, and reformers even made several tentative attempts to do something about primary justice. However, because they lived in an era of a still unchallenged presumption of private prosecution, their efforts only reinforced the power of aldermen and private prosecutors.

Concerns about order for early nineteenth-century American lawyers and jurists were not only the result of a perception of disorderly people or institutions but a predilection of the legal mind. Rooted in the eighteenth-century republican anxiety over the fragility of liberty and the strength of corruption, early American lawyers were preoccupied with the law's ability to impose order upon, and give definition to, the nation. Thomas Paine set the tone when, in the course of arguing for the superiority of republics over monarchies, he made the simple point that in America, "THE LAW IS KING."[2] This was, of course, because the people in a republic made even the most fundamental law. As a result, law became not just the substance but also the symbol of sovereignty, and popular legal activism, of which private prosecution was a part, became widespread. As a result of this, disorder within the law itself became a concern of jurists and legislators.[3] All of their attempts during the late eighteenth and early nineteenth centuries to restore order to the process of prosecution nevertheless remained wedded to the fundamental notion that popular involvement and private initiative were the foundation of law and order.

The first complaints were actually about the people having too *little* access to the law. Dissatisfaction surfaced in part because of revolutionary-era upheavals that extended political participation and diminished deference among ordinary men.[4] Democratic passions also touched the courts. The administration of justice became markedly more unruly during the late eighteenth century. Controversies arose that revealed how deeply rooted the informal procedures of justices of the peace already were in the city's life. Complaints about "trading justices" during the Philadelphia elections of 1786 raised issues such as the abuse of the fee system and the access to justice for the poor. For over a year, critics repeatedly accused government officials, especially justices, of charging excessive fees and thereby enriching themselves at the expense of the city's poor. Critics suggested that they inhibited access to the law for those least able to afford the inflated fees. This may or may not have been the case, but the charge of "retailing" justice did reflect a popularization of criminal justice which allowed less scrupulous magistrates to charge excessive fees and abuse their authority.[5]

One consequence of this controversy was the elimination of elections for aldermen when Philadelphia was reincorporated in 1789, but the minor judiciary resurfaced as a concern during the first decade of the nineteenth century. The structure and power of the judiciary became a major issue in the struggle between Jeffersonians and Federalists in Pennsylvania, partly because the principles of arbitration had become central to the legal process.[6]

After the Republican triumph of 1800, the Jeffersonians in Pennsylvania became deeply divided into a moderate faction of Philadelphia merchants and lawyers led by Governor Thomas McKean and a radical faction centered in the countryside but led by the urban radical agitator William Duane. Rejecting the moderates' efforts to revise the court system to meet the needs of "the extension of Commerce and Agriculture," rural radicals demanded a "plain and simple" legal code and a system of arbitration that would "allow laymen to plead their own cases." Echoing the sentiment of farmer and New Hampshire Supreme Court Justice John Dudley that "it is not law we want, but justice," the radicals attempted in 1802 to extend the jurisdiction of justices of the peace; justices were almost always laymen and their procedures often resembled arbitration, which the rural faction wanted included in reform legislation.[7]

The radicals succeeded with the legislators, but McKean vetoed their law. This spurred Duane and the Philadelphia radicals into action. They had not been involved before for a variety of reasons, including the commercial orientation of even radical urbanites and Duane's lack of personal interest in the issue. But Philadelphians, especially the poor and artisan groups for whom

Duane spoke, had sufficient reason for hostility toward lawyers, if not the judiciary.[8]

Their resentment against lawyers became explicit in 1805 when Duane successfully aroused Philadelphia voters in an election that turned largely on the question of judicial reform. The chief campaign piece, published by Duane and entitled "Sampson Against the Philistines," was largely an attack on lawyers and "the abuses upon which they thrive; the tyranny which they display in courts." Its proposals included excluding lawyers as far as possible from all trials and having the state pay them a fixed salary when their participation was necessary, having all cases heard before local courts with the right of appeal severely limited, and requiring arbitration if either party desired it. Duane added that criminal courts had to be informal and local as well in order to protect people from "the terrors of *anonymous* prosecutors." Duane's faction carried Philadelphia County in 1805 although McKean won the election. Perhaps the late entrance of the Philadelphia radicals into the judicial reform fray reflected not so much the commercial orientation of *all* Philadelphians as the general satisfaction the city's less commercially inclined lower orders felt with the local justice's courts, which they were fashioning into accessible and informal tribunals; but lawyers, who could use those same courts in ways threatening to these same people, were another story. When *they* became the issue, urban radicals responded.[9]

Their response made a difference because, even after McKean's re-election, the arbitration and extension of justice's jurisdiction laws remained in force. In 1806 the legislature passed the law allowing aldermen and justices to settle assault and battery cases in their offices, which also encouraged litigation.

These were very conservative changes that failed to tamper with the structure of the criminal law and maintained traditional assumptions. For example, the legislature never would give the minor judiciary the power to judge assault and battery cases. Later in 1806 (and again in 1832), lawmakers rejected a proposal that would have given aldermen and justices final jurisdiction over misdemeanors, preferring the tradition that kept decisions about guilt and innocence in indictable, even if petty, offenses in the hands of judges and juries.

Enacted against the backdrop of considerable support for the informal methods and wide jurisdiction of aldermen and justices, new laws only strengthened the system of private prosecution.[10] The most important thing about the entire episode, seen in the context of widespread litigation, was the combination of hostility toward lawyers and respect for the law and the courts. This peculiar blend of commitment to the law and suspicion of the lawyers' control of the process of litigation was central to the development of criminal justice and the persistence of private prosecution in the nineteenth century.[11]

Private prosecution and the concern for order within the legal system also influenced the first members of the Philadelphia Society for Alleviating the Miseries of Public Prisons (PSAMPP). Horrendous, overcrowded prison conditions, made worse by improper and pretrial confinements, were the immediate reasons for the founding of the PSAMPP by Benjamin Rush in 1787. It rapidly became the leading source of criticism of abuses of criminal prosecution. PSAMPP members were the elite of the Quaker-dominated philanthropic community of Philadelphia—ministers, physicians, prominent merchants and their sons, all of them well-to-do and dedicated to humanitarian causes. Among them were the Reverend William White, Roberts Vaux, Caleb Lownes, Dr. William Shippen, Benjamin Franklin, Tench Coxe, publisher Zachariah Poulson, and four sons of the celebrated merchant Caspar Wistar. Of the first 340 members, 136 were also members of the Society of Friends. When the board of prison inspectors was established in 1790, ten of its twelve members belonged to the PSAMPP.[12] Rush and Vaux especially were frenetic conservative reformers concerned with the criminal justice process in large part because of their conviction that the orderly legal process itself could reform criminals.[13]

For the first third of the nineteenth century, the PSAMPP was primarily concerned about prison overcrowding. The problem was simple: overcrowded prisons eliminated any possibility of salutary prison discipline and thus reformation for those needing it, and the indiscriminate mixing of inmates of all kinds was a palpable injustice to the poor, untried, and child prisoners. The solution, however, was more complicated. Despite the construction of several new penal institutions during these years, the society repeatedly bemoaned the "intolerable" conditions of them all. They described the Arch Street Prison in 1830 as a "mass of vice, whose contaminating influence must be felt by everyone who unhappily is in it."[14]

Controversy over the judiciary had barely subsided when the society believed it had discovered the reason for this problem. Roberts Vaux, the most prominent member of the visiting committee that regularly inspected the prisons, wrote in 1809, "The Committee are concerned to state that some of the magistrates of the peace, appear to use their authority rather to enrich themselves than to serve the purposes of publick justice." By the early 1820s, the society was accusing magistrates of making "many hundreds" of "unjust and illegal" commitments. In 1833 a committee investigating a deadly outbreak of cholera in one prison concluded that "most of the cases of imprisonment for minor offenses would not be heard, except for the costs which accrue upon them." The underlying cause of the disease was, according to the committee, the practices of the magistrates. The desire for fees was being encouraged by the "advantage . . . given to the magistrate who transcends the proper exercise of authority."[15]

Soon after the cholera epidemic, an exasperated PSAMPP asked its counselors, Joseph Ingersoll and George Wharton, for advice about the powers of magistrates and ways to prevent improper commitments and discharges. The attorneys reassured the society that many of the magistrates' practices were indeed illegal, but they could not suggest much to do about it. The society thought the solution was simply to turn the system against the magistrates and asked Ingersoll and Wharton to prosecute those guilty of "violations of the law," but there is no record that the counselors ever prosecuted a case.[16] The attention given the abuses of magistrates by prison reformers, nevertheless, did bear some fruit. The state legislature tried to remedy the problem of illegal fees with an 1814 law requiring a justice to pay the injured party $50 if he was convicted of receiving illegal or excessive fees. In 1824 magistrates were made liable for the costs in a suit to recover illegal fees, and in 1827 they were made liable for the $50 fine even if the illegal charge was imposed out of ignorance and without corrupt intent.[17]

The PSAMPP was more successful in its campaign for new institutions, which produced a major step forward in the centralization of Philadelphia's penal system and a significant, if lesser, improvement in their classification of prisoners. The two most important new institutions were the house of refuge, opened in 1828, and the Philadelphia County Prison, or "Moyamensing" as it was familiarly called after the suburban district in which it was located, opened in 1835. The former, designed to separate vagrant and delinquent children from adult offenders and to transform them into useful citizens, drew wide support from Philadelphia's leadership community after the PSAMPP began organizing public meetings to raise funds for it in 1826. The county prison, four years in construction, was designed after the "separate system" of the nearby Eastern State Penitentiary, originally devised by members of the prison society. All convicts, including vagrants, were to be held in separate cells. To manage the new prison, the board of prison inspectors was reorganized, its twelve members now appointed, four each by the mayor, quarter sessions judges, and district court judges. A major new power, designed to prevent overcrowding, allowed the inspectors to discharge anyone committed for vagrancy by an alderman or justice.[18]

All of this activity put the magistrates in a rather negative light with some legislators. The argument that persuaded the assembly to reject a summary justices court for misdemeanors in 1832 stated plainly that "the people of Pennsylvania . . . have reason to know that there are many ignorant and some profligate men in that class of magistrates; and in the opinion of the committee their power over the property and personal liberty of the citizen is quite as extensive as it ought to be." To put a criminal court under the control of a justice in every village or ward would be to encourage judicial consideration of "every petty assault and battery, or trifling offence," in opposition to the public interest and the effort to keep these cases out of the courts. By the early 1830s, then, thanks in large part to the efforts of the prison society, it was becoming clear that the culture of criminal prosecution was quite different from the elite and paternalistic ideal prevalent at the turn of the century.[19]

By 1840 the contours of primary justice in Philadelphia were even clearer. Universal manhood suffrage, the expansion of the number of elective local offices, and the rise of popular journalism that concentrated on news of crime and the courts were among the factors contributing to the extension of the informal practices of primary justice and to popular awareness of them.[20] Although aldermen were still appointed for life by the governor, they had become officials intimately connected with local politics. After about 1815, disgruntled Federalist elites largely withdrew from politics, leaving the field to the Jeffersonians, who had already been feuding among themselves and who now became fragmented into rival factions that were led by powerful personalities like John Binns and William Duane. Dominated by issues based on local differences and leaders, these factions demonstrated little stability or longevity, and their followers showed little loyalty or discipline. Democratic ward meetings during the 1820s were already notoriously raucous and divided.[21]

Jacksonian democratic reforms heightened these aspects of politics. Saloons and fire companies became informal neighborhood political headquarters for factions that, after Jackson's bank veto, coalesced into parties. Conservative Democrats and old Federalists who were concentrated in the central city provided the Whig party with substantial support, and after a statewide anti-Jackson coalition captured the statehouse in 1835, party rivalry returned to Philadelphia politics. Party competition was heated, and local political activists received appointed office as rewards when their party was successful in elections, including those for governor. Aldermen, such as

Morton McMichael, a future prominent Whig and Republican who until 1838 was a conservative Democrat, were among these activists. The political connection was not lost on the critics. Journalists accused aldermen of ignoring honest constables in favor of dishonest friends whom they illegally deputized and of accepting people as bail who clearly could not be responsible for the amount of money involved.[22] "In no part of the country is the administration of justice more corrupt" than in Philadelphia, asserted one critic, mostly because magistrates were political appointees and paid by fees.[23]

During the late 1830s, reformers made several attempts to limit the power of the minor judiciary, turning first to the structure of the criminal courts. Three criminal courts served Philadelphia County: the mayor's court for the city; the recorder's court for Northern Liberties, Spring Garden, and Kensington; and the quarter sessions for the rest of the county. Each court held sessions four times a year. Two things bothered PSAMPP reformers about this structure. First, quarterly court sessions meant untried prisoners and witnesses could spend months behind bars awaiting trial. When the trial was finally held, many other witnesses—most often defense witnesses—could no longer be found. The quality of justice was thus materially reduced. Moreover, the inconvenience of initiating a prosecution and having to wait months for a trial dissuaded many strangers and persons unfamiliar with the Philadelphia courts from bringing "the culprit to justice." Second, confusion about which court to use also discouraged prosecutions and contributed to the problem of pretrial detainees. With so many overlapping authorities, there was no central body to which returns of cases were sent, no body that could oversee the commitment practices of the magistrates. Unscrupulous prosecutors and magistrates could too easily fail to return a case and keep a poor defendant helplessly incarcerated for months.[24]

Prompted by the prison reformers, Philadelphia County legislator Samuel F. Reed submitted a bill in 1838 to reorganize the criminal courts. Reed proposed to abolish the mayor's court and the recorder's court, remove criminal jurisdiction from the quarter sessions and place it in a new criminal court that would serve the entire county. This court would hold bimonthly sessions and receive weekly returns of all untried prisoners in order to schedule an immediate trial or discharge. The *Public Ledger* quickly assumed a leading role as advocate of the new court. The paper estimated that the average wait in prison for an untried person was six weeks and that the prison population averaged 200 untried prisoners a day in 1837. During that year, the mayor's court alone failed to convict 164 persons imprisoned before trial, some for as long as eight months. A few days later, the *Ledger* announced that these issues of the paper were in greater demand than any previous and that "men of all parties, and in every condition in society, have eagerly sought to sign petitions for the new court."[25]

There was, nevertheless, substantial opposition to changing the county's criminal courts. As would be the case with all attempts to reform the structure of city government, it was rooted in politics. Local politicians objected to any tampering with a system of government that placed most of the power in their hands, and aldermen especially resisted any innovations that would limit their autonomy. Party considerations also entered in. A centralized court system would surely mean a loss of patronage for the mostly Democratic county politicians and a dominant position for Whigs from the city. Thus, all seven city representatives supported the bill, and of the eight representatives from the county, all but Reed opposed it.[26]

The bill passed and the court of criminal sessions commenced business in April 1838. The *Ledger* proudly took much of the credit and again stressed its primary reason for supporting the new court. The major beneficiaries of the change would be those victimized by "that system of oppression heretofore exercised by petty magistrates" who, by committing people to prison on false accusations, had reaped "a harvest of fifteen hundred to two thousand dollars annually, when the legal emolument of such magistracy, honestly administered, would not have exceeded two or three hundred." The weekly returns of untried prisoners would check this practice.[27]

Reformers like the *Ledger*'s editors soon realized how ineffective the new court would be in restraining private prosecution, but even before this, they learned how powerful the aldermen were. Shortly after the passage of the court reform bill, the emboldened critics of the minor judiciary sought to strike at them even more directly. In March 1838, the state's constitutional convention was finishing its work in Philadelphia and contemplating a series of changes in the powers and tenure of aldermen. Because the structure of the minor judiciary was fixed by the state constitution, any changes in that office would have to be included in the new document. The *Ledger* and other consistent critics of the minor judiciary had been strongly urging the convention to limit the authority of the aldermen since its opening the previous spring.[28] But two things made any such changes impossible. One was the democratic thrust of the age, which only strengthened aldermen and other local politicians who naturally resisted change. The other was the opposition of conservative members of the legal establishment such as John Bouvier and John Sergeant, who supported strengthening the courts of record but opposed tampering with the traditional mode of initiating the criminal justice process.

The subject was first considered in July 1837. The judiciary committee of the convention recommended only that justices and aldermen be elected for five-year terms instead of being appointed by the governor for good behavior. Even this proposal spurred vigorous debate. Many representatives from rural counties believed that the problem was not that justices were appointed but that there were too many of them. They had no trouble with limited terms of office but favored appointment in order to keep the office free from the even greater temptations to favoritism that electoral politics would occasion.

Several Philadelphia delegates maintained that the larger problem was the fee system. They emphasized that poor people were almost entirely dependent on justices and thus subject to corruption from which they had virtually no redress. Fixed salaries and frequent elections would remove temptations to corruption and give the poor a way to combat oppressive magistrates. As one delegate insisted, "If there was one thing more than another from which the poorer classes suffered, it was the arbitrary and unfair practices of their Magistrates. They suffered more on this account, than if they were living under any foreign Government." This reasoning was persuasive, but it unfortunately failed to consider the possibility that the poor also benefited from the actions of the aldermen and that elections might reinforce rather than erode their authority.[29]

Aldermen, most of them already influential local politicians, were not too worried about the prospect of standing for election although they naturally preferred lifetime appointments. Most delegates defended their methods of administering justice, and the most prominent of their defenders was the widely respected president of the convention, John Sergeant. Sergeant's traditional sense of legal order led him to give the magistrates the benefit of the doubt and to defend traditional arrangements, even as it had led him to be a leading prison reformer. Condemnations of justices were based on "slight hearsay evidence, and vague, unfounded generalities." Elected magistrates would never find for a stranger against a constituent or a friendless constituent against a politically influential one. Magistrates were "respectable men" operating under a system that was wisely adopted only fourteen years after an elective system was found wanting. Sergeant urged their vindication through the continuation of the system of appointment for good behavior. He and several other Philadelphia attorney delegates, such as Charles Ingersoll and Joseph Doran, did support fixed salaries but as an affirmation of traditional legal practices. In this way, they were addressing the concern that there not be two systems of justice, one for the rich and one for the poor. Putting justices on the same footing as judges—appointed officers on a guaranteed salary—would elevate them and afford them the same respect as judges, respect that Sergeant clearly believed justices and all representatives of the state deserved. But there were some serious practical objections to this idea. Some delegates claimed that salaries would cost the state too much, remove a wholesome restraint on frivolous litigation, and pay equal amounts to justices who handled widely differing numbers of cases.[30]

Proponents of change had difficulty getting their colleagues to agree on anything. Both salaries and frequent elections raised serious problems. As long as all assumed that the minor judiciary was necessary, that it should handle the legal business of the poor, and that it be the site of the initiation of the criminal justice process, there was no sure way to protect against excessive litigation and some corruption. Also, delegates from rural areas had no interest in paying for salaries that might limit the access to justice for poor people in the city. The proposals to pay salaries and hold elections every three years were easily defeated. The committee's recommendation for elections for five-year terms was approved by a single vote, and during the winter sessions in Philadelphia, the delegates agreed to allow no more than two justices or aldermen per ward, borough, or township "without the consent of a majority of the qualified electors within" that district. In accordance with this, one of the few changes in the structure of government that was made by the convention, the legislature set the first elections for 1840 and allowed only one aldermen per ward in the city and the incorporated districts of Philadelphia County.[31]

The 1838 constitution was a politician's delight, notable mainly for increasing the number of elective offices in the state and extending the suffrage for white men. The compromise on the minor judiciary was in keeping with this trend, but it also reflected the strength of traditional notions of local government and the legal process. Throughout their debates, delegates never questioned the necessity of the people's bringing private prosecutions to the minor judiciary, never proposed a comprehensive alternative. In a law enforcement system without a police force, private prosecution and the minor judiciary were essential. This left delegates facing the same paradox that judges and jurors faced every day, dissuading people from using the courts while insisting on a strong system of criminal justice. Was not the frequent use of the courts by the people, especially poor people, gratifying evidence of belief in, and respect for, the law? Would not a reduction in use of the courts be a worrisome sign that the law could be broken without consequence? How could one be sure that only trivial cases would be discouraged and not serious, legitimate crimes?

Although the revelations of reformers and journalists which preceded the convention made everyone sensitive to what the critics characterized as the abuses of the magistrates, the constraints of the moment left delegates with few options for correcting these abuses. Direct election was a popular reform in the Jacksonian age, but it could only be an effective restraint on the magistrates if the voters felt abuse where the delegates saw it and turned the offending magistrates out of office. The convention's reinforcement of the traditional structure of criminal prosecution did as much to legitimate the activities of magistrates and private litigants as it did to restrain them. The cumulative effect of all the changes since 1800 was to strengthen the foundation of private prosecution and the minor judiciary, despite the harsh criticism directed at the aldermen by some reformers. Now, with the direct election of aldermen about to strengthen their ties to the ward-based parties that controlled Jacksonian democracy, the aldermen were about to become even more important members of their communities.

Aldermen and Politics, 1838–1850

The few reforms enacted before 1840 had done little to restrain the aldermen and their constituents, and there was little reason to believe that the upcoming elections would do so either. As, in the wake of democratic reforms, local politics came to parallel the local structure of the state, and as aldermen became central figures in both, private prosecution and the informal practices of primary justice were only apt to be reinforced.

Two years passed between the completion of the state constitution of 1838 and the first election for aldermen. During the interim, criticism of private prosecution remained much as it had been before: there was too much of it, it was handled too informally, and the greedy minor judiciary were to blame.[32] "Some . . . are in the daily habit of fomenting quarrels between the ignorant and vicious, that they may reap the fruits of their controversies, encouraging them, in the first instance, to fight and brawl, and then exacting from them sums of money to obtain protection from the proper course of the law." Aldermen allowed their constables to make arrests for "trifling causes," sent the arrested person to prison, and awaited the appearance of a friend of the accused who could pay the costs to procure a discharge.[33] Grand jurors continually complained that aldermen either settled too many or too few cases, reflecting their continued relative powerlessness in the criminal justice process.[34]

Criticism of the alderman-litigant relationship implicitly recognized its usefulness to many people for the resolution of personal disputes, and the election confirmed it. The legislature scheduled the first election of aldermen for 20 March 1840. In mid-January, the campaign began, and politics quickly became a dominant issue. "A Constant Reader" urged the *Ledger* to plead with people to make "moral honesty" the only basis for the selection of a candidate "so that we may make an effort to clear the magistracy of the rubbish of party," but this was wishful thinking in an age of raucous partisan local politics.

With the emergence of the Whig party during the first half of the 1830s, politics in Philadelphia became especially intense. Conservative Democrats, always whiggish in economic matters, began joining the Whigs in substantial numbers during the unsuccessful campaign of William Henry Harrison in 1836. That election established Whig control of the city and Democratic control of the suburbs, a pattern that would dominate Philadelphia politics for two decades. While wards throughout the county tended to be dominated by one party, the strength of the parties in the county as a whole was relatively equal. The ability of ward party organizations to mobilize voters was key to the success of either party in a close election, which the national contest of 1840 promised to be. Seeing the aldermanic elections as an important early test of party strength, the ward politicians took firm control of the selection of candidates. "Franklin" wrote that, in his ward, all of the candidates were unqualified, "mere party politicians [who] fancy that they possess claims for being elevated to the office of Alderman in proportion to their political influence at the ward tavern." The editors of the *Ledger* agreed that "small ward politicians have taken the matter under their exclusive charge" and regretted that the "importance of choosing proper persons to fill these offices seems not to be duly appreciated by the people."[35]

In the weeks that followed, an unprecedented discussion of the aldermanic office unfolded in Philadelphia's press, concentrating on the importance of aldermen to the community and the basis for many citizens' choice of candidates. Newspaper editors asserted that "a large portion of them are ready to cast their votes upon personal or political grounds, without any concern as to the qualifications of the applicant. This is clearly wrong. . . . If [magistrates] are disposed to pervert their official power to improper use—if they promote litigation, encourage strife and foster disputes, they are pests." This was especially the case among the "humbler classes," where, for example, wives frequently complained of improper treatment at the hands of their husbands, "and in too many cases, it must be confessed, her complaints are well founded." These people depended upon the alderman to recommend "conciliatory measures" in order to prevent not only criminal cases but also "perpetual misery" between the parties.[36]

The alderman was, in short, "an example for imitation; and if he misbehaves, he is, to a certain extent, the author of mischief."[37] The editors implied that only aldermen who adopted the paternalistic posture of settling disputes, quieting passions, and discouraging litigation would genuinely serve the public interest and prevent crime. Although, understandably, the model magistrate for reform-minded journalists seeking to discredit politicians, this type of alderman was a relic. Where domestic violence was concerned, an equally strong case could have been made for the flexible response of aldermen and private prosecutors, which included at least the threat of imprisonment and criminal prosecution.

Litigation and party affairs directly involved perhaps the majority of Philadelphians with the city's politics and government. Voters exercised citizenship through local political organizations that were led by their neighbors and were able to dispense influence and patronage. Everyone, even people excluded from the franchise, could also participate in forging the bond between the community and its politicians through the mechanism of private prosecution. The election campaign revealed the power of this dual bond.[38]

Partly in response to the endless criticism, a number of nonpartisan and "people's" candidates for alderman appeared, all echoing the sentiment that aldermen were too important to be chosen on the basis of party affiliation. The most prominent of the nonpartisan candidates was Spring Garden Alderman Morton McMichael, who was supported by a committee of 116 residents of his ward and enthusiastically endorsed by the *Ledger*, the voice of nonpartisanship in Philadelphia. McMichael was, however, hardly free from partisan attachments. He had been a leading conservative Democrat for most of the preceding decade but, by 1838, had become attracted to Whig economic positions and was in the process of making a political transition. Later to become sheriff, mayor, and a leading county Republican, McMichael was only a momentary nonpartisan, and was the only candidate in the county to run unopposed.[39]

Most other races were hotly contested among Democratic, Whig, and nonparty candidates. Some of the latter, such as George Gilbert of Pine Ward, were partisans in all but formal affiliation. Among Gilbert's supporters were such young Democratic politicians as William D. Kelley and William McMullin, a future alderman and postwar Democratic party boss.[40] In contrast, Adam Seckel of Cedar Ward was undoubtedly an independent. Seeing the election as evidence of how "party politics run so high as to corrupt the fountain of Justice," Seckel not only ran for office but also attended and attempted to participate in party meetings, at which he was silenced, called a traitor, and labeled "contrary to all usages of the party," as he undoubtedly was.[41]

For the most part, party organizations proudly ran their candidates for alderman and defended the proper role of partisan politics in the selection of judicial officers. They claimed that, when the constitutional convention made the office elective, they intended for it to be controlled by political parties, which surely was true of the politicians who supported the proposal. Party newspapers like the national *Gazette* published statements that connected organization to ideology, asserting the importance of political principles ruling even in local matters and suggesting that, because party predilections influenced the decisions of aldermen, party supporters should be concerned with having their man elected.[42]

The election itself vindicated the politicians or, from the perspective of the independent *Ledger*, "furnished a melancholy proof of the evil influences of the 'monster, party.' " Only McMichael and a few other independents were elected. Despite his many supporters, George Gilbert was soundly trounced. Adam Seckel ran a distant third in a three-man race. Though the *Ledger* and others critical of aldermen no doubt saw the widespread triumphs of party politicians as evidence of the indifference of citizens to the honest administration of the law, it might better be seen as an affirmation by voters of the party system.

Despite the protests of reform-minded citizens and editors, aldermen and the ward political organizations were providing an essential community service. Access to the law on a pay-as-you-go basis was popular, and even if there was more than a hint of corruption involved, most communities felt no widespread need to reject the kind of men who had been offering this service. Given the rapid population turnover in the city, the minor judiciary and their allied political and social organizations were important sources of stability. Already, at least (or especially) on the most local level, aldermen and their political party colleagues were "mediat[ing] . . . the role of the working class in municipal government." As a result of the dual bond that aldermen and political parties had forged with the city's people, their power had reached new heights. They were in a position to limit severely the possibilities for change in city government and thus to influence not just the conduct but also the reform of criminal justice.[43]

Corruption and the Courts

According to most students of nineteenth-century criminal justice, "the people, speaking through the political machines, preferred corruption." According to many critics of the early 1840s, corruption was what the people got.[44] The rise of Jacksonian party politics provoked the first sustained effort to expose and remove allegedly corrupt links between local government and party politics in Philadelphia. Totally unsuccessful though it was, this campaign raised the issues and introduced some of the characters that would play major roles in subsequent attempts to restrain private prosecution.

Most of what judges, grand jurors, and editors said about criminal justice was already very familiar, but they also boldly accused aldermen of outright corruption. "It appears that several of them have made attempts to extort money from people" by forcing larceny prosecutors to pay illegal fees for the return of stolen property that had been recovered from thieves. In fact, aldermen were now increasingly charged with crimes. Alderman Redman was held on a charge of misdemeanor in office for refusing to issue arrest warrants in an assault and battery case unless the prosecutrix paid $1 per warrant. A jury convicted Redman of taking illegal fees and fined him $50. He claimed futilely that the case was a malicious prosecution by persons who had lost four previous cases that had come before him. In addition, a grand jury indicted Alderman McCall and others for abetting the escape of a prisoner; and an "uptown" alderman was sued for money given to him by a defendant which he never turned over to the intended recipient.[45]

Aldermen and their greed remained a public issue with the enactment of two new laws in the summer of 1842. One was the long-struggled-for abolition of imprisonment for debt, the other was a requirement that aldermen deposit with the county treasurer a quarterly statement of fines received. Aldermen lost a potent source of income and were made publicly accountable for a large share of what remained. "A Citizen" wrote in November that, as a result, "it is feared that some [magistrates will] begin to resort to means of raising money not strictly consistent with justice and good morals."[46]

Perhaps some did. A January 1843 grand jury thought so, suggesting that the number of aldermen of high honor and integrity were few, that they abused their powers according to whether "the defendant may or may not be entitled to *vote*," and made a mockery of justice by accepting so many "bills for chicken stealing, fifty-cent larcenies, etc., whilst grave offences remain unchecked." Alderman Houston Smith certainly did not prosper. He resigned in February 1843 because, since the abolition of debt imprisonment, the office had "become almost worthless, as a matter of profit, to all but a favored few." Few aldermen, however, followed Smith's example. One correspondent for the *Ledger* believed, in early 1843, that the system of selling justice was the central problem of criminal justice in Philadelphia. He suggested that "in all criminal matters, [the people] have the right to reparation and justice, free of costs or charge."[47]

The connection between private greed and corruption in government transcended criminal justice during this era. It came before the courts in 1839 as a consequence of mismanagement of funds, frauds, and forgeries engaged in by the directors of the Norristown Railroad Company and the Schuylkill Bank. With depression deepening in Philadelphia and elsewhere, the *Ledger* asked why none of the culprits had "been visited with the vengeance of the law. . . . If the rogue in rags who steals a trifle from his neighbor is properly a subject for penal inflictions, the rascal in purple and fine linen who defrauds hundreds, perhaps thousands of their honest earnings is certainly not less so."[48]

The next week, criminal sessions judge and elder local legal scholar John Bouvier repeated this question while instructing a grand jury to investigate the collapse of the Schuylkill Bank, but Bouvier went even further, explicitly linking criminal justice and the specter of social crisis raised by the depression. He suggested that the entire web of law and justice would crumble if the "poor starving wretch" who steals and is imprisoned saw the "respectable offender" who robbed widows and children go free. Respect for law would evaporate and with it something nearly as important, a healthy disrespect for the fevered rush "to make a fortune by a dash, regardless of the means." A spirit of speculation had "swept over the land and carried away the frail virtue of those who became its worshippers." Bouvier impressed upon the jurors their responsibility not only to "let not the poor man be able to say there is one kind of justice for him, and another for the rich" but also to make sure that "enterprise . . . with industry . . . be cherished, but the . . . gambling and dishonest speculator . . . be discountenanced and discouraged."[49]

Part of the reason for this being so important was that greed directly affected the substance of justice. Corruption in the courts included allowing well-heeled defendants to escape prosecution. Court reporters believed that it was commonplace for "respectable swindlers" to go unpunished. When Mary Ann Costill, a black girl, was committed, indicted, tried, convicted, and imprisoned for larceny within two hours in May 1841, the reporter noted that "unfortunately for Mary . . . she was not a noted forger or pickpocket or she might have fared better, and perhaps escaped altogether."[50]

The issue of corruption in the administration of justice became, by the middle of the decade, one aspect of a widespread controversy over corruption throughout city government. Corruption was, of course, the symbolic theme that stood behind the Jacksonian assault on the national bank, and the depression only fueled resentment against speculators, government officials, and others who seemed to profit from secret bargains while the majority suffered. Political outsiders, opportunists, and self-styled reformers jumped on the bandwagon of dissatisfaction that had arisen by the middle of the decade, and they seriously disrupted the local party system.

The campaign against corruption began with typical charges of aldermanic misbehavior.[51] Then, in 1847, the entire public and legal system of the county, in particular the fee system under which most public offices operated, became the target of charges of corruption. The campaign to expose the illegal practices of officials was led by maverick attorney William R. Dickerson. Early that year, Dickerson formed a committee to investigate and propose remedies for the malpractices of county officials. At the same time, he began publishing a series of articles in local newspapers, and finally in pamphlet form, under the title *The Letters of Junius*. These short pieces detailed the corrupt practices of each office on "state house row," where the courts and public offices were located. The *Letters* provoked considerable controversy, as well as the ire of most of the officials assailed. As a result, public meetings organized by Dickerson to demand an end to the practice of taking illegal fees received considerable attention.

Dickerson himself was a controversial figure. Frequently a candidate for political office, his strongest ties were to the nativist parties that captured the votes of many disgruntled Democrats and conservative Whigs, the organizations that were most responsible for upsetting local politics during the 1840s. Dickerson belonged to the Native American party, and he may have had links to nativist workingmen's organizations as well. Combining a vaguely radical economic appeal with hostility towards immigrants and Catholics, the Native Americans were quite successful in local elections during the depression's darkest years after 1842. In 1846 Dickerson expected to be appointed to a patronage job by a newly elected Native American sheriff but was passed over. Angered at the rebuff, Dickerson wrote the *Letters* exposing the system of patronage and corruption to which he was denied access.[52]

For obvious reasons, the office of sheriff received extensive criticism from Dickerson, but this was no more than he heaped on the judges of the quarter sessions. Sparing only Judge Anson V. Parsons from his wrath, Dickerson accused the judges of being appointed solely because of their political connections. In their roles as common pleas judges, these men entrusted relatives with the lucrative task of appraising estates. They set confusing court schedules, allowed cases to be called when parties were not present in order to maximize forfeited recognizances, and never interfered with the attorney general's capricious handling of cases. Judges allowed underlings to extort court costs and illegal fees from prosecutors, sold liquor licenses illegally, and accepted bribes to ignore cases. Dickerson implied that fees never paid to witnesses and forfeited recognizances that were never paid into the county treasury were pocketed by the judges themselves, and as far as justice went, rare was the case that was prosecuted to judgment. The court had "lost its high character . . . its moral influence in our community." Better to do away with the court altogether and return to the decentralized system in which most judicial power was exercised by the mayors and aldermen.[53] Aldermen actually received little criticism in the *Letters*. Dickerson accused them of illegally requiring prosecutors to pay costs before judgment and extorting fees from parties in petty violence cases, but he included them almost as an afterthought. The real targets of the *Letters* were the officials of the higher county offices.[54]

Yet this was still a system in which most judicial power was exercised by aldermen. Dickerson's charges encompassed most of the elements of the informal relations between minor court officials and the citizenry. He believed that the corruption inherent in these relations included the quarter sessions bench, but he had evidence only of some ordinary abuse of patronage. In fact, judges were ambivalent concerning these informal relations. They understood that corruption was often inimical to justice and felt burdened by the caseload and the relative powerlessness of their offices. Yet they also knew how crucial popular participation was to the authority of the law and that participation was dependent on informal relations. So they tolerated them, reluctantly, but hardly with the venality suggested by Dickerson.

Nevertheless, the *Letters* were noticed, in large part because of the context of popular criticism of political economy which the lingering depression inspired. Soon after they began to appear, another popular pamphlet appeared that romanticized Philadelphia's youth gangs and made the related argument that "justice is only brought to bear on and to smite those persons who are poor and unfortunate," unable to "flatter and interest its minister." A similar impression of justice in Philadelphia was offered in radical journalist George Lippard's *The Quaker City*, also published in 1847 and one of the most popular American novels of the era.[55]

Corruption also became the theme of grand jury presentments on aldermen in 1847. The presentments expressed concern over the great number of persons who were committed to prison by magistrates against whom no witnesses ever appeared and who seemed to be languishing in prison. One inquest suggested that blacks and other poor persons who could not pay fees to aldermen were especially likely to be found in such circumstances. Another proposed that prosecutors also be required to post bail to ensure that they appear for the trial of defendants waiting in prison. A grand jury in April 1847 was particularly direct. Claiming that the law was "never intended to be the vehicle of private malice," the jury extolled the positive effects of ignoring bills and charging prosecutors with the costs. However, this was not enough. There was "one source from which this evil has originated," specifically "a want of discrimination . . . and undue attention to the interests of the public" on the part of aldermen. This public was defined by another inquest that year as "nearly always . . . if a distinction in classes may be made . . . the lowest grade in society." Aware of the relationship between poor litigants and aldermen, each grand jury during 1847 urged that aldermen settle these cases and requested the power to place costs on the aldermen as well as prosecutors, especially in cross-prosecutions.[56]

Because they were officers of the court, but only for brief periods, grand jurors were inclined to interpret the activities of the minor judiciary as corruption. They saw clearly that the actions of aldermen were relatively autonomous and encouraged popular use of the criminal law in circumstances they believed to be unsuitable for official intervention. Since their involvement with criminal justice was only fleeting, grand jurors were less sensitive than judges to the important positive function of this process and were, therefore, much more scathing in their condemnation of it.

With the publication of the *Letters of Junius* and the monthly grand jury presentments, pessimism about the effectiveness of criminal justice was becoming widespread. Judges and journalists questioned the honesty and consistency of jurors, witnesses, and lawyers.[57] The PSAMPP praised a law that required public returns from the criminal courts and prisons. In this way the practices of the system would be known: who was incarcerated, why, how they were treated, and how the cases proceeded through the system. "The truth is, that there are great abuses which are not considered by either local officers or the citizens generally."[58]

Dickerson had intended to mobilize many more people than just pamphleteers, prison reformers, and grand jurors. The first public meeting he called to act on his charges sent resolutions to the legislature requesting that all public offices be made salaried, that judges lose all patronage power, and that aldermen *not* be permitted to settle criminal cases. The major public response to these charges, however, did not occur until after all the letters were published in the spring of 1848. After a lecture by Dickerson at Franklin Hall, several of the 1,500 present organized a Committee of Fifteen to investigate the charges. William J. Mullen, a well-to-do jeweler, was elected chairman of the group. Born in Lancaster in 1805, Mullen had made his way to Philadelphia while still a child, was apprenticed as a jeweler, and became the first American to successfully manufacture gold watch dials. This brought him an annual income of over $10,000, and like many successful artisans-cum-businessmen of this era, he fell under the influence of the Second Great Awakening. Soon he was prominent in independent politics, labor reform, and philanthropic causes. Mullen helped organize the local Free Soil party. During the harsh winter of 1846, he operated a soup kitchen for the poor in the Baker Street area and founded the Moyamensing Soup Society. The next year, he became leader of the Cadets of Temperance, and in 1847 he founded and became the first president of the Philadelphia Society for the Employment and Instruction of the Poor. Located in Mullen's home district of Moyamensing, it was one of the first secular voluntary associations in the United States devoted to assisting the poor, and Mullen was its "life and soul." His association with Dickerson and the Committee of Fifteen marked the beginning of an involvement with Philadelphia's criminal justice system that would become central to his incredibly broad thirty-year career as a benevolent reformer.[59]

Throughout 1848 and early 1849, the committee held sparsely attended public meetings at which Dickerson and others complained of corruption. Despite receiving little cooperation from county officials, the group pressed on with its investigations.[60] The first report of the Committee of Fifteen was issued in March 1849 and printed in four local newspapers as a paid advertisement. This report was even more scathing than Dickerson's *Letters*, combining Dickerson's concern over official misconduct with Mullen's concern for the poor. Officials of the criminal court and aldermen were charged not only with corruption but also with the regular oppression of the "poor, unfortunate and distressed individuals" who were defendants in criminal cases. Claiming that Philadelphia's prosecuting attorneys had received over $70,000 in undeserved fees, the committee reasoned that these men belonged in a seat alongside the defendants in the prisoners' box. They repeated contentions that any defendant with money or connections could avoid conviction, that political considerations entered into judicial and prosecutorial judgments, and that judges and prosecutors manipulated the daily press to besmirch the reputations of persons brought before them. The courts were "a den of official tyranny and human depravity." Lectures given by judges to the poor persons convicted of trifling offenses ("in order to keep up the appearance of a faithful and impartial administration of the criminal law") were a "judicial farce . . . nine-tenths of which would much more appropriately apply to the Commonwealth officers than the defendant at the bar." Such public reprimands, reported fully in the press, destroyed the spirit of the defendant and were "the ruin of many a worthy man."[61]

Aldermanic justice was no better. Aldermen issued warrants and held persons to bond for deeds that were not crimes, such as using abusive language. Of aldermen's warrants, 95 percent were issued on complaints that were not sufficient to justify an arrest. Of the persons arrested, 90 percent had to pawn property in order to raise the money to avoid prison, bringing aldermen "for one description of cases" at least $35,000 in illegal fees annually. For one dollar, anyone could "have any person arrested, bound over, or committed to answer at the criminal court." Aldermen "pretend[ed] to administer the law"; the system "appears only to be for the purpose of oppressing the poor and unfortunate, and to extort from them illegal fees."[62]

This public attack on the minor judiciary only emboldened grand juries. Now their monthly demands that aldermen settle trivial cases were couched in especially harsh language. One jury insisted that some magistrates not only failed to settle cases but excited the parties' passions in order to increase fees. Another condemned the "venal and mercenary conduct of the magistrates" who fostered criminal cases. Yet another accused magistrates of turning the families of persons committed in such cases into paupers.[63]

The committee, going beyond the *Letters*, took as its theme the consequences of official corruption. Its emphasis on palpable injustice and oppression of the poor reflected the influence of William J. Mullen. To him, the vast majority of minor cases were instances of oppression; the vast majority of defendants, clearly victimized. The very fact that citizens could so easily initiate a prosecution was for Mullen the system's major flaw. It was not just that Mullen, like Dickerson, failed to see the importance of private prosecution to the authority of the law; rather, this very system of justice had become for Mullen, like the changing economic relationships of his time, a form of exploitation that was creating the poverty he had been vainly trying to fight.

Certain that the victimized public would share its outrage, the committee urged Dickerson to run for sheriff in the election that October. The committee distributed some 17,000 copies of its *Report* to citizens as part of the campaign and claimed that they could not meet even one-tenth of the demand. Though the court and its officers were allied against him, Dickerson's *Letters* prompted the senate to investigate his charges of nepotism, and the result was the passage of a law prohibiting judges from appointing relatives to positions with the court. The committee smugly asserted that Dickerson was the favorite in the election for sheriff.[64]

The confidence of the Committee of Fifteen and all supporters of political reform was rudely shattered on election day. Dickerson garnered slightly over 3,000 votes, about 6 percent of the total, running a poor third. Having mistaken a part of the criminal justice process in Philadelphia for its entirety, Dickerson and his supporters were unrealistic in believing that they could have done any better. Private prosecution represented the dignity and citizenship of Philadelphia's poor and working classes at least as much as it represented their oppression. Elections provided an opportunity for voters to affirm their relationship to the aldermen by registering their allegiance to the political organizations of which these officials were sometimes prominent members. In this, as in previous elections, the voters did just that.[65]

The reformers' failure was rooted in the very conditions Dickerson had exposed. Corruption was normal. Primary justice was no more, perhaps even somewhat less, corrupt than other parts of city government. Most public officials worked under the fee system. Favoritism and corruption were only extensions of the particularism that was the foundation of local government. The legitimacy of the fee system invited corruption, and in small ways, this was not necessarily a venal thing. Reformers had thus set an imposing agenda for themselves. Not only would they have to dismantle and reconstruct an entire system of local government, but they would first have to convince at least a substantial and powerful minority of their fellows that the system was illegitimate.

Dickerson continued to carry on for a time. In 1850 he ran for district attorney and again received about 6 percent of the vote. For the next few years, he continued to speak against official corruption at public meetings, finally returning to his political affiliation with the nativists. William J. Mullen, alone among the committee members, maintained his interest in the abuses of the criminal courts. More than anyone else, he would be responsible for carrying forward the crusade begun by the Committee of Fifteen and for making the criticism of the first half of the nineteenth century the basis of the reforms of the second half. He would soon be heard from again.[66]

As the nineteenth century passed its midpoint, private prosecution and the minor judiciary of Philadelphia were thriving. Despite decades of criticism, the aldermen were more entrenched in the city's neighborhoods and political system than ever. They commanded the business, respect, and, on election day, the votes of the people who mattered most, the ordinary residents of their wards. While legal and prison reformers had some success in tinkering with the law and constructing new institutions, critics of the courts and politics could only watch as the aldermen and their informal methods of enforcing the law became ever more firmly established.

Nevertheless, the stream of criticism that culminated with the Committee of Fifteen had some effect. Public discussion of the fee system had become greater than ever before. Sentiment for its abolition entered regular political discourse, never really to fall out of it again. More importantly, a tradition of reform activity that held the minor judiciary in high disrepute had been established. Reformers after 1850 would always be primarily concerned with politics and the question of who would rule the city, but because aldermen were politicians, and because the manner in which they governed (which included criminal justice) was the central issue animating municipal reformers after mid-century, criminal justice became a part of their agenda. For them, the legacy of criticism of aldermen and private prosecution provided both ammunition and legitimacy.

Part III The Rise of State Prosecution

6. *The Origins of Police Authority*

In May 1838, construction was completed on Pennsylvania Hall, intended by its managers to be the main meetinghouse for reformers of all stripes. The hall opened with a series of meetings featuring many prominent abolitionists. On Wednesday, 16 May, a hostile crowd gathered at its doors; by Thursday evening, it had swelled to three thousand people. Late that night, the crowd torched the hall, and, as the mayor and his small band of watchmen looked on, it burned to the ground. No one heeded their calls to support the law. Firemen either refused or were prevented from attempting to extinguish the fire. The next night a mob attacked a Friends' orphanage for black children and set it ablaze, but the police and firemen fought past the mob and saved the building.[1]

A committee appointed by the city councils to investigate these events severely criticized the mayor and police and observed that "were our preventive police invested with greater powers, our city might have been spared the events of May 16–17." Though no one present "had any desire to arrest the progress of destruction" or support the mayor and the law, the committee added that, because conditions such as these had been rare, a strong police force had "never yet been required. . . . A moral force . . . has heretofore always sufficed to preserve the public peace."

As deeply rooted and disturbing to some reformers and jurists as private prosecution and the power of the minor judiciary was, the matter that, in the end, prompted the first major change in Philadelphia's criminal justice system was riot and disorder. Neither private nor state prosecution was capable of stemming the unprecedented but popular violence that erupted in the streets of the city beginning in the 1830s. Between 1837 and 1850, as the determination of the judiciary to intensify state prosecution and the punishment of rioters grew, support for expanding and improving the city's police force increased. When this was finally accomplished, the apparatus of state prosecution was greatly augmented, the mandate of the police to keep order on the streets was crystal clear, and the dominance of private prosecution over criminal justice in Philadelphia had begun to erode.

Direct attempts at reform and efforts to restrain private prosecution made little contribution to the development of state prosecution. Instead, it emerged piecemeal, as a response to the increasing erosion of public order, primarily through the haphazard growth of the authority of the police. Because the development of state prosecution was not at first the result of reform, it led inexorably to the strengthening of ties between policemen and aldermen, ties that were similar to those the aldermen had with private prosecutors. This, in turn, had the ironic consequence of strengthening aldermen and thus private prosecution as it provided the beginning of an alternative to private prosecution. It also compounded the problem of preventing disorder and punishing illegal popular recreations by making state prosecution as ineffective as private prosecution in these matters.

By the mid-1840s, these patterns had become so firmly established that the city was powerless to prevent the violence that raged on its streets. As a result, an elite movement in favor of a professional police arose. This was the first major organization of municipal reformers in Philadelphia, and their success set the groundwork for their successors. But in order to achieve an effective police force, the reformers would have to compromise with the ward politicians who had, by 1850, become a powerful force in both private and state prosecution. In the end, while this would compromise the efficiency of state prosecution, it would also make it possible for both reformers and politicians to accept the transformation of criminal justice.

State prosecution had a distinctly secondary position in criminal justice during the first half of the nineteenth century in Philadelphia. When state prosecution did take place, the two bodies responsible for case initiation were the police and, to a lesser extent, the courts themselves. Though relatively small in number, these two groups of prosecutions had important effects. In minor police cases, the minor judiciary established informal methods of adjudication similar to, and as intractable as, those employed in private cases. In most serious police- and court-initiated cases, these same methods and public indifference made prosecutions virtually impossible to sustain. Both led to the endemic disorder that provoked the professionalization of the police and the eventual decline of private prosecution after 1850.

For most of the first half of the century, Philadelphia's police force consisted of a handful of men who guarded the city at night and who could initiate a criminal proceeding through an arrest. As late as 1831, the city had only 106 part-time night watchmen and eight daytime constables. Each suburban district also had its own smaller force.[2] Only minor changes occurred for the next fifteen years. In 1833, following the bequest of financier Stephen Girard, the city was divided into four sections, each with six day policemen, thirty night watchmen, one watch captain and lieutenant, and three inspectors.

In 1835 the numbers were increased slightly to a total of 176 officers, all under the control of the mayor.[3]

Such a police force was not capable of acting as a powerful instrument of state enforcement of the criminal law. As a result, through the first half of the century, police prosecution consisted of little more than the apprehension of drunks and vagrants.

Minor Police Cases

Though the watchmen and day police were effective only in relatively minor breaches of public order, these cases had enduring importance. The disposition of them, like all criminal cases, was under the control of the minor judiciary. The aldermen developed methods for handling them that, on the surface, resembled those used in private cases, but these methods also set the groundwork upon which the future relationship between the aldermen and the police would be built. Aldermen developed a powerful interest in police cases which would come to rival their interest in private cases and help determine the course of change in the criminal justice system.

Arrests for drunkenness were the simplest police actions. They comprised by far the largest number of arrests and established the vulnerability of the poor to state prosecution. Most arrests of drunks were routine matters, but they were frequent enough to keep the small force of watchmen quite busy. On any one day, many might be apprehended.[4] The typical drunk was probably sleeping or stumbling about the streets, and the watchman quickly and quietly whisked him off to jail.[5] Drinking was, however, a popular activity in the United States before 1850, and many a tippler believed that it was his right to be drunk. A few expressed this conviction by resisting arrest. Francis Stewart was shouting, "Who wants to drink?" in front of a theater one evening and was admonished by the watchman. After first asking the watchman to accompany him to a public house, Francis then rejected the officer's advice that he cease tippling with a blow to the officer's jaw. He was charged with assault as well as intoxication.[6]

An arrest was only the beginning, however. A charge of drunkenness was also the substance of a criminal case. Like other minor cases that began with a police arrest, drunkenness was a "summary" offense, which meant that aldermen and justices had complete jurisdiction over them. They could convict and sentence the accused without a jury trial, and their decision was final. The punishment for drunkenness was a fine of 67 cents ($1.50 after 1841) or twenty-four hours imprisonment.[7]

Most of the time, defendants accused of drunkenness were convicted. Usually they paid their fines without a fuss, but some tried to fashion a defense. Matthias Snell, for example, was found by a watchman on a February night staggering about the streets, his soaked clothes smelling of whiskey. He claimed that he was only returning home after visiting a sick friend and had been the victim of his own generosity. He had offered to help a "wagoner" lift a barrel of whiskey off his wagon, but the barrel broke open and drenched them both. The alderman was unconvinced, and Snell was fined despite his protests. Others claimed that they had been forced to drink by friends, did not know intoxication was against the law, or had only had one drink. A sailor on liberty tried explaining to the mayor that liberty was "for getting drunk." None of these defenses worked.[8] Only a few ever did. If an accused drunk was especially young, a first offender, or from outside the city, the case might be discharged, usually with a warning from the magistrate, but in general, the arrest was the determining factor in intoxication cases, and conviction followed almost automatically.[9]

Public intoxication was really the offense over which the police exercised authority. The majority of people who became drunk in public places were poor and working people, many of them unable or unprepared to pay the fine to which they were sentenced. Instead, they were forced to suffer a day's imprisonment. On a typical day, the court reporter remarked that most of those fined "appeared as though they had not looked with pleasure upon a dollar and a half for a long time past."[10] Those who resisted arrest, and some who had not, were also held on bail to keep the peace. This was an onerous burden for the typically poor drunkards who had difficulty paying even their fines. When people could not meet the bail, they were held in prison indefinitely, usually until discharged by the inspectors or, as some claimed, until the magistrate received a "sufficient consideration."

The magistrates who actually passed sentence on drunks were only of secondary importance because they exercised little discretion, applying a routine punishment to the charge entered by the officer. Magistrates used their power to keep a person in prison only in the relatively rare instances in which a peace bond was requested. Though magistrates certainly did not mitigate the consequences of police action in drunkenness cases, their behavior was consistent with that in private cases. Because the fee system made it in their interest to accept all charges, they treated intoxication cases just as they did most others. Drunkenness arrests captured one aspect of police prosecution, the vulnerability of the lower classes to arrest, better than any other group of cases because they were the least manipulated by the relationship of those people to the minor judiciary.

Vagrancy and disorderly conduct were much more complicated. The magistrates played a much more active role in these cases, establishing a relationship with policemen and a pattern of prison commitments that became the foundation upon which state prosecution was built and that brought the aldermen as much rebuke as did private prosecution.

The legal penalty for vagrancy was one month's imprisonment. Disorderly conduct was simply a form of vagrancy; persons adjudged to have been disorderly were supposed to be treated just like any other vagrant, but they were not. Aldermen committed people to prison at widely different rates for the different minor offenses. Alderman Amos Gregg's late-century pattern was much like those of earlier magistrates. Gregg committed 25 percent of those brought before him for drunkenness, 11 percent of those accused of disorderly conduct, and 7 of the 8 persons charged with vagrancy.[11] The variation in commitments by Gregg was typical even if his pattern was idiosyncratic. For the city as a whole, one was more likely to be committed for disorderly conduct than for drunkenness and virtually certain to be committed if arrested for vagrancy. In fact, each year the number of vagrancy commitments easily exceeded the number of arrests, suggesting either considerable private prosecution of vagrants or, more likely, an aldermanic penchant for committing people arrested on other charges as vagrants.

Not only did the likelihood of a prison commitment vary from charge to charge but so did the length of time a person remained in jail. Drunks generally remained in prison for the legally stipulated period of 24 hours. However, prison terms for both vagrants and the disorderly departed widely from the 30 days the law prescribed. The disorderly remained in jail for an average of 9 days before 1854, and vagrants were held for 22 days.[12] No one imprisoned for disorderly conduct ever served a 30-day term. The magistrate who made the original commitment released roughly one-third of them, much like they released those committed for indictable offenses. Although prison overcrowding was often the ostensible reason for this practice, the actual process of releasing prisoners early opened a wide field for manipulation and possible corruption by aldermen.

Vagrants were always sentenced according to law to thirty days imprisonment. The circumstances under which most vagrants were arrested did not differ much from those under which drunks were arrested. Watchmen found them intoxicated and either disorderly or asleep in public. The difference was that vagrants either requested a month's confinement or were well known to the magistrate as dissolute persons incapable of supporting themselves. Repeat offenders and very poor persons, often arrested in large numbers in the dingy rooms and cellars in which they congregated, were likely candidates for such treatment. Sixteen persons—twelve whites and four blacks—were punished as vagrants after having been arrested for drunkenness in a "beastly haunt" in Moyamensing in 1841.[13] William Thompson was committed on 22 December 1841, released 21 January 1842, and after sleeping out for three nights, requested another thirty days on January 24. "Such cases occur very frequently," noted the court reporter.[14] Sometimes magistrates committed common drunks to prison for thirty days as vagrants. This did not occur frequently, but may have been among those frequently complained-of cases in which magistrates released vagrants before the expiration of the thirty-day term.[15]

Cases of common vagrancy reflected the main utility and original intent of the law as a device for providing temporary shelter for the homeless. Vagrants were supposed to be homeless people with no obvious means of support. When the watch found someone wandering aimlessly about or sleeping in a barn, yard, cellar, or street, that person was vulnerable to a conviction for vagrancy unless he or she could give proof of having a means of support. According to the prison inspectors, "vagrants, as a class, have very little of a positive character, they deserve the designation of unfortunate rather than of criminal. They are human beings demanding the sympathy of the virtuous and the Christian."[16] Nevertheless, vagrants were treated as minor criminals. However, in contrast to drunkenness, the minor judiciary was the more active party in these cases. People from outside Philadelphia who could have been committed as vagrants were frequently told to leave the city. In 1837 the mayor sent one New Yorker back home and warned local authorities that "the paupers of that city are coming upon us in shoals; a stop must speedily be put to these inroads, or we shall be overrun with the vermin."[17] Magistrates also used their authority to discharge vagrants before the expiration of their terms. Although over half of the vagrants who were sentenced to thirty days served the full term, those released early served on average only thirteen days. The prison inspectors usually authorized releases, but over one-quarter of them were authorized by a magistrate, usually the committing magistrate.[18] The reasons for this are not at all clear. According to law, a discharge by a magistrate was legal only if he had taken security for an appeal, but the PSAMPP repeatedly noted that they had "not been able to find that any such appeal has been prosecuted."[19] Prison crowding may have been a motivation, especially for the inspectors, but critics insisted that magistrates released vagrants prematurely either because they received a payment in the prisoner's behalf or because they wanted to make the unfortunate vagrant susceptible to another commitment (and thus earn the magistrate another fee). The prison inspectors' role might have been in part an effort to prevent these practices, but for whatever reasons, the minor judiciary exercised discretion in vagrancy cases, which could suit a vagrant's wishes either to be released before the expiration of his term or sentenced to an additional one.

Vagrancy was a clear example of the minor judiciary's stretching the law and establishing an independent relationship with people arrested by the police. However, vagrancy cases were not distinct from others in the broad category that included disorderly conduct, breach of the peace, and minor assault. These accounted for the greatest number of prison commitments and encompassed chronic drunkenness, public unruliness, and minor personal violence. Magistrates had complete discretion over how to handle these cases. Some they no doubt considered vagrancy, but others they labeled anything from simple drunkenness to an indictable offense. Most of the time, magistrates treated them as disorderly conduct or, what was virtually the same thing, breach of the peace.

People who were considered vagrants by others often found themselves repeatedly imprisoned on these charges. In 1822 Bartholomew Wistar of the PSAMPP complained that some aldermen were imprisoning "persons (till discharged by the courts of law) for offenses not indictable, instead of sentencing them, as vagrants, by which many unfortunate prisoners have been confined nearly three months, when the extent of their sentence, as vagrants, could not have exceeded one month." A year later, the society explained that the problem was more often premature than delayed releases. "Certain magistrates make a trade of committing and discharging these poor wretches, and, in order to evade the law, commit them as disorderly instead of vagrants, which they really are."[20] Reformers believed that the magistrates' habits of committing vagrants for disorderly conduct and releasing them quickly was as much a cause of overcrowding as was private prosecution. Some people who should have been treated as vagrants were confined under thirty-day sentences three times in the same month![21]

According to reformers, the cause of all this was clear. "The . . . Committee can see no object but that of a paltry fee for commitment," the PSAMPP observed in 1820.[22] The law allowed magistrates to commit "disorderly persons" to prison as vagrants, but this term was so vaguely defined as to leave magistrates with considerable latitude in making such commitments.[23] The reformers charged that magistrates committed people arrested for disorderly behavior as they did vagrants, but because they were neither destitute nor homeless, they paid the magistrate a small sum in order to procure a release.

Disposition of disorderly conduct and breach of peace cases varied greatly. The average time served for disorderly conduct before 1854 was 9 days, and for breach of the peace 10 days, but there was great variation among the magistrates, reflecting the questionable practices involved. For example, the average time served by those committed for disorderly conduct by the mayor was 4 days; by Alderman McGarry, 10 days; Alderman Loughead, 17 days; and Alderman Hoffner, 21 days. Aldermen Hoffner and McGarry were the most frequent users of the breach of the peace charge—another example of the variability of the process—yet Hoffner's commitments resulted in prison stays of 19 days while McGarry's lasted only 5.[24]

These figures suggest that the handling of disorderly conduct cases was more complicated, and for a defendant more chancy, than the reformers' complaints would have had it. Aldermen were by no means alike. Some committed people for one charge more frequently than another; some released people quickly while others left them incarcerated for relatively long periods of time. Critics believed that very short stays in prison indicated extortionate behavior by aldermen, yet the shortest stays of all followed commitments by the mayor, who was presumably the least likely to be so personally corrupt. Some corruption was undoubtedly involved, but the complicated commitment patterns may just as well have indicated a process of particularistic case disposition. By law most of these cases should have been either one-day drunkenness or thirty-day vagrancy commitments, but aldermen may have reckoned, and the examples of typical cases suggest, that many incidents fell somewhere between the two. Disorderly conduct and breach of the peace were charges that provided a means for circumventing these limits, for apportioning the punishment to fit the crime. Such behavior suited the aldermen's need to remain popular in an era of private prosecution, and the informality and flexibility provided defendants with more maneuverability than they would otherwise have had. All this made the negotiation of cases of minor disorder, even when police-initiated, very much like private prosecutions (which, as we have seen, some of them were), and this accounts for the deep-rootedness of the entirely customary and nonstatutory practice of punishing people for disorderly conduct and breach of the peace.

At the same time, this process was likely to make alderman receptive to police prosecution and to annoy the prison keepers and inspectors. Both kinds of commitments were strictly illegal and both contributed to the overcrowding and unruliness of the prison. It was, no doubt, effective for critics to accuse aldermen of gross misconduct when arguing that the prison inspectors should interfere and release prisoners on their own, but the complexity of the process, as well as the difficulty the reformers had in disrupting it, casts doubt upon their simple picture of aldermanic corruption.

Still, greed played a major role in determining how magistrates handled these cases. By far the most common action they took was to hold the accused in bail to keep the peace. The amount of the bail could be as little as $50 or as much as $500, usually $100 or $200. This was a lot of money, and those who could not pay were committed to prison until they could raise sufficient funds or otherwise procure a release from the prison inspectors, committing magistrate, or criminal court judge. Many, perhaps most, commitments for disorderly conduct and breach of the peace were made in this way and served as the prime source of accusations that aldermen committed persons capriciously and settled cases for illegal fees.

Cases of this kind occurred virtually every day and included almost any activity that could be considered disorderly. Noisy dance parties and simple fights—such as the one between Clarissa Williams and Matilda Anderson, friends "of long standing" who could not agree on whose turn it was to pay for the next round of drinks—were typically the stuff of disorderly conduct cases. People frequenting neighborhoods known to be disorderly might be arrested on any pretext. Sarah Hays and Thomas Firth were arrested in 1839 for kissing on the street in just such a place. Though the mayor knew of no law prohibiting kissing, the reputation of that part of the city provided sufficient grounds for him to hold them in $100 bail to keep the peace.[25] Police and magisterial practice clearly confirmed Judge Anson V. Parsons's sense that the term disorderly was "very extensive in its signification."

Rare but also instructive were the occasions upon which the magistrate committed disorderly persons as vagrants as he was supposed to. One day in 1838, the mayor committed two black girls for thirty days for throwing bricks at a house in Sasafrass Alley, one of the city's most squalid streets. They were so shocked at the sentence that they immediately attacked a woman who had testified against them, causing a riotous "scene of a most extraordinary and ludicrous character," sending even the mayor into "a hearty laughing spell." Spectators cheered as the constables threw themselves into the fray, attempting to separate the combatants, who then received an additional assault and battery charge for their conduct.[26] What was ludicrous to the court reporter must have seemed like a gross abuse of power, even discrimination, to the girls who were excluded from the normal channels of informal justice.

Philadelphia's minor judiciary thus established an extralegal mechanism for exercising authority over the minor public disorder that was increasingly common in the antebellum city. Treating all those arrested as vagrants would have overcrowded the prison and been impossibly harsh, so the magistrates developed a practice that maintained, or even increased, their income, supported the police's power to arrest, and afforded offenders with a way to procure a relatively quick release from custody. Informal aldermanic justice operated in the interests of everyone involved in these minor cases, with the exception of those with absolutely no resources or friends and no desire to remain in jail. People arrested were still, however, subject to the power of the police; aldermen and justices may have mitigated this but did not eliminate it. Before 1850, by building on the informal practices developed in private prosecutions, the aldermen fashioned a method of treating minor police prosecutions that appeared to compromise the power of the police, but actually this method set the groundwork for a connection with the police that would ultimately undermine the power of private prosecutors.

Although people arrested exerted some influence over them, the primary lesson of minor police cases was that the public disorder of the lower classes was subject to the repressive activity of the state. This lesson was not lost on the journalists who covered the proceedings at the mayor's office, where many of these cases were heard. Reporters were often outraged by the mayor's occasional habit of granting well-dressed or otherwise well-to-do prisoners private hearings. When a "gentleman" was taken into a private room for an examination in 1836, the reporter huffily remarked that "the influence which dress exercises in the mayoral office was never more strongly evinced." On another occasion, the reporter noted a workingman's hearing and added that "the person has the misfortune to be a mechanic, and was consequently examined in public courtroom, but two rowdies of a better sort, dressed in fashionable costume, were invited into the private office to whisper their peccadilloes. The custom smacks of the system of privileged orders."[27]

The exceptional treatment of "respectable" miscreants proved the rule. Their indiscretions could be overlooked because the larger problem of public disorder was a problem of the lower classes. This was the concept that set the police off from other elements of the criminal justice system, even in this period of its infancy. The ability of the minor judiciary to cushion the power of the police, the relative inadequacy of the police force itself, and the righteous indignation of reporters at the idea of a criminal justice system designed especially to punish the poor kept this aspect of police cases in the shadows. But it was still there, ready to blossom once the police became the centerpiece of the criminal justice system.

Serious Crime

The same informal methods used by aldermen in private prosecutions and minor police cases had a different effect when applied to state-initiated prosecution for indictable crime. Although this was a relatively rare event before 1850, its general ineffectiveness anticipated the failure of the state to control serious disorder in the streets. Prosecution of indictable crime was a distinctly minor part of police work before 1850. Most of the cases that the police prosecuted were indistinguishable from routine private prosecutions and were treated by the aldermen in an identical manner. Larceny arrests, for example, usually occurred when an officer discovered someone in possession of property he suspected was stolen. Benjamin Henry could not give a satisfactory explanation of how he came into the possession of six chickens and a guinea fowl, so he was committed to prison.[28] Thefts often occurred in public places, especially in bar rooms and guest houses. Larcenous guests slipped out of hotels unnoticed until some of the establishment's property was found to be missing. William Ross, a young newlywed, took some furniture from Mrs. Thoburn's boarding house, in which he had been living. A police officer found him in his new home, tastefully adorned with Mrs. Thoburn's property.[29] Thieves also coveted jewelry, especially easily snatched watches and pins, for its monetary value. Thefts of commercial property involved shoplifting anything from food to plumbing equipment from stores and stalls.[30]

As with private cases, magistrates usually accepted the charges. In only two types of cases did a magistrate ever release a prisoner whom the police charged with larceny. Sometimes the officer was wrong, and the accused could prove it. Racism and extreme poverty made a black's possession of almost anything of value grounds for a policeman's accusation of larceny. An eighteen-year-old black man who was wearing new shoes and new pantaloons was arrested for stealing them. He was able to prove to the mayor that he had purchased them and was released. The mayor might also release a prisoner in a case of extreme hardship. A "hard-working" Irishman stole some wood to provide heat for his family, having no money left after paying rent. "His honor, after a feeling reprimand, in which he remarked that in some instances crimes were committed through depravity of heart, in others, from necessity, and his case seemed to be an instance of the latter, declared he would, for the sake of his wife and family, forgive him, but if ever he was convicted again of the slightest larceny, he would punish him severely." Although cases like these were reported frequently, only rarely were suspects completely discharged or exonerated by the minor judiciary.[31]

Nevertheless, there were avenues of escape for those arrested. Serious crime was unlike the mass of petty acts that dominated the business of the minor judiciary. To whatever extent there was a real criminal underworld before mid-century in Philadelphia, people arrested for serious property crime were part of it. They tended to have either money of their own or connections with others who did. The same structure of informal justice that petty offenders used to soften the impact of arrests was sometimes used by serious criminals to avoid prosecution altogether. In the typical petty case, the accused received a small reward for a small payment. Here, the stakes were higher. For example, after a visiting businessman was robbed of $500 in 1837, the persons responsible "were arrested on a day or two after the robbery, and had a hearing before *one* of the Aldermen, who liberated Jane Anderson on paying $15, Samuel Murray on paying $5, and Levina Johnson on paying $12, and Nancy Murray, *the principal* paid from $20 to $30, and was only committed for a further hearing!"[32] Of course, this did not completely negate the significance of the arrest. The informal "fine" assessed by the magistrate was a form of punishment though a far milder one than a trial would have brought. Under these circumstances, neither the magistrates nor the thieves were likely to object. The minor judiciary were again the pivotal figures in criminal justice, their offices again the places in which the most important decisions about punishment were made.

Before 1850 the police frequently provoked the serious crimes that they prosecuted. Very often, they prosecuted people for attacking them, usually while resisting arrest. When watchman Vandersmith tried to arrest disorderly Mary Bradley on Dock Street one afternoon, Dick Smith and three companions attacked him. Dick was bound over. When three men attacked some officers attempting to make an arrest in Spring Garden, they severely injured not only the policemen but also the man they were attempting to rescue. Attacks on officers were also unprovoked. The ubiquitous "gang of rowdies" attacked Moyamensing watchman Philip Brady one Sunday night in 1837 and beat him so badly that his life was threatened. This was the third such assault that week. Other attacks were more surreptitious. City watchman Steel was standing and "crying the hour" in Cressons Alley in 1850 when a resident reached out of a third story window and dropped a large stone, missing Steel's head by six inches.[33]

Arrests for indictable crime were rare before 1850 and contributed little to the emerging culture of state prosecution. More important were the periodic attempts of the court itself to initiate prosecutions.

Court Prosecutions

The courts of record conducted prosecutions from time to time before 1850, in a few narrowly defined areas. These attempts at state prosecution fared even worse than the others, despite their lofty origins.

Gambling and unlicensed liquor dealing, often conducted together in the same establishment, were thriving activities in Jacksonian Philadelphia. "We have reason to believe that gaming flourishes in this city, to a horrible extent; that it is connived at in high places; that laws against it are almost openly set at naught, with the implied encouragement of those whose duty it is to execute them." Critics accused police officers of taking bribes from keepers of unlicensed tippling houses, noting that beats that included many such establishments were eagerly sought after by watchmen.[34]

Ward constables, however, and not regular watchmen were the officers responsible for alerting the criminal court to the names of unlicensed liquor dealers. Tippling house cases were usually initiated under judges' instructions to the constables to report each month to the court all unlicensed taverns operating in their wards. Primarily deputies of the aldermen, constables were paid per-case fees and were well connected in their wards to, among other notable residents, the saloon-keepers. Their control of the decision to initiate a case, failure to attend to the details of filing a charge, and manipulation of the fee system thwarted the courts' efforts to enforce the liquor license laws. When challenged to explain their neglect of duty, constables responded that the $5 they received each court session for this task was not "adequate pay" for the work involved.[35] Ward constables spent the bulk of their time attending aldermen's offices and serving the warrants they issued. Many developed close relationships with aldermen, so it was not surprising that the real cause of the constable's neglect was laid at the magistrate's doorstep.

The criticism was borne out by the conviction rate for liquor cases, 8 percent. Only 22 percent of liquor cases reached a plea; only 15 percent of the cases that went to trial resulted in convictions. Although defendants in liquor cases stood an excellent chance of avoiding conviction, two-thirds of all those found guilty were convicted by their own pleas. The reason for this was the sentencing pattern; all of the defendants in the sample convicted by trial were sentenced to prison terms, and all who pleaded guilty were fined. Prison terms were short, averaging two months, and the fines were heavy, averaging $40. Nevertheless, a fine was certainly preferable to a tavern-keeper who could probably afford it. The court also probably favored fines in these cases because they provided a rare opportunity for generating income, whereas prison terms were a drain on the county's resources, and because, under ordinary circumstances, judges recognized that the liquor trade could not be suppressed but only regulated. Here, then, an incentive for something like plea bargaining existed for both sides. If it became clear that the court intended to pursue the case, most defendants concluded that, rather than risk even the small possibility of a prison term, one might just as well plead guilty and accept a fine. No doubt, the intention to pursue a case must have been a shock to a defendant. Almost one-quarter of liquor cases were dismissed, and over half were simply not acted upon.

Frustration was the primary result for court officials who wanted liquor laws enforced. Tippling house cases were prosecuted irregularly. Periodically, the court placed special pressure on the constables to make returns of unlicensed houses, usually during one court session each year.[36] However, there were times when the court made especially strenuous efforts to enforce the license laws. In early 1841, for example, the new court of general sessions tried without success to prosecute unlicensed liquor dealers. The judges were attempting to bypass the clerk of the court, who was accused of receiving payments for keeping the cases from the grand jury, but they were frustrated because the constables reported only dealers about whom they had no direct evidence, following the letter but not the spirit of the court's instruction.[37]

When the court of quarter sessions was reinvested with criminal jurisdiction in 1843, its new group of activist judges announced a policy of active prosecution and severe punishment of unlicensed liquor dealers.[38] The judges ordered the constables into court and publicly examined each of them about their returns, confronting them with gossip and accusations regarding the number of unlicensed houses in their wards, threatening to prosecute them for misdemeanors in office if they failed to return even one illegal house to court. As a result, many liquor cases were prosecuted in 1843 and 1844. Within a few days of the beginning of the November 1843 session, the grand jury returned 73 indictments. On 20 November the court tried so many cases that it required two juries to hear them simultaneously. Jurors convicted 15 of 35 defendants that day, and fined them from $20 to $50. They acquitted 10 but saddled 5 of them with the court costs. Because the prosecuting constables did not attend, 10 cases went untried, prompting the judges to announce that all constables were to attend the next day or face criminal charges. And so they did. The court tried all 14 cases on the docket for 21 November. Ten resulted in convictions, 4 in acquittals, and in 3 of the latter, the defendants were assessed the costs. The judges told the convicted defendants that they could expect prison terms upon a second conviction.[39]

The court could not, however, sustain this record. Though many tippling house cases appeared on the dockets in 1844, the rate of conviction returned to its typically low levels. Grand jurors dismissed over half of the bills. In response to questioning from the bench, the jury foreman explained that the constables had decided to exploit the climate created by the judges to their own advantage. "A great many suits had been instituted against persons for keeping tippling houses, evidently with the view of extorting money from the persons so charged." The judges' determination unleashed the constables. So, even more than ordinary private prosecutors, the constables found the temptations to abuse the system impossible to resist. It had become open season on liquor dealers. The grand jury had no recourse but to dismiss bills and place the costs on the clearly culpable prosecutors. The reformist zeal of the new bench was quickly thwarted by the fee-system-based corruption that was the hallmark of the era. For the rest of the decade, the court tried liquor cases irregularly as constables made their perfunctory returns. Those few defendants who were convicted were fined anywhere from one cent to $50. Most cases went untried because of the inattentive manner in which constables made returns. They used old lists and thus returned many houses that no longer existed, had licenses, or had changed names.[40]

In liquor cases, the judges' determination to prosecute was thwarted by the informal relations between constables and liquor dealers, much like the informal relations that so often determined the outcome of minor police cases and assault and battery prosecutions. The difference was that, in these cases, the collusion between officers and citizens was designed to avoid the law altogether, not to mold it to the participant's desires. Furthermore, the active law enforcement designs of the court were foiled here, and this was potentially even more dangerous than the consequences of private prosecution.

Similar obstacles faced prosecutions of the keepers of brothels and gambling houses, which court officials from time to time instructed the police to initiate. Both were prime examples of the ineffectiveness of law enforcement to suppress popular activities before 1850. In 1843, at the same time that the new quarter sessions judges put pressure on constables to return tippling house cases, the judges urged the grand jury to accept all bills for bawdy houses or houses of prostitution. Few, however, were ever presented to jurors, and when they were, jurors generally treated them only as disorderly houses. Gambling cases also rarely entered the courts of record during this period. Private citizens rarely felt a need to prosecute. When the police attempted to initiate a case, gamblers, like brothel-keepers, had an easy time dissuading them. In 1847 the legislature did pass a law forbidding the operation of private lotteries. Davis Bartram was the first person tried under the law in June of that year, but as with other gambling cases, it was difficult to find a witness eager to see Bartram jailed. He was acquitted and the law was used infrequently, at least in Philadelphia.[41]

State prosecution of indictable offenses was a rare and ineffective aspect of criminal justice before 1850, subordinated both in numbers and spirit to private prosecution, just as the police and court officials were subordinated, in practice, to the aldermen. Nevertheless, along with those developed in police prosecution of minor crime, the methods of case disposition that the minor judiciary and their constables employed in court-initiated prosecutions were the basis of their treatment of the more numerous similar cases that the police would initiate after 1850. These methods were very important because, out of them, the aldermen would fashion a relationship with policemen that came to rival their relationship with private prosecutors. This would not only help to determine the character of the policed city but it would also help to determine the remaking of primary justice.

Of more immediate importance, though, was the ineffectiveness of police- and court-initiated prosecution to restrain disorder and popular illegal activity. On this front, after 1837, things got quickly out of hand, and out of this a mandate for the police would be forged, ushering state prosecution into a new era.

Fire Companies, Civil Disorder, and the Courts

If the criminal justice system had difficulty in controlling violent incidents between individuals, it was even less successful in cases of collective violence. The criminal courts stood virtually alone as the state's everyday means for dissuading people from rioting. Even before the depression, beginning in 1837, citizens complained of "gangs of riotous boys which infest the city of Philadelphia." Public violence occurred repeatedly, stemming from labor disputes, religious and racial tensions, and the disorderly behavior of groups of young men. The most spectacular events were a battle between Protestants and Catholics, following an Orangemen's demonstration in 1831, and an attack by antiabolitionist whites on the black community of Moyamensing in 1834. The most common were minor disturbances by groups of boys and young men who gathered on street corners, making noise, insulting women, defacing property, shouting fire, and fighting among themselves.[42]

The police, however, probably because of their physical disadvantage, avoided arresting corner loungers. On those few occasions before 1850 when they did, the magistrate took the ordinary step of binding the boys over to keep the peace. Sometimes the mayor called in the boys' parents and scolded them too. "It is boys such as these that cause all the riots which disgrace our city, and they should be punished severely," he told three families in 1838, but the mayor only held the boys in $300 bail to keep the peace and sent them home.[43]

Serious public personal violence occasionally resulted in police action. Even the brandishing of a weapon in a threatening manner was sometimes enough to induce a magistrate to send an assault case to court.[44] Magistrates always bound over people arrested for beatings that resulted in serious injury. Usually they were the result of an attack by gangs or groups of "rowdies" on a single person who was unprepared or unable to defend himself. One night in 1841, watchmen arrested two men for a number of beatings in front of the Walnut Street Theatre and also accused them of planning "a conspiracy to create a disturbance at that Theatre."[45]

Riot prosecutions, however, were much less common than riots. Most of the incidents that prompted the untrained and unarmed police to make arrests for riot were relatively minor. John Emory was "entertaining the inhabitants of Race Street" with some songs one Saturday night. One resident was not so pleased with the performance and wound up in a scuffle with John, whom a watchman arrested and held for inciting to riot. Other riot charges resulted from what were really neighborhood brawls. One took place among black residents of Apple Street and resulted in the commitment of six persons for riot. The watch arrested four Irish immigrants for a similar fracas in 1836, but this time, though "inclined" to bind them over, the mayor, "in consideration of their apparent poverty," let them go with a severe warning.[46]

After 1837, Philadelphia faced a virtual epidemic of violence and disorder. "Outrages" committed by gangs of boys and young men on peaceful citizens became daily events. Most typical were disturbances caused by fire companies and their affiliated youth gangs. During the late 1820s and early 1830s, the membership of Philadelphia's volunteer fire companies gradually changed from men in middle-class occupational groups to younger working-class men, organized according to neighborhood and often religion. This was especially true of the newer companies organized during the 1830s in the increasingly populous, largely immigrant suburban districts of Moyamensing, Southwark, Kensington, and Northern Liberties.[47]

The class-conscious organizations of workers that had led successful strikes and wielded considerable power through Philadelphia's General Trades Union were crushed by the depression. Into the gap they left stepped organizations that stressed cultural and community identity: temperance societies, bible societies, ethnic clubs, nativist political parties, and fire companies. The latter, now with clearly established geographical, ethnic, and political loyalties, were perhaps the most important groups of all. Their rivalries, especially those between Catholic and Protestant companies, became fierce. Many of the companies had affiliated youth gangs with ominous names such as the "Killer," "Rats," and "Bouncers." Firehouses became important centers of working-class male leisure, and fires became regular occasions for competition and sometimes for full-fledged riots complete with deadly violence. Companies even started fires in order to provoke competition and violence, and youth gangs frequently fought without even that excuse.[48] Fights became matters of honor, and triumphant warriors became heroes in their communities. From this point on, the volunteer fire department became the prime source of street disorder in Philadelphia.[49]

Because the disorderly activities of fire companies and their youthful adherents were so widespread, magistrates rarely exhibited leniency when fire company members were brought before them. A boy arrested while running with the American Engine Company in 1839 pleaded self-defense, but the mayor held him over for trial, claiming that "these occurrences were so frequent and the peace of the city so often disturbed by them, he felt it necessary to send every case of the kind to court, hoping that such means would have a salutary effect and check the evil." The rioting, however, never abated.[50] Probably only a minority of those arrested were ever convicted or sent to prison. Judge Bouvier, in the course of blaming on mobs the spirit of violence created by the vast number of individual assault and batteries, described how cross-bills for assault and battery effectively kept the court from punishing the disorderly. He suggested that grand jurors ignore bills arising from private fights and, instead, find indictments for affray against both parties to a public altercation.[51]

Sentiment favorable to strengthening the police first emerged in 1838 as a result of the Pennsylvania Hall riot, but the committee that investigated the riot was anything but clear on the matter. They implied that the managers of Pennsylvania Hall had not respected the moral sentiments of the city, which, because of Philadelphia's proximity to the South, were generally proslavery. The committee thus implied that the managers got what they deserved, and no one was brought to answer for the destruction of the hall.[52]

The equivocal position adopted by the committee that investigated the burning of Pennsylvania Hall would not last for long, however. Violent public disorder intensified during the early 1840s, and it increasingly involved ethnic, religious, and neighborhood issues. During these years, conditions deteriorated in Philadelphia.[53] Economic collapse crushed labor organizations and reduced wages, and additional immigration to the city increased competition for work. Already accustomed to private and public violence and chafing under economic distress, Philadelphia's workers became increasingly hostile toward one another. Fear and prejudice were intensified by cultural and ethnic organizations. Catholics had the church; Protestants had Bible, temperance, and nativist organizations, and the resurgent American Republican party; both had numerous fire companies. Seething hatred between these two groups, and between both of them and blacks, bubbled to the surface.[54]

Civil violence between groups of young working-class men consisted of continual street fights and occasional large-scale riots. During 1840 the *Ledger* maintained that one-third of the communications they received concerned "street disturbances, gatherings of wicked boys, drunken riots, misbehavior of prostitutes, and of rowdies generally." Typically, the editors attributed these disturbances to "worthless and negligent officers" whose tenure in office was dependent upon the citizenry's allegiance to partisan politics.[55]

Politics was part of the problem but not quite in the way the *Ledger* maintained. The ethnic tensions that sparked so many disturbances were intensified by politics after 1840. The stable second-party system that had developed in Philadelphia by the mid-1830s did not last long. Just after the 1838 constitution increased both the number of voters and elective offices, ethnic and cultural issues became prominent in the wake of the depression. Out of this mix came a revival of nativist parties that drew support away from both Whigs and Democrats. By 1843 the nativists were a major political force in Philadelphia, and in 1844 their alliance with the Whigs drew enough support from suburban Democrats to elect eight state legislators. Philadelphia politics was already on the road to the third-party system; more importantly, the legitimacy that politics gave to ethnic rivalry only emboldened the fire companies.

With ethnic tensions increasing, young men were joining or forming fire companies in unprecedented numbers. Most of the sixty-eight companies founded in Philadelphia between 1826 and 1852 were organized during the depression years of the early 1840s. Supported by "resourceful neighborhood followings," companies "focused their anger on neighboring, political and/or ethnic groups and fire companies" and fought "to regulate who lived near them, who socialized at their pubs and taverns, and which companies serviced their people." One chagrined observer characterized working-class Philadelphia of the 1840s as being under the "absolute and uncontrollable rule of the Volunteer Fire Department."[56]

The intensifying violence of the early 1840s prompted criminal court judges to step up their efforts to enforce order. At every turn, however, the limits of the criminal justice process frustrated them. Reliance on private prosecution gave rioters, as it did other citizens, the means with which to avoid conviction. A committee of city residents that was seeking information on riots among "persons calling themselves firemen" asked Attorney General Ovid F. Johnson, in September 1843, to provide information on court disposition of riot cases. They inquired about nine specific cases. None ever went to trial, either because witnesses could not be found or settlements were arranged. When trials occurred, evidence was so contradictory that no guilty party could be clearly determined. Most riot cases were marked by cross-bills, and trials turned into exercises in futility, with each side flatly contradicting the other. Juries simply acquitted everyone. Johnson admitted that, though cases had been returned to court every session for years, few convictions resulted. "Those who are not familiar with the administration of justice in our courts can form no adequate idea of the obstacles in the way of arriving at the truth in those class of cases. It seems little short of an impossibility." The confusion of a riot, the fact that most witnesses were adherents of one side or the other, the cross-actions, and the contradictory testimony in the context of the legal system's presumption of innocence all contributed to this "impossibility." Eighty-three riot charges between September 1841 and August 1843 resulted in sixty-eight indictments and six convictions. A grand jury, in November 1843, noted that they could only find indictments in cases presented to them, but the "hazard of making an arrest" at a riot scene and the problems of the courts made the difficulty of "detecting and bringing [fire rioters] to punishment . . . very great."[57]

The new quarter sessions judges' attempt to suppress unlicensed saloons in 1843 was also an aspect of their struggle to quell disorder. Saloons proliferated in working-class areas, and drinking was deeply imbued in the culture of the city's many journeymen. Taverns, many with ethnic cultural flavor, were places in which the drinking habits that workers had established in their workplaces could be continued. Gangs, fire companies, and political organizations were affiliated with neighborhood saloons; political leaders in these areas, including some aldermen, were sometimes tavern-keepers.[58]

Although the court's resolve was also thwarted here, the effort resulted in praise for the judges.[59] Reformers heaped praise on Parsons and his fellow jurists. The 1843 Eastern Pennsylvania Temperance Convention singled out judges Anson V. Parsons and Edward King as the most effective temperance men on the bench. Journalist George G. Foster lauded Parsons for his unflinching manner and called him "a terror to evil-doers." An 1844 grand jury congratulated the judges for their energetic efforts to stem the liquor trade. Temperance activists opposed proposals to remove the licensing power from the quarter sessions because of the judges' "conformity with the enlightened and humane spirit of the age." One called their work "a great moral revolution . . . in the administration of the criminal law" and gave most of the credit to Judges King, "an ornament to his profession," and Parsons, "a formidable rival to the President Judge."[60]

The judges also applied their activist spirit to riots. Soon after assuming the bench, Judge Joel R. Jones refused to lower an accused fire rioter's bail and promised to sentence all those convicted to "imprisonment for a term of years" even though it "may operate hard in a few instances." Judge Parsons assured the city that "no member of the bench will shrink from a faithful and energetic performance of his duty." He called on all citizens "who desire the protection of the law . . . to take the necessary means to obtain it" by bringing prosecutions against violent fire companies and any public officers who failed to do their duty to prevent riots. Parsons expressed confidence that the court and the traditional method of enforcement, private prosecution, could effectively contain the violence.[61]

When it came time to act, however, the new judges imposed only fines or short prison terms on convicted rioters. Though Parsons recognized the leniency of the sentences, he noted that, to separate poor young fathers from their families, even for a month, was a difficult and painful duty. The problems for the court were deeper than just the obvious injustice of severely punishing the generally poor rioters, however. The judges' reliance on private prosecution shackled them as it had their predecessors. Not only did it give rioters and other offenders opportunities to avoid legal punishment, but it kept the court dependent on pleasing the public in order to encourage the necessary public use of the law. Though judges did occasionally punish a convicted rioter harshly, the vast majority of persons accused of riot escaped either conviction or lengthy imprisonment. Surely jurists could not have been pleased by the way rioters avoided punishment, but it did have a positive consequence for the administration of criminal justice. Frequent convictions and severe sentences for poor and often popular volunteer firemen were not conducive to the continuation of private prosecution, to which the judges remained committed and to which the city still had no alternative. Parsons often voiced this component of legal thinking, and it was echoed by Judge Jones when he advised a reluctant larceny prosecutor in 1844 not to worry about a potentially severe sentence. "If people were less tender on this point and more prosecutions were brought, there would be less crime." Though ill-suited to riot prevention, the administration of criminal justice in riot cases did reinforce the precepts of the criminal justice system's foundation, private prosecution.[62]

Given the weakness of the law, it was not surprising that through 1843 and early 1844 the scale of street violence increased. Youth gangs were especially responsible for riots "replete with arson, shootings and murder." They fought with or without the excuse of a fire and sometimes attacked citizens who were not connected in any way to fire companies.[63] In a January 1844 riot among three fire companies, the armed combatants were cheered on by "small boys from ten to fifteen years of age" who procured weapons for the firemen. Several were shot and beaten, and one was assumed dead. When three aldermen attempted to calm the crowd, they were stoned. At a riot the previous summer, Alderman Hoffner was beaten nearly to death in a futile attempt to arrest the participants.[64]

The failure of civil authorities to suppress fire riots and other violent incidents through early 1844 revealed the vulnerability of the city to severe disturbances based on its deeply rooted cultural rivalries and increasingly volatile politics of ethnicity. Shortly thereafter, the extent of that vulnerability was unmistakably demonstrated, and the city would never again be the same.

Riots and the Police Mandate

The issue of civil disorder and the appropriate state response to it changed irrevocably in 1844. Besides the legacy of civil disorder and ineffective law enforcement, the foundation of the 1844 riots was the revival of anti-Catholic bigotry that swept the city and nation, provoked in Philadelphia by the Catholic demand to use their own version of the Bible in the public schools.[65] As a result, the Bible societies and temperance societies resurgent since the late 1830s adopted an increasingly anti-Catholic tone. Working-class nativists, attracted to the anti-Irish and anti-"accumulator" ideas of such groups as the American Republican Association, organized their own Order of United American Mechanics, led by artisans but composed mostly of "boys and young men never subject to [party] discipline . . . much the same human material that filled the ranks of the city's violent fire companies and street gangs." That such inflamed feelings among an already violence-prone population led to riots, especially in the context of the weakness of the authorities, was hardly surprising. A major riot between blacks and Irish erupted in August 1842 and was quelled only when the mayor mobilized seven militia companies. Strikes by Irish weavers in Kensington and Moyamensing frequently turned violent, pitting the Irish against native law officers. Aldermen attempting to arrest rioters were stoned and beaten off; grand jurors could only issue futile pleas for peace. The culmination of the disturbances was the "Nannygoat Market" riot of January 1844 in which a posse and the sheriff himself were severely beaten. Twelve militia companies finally quieted this battle, but it cemented hatred of the Irish in the minds of many natives.[66]

All the ingredients for a truly major riot were present in Philadelphia in the spring of 1844. Only a spark was needed, and it was provided in early May when a group of American Republican Association members from Spring Garden took the provocative step of holding a political rally in the middle of largely Irish Kensington. Catholics disrupted it, heckling and stoning the small group of nativists into a local temperance hall. "Native Americans" responded to this by calling a citywide rally at the same spot. A much larger crowd assembled the next day, but the Irish of Kensington, hardly discouraged by the first confrontation, were prepared again to meet what they considered an even more insulting invasion of their community. Fighting began between Catholic hecklers and some of the nativists, and by the time the rally disbanded, several had been killed by snipers.[67]

Nativists called another demonstration the next afternoon in Independence Square and advised all to "come prepared to defend" themselves. After inflammatory speeches, a crowd of several thousand set off for Kensington. Shooting resumed and over thirty buildings were set on fire. Many Catholics fled the city. The next day, mobs, composed mostly of boys, burned two churches that had been left virtually unguarded by either the militia or the watch. By this time, authorities were in a panic. Without a police force and with a militia composed largely of the friends and neighbors of the rioters, the situation seemed out of control. Peace was finally restored by the arrival of country militia companies, the instructions of Governor Porter to the militia to shoot rioters, and the organization by the aldermen of each ward of an armed "peace police" that patrolled the city for nearly a week.[68]

The Catholic victims of the riots received little sympathy. The grand jury, which was already in session, kept abreast of the riots and condemned the participants. Immediately following the restoration of peace, the grand jury embarked on an intensive investigation of the conduct of the authorities and "the origin and cause" of the riot. Judge Parsons concluded his charge by insisting, as he had in the past, that responsible popular use of the law by aggrieved citizens could have prevented violence: "The LAW is sufficiently strong and powerful to protect ALL; and gives a complete redress for any wrong or injury which one inflicts upon another."[69]

The grand jury's presentment criticized "the very imperfect manner" in which the law had been enforced but blamed the entire disturbance on the Irish Catholics. They concluded with one of the earliest pleas for a consolidated county police force, but this conclusion made less of an impact than their virtual exoneration of the rioters. Judge Jones encouraged this in his charge to the subsequent grand jury in early July. Though his remarks were devoted primarily to the inadequacies of the authorities, his opening statement on the causes of the riots focused on "idle vagabonds . . . criminals and foreigners. Foreigners especially." Because they had no respect for self-government, foreigners flaunted authority and were "a constant element of disorder." Given the ubiquity of the prejudice against the Irish, it was no wonder that the courts had virtually no success in punishing rioters. Only 18 of the 633 persons committed to prison in May 1844 were connected with the riots; only 10 of the 72 persons indicted in the riots were convicted and imprisoned, and most of them were Irish. Morton McMichael, now the sheriff, and the police magistrate of Kensington, Alderman Hugh Clark, were acquitted of negligence charges.[70]

Naturally emboldened, thousands of nativist men and boys paraded on 4 July to honor the victims of the May riots who had become martyred heroes of the cause. Afterwards, some Southwark nativists observed muskets being delivered to a local Catholic church, which, unbeknownst to them, had been ordered by the governor for defense against a possible attack. A crowd assembled, on 5 July, in front of the church, which was located in a working-class district composed of both Catholic immigrants and native Protestants, and the militia found the entire cache of arms and removed them. However, early on the morning of 7 July, the church was besieged, and the militia was forced to relinquish it to the mob.

By dusk, moderate nativist leaders had quieted the crowd, but the militia in the city was unaware of this. Knowing only that the church had fallen to the mob, and fearful of further violence, General Cadwalader and two hundred of his militiamen set off for Southwark, determined to tolerate no resistance. When the startled crowd milling about the church met the militia, they refused to disperse and a scuffle ensued. Under orders to fire if faced with trouble, the militia opened on the crowd and killed several people. By the time hostilities ceased the next afternoon, fourteen were dead, including a number of bystanders, and over fifty were wounded.

The Southwark riots were the first occasion in Philadelphia's history in which the militia had fired on citizens. Most of the city's elite and thousands of others signed a petition that was sent to the governor supporting the militia and expressing the idea that, in times of riot, those not actively trying to oppose the riot should leave, or else be considered rioters. So much for outrage at the killing of bystanders by the militia. The petition proposed not a police force but a permanent militia regiment to be kept in the city under the mayor's control.[71]

Among at least some prominent Philadelphians, however, sentiment for an improved police force increased in the wake of the July riots. A lengthy response to the petition, entitled *Street Talk About An Ordinance of Councils, Passed the Eleventh of July 1844 Organizing A Military Force For the Government of Philadelphia*, voiced opposition to the permanent militia plan, calling it an invasion of constitutional rights and pointing out that the militia escalated the violence in Southwark. *Street Talk* implied that, because the city governments "have no police," military rule would be necessary at the sign of "even the most impudent breaches of order." It, therefore, requested that the city councils "give us what all other large towns possess, namely—a civil police, to prevent disorder . . . give us a little prevention, and we will ask less cure."[72]

The grand jury that investigated the Southwark riots also preferred a civil police to a military solution. As was the case with its predecessor in May, the inquest blamed the riots more on the Irish than on the nativists, but this jury dug deeper. The original attackers, and most of the rioters on both sides, were "a class, whose depravity seeks every opportunity to violate the rights of others." They were the "pests of society, disturbers of the peace, the cause of riots, tumults and murder." The jury called for the disarming of all fire companies and the organization of a 450-man police force for the entire county, which would be distributed to each district, would be controlled by the civil authorities of each, and would come together only in order to quell riots.[73]

The major concern of those proposing new measures of law enforcement was the failure of civil authorities to respond effectively to the riots. Only a handful of citizens responded to the sheriff's and aldermen's summonses to form a civil posse. Although it possessed the requisite force to disperse rioters, the militia was also a flawed solution. It could only be mustered after a disturbance began and the riot act was read. When the mayor or other civil authorities requested that the governor activate the militia, he always did so, but the first companies to be activated were locally based and often made up of neighbors and even relatives of the rioters. The failure of the militia in Kensington to use force was a result of the reluctance of civil authorities to give an order to one group of their constituents to fire upon another. The mob in Kensington had already shown what might happen to an unpopular official;

they had burned the house of Police Magistrate Hugh Clark. The only way to be sure militiamen would use the force at their command was to employ companies from outside the city, but this could only be a second step, and it carried the danger of escalating the violence before ending it. Finally, the authorities proved either unwilling or unable to round up rioters after the events. In neither riot was anyone arrested afterward; only those caught at the scene were charged. Of these, but few were convicted—only four of nineteen indicted in the Southwark riot. Those who were convicted faced only a few months imprisonment at most.[74]

Both propolice and promilitary factions saw their proposals as attempts, in part, to relieve elected officials of the responsibility of ordering an attack on the electorate. Horace Binney included a riot act in his militia proposal that put the mobilized forces under strict military command; the authors of *Street Talk* claimed that, with an effective regular police force, magistrates could "act without half the crowd's knowing they are there."[75] *Street Talk*, though published anonymously, was probably the work of a group of Philadelphia's elite, including former mayor John Swift and the merchants Edward P. Cope and Francis Wharton, who formed the first proconsolidation faction in the city. Supported by the *Ledger*, which proposed county consolidation in the days immediately following the July riots, these men held a large meeting in the early fall in which they defined consolidation as simply a movement to unify and professionalize the police. More was involved, however, and as a result, most of the city's elite opposed consolidation. The lawyers, city bondholders, and incumbent officials in all the districts were loathe to upset the political status quo. Whig city officials feared losing power to the Democrats who dominated the districts; bondholders feared a decline in the value of their investments if the city merged with its poorer neighbors. No patronage employee anywhere wanted to risk his party's removal from office. Led by Binney, opponents countered the consolidation proposal with one for a "standardized and somewhat co-ordinated police system" and a comprehensive riot act that would give the sheriff authority to employ all of the county's police during a riot and to call for the militia if the police proved inadequate. The militia would remain under military control; soldiers, police, and civilian posses would be absolved of all liability for any life they took after the sheriff had called upon the crowd to disperse. Anyone remaining at the scene would be presumed a rioter; there would be no more innocent bystanders.[76]

The Binney group's proposal was much like the one offered by the grand jury, and it became substantially the law in April 1845. The force in the city, Southwark, Spring Garden, Northern Liberties, Kensington, and

Moyamensing would consist of no less than one officer per 150 taxable inhabitants. More than enough policemen already existed in the city to meet this requirement; its real effect would be to establish a small force in each of the districts. Each district's force would be completely independent of the others' except in times of riot.[77]

In real terms, improvement in the size and organization of Philadelphia's police was only slight. Tradition and interest had prevented any significant change from occurring in Philadelphia's law enforcement and criminal justice system, but the weaknesses of this system were now clearer than ever. As a result, some of the city's elite, and some of those within the criminal justice system, had become supporters of a preventative police force.

The ranks of supporters of the police grew over the next several years, as the police force established in 1845 proved to be thoroughly inadequate. No major riots occurred until late 1849, but the depredations of fire companies and gangs became legion, especially in the suburbs. Many of the rowdiest fire companies and youth gangs were from Southwark and Moyamensing, where they and their associated political clubs and saloons were the strongest formal organizations among poor whites. Southwark and Moyamensing were among the best Democratic areas in the city. Already, in 1845, some fire companies and gangs were beginning to wield substantial power within the party. The Catholic Moyamensing Hose Company, for example, became closely affiliated with the Keystone Club, an organization of Democratic ward workers, and the most prominent gang of the era, the Moyamensing "Killers." The leader of the Keystone Club, also a fire company member, was William McMullin. The son of a Moyamensing grocer, McMullin's life became centered on the city streets at a very young age, and it never left them. He was one of the principals in the riots of 1844, and in order to escape retribution, he joined the navy for a brief time. When he returned, he and other Moyamensing Hose Company members acted regularly as Democratic poll watchers. McMullin excelled at this because of his great physical strength, an important asset when disputes about voter eligibility arose. After enlisting with the rest of the Hose Company for duty in the Mexican War, McMullin returned to Philadelphia for good in 1850, resumed leadership of the Company, and became president of the Keystone Club.

Southwark was less solidly Democratic than Moyamensing. The nativist American Republican party gained strength there among formerly Democratic Protestant workers during the early 1840s and managed to control the district's politics for the rest of the decade. The local Weccacoe Engine Company allied with the "Americans" and with a notorious gang known as the "Rats," but its Catholic rival, the Weccacoe Hose Company, remained Democratic and joined forces with the "Bouncers" gang. Repeated battles ensued between these fire company and gang alliances and also between the "Killers" and the nativist Shiffler Hose Company (named for a young man shot by McMullin during the Kensington riots), which was located near the Southwark-Moyamensing border.[78]

The inability of the city's criminal justice system to control public violence was making Philadelphia a national embarrassment. Fire companies and gangs were becoming one of Philadelphia's most notable features. One grand jury noted with chagrin that the city's firemen were "remarked upon on both sides of the Atlantic." George G. Foster devoted a full piece to them in a series of articles on Philadelphia, published in 1848, in which he blamed the violence on "ruffians and rowdy apprentices" who were tolerated by the authorities in the suburbs because of political influence. The "Killers" were thoroughly romanticized in an 1847 fictional pamphlet entitled *The Almighty Dollar: or, the Brilliant Exploits of a Killer*. In this the gang was likened to the Jacobins of revolutionary France, leading a political upheaval of "the ground down and oppressed . . . putting down aristocrats, monopolies, and the DOLLAR'S MISRULE."[79]

Such sentiments echoed the radicalism of the pre-1837 democracy, but the behavior of fire companies and gangs belied them, and the criminal justice system remained unable to do anything about it. Judges regularly instructed grand juries to investigate firemen's riots, especially those that occurred when there was no fire or alarm, but to no avail. The January 1848 grand jury, because of "the evident determination on the part of witnesses to give no information," could find no indictments against participants in a series of riots between the Fairmount and Good Will Engine companies. The books and papers of the Fairmount Company, subpoenaed by the jury, mysteriously disappeared as soon as the request was made. As if this was not enough, the courts were further hampered by the familiar practice of cross-prosecution, which was now sometimes even instituted against policemen who dared arrest disorderly fire company or gang members.[80]

Each time a grand jury expressed its frustration, it recommended that a law be passed giving the court the power to disband riotous companies and to prohibit minors from being members. Finally, in March 1848, the legislature passed such a law and at the same time slightly enlarged the police system in the city proper. The city was divided into four districts, with a total of 200 night and 34 day policemen. Officers were required to attend all fires and preserve the peace.[81]

The attention of criminal justice officials quickly turned to youth gangs. Judge Parsons declared that their attacks on innocent citizens, blacks, and each other were the city's greatest scourge. Fire companies were now less frequently troublesome, thanks to the new law. Actually, only three companies were declared out of service during the law's first year of operation, but the prohibition of membership by minors shifted many of the most disorderly to affiliated youth gangs, simultaneously making gangs an even greater problem and charges of riotous conduct against fire companies more difficult to prove. The result was a reported increase in the number "of disorderly young men and boys . . . held to bail" and sentenced to short prison terms during 1848 and early 1849. The young men involved blamed their troubles on the decline of traditional apprenticeship and the absence of any system of education to replace it. Gang members, harassed by the police for congregating in dugouts and on street corners, complained of having "no place to go." This was echoed by other citizens. Some of those opposed to the city's mobilization of troops to quell riots suggested that the city concentrate instead on prevention, claiming that the education of many of the rioters had been "shockingly neglected" by the city.[82]

In any event, the relative calm among fire companies ended in 1849. That June a terrible riot occurred in Moyamensing between old rivals, the Franklin and Moyamensing Hose companies; at least seven people were shot, and several others were seriously injured in other ways. A twenty-one-year-old man died of gunshot wounds. The police act of 1845 was of little use in quelling this riot. Neither the mayor of the city nor the police magistrate of Southwark responded to the sheriffs' request that their police forces be made available for riot duty, in clear violation of the law's intent. As a result, the police arrested only two participants at the scene. The court expressed its condemnation at the time and again a few weeks later when a jury acquitted the arrested rioters. "I doubt very much whether twelve other men would have rendered such a verdict," Judge Parsons remarked, apparently unimpressed by the general applause that greeted of the verdict.[83]

Firemen's riots again became regular events in 1849. The court declared eight companies out of service because of riots during the year. Violence greeted arresting officers; complaints reappeared that most officials would not interfere with the activities of the politically powerful companies. Meanwhile, the violence of youth gangs continued unabated. One result of the evident ineffectiveness of the police and fire company laws was a hardening of the posture of court officials. A September grand jury called strongly for consolidation of the city and reorganization of the fire department. Judge

Parsons relinquished his belief that private prosecution and reliance upon the law were sufficient protection against crime and disorder. Consolidation "for the purpose of having an adequate police department for the suppression of riots" was now the "only efficient mode" of protection. Judge Kelley agreed with great reluctance that an "armed police" was becoming a necessity.[84]

If consolidation received a boost from the enlistment of the quarter sessions judges among its supporters, another major riot on election night, 9 October, provided an even greater impetus for change. That night members of the "Killers" made one of their not infrequent assaults upon the black community, their target a Moyamensing saloon known as the California House, which was operated by a black man and his white wife. After some preliminary fighting and shooting, the "Killers" put the torch to the saloon, where many of the assaulted blacks had taken refuge. As the fire spread, the gang and its allies surrounded the block and prevented any fire company from trying to extinguish it. Three people, including one fireman, were killed, and many others were wounded. The militia was called out, the governor offered a reward for the arrest of the rioters, and the entire episode was depicted in the novella *The Life and Adventures of Charles Anderson Chester, the Notorious Leader of the Philadelphia "Killers."*[85]

By November a resurgent consolidation movement had gained considerable momentum. Members of the city elite such as State Senator Eli K. Price and industrialist Matthias Baldwin joined court officials at its head. Thousands attended a mass meeting and sent an appeal to the legislature. Grand jurors continued to support consolidation into the spring of 1850; they also proposed the arming of police stations and the replacement of the volunteer fire companies with a paid department that could also serve as an auxiliary police force. The emboldened quarter sessions judges imposed particularly stiff sentences on the convicted rioters, of whom there were a greater number than ever before thanks to the governor's rewards. Eleven rioters were sentenced by Judge Parsons to terms ranging between one and two years.[86]

Resistance to consolidation remained strong, however, among the Binney faction and the officeholders who stood to lose power. Thwarting consolidationist plans was still not difficult since any such change had to be made by the legislature where the populous county districts wielded great influence. Leaders of the various districts proposed to the legislature that the police of the county be unified but that the political boundaries be retained. On 3 May 1850, the legislature adopted their plan. In addition to the already existing police forces in each district, a new marshal's police was established for the county. The police were distributed among the suburbs and the four city police districts and were to act within each district both independently and in conjunction with the regular police. Their major responsibilities were to arrest idle, suspicious, or disorderly persons and to respond to the marshal's call to put down riots anywhere within the county. The marshal was to be elected for three years and to select officers from nominees chosen by the district councils or commissioners of each district. The number of policemen in the city was thus increased to 189; by 1852 the number for the county reached 705, as high as it would get until the 1880s. As part of the same act, the public prosecutor's title was changed to district attorney, the office was made elective, and he was required, for the first time, to "sign all bills of indictment and conduct in court all criminal or other prosecutions in the name of the commonwealth."

Nativist John Keyser, formerly a police lieutenant in Spring Garden, was elected as the first marshal. Philadelphia thus got a metropolitan police force capable of stopping and preventing riots, the second such force in a major American city. New York had established one five years before, and Chicago and Boston would do so a few years later. Like these other police forces, Philadelphia's was expected to keep the streets free from violence, especially collective violence. Policemen were instructed, therefore, to keep a close eye on potential troublemakers, and for this job, Keyser chose mostly neighborhood toughs with close ties to fire companies, young men who could become a "strong-armed force prepared to slug it out with fire gangs."[87]

After the establishment of the marshal's police, major riots became markedly less common. This satisfied one great impulse toward consolidation and corrected the most frightening weakness of the criminal justice system, but it did little else. It addressed few of the political, structural, or legal issues that still affected city government and that supported private prosecution, and it hardly made a dent in the authority of the aldermen. It did, however, put a new and permanent mode of law enforcement on the streets every day and augmented the power and discretion of the public prosecutor. An alternative to private prosecution had arrived.

7. *Consolidation and Compromise*

The marshal's police may have embodied a new theory of preventative policing, but they also strengthened the old practices of criminal justice. Between 1850 and 1854, the relationship that aldermen had established with the new police force's puny predecessors blossomed, making police prosecution a formidable part of criminal justice and also further empowering the minor judiciary. This, in turn, reinforced private prosecution and the power of ward politicians.

In response, critics of criminal justice intensified their demands for change. Temperance reformers recruited judges and grand jurors to their cause, and prison reformers sought to carve out a place for themselves within the criminal courts. Municipal reformers included the centralization of primary justice in their larger demand for the consolidation of city government. Behind their actions stood the principle that the law should be enforced by independent state action and need not necessarily rely on the voluntary action of aggrieved citizens. Without articulating it, perhaps even to themselves, reformers were becoming supporters of an administrative state, pushing the law from an era of social laissez-faire into an era of public social policy.

This was just the beginning, however. Reformers could not achieve their goals without compromising some of them, partly because of their own uncertainty about what they were doing, partly because of the strength of their opponents. Ward politicians forced reformers to adopt a structure of city government that ensured a wide field of control for politicians in the criminal courts and the consolidated city generally.

Still, consolidation and its supporters had a major impact on criminal prosecution and the future of reform. A consolidated city meant a consolidated police force, one much more conducive to concerted state efforts at criminal prosecution. The creation of police stations with aldermen sitting as magistrates in each drew the center of gravity in criminal justice away from private prosecution and toward the police, and it provided some aldermen with lucrative posts that were tied directly and exclusively to the police. In addition, the criminal court and its judges established close formal ties to local reformers. Equally important was the fact that the consolidated city offered aldermen and other politicians a much wider field of action and paved the way for the shift in power from ward-based to citywide parties, a shift that also contributed to changes in the practice of criminal justice.

The Marshal's Police

John Keyser was elected marshal on 1 March 1850, and the force hit the streets on 21 November. Many Philadelphians were skeptical about the marshal's police. Consolidationists had lost their best issue, and they tried their best to get it back. Judge Parsons called the measure a "palliative" and warned that, unless the city was consolidated, there would be "a constant increase of crime in its various forms." Other supporters of consolidation pointed out that, under the 1845 law, the police of the various districts were already empowered to join forces to quell riots. After a watchman was murdered in Moyamensing during the summer of 1850, many people believed that, as long as the districts dominated by gang members remained independent, the police would never be able to safely patrol the streets. Critics also wondered whether rioters in Moyamensing, for example, would be anything but further incensed by the arrival of officers from another district, who would seem like hostile invaders. At a large consolidationist rally in early November, Parsons argued that the police of each district were often connected with the riotous gangs and that, without consolidation, there was no hope for peace.[1]

Despite the ability of the marshal's police to arrest unprecedented numbers of people, many of these fears proved to be well founded. Marshal Keyser chose officers connected to nativist gangs and fire companies. Catholic companies regarded the police less as representatives of the law than as their traditional rivals. The "Buffers," a gang affiliated with the Keystone Club, challenged opponents: "Go and get John Keyser and all of his Police; / Come up to the Market, and there you will see fun, / To see the Buffers thump old Keyser, and make his puppies run." Other gangs' boastful songs also expressed the belief that the police were merely old adversaries in new clothes. The "Bleeders," for example, told of being attacked one night by "a band of ruffians . . . they called themselves Police." When Keyser's term expired, the new Democratic marshal replaced most of the nativist policemen with Democrats, many of whom were also gang members. One of the new lieutenants was Keystone Club leader William McMullin.[2]

Since the marshal's policemen were members of the city's most disorderly groups, even on duty they often displayed precisely the behavior that they were supposed to suppress. Lack of discipline and lax enforcement of the law were prominent features of the marshal's police. Repeatedly, Keyser confronted his men with charges that they spent too much of their time in "grog shops, taverns [and] houses of doubtful reputation." In a speech to his men at the end of the first year, Keyser warned that too many of them were "worthless, drunken, and totally unfit" to serve on the force. He dismissed seventy-three officers for intoxication and disorderly conduct during the year, over one-third of the force.[3]

Policemen also often failed to appear in court and publicly fought with other policemen, a result of what one grand jury called "a spirit of rivalry between the different police organizations of the city and the districts." Officers failed to report for roll calls; lieutenants failed to call the roll. Keyser "repeatedly heard of officers lounging about the taverns, playing dominoes and drinking, while their beats were left exposed to rowdies and outlaws." Given even the lieutenants' laziness, Keyser "did not wonder that so many complaints were made of the inefficiency of the Department." One came from the Rosine Association, which accused the police of raiding and closing brothels only to "absorb all the money that could be drained from the unfortunate women" and then allowing them to resume business in other parts of the city, thus contributing to the spread of prostitution.[4]

Conflicts over jurisdiction, rivalries among district divisions, and laxity on the job kept the county's police ineffective.[5] Still, the marshal's police had a major impact on the streets and criminal justice system of Philadelphia, stemming from their greatly enhanced power to make arrests. This was, in part, simply a matter of increased manpower, but it was also a result of the logic behind professionalizing the police. In order to effectively prevent disorder, the police had to be able to watch and, if necessary, detain people they considered likely to commit crimes. Even before the marshal's police was created, the *Ledger* had pointed out that the police too often arrested persons on suspicion and without sufficient evidence although such an arrest usually took place after a crime. The practice was "too lose, vague and undefined." No person was safe from arrest where he was not known, but, more to the point, "in some cases the poverty of a man is made to justify an arrest on suspicion, though establishing a doctrine of the most pernicious tendency."[6]

Pernicious or not, after the new police law took effect, the doctrine of arrest on suspicion was tacitly extended to the arrest and surveillance of people in advance of a crime. The *Rules for Regulating* directed each officer to "report . . . all suspicious persons and places . . . where idlers, gamblers, prostitutes, and other disorderly and suspicious persons may congregate." Further, the *Rules* instructed policemen to "promptly arrest any and all disorderly persons, thieves, burglars, pickpockets, and persons found prowling in the streets under suspicious circumstances, who cannot give satisfactory explanations as to their business and intentions." The new rules equated idleness and poverty with crime. "As a general thing, any idle, able-bodied poor man has no right to complain, if the eye of the police follows him wherever he roams or rests. His very idleness is an offense against all social laws." For the first time, the state encouraged its representatives to act among the poor in the same manner that the poor had been acting among themselves—to bring criminal prosecutions against people on trivial grounds, even when no real crime had been committed. Of course, there was a major difference between the two. Policemen were not seeking to redress some perceived injustice or influence their personal affairs; rather, they were (in theory) seeking to punish minor disorder before it got worse, to nip serious crime in the bud.[7]

Although there was a considerable gap between the design and execution of the new policy, the police made many more arrests than ever before. More arrests meant more cases initiated by policemen before the county's aldermen, and more police cases meant the intensification of the already established relationship between the two. Judges, grand jurors, District Attorney William B. Reed, and Marshal Keyser all made it plain that aldermen were attempting to treat police cases like private cases by making private settlements with the parties. An 1851 grand jury first raised the issue in comments concerning arrests for "gambling and other misdemeanors" which had partial hearings before aldermen but which were not returned to the court. Meanwhile, the *Ledger* worried that "the majority of cases" that began with police arrests "have been lost sight of, and the prisoners have been let go." The quarter sessions judges more than once reprimanded policemen who simply failed to appear for the trials of people they had arrested and implied that, in some of the cases, commitments were made merely for the costs.[8]

The next year, Marshal Keyser defended his men and pointed his finger at the aldermen. In September he told the court that over one hundred fire riot arrests were never returned because they were settled by aldermen. He blamed the inability of the police to stop the fire rioting on "the unwarrantable interference of the magistrates" and noted that the practice was not new. Alderman Elkinton protested his own innocence and promised that the riot cases brought to him would come up during the next term of the court, but he left the general charge unchallenged. When the cases went to trial in December, Judge Kelley echoed Keyser's remarks, asking "the public to investigate . . . how hundreds can be arrested and only about ten brought to trial."[9]

In some districts, the police were also accused of making arrangements to bring all their cases to certain aldermen because of the magistrates' political affiliation. Since both jobs were closely tied to ward politics, this was hardly surprising. In 1853, after an excluded alderman complained, the marshal agreed to furnish District Attorney Reed with a weekly list of all arrests on which aldermen held hearings. Reed announced that he would release prisoners charged with misdemeanors who had been in prison over one week, unless a specific return was filed. Any other process was a misdemeanor in office, and Reed promised to so regard all settlements of police cases by aldermen.[10] One of the first threats of independent prosecution made by the newly empowered district attorney was directed at the minor judiciary, a very early sign of the inherent conflict between the two. Significantly, this was provoked not by private prosecution but by the aldermen's relationship with the police. Partly this was because the district attorney could much more easily prosecute official misconduct, but it also reflected how completely the new authority of the police became entwined with the old authority of the aldermen.

Antebellum Reform and Criminal Justice

One of the high points of reform in nineteenth-century America occurred in the early 1850s. Nativism, abolitionism, and temperance were changing the social and political face of many American communities. In Philadelphia the strength of nativism had already been demonstrated during the forties. Now the quieter influence of more sober reform would have its greatest impact on the city and on criminal justice. New reform issues, and finally reformers themselves, became an active part of the criminal justice system. This was partly another response to the deficiencies of private prosecution, but it was also a response to the obvious problems with the new police. Either way, antebellum reformers contributed to the articulation of a new concept of criminal justice that complemented even as it criticized police prosecution.

Different types of reformers had, of course, been of central importance to criminal justice before this time. Although the early prison reformers especially were forerunners of antebellum reform, the sometime subtle differences between them were important. Elite prison reformers such as John Sergeant and the leaders of the PSAMPP were traditionalists primarily concerned with order. They combined support for coercive institutions such as prisons and the police with a continuing commitment to established legal procedures.

The reformers of the 1850s, inspired by the humanitarian and optimistic vision of evangelical Protestantism, were also concerned about social order, but they combined this with a greater interest in social conditions and a willingness to abandon legal tradition. Temperance reformers were the first to affect criminal justice, by enlisting the support of the judiciary. Local temperance activists had been advocating special institutions for drunkards since the late 1820s and led a chorus of cheers every time the court took aim at tippling houses.[11] These activists became permanently organized statewide in 1834 and, by the mid-forties, were campaigning feverishly for more restrictive legislation and more stringent enforcement of existing laws. "Intemperance is the main-spring of most, if not all of our social disorders," asserted one grand jury in 1846. Judge Parsons encouraged these views, urging the indictment of all tippling houses because it was there that young people learned how to ignore the law with impunity. In 1847 newly appointed Judge William D. Kelley instructed a grand jury to investigate tippling houses in the Baker Street and Seventh Street area. Judge Kelley believed "that the crime, disease and misery there to be found was mainly to be attributed to the existence of tippling-houses."[12]

As we know, the court was nonetheless powerless to halt the spread of unlicensed tippling houses. Opponents of temperance urged the state to use liquor licenses to raise revenue rather than restrict consumption. They reasoned that the quarter sessions policy of reducing the number of licensed houses only cost the state money, that unlicensed houses paying no legal fees had replaced the licensed houses, and that the court was unable to suppress the unlicensed houses. Why not admit defeat, raise the fees, and license any dealer who could pay? This argument was very persuasive to the revenue-conscious and hardly teetotaling legislators in Harrisburg, and in April 1849, they changed the licensing laws for Philadelphia County. Minimum fees were raised from $5 to $50; maximum fees increased from $200 to $350. The licensing power was taken from the quarter sessions judges and given to a board of appraisers that assessed each dealer, calculated the fee, and sold the license. Brewers and distillers were also assessed and licensed. The law's supporters claimed that the county would receive $125,000 annually from the new licenses.[13]

The new law gave temperance advocates even greater influence over criminal justice. By 1850, in the wake of Neal Dow's efforts in Maine, the temperance movement had become dominated by prohibitionist thought. Although a "Maine law" was never passed in Pennsylvania, the crusade for one was influential. Prohibition's strength during the early fifties rested on the widespread support of the state's clergy, but its influence touched the judges and prosecuting attorney of the criminal court.

The quarter sessions judges became associated with temperance as the direct consequence of the court's failure to restrain the spread of drinking houses following the license law of 1849. They reported that the number of licensed taverns had increased from one per 112 taxable citizens to one per 44 between 1849 and 1853. Grand jurors never ceased reminding the city that there were also almost as many unlicensed houses that were run by people who were unwilling or unable to pay the license fees.[14]

Judges became leading members of temperance societies, regular speakers at their meetings, and marshals of their parades. Stripped of their control over licensing, the judges used the bench to wage a propaganda campaign against liquor. Parsons asserted that Philadelphia was "one vast groggery," tempting "thousands of our fellow men . . . into the great army of hard drinkers." The result was "the ruin of many of the most promising young men among us." Poverty and crime were the necessary consequences of the spread of taverns, as "no one who will sit with me in this Criminal Court for two months . . . will doubt." Judge Kelley boldly stated that "without exception," every case that had come before him was the result of intemperance. Grand juries saw drinking houses as the wellsprings of disorder, "night haunts for the incendiary and assassin [and] the special rendezvous for gangs of lawless individuals." William J. Mullen, by now a veteran temperance advocate, wrote and distributed a pamphlet that criticized the liquor law and quoted extensively from the quarter sessions judges.[15]

Judges, jurors, and temperance activists made great use of statistics that demonstrated a simultaneous increase in crime and the number of saloons. According to a petition to the legislature asking for the repeal of the license law, these crimes were "promoted by the excitement, passions and debasement generated by the use of intoxicating drinks; and it is probable that nearly all of these cases had their origin in intemperance." Mullen claimed that, if liquor was prohibited, the number of criminals would be reduced "to one-twentieth of their present amount." A 33 percent increase in commitments during 1850 (from 5,799 to 7,687), which included a doubling of intoxication cases and was the largest increase the city had ever seen, prompted a sharp response in early 1851. Parsons called it "a sad commentary on the condition of crime and morals in the community" and claimed that the license law was its first cause. The *Ledger* argued that the license law was more responsible for the increase in commitments than even the indiscriminate practices of aldermen.[16]

Reformers also used statistics generated by the police. Mullen claimed that the number of arrests jumped from 7,000 in 1848 to 25,000 in 1850. The temperance petitioners said that 5,987 cases of drunkenness and disorderly conduct came before the mayor during 1850. These figures are probably too high; they exceed considerably those reported by the newspaper and the police themselves, who recorded only 7,076 arrests between 21 November 1850 and 1 July 1851. Nevertheless, there was undoubtedly an increase in arrests and prison commitments beginning in 1850, the first full year under the new law. However, this was also the first year of the marshal's police. The steep rise in arrests and commitments was as much the result of more and better-organized policemen patrolling the streets as it was the result of drinking houses proliferating under the license law.

In late 1851, the judges' connection with reform gained further impetus from the county's first judicial election. The necessity of conducting campaigns put judges in direct contact with reformers who were members of political parties and required the judges to confront the major political issues of the day. In the local politics of 1851, no issue was bigger than temperance.

The bench was made elective by a constitutional amendment affecting all of Pennsylvania. Three judges were elected in October 1851, one a president judge with a ten-year term, the other two with five-year terms. Among the sitting judges, only William D. Kelley won.[17] Kelley, an immensely popular local politician, was the best example of a judge who had been influenced by reform sentiments and political considerations. After his youthful days as a locofoco Jacksonian (and fire company member) in Philadelphia, Kelley spent several years in Boston where he came under the influence of Orestes Brownson, George Bancroft, and the most radical wing of the Massachusetts Democracy. He returned to Philadelphia in 1839 to study law with leading Democrat James Page, bringing with him the idealism of his workingman youth, the reformist sentiments of the Boston radicals, and a passionate commitment to the Democratic party as the vehicle for his principles. Like many other radicals of artisan roots, Kelley was committed to variety of reform causes, including abolitionism and temperance. These commitments led Kelley into the Republican party by decade's end, but now, in his first run for an elected office, his commitments introduced him to the peculiarities of party politics.[18]

Kelley had passed the bar in 1841, had worked hard as an advocate of Governor Francis Shunk's reelection in 1844, and had been rewarded with an appointment as deputy attorney general for Philadelphia in 1844. The next year, he was appointed by the governor to the common pleas and quarter sessions bench. By the late forties, however, Kelley was beginning to move away from the mainstream of the Philadelphia Democrats. He had never been comfortable with the ward leaders, their ties to violent gangs and fire compa-

nies, and the antiblack and abolitionist violence that they frequently provoked. Then, when the conservative supporters of James Buchanan took
control of the party and repudiated the Wilmot Proviso in 1847, Kelley threw
his support to the fledgling free-soil movement.

When the election of 1851 arrived, Kelley found himself in an odd
position. The first election for district attorney had taken place in 1850, and
the ward politicians of both parties were anxious to have their man win. This
was one of the first countywide elections in Philadelphia's history and an
important test of strength. The Democrats, accustomed to controlling the
elections in the suburbs that they dominated, made sure they would win by
falsifying the returns, but the defeated Whig, William B. Reed, contested the
result. When the case came before Kelley and the other Democratic common
pleas judges, party leaders put intense pressure on them to overlook the
evidence and place the party's interests first. The judges refused and declared
Reed the winner. A chasm was growing between the idealistic Kelley and the
parochial, conservative local Democratic party, increasingly dominated by
Kelley's probank, proslavery rivals. At the same time, the judge's popularity
made him attractive to other parties, and so, despite the Democrats' refusal to
nominate him or the other two incumbent judges, Edward King and James
Campbell, Kelley ran as an independent in the judicial election. Supported by
reform-oriented, free-soil Democrats, Whigs, William J. Mullen's Workingmen's party, and even a faction of the nativist American Republicans, Kelley
finished first in a five-man race for the two associate judgeships. The other
successful candidate was the protemperance Native American candidate, Joseph Allison. In a separate contest, Democrat Oswald Thompson was elected
president judge.[19]

The new judges were no more successful than their predecessors in
enforcing the liquor laws. Conviction rates for liquor cases were especially
low during the years after the change in the license law. As in the past,
constables were unwilling to investigate liquor dealers for the paltry fee of 50
cents per day. Instead, they filed returns from memory or from outdated lists,
ignored newly established saloons, and harassed licensed ones. Even when a
case reached the court, grand jurors too often found themselves "compelled
. . . to grope in the dark" because the testimony was "not of a character
altogether satisfactory." Although the courts still sometimes made a strong
effort—191 indictments in January 1853, for example—they continually were
frustrated.[20]

So court officials instead fashioned themselves as guardians of community morals and concentrated on political agitation. Judges Kelley and

Allison became regular speakers at temperance and prohibition rallies. Grand jurors regularly used their presentments to appeal to the legislature to change the law. Increasingly, they supported the total prohibition of liquor in Pennsylvania.[21] A March 1854 presentment was almost entirely a prohibitionist tract. Its conclusion—"What is the remedy for this terrible scourge! Nothing but a prohibitory law!"—was a call to action directed not at criminal justice officials but at the electorate and the legislature. The report of the 1854 State Temperance Convention included a lengthy presentation of statistics on liquor consumption and criminal justice, with quotations and letters by judges and grand jurors. The county's court of quarter sessions was in the forefront of one of the era's foremost reform crusades.[22]

The judges were comfortable with their involvement in a reform crusade in part, like Kelley, out of conviction but also because they were more interested in being politicians than jurists. Most had larger ambitions and used their positions on the bench as stepping stones. Like Kelley or Judge James Campbell (an intimate of James Buchanan), many received their posts as political rewards, but unlike aldermen, their ties were to state and national party interests rather than to local ward politics. Several went on to achieve state and national office: Kelley in Congress for thirty years, Campbell as Franklin Pierce's postmaster general. Both Republican Edward M. Paxson and Democrat James R. Ludlow became prominent members of their state party organizations after the Civil War, and both ran for statewide office. The post-1850 quarter sessions judges were a breed apart from the minor judiciary, more likely to be attracted to both social and political reform movements, and increasingly more willing to accept innovation in the law and disruption of the power of local politicians.

Prohibition was defeated in Pennsylvania in a public referendum in 1854, and soon afterwards, temperance activism waned in the courts and the state at large.[23] Nevertheless, by enlisting the judges' support and by so explicitly making the connection between criminal justice and social reform, temperance advocates encouraged judges to assume a reformist posture on the bench and prepared them to be receptive when prison reformers sought a place within the criminal courts. Members of the PSAMPP were regularly struck by the "instances [that] often occur of persons being committed to prison who are either entirely or comparatively innocent of crime, who for want of qualified persons to interest themselves in their behalf become the victims of others who are influenced by sinister motives." In order to assist these victims of oppression, the society proposed in 1850 that they be given permission to employ a prison agent who "would probably be a means of restoring in some degree those illegal and inhuman schemes so often employed to the injury of those, who are ignorant or friendless."[24]

As members of the visiting committee of the Prison Society watched the untried department become ever more crowded over the next few years, they maintained their support of the prison agent idea. In the autumn of 1853, William J. Mullen, until then a relatively quiet member of the Prison Society, began visiting the prison daily as a member of the visiting committee. Fresh from political frustrations in the temperance and antislavery movements, Mullen lashed out at the aldermen, who, "scarcely responsible to any authority," committed persons "on every pretence, and in many instances without sufficient evidence." Prisoners waited for trial for an average of two months, sometimes as many as seven, pleasing "intemperate or malicious prosecutors" and enriching the committing magistrates. In his first two months of daily visiting, Mullen arranged the release of 122 prisoners.[25]

Mullen was clearly acting as the Prison Society had envisioned the prison agent would. The society had appointed one James Adamson an agent to assist discharged convicts in 1851, but he does not seem to have ever taken this job seriously. Mullen assumed his duties informally and also insisted that an agent was needed to care for the "unfortunate class" victimized by aldermen and irresponsible prosecutors. In January 1854, the society adopted rules for the office of prison agent and received the support of the quarter sessions judges. Mullen was elected as the first prison agent and was to be paid by the Prison Society through subscriptions raised from the public. By August the prison inspectors joined the society as official sponsors of William J. Mullen, prison agent.[26]

In addition to his political and propaganda activities, Mullen was still the only Moyamensing resident and the driving force on the Board of the Philadelphia Society for the Employment and Instruction of the Poor. He believed that the poverty in his midst was a result of "gross imposition" upon the area's population. These people, the object of his charitable efforts

> may almost be called bondsmen of certain depraved individuals upon whom they live in a helpless state of dependence; who are the purveyors of everything; who rent them the offal scrip, the basket or hand barrow, with which they are to earn their daily pittance; who buy from them the rags, bones, and glass or paper they collect in the streets, and pay them in broken victuals—their dainty food—the poisonous liquor which is to drown their cares, and their lodgings—the night's straw upon which they are to sleep off its fumes.[27]

A few others supported Mullen's perception of poverty as the fruit of a much larger web of economic dependence, a conclusion that Mullen no doubt had drawn from his experiences in the Industrial Union and other working-men's political activities. The Rosine Association supported this view from the narrower perspective of women and the causes that led to prostitution. Pay female labor better, redress the "unequal state of society," and prostitution would wither away. No woman who could support herself without having to sell herself would choose the immoral path, the Rosines believed.[28]

The emphasis on oppressive social and economic conditions and on the exploitation of the poor was absolutely central to Mullen's and other benevolent reformer's approach to criminal justice. In this view, there was little difference between abusive employers and landlords, liquor dealers and aldermen. All contributed to keeping the poor in rags, and all profited from it. Mullen connected criminal justice to poverty in a new way, as a cause rather than a consequence. Philanthropy thus had a direct role to play in the criminal justice process—to assist its victims just as it would the victims of any other form of exploitation.

Mullen was nothing if not a philanthropist. Since his experience on Committee of Fifteen in 1848, he had been president of the Industrial Union, the Independent Workingmen's Convention (which nominated Judge Kelley in 1851), the American Emigrant's Friend Society, and the Mullen Beneficial Temperance Society. He was also a member of the International Order of Good Samaritans and the Managers of the Moyamensing Soup Society; an official at the 1851 and 1852 National Industrial Congresses, an 1853 Prohibition Convention and Maine Law celebration, and various temperance, land reform, and antislavery meetings. He wrote popular temperance pamphlets, was active in the ten-hour movement, and ran for Congress on the Freedom and Democracy ticket in 1852.[29]

Mullen was one of the best examples of a middle-class reformer who was deeply concerned with the conditions of working people, no doubt because of his origins as a workingman himself. But as he moved out of the working class, his energies became directed less at labor's struggle against capital and more at the struggle against demoralizing habits and the plight of the poorest members of the working classes. No longer engaged in manual labor, Mullen found himself more comfortable with other philanthropists than with workingmen, more at ease in working to reclaim the oppressed poor from their victimizers than in helping self-motivated workers in battles against their employers. For Mullen, working-class radicalism moved easily into philanthropic benevolence; his intense humanism remained the same, but his relationship to those for whom he was working changed dramatically. Mullen went from comrade to benefactor and, in so doing, personified an essential aspect of the reform-minded middle class (tied to benevolent institutions and the state and allied with neither capital nor labor) that was just beginning to emerge as the nineteenth century passed its midpoint.[30]

Mullen, and the prison agency in general, also represented an increasingly popular new view of criminal justice. According to this view, poverty and dependence, on the one hand, and widespread corruption, on the other, had turned the minor judiciary into just another mechanism of oppression. The prison was filled with people who did not belong there, who had been delivered to its cells by corrupt officials and the system of private prosecution. Poor people needed not only to be saved from such injustice but also to be relieved from the economic dependence that had made them vulnerable to magisterial oppression in the first place. In order for the state, with the help of reformers, to achieve this, criminal justice would have to be controlled by independent officials outside of the traditional relationship of the minor judiciary and the citizenry. The prison agency created for William J. Mullen perfectly met this need for a change in the criminal justice system, a change that had been so ardently desired by Mullen and his associates a few years before when they were serving on the Committee of Fifteen. The prison agency was not merely a short-term expedient. Its supporters intended it to be a permanent fixture in the criminal justice system as long as the courts and prisons were dominated by poor people who were as much in need of relief as punishment. Official power had been given to a reformer which invested him and other officers of the court with the discretion that had until then been primarily held by aldermen and private litigants. Through the criminal justice system, the prison agent became one of the first benevolent reformers to assist the dependent poor directly through the state.

Consolidation

The inefficiency of the marshal's police and the insertion of antebellum social reformers into the criminal justice process had contradictory effects on criminal justice, but they both kept the spirit of consolidation alive in Philadelphia. When it came in 1854, consolidation of the independent districts of Philadelphia County into one city represented the impact, less direct but no less important, of yet another group of reformers on criminal justice.

Consolidation was designed to provide Philadelphia with some of the administrative resources and flexibility necessary to govern and service a big city. The coalition that brought the consolidation movement to fruition was the foundation of the countywide political organization that would take control of the new city after the event. The formation of this organization provoked conflict between the informal and localistic traditions of ward politics (best represented by aldermen and well illustrated by the conduct of private prosecution) and the metropolitan consciousness of those who supported citywide institutions. A battle between ward-based machine politicians and municipal reformers over the imposition of centralized government on the neighborhood-oriented but rapidly growing metropolis resulted in the compromise that was consolidation.

Its obvious consequence for criminal justice was the creation of a single, uniformed, citywide police force. This was, of course, the basis for most of the demands for consolidation in Philadelphia since the riots of 1844, but after 1850 this argument had lost some of its force. Despite its many problems, the marshal's police was relatively successful in meeting its mandate to stop major riots, at least at first. Judge Parsons, though still an advocate of consolidation, conceded early in 1851 that the marshal's force had "done more for the arrest of criminals, the preservation of good order, and the suppression of crime, than the whole police force of both city and county for the last five years." As late as February 1854, the eve of consolidation, the *Evening Bulletin* boasted that Philadelphia was "the quietest and most orderly city in the union." Opponents of consolidation gloated; there was "no longer any reason for consolidation . . . it will be wiser to 'let well alone.' "[31]

The practice of making blanket arrests for suspicion and disorderly conduct by the marshal's police, and their attendance at all fires, had a quieting influence. The police seized people at fires on charges of inciting to riot, either with words or deeds, and thereby aborted disturbances before they could develop. Sometimes it provoked bloody fights between the police and their intended prisoners, but the practice worked. For the first sixteen months of the force's existence, not a single fire company was declared out of service for riotous conduct, and throughout the four years of the force's existence, there was no repetition of the deadly full-scale rioting that marked the 1840s.[32]

However, there were, as we have seen, problems that surfaced rather quickly. The most damning from the consolidationists' perspective was the force's failure to put an end permanently to the smaller-scale violence of the fire companies. In the year between March 1852 and March 1853, the court declared ten companies out of service, as many as in the worst previous twelve months. During 1852 there were sixty-nine fire riots. Throughout the summer, fire riots were almost daily events. At summer's end, a grand jury revived the demand for the abolition of the volunteer system. Judge Kelley called it "one of the worst systems that can be imagined." Fear was again aroused that "rowdy fire companies will become the schools for the training of an "army of young rioters," which would result in "the corruption and ruin of the rising generation."[33]

Marshal Keyser responded to the grand jury by ordering policemen to arrest minors who ran with fire companies. They did so, and the courts often treated the young men harshly. Alderman Elkinton held ten boys to bail one day in August 1852; Judge Kelley sentenced seventeen to prison terms of from three to twelve months in December. When citizens requested that fire companies be disbanded for riotous conduct, the judges generally responded.[34]

Nevertheless, a variety of factors rendered the court's efforts ineffective. Too often to suit the bench, jurors acquitted defendants in riot cases. Disbanded fire companies continued to function. More important, the informal relations of the criminal justice process interfered. Aldermen occasionally settled fire riot cases without returning them to court or tried to dissuade private prosecutors in riot cases from pursuing criminal remedies. The quarter sessions judges implicated the police in this process as well. Judge Kelley cited the "indisposition of the Marshal's Police in reporting to the Court companies who violate the law" and lamented, that without the cooperation of the aldermen and police, justice could not be done even though "the Court had done its duty and the District Attorney had done his." At one moment of extreme exasperation, Kelley lashed out at the "utter inefficiency of the police in preventing disturbances and bringing offenders to justice."[35] "The remedy is with our citizens," declared one of the grand juries, in what became a monthly ritual of recommending replacement of the volunteer system with a centralized and salaried fire department. The jurors' reference to "citizens" did not mean the traditional reliance on private prosecution but the legislative remedy of consolidation and abolition of the volunteer fire companies.[36]

Professionalization of the fire department, like professionalization of the police, became one of the administrative demands of the metropolitanists who ushered in consolidation. Led by state senator and real estate lawyer Eli K. Price, advocates of consolidation never ceased their efforts even after they were thwarted by the creation of the marshal's police. Police reform never regained its place as their major issue, but all of their fundamental demands for improved and expanded city services were of a piece with it. Criminal court judges played their part in support of consolidation. A reform of the fire department "would be hailed by us . . . joyfully," the judges told one committee of citizens promoting the change. A successful consolidation movement would provide the basis for both an effective police force and a peaceful fire department.[37]

The metropolitan vision of supporters of consolidation was in direct opposition to the localism upon which private prosecution thrived. Consolidation rode to victory in the election campaign of 1853 primarily on Price's argument that Philadelphia needed to be unified, its city services streamlined and efficiently organized if it was to "sustain the rivalry of other cities seeking to absorb her trade, wealth and population." The residential districts and the commercial city would be joined in a new partnership; professional police and fire services would be joined by rationally organized and properly graded streets, a metropolitan board of health, and a single process of tax assessment and collection. And, not unimportant to the increasingly boosteristic spirit of the mid-nineteenth century, consolidation would make Philadelphia geographically the largest city in the union and make it second to New York in population.[38]

Before this spirit could prevail, however, the resistance to consolidation that had been so strong for years, especially in the suburbs, had to be overcome. It was never completely eliminated, of course, but several factors had combined by 1853 to undermine its strength. One was dismay at the continuing disorder of fire companies, another was the rising value of land in the suburbs, which blunted the argument that they would be financial liabilities for the wealthier city. Concessions made by consolidationists to the suburbs, such as a lower tax rate for rural areas and absorption of all existing debts, also helped. Perhaps most significant of all the factors, though, was the abating of purely political resistance. The fears held by both the Whigs, who dominated the city, and the Democrats, who dominated the suburbs, that the other party would gain control of the consolidated city weakened considerably as a result of the increasing strength of minor parties and the relative balance between the two major parties in the county as a whole. Both could now reasonably expect to attain power, and as it happened, both did within two years.[39]

Still worried about political resistance, however, consolidationists formed their own party at a mass meeting in July 1853 and chose a slate of candidates for the legislature. By the time the October elections rolled around, every party had endorsed consolidation, assuring a triumphant result. Immediately afterward, a committee of over one hundred citizens from throughout the county wrote a new city charter to present to the legislature. Sheriff Morton McMichael was the chairman, and most of the city's elite, including the judges, were members. Horace Binney finally gave up his opposition, admitting the necessity of order and conceding that the financial advantages to consolidation outweighed the political disadvantages. Eli K. Price, elected to the senate as a consolidationist candidate, was committed to guiding the bill through the legislature. In December the document was completed, and Price introduced it in the state senate. Two weeks later it passed. Twelve days later, under the guidance of Matthias W. Baldwin and William C. Patterson, also avowed consolidationists, it was passed by the assembly, despite the pleas of some officeholders from the county who feared for their jobs. On 2 February 1854, the Consolidation Act became law. Its long-time advocates beamed. Consolidation was, they exaggerated, "a striking rebuke to pot-house politicians, managers of conventions, tax-collectors and pullers of the small wires."[40]

The law directed the city councils to organize a police department and, if necessary, a fire department. The judges urged that both be done immediately, but the councils concentrated first on the police. The law provided that the marshal of police remain at the head of the department and the mayor appoint the policemen, but it left the size of the police force and its organization up to the councils. The councils ultimately decided upon an 820-man force, divided into fourteen police districts, corresponding to the ward divisions of the new city. This gave the city a better-organized but no larger police force than it had before. More important were the changes made in the minor judiciary. Consolidating the police led to the first reform of the structure and powers of the minor judiciary in over half a century. Councils were instructed to elect one alderman to serve as committing magistrate in each police district, at an annual salary of $500. Each district would also have a police lieutenant and two sergeants. All rules for the police were to be made by the mayor; each officer was also paid an annual salary of $500 and could accept no gratuities. In order to remove the foundation of the corrupt ties between the police and the aldermen, the Consolidation Act also provided that no aldermen could receive any fees in criminal cases.[41]

The first election for mayor of the consolidated city took place on 6 June 1854. The city triumphed over the districts in this contest, as Nativist-Whig Robert T. Conrad defeated Democrat Richard Vaux. Conrad, a former judge who was known for his sour demeanor, promised to appoint only nativists and no immigrants to the police. The rules established for the police retained the former instructions that officers should disperse and arrest idle and suspicious looking men, using familiarity, dress, age, and state of sobriety as their guides. The professional police, in the context of consolidation and the abolition of the fee system in criminal cases, was a major part of this early step in the "shift from a community experienced directly and informally to one that was perceived as a formal abstraction." The attempt to formalize the aldermen's relationship with the police, and the construction of ward boundaries that completely obliterated the ethnic and localistic identities of preconsolidation political communities, major examples of this, bore directly on the traditional practices of criminal prosecution.[42]

Though similar in important ways, consolidationist police reformers and prison reformers were quite different groups with different agendas. Also, neither group worked with a well-thought-out program. Still, they created two criminal justice institutions that were fundamentally unlike those in existence previously. The difference was the assumption that the police and the prison agent would take positive action as representatives of the state to implement social policy and activate the criminal justice process; they would neither wait for a citizen's complaint nor be dependent on a citizen's fee.

Yet the people who would be on the receiving end of the actions of these two new agencies—the surveillance and suppression of the police, the benevolence of the prison agent—were precisely the same people who had so avidly used the criminal courts under the system of private prosecution. The "rebuked" politicians were often the very aldermen whose neighborhood bases and primary source of legal income seemingly had been destroyed. Neither group simply acquiesced to these changes. The very process of enacting consolidation anticipated this since, in order to gain the support of the politicians, consolidationists held out the promise of the ever bigger rewards that would be forthcoming from control of the larger wards and, perhaps, even the consolidated city. Among the first politicians to benefit from this bargain were the fourteen aldermen who would be chosen police magistrates. Consolidation's triumph, then, was also its compromise. Despite the importance of the changes made since 1850, the old battle lines had not disappeared. Party politics and criminal justice in Philadelphia were about to enter a new stage, but with alderman, policemen, and private prosecutors still major players.[43]

Part IV The Decline of Private Prosecution

8. The Impact of Consolidation

Almost immediately after the consolidated police began service, officers established a relationship with the police magistrates which rested squarely on the experience of the marshal's police and its predecessors. Like the earlier pattern of primary justice in police cases, its informality resembled private prosecution, but its greatest importance was that it cemented a link between the minor judiciary and the police which would more than rival private prosecution.

On the whole consolidation was, in many ways, illusory. Its success depended in large part on the acquiescence of the same politicians whose activities it had been designed to control. Building on the old practices of primary justice, aldermen remained in control of criminal prosecution, profiting now from police cases in ways unheard of before. Building on the formerly submerged aspects of police authority, the police carved out a new arena of law enforcement in the city's streets. The procedures of ward politics intensified with the rise of a citywide political machine. As a result, the police became closely tied to both the existing structure of primary justice and the new structure of urban politics, the courts moved even further out of the control of the judges and grand jurors, and the administration of justice was anything but a tidy matter.

It was, therefore, not long before the reformers were busy again. Prodded by some of the aldermen themselves, reformers developed a logic that saw private prosecution as the root of the new problems of criminal justice and disempowering private prosecutors as the solution. This would, they hoped, further both the rise of the administrative state and the decline of machine politics, but as some aldermen already understood, and as time would tell, it would primarily further only the former.[1]

The Police and the Aldermen

The city was divided into fourteen police districts in 1854, and the new police began service late that fall. They worked on a rotating schedule of day and night patrols, with two-thirds of the officers on night duty.[2] The police department was slightly reorganized several times over the next two decades.

In 1855 the number of policemen was reduced from 820 to 650, the number of police districts was increased to 16, and the number of committing magistrates was reduced to 1 in each police district.[3] Afterwards, as the city grew, so did the number of police districts. A seventeenth district was carved out of the first two districts in 1866; an eighteenth was created in 1867. Small forces of harbor police and park police were created in 1860.[4] The number of regular police then remained stable until the force was reorganized under Mayor William S. Stokley in 1871. He increased the number of patrolmen to 1,000, the number of districts to 24, and reorganized the structure of command.[5]

Instructed by their nativist leader, Mayor Robert T. Conrad, to maintain a policy of aggressive patrolling and arrest for minor, especially liquor-related, offenses, the new police had an immediate impact on the city. Even in the absence of the fee system, the new committing magistrates found their offices more lucrative than ever before, thanks to the great number of arrests inspired by Mayor Conrad in 1855. Blaming crime on "perverted immigration," Conrad gave the police blanket authority to arrest people who were considered likely to run afoul of the law. "The only police worth the cost of its maintenance . . . should be a system overspreading and guarding the whole community, rendering it impossible, or most dangerous, to attempt the commission of crime." He ordered the lieutenants in each district to suppress all "policy houses, disorderly public houses, gambling houses, club houses, dance houses, houses of ill fame, and other places where inebriates, minors and known violators of the law assemble," warning that "those who neglected to take the proper steps to bring offenders to justice would do so at the risk of their places." The mayor also instructed his officers to disperse all groups loitering on street corners and arrest as disorderly anyone who resisted. He even attempted to seize police reports and shield them from from the view of reporters in order to "prevent the public from knowing what the officers . . . were doing."[6]

Conrad's new policemen went to work with understandable zeal. During their first year of service, they made arrests at the rate of one hundred per day, far exceeding past practices and prompting immediate criticism.[7] Just five days after entering service, a posse of police raided and disrupted a German festival; the *Ledger* immediately blamed the mayor's nativism. During the following month, a case reached the quarter sessions that involved Conrad's instructions to disperse groups in the streets. An officer demanded that three men who were talking quietly in front of the home of one disperse, but they refused. The officer arrested one man on an unspecified charge. Judge Kelley of the quarter sessions discharged the man, placed the costs on the officer, and said that "he had never heard of a more gross outrage upon the rights of American citizens." A common council member accused the police the next summer of repeatedly making improper arrests and engaging in the virtual entrapment of citizens; he concluded that "the course of the policemen was calculated to increase crime, by oppressing the people."[8]

Such emphatic direct criticism of the police diminished after the first few years, but it never entirely disappeared. Prison Agent William J. Mullen, who in 1855 began pursuing the release of people "unfairly or improperly" imprisoned, was a major source of continued complaint. In the winter of 1858, Mullen persuaded the Prison Society to form a committee to investigate the "misconduct" of a Lieutenant Sawyer, one of "several instances" of police misconduct of which he had become aware. His reports to the society repeatedly accused policemen of perjury and "many remarkable cases . . . of improper arrest." As early as 1861, he prompted the PSAMPP to remark in its influential journal that "the police . . . is open to bribery and corruption." In January 1862, even the *Ledger* wondered whether the police arrested "a great number of innocent persons" and, a few days later, reproached the many officers who "seem to think that no discrimination is required of them in making an arrest, but that they can beat and maul any citizen . . . provided he considers it proper to make the arrest."[9]

When critics of the police looked for a reason behind all of the improper arrests, they looked first to the corrupt ties between police officers and the aldermen rather than to the ideal of a preventive police force. The councilman who described police oppression also pointed out how aldermen cooperated with the police by settling the cases resulting from improper arrests. Repeatedly, reformers and grand jurors stated the belief that policemen and aldermen had conspired to arrest and imprison poor people. One jury remarked in November 1855 that "some system is in operation among the Aldermen and Police of this city, whereby this thing is done, which is not only a heavy expense to the city, but a great injustice to the person imprisoned." When the Reverend Benjamin Sewell tried to interfere with this "system" following the fatal beating of an improperly arrested black girl in 1858, he claimed that he could find no alderman who would give the suspected officer more than a "mock hearing." Prison Agent Mullen bluntly charged that aldermen paid policemen to arrest repeatedly released convicts so that they could keep extorting money from them.[10]

In August 1858, one group of reformers felt it had discovered the basis of the link between aldermen and policemen in the practices of private prosecution. Policemen, they claimed, had "monopolized" the business of serving criminal warrants by neglecting their duties and instead attending aldermen's offices in order to obtain warrants. But if old habits lingered, reformers were just as certain that policemen and aldermen were developing new ones. Probably the most explicit lament about the unfortunate consequences of their relationship was made by Rosine Association members in 1855; they commented that disorderly conduct arrests covered "a multitude of transgressions or misfortune," but most often were the result of "merely the cupidity of the policeman and alderman, who hoped each to get a dollar from the unfortunate one, or through some sympathizing friend, for their release."[11]

Critics, however, never entertained the notion that there were also favorable consequences of informal justice, nor were they able to demonstrate that policemen actually profited from corruption in arrests for minor offenses. It remains unclear whether policemen made so many arrests because of corruption or simply because they were expected to do so by their supporters and superiors. Of course, these were hardly incompatible motives, and there was still considerable suggestive evidence that at least aldermen did profit from these arrests. One manner in which they did so involved an entirely new form of illegality.

After 1854 aldermen were required to pay into the city treasury all fines and fees they collected from the cases they heard. According to their critics, they rarely ever did so. In August 1855, a court reporter asked, "What becomes of the fees" in all the new drunkenness arrests? Neither aldermen nor policemen were entitled to the fees chargeable to arrested drunks, but magistrates were still collecting the $1.25 to $2.50 in costs prescribed by the fee bill. The reporter implied that they either kept the money or shared it with the arresting officers.[12]

During the next two decades, critics looked at the amounts actually paid to the city and asserted their charges more boldly. Complaints that aldermen kept fees improperly became regular features of reformers' and journalists' accounts of aldermen's activities. The *Ledger*, in November 1855, estimated the average daily fees for drunkenness alone at $150, but Prison Agent Mullen reported that the total amount paid by the aldermen in 1855 for all cases was only $900! Only a handful of aldermen submitted any money to the city each month in 1857, and just $3,662.36 was paid into the treasury by aldermen in 1858. "The law requiring committing magistrates to pay to the city treasury all fines and penalties received by them monthly appears to be nearly obsolete," stated the *Ledger* after only three magistrates made returns for June 1862. By August 1864, the editors commented that the payment law was "disregarded by nearly all the magistrates in the city"; $27 had been received by the treasurer since January.[13] Returning fees to the city treasury would have meant that aldermen could not keep even those fees that previously had been legal. This was one innovation of 1854 that they steadfastly resisted.

If there were new charges of corruption that hinted at the expansion of informal justice, there were old ones as well. According to one critique, aldermen were still guilty of extorting illegal payments for a release from people they had imprisoned, only now it was for the new, but still nonexistent, charge of "drunk and disorderly." By the summer of 1855, the prison inspectors specifically attributed prison crowding to the fact that "many of the Aldermen commit drunken and disorderly individuals . . . for thirty days, when the law directs that drunkards shall be imprisoned for twenty-four hours." In December a new board of inspectors adopted a regulation prohibiting the discharge of persons committed for drunk and disorderly conduct without the endorsement of one of the inspectors. They noted that "there are but few of the committing magistrates who commit for drunkenness"; most made thirty-day commitments and charged between $1 and $5 for a release, depending on the resources of the prisoner.[14]

The situation that resulted was similar to the one prevailing before 1854, but now on a much larger scale. Many of those arrested who should legally have been committed for either drunkenness or vagrancy were instead committed without a specific sentence or for thirty days as drunk and disorderly. The police clearly provided the opportunity for the concoction of this new charge. Drunk and disorderly commitments were negligible before 1855; in 1856 they accounted for 21 percent of the total. According to Mullen, "It is believed in all cases, where commitments are for a certain and definite period, the record of convictions upon the Alderman's docket is altogether defective, and the defendants falsely imprisoned." Critics charged that aldermen preferred thirty-day commitments over simple drunkenness commitments because this gave magistrates the opportunity to generate income equal to that which by law was "allowed to six of them."[15]

There is no certain way to gauge the actual extent of aldermanic extortion in these cases. One way to get a glimpse of it is to examine how those committed for thirty days were released. If the critics were correct, those who paid were released by the committing magistrate, and those who did not pay were released in some other fashion. Most of those committed for thirty days and not discharged by the committing magistrate were released before the expiration of their terms by the prison inspectors.[16] The average time that prisoners served for drunk and disorderly conduct after 1854 was only five days; however, the inspectors released 64 percent of them, and the committing magistrates released only 23 percent. If extortion existed, or was intended, it was not successful as often as critics implied.

Nevertheless, the informal processing of arrests and commitments for minor crime was always a central feature of police prosecution after consolidation, and court officials could do little to change it. By 1869 aldermen had long since resumed making prison commitments for unspecified misdemeanors and the nonexistent offense of breach of the peace, as well as for drunk and disorderly. In order to relieve the prison of inmates and the court of the pressure of prison cases, Judge F. Carroll Brewster instructed the inspectors in 1869 not to receive prisoners committed for such general offenses as misdemeanor or breach of the peace unless the specific criminal act was described on the commitment and not to discharge prisoners unless they were released before the return of the case to court and with the consent of the prosecutor. As a result, such commitments, which had risen to 43 percent of the total in 1868, fell precipitously, and simple drunkenness commitments increased from 12 percent in 1868 to 19 percent in 1869.

An unintended effect of the judge's instructions was that the inspectors ceased discharging persons committed for breach of the peace because the inspectors took the order to mean that such commitments were indictable offenses, not that they were entirely improper. As a result, aldermen began making more breach of the peace commitments than ever before. These grew from 4 percent of all commitments in 1868 to 25 percent in 1870. Time served was nearly identical to that for drunk and disorderly, just over five days, but magistrates discharged half of these prisoners, and the inspectors discharged only 40 percent.[17] Critics believed breach of the peace commitments were simply replacements for the drunk and disorderly commitments, "retaining under [the magistrates'] control very many cases which were not really breaches of the peace."[18]

The confused inspectors asked the court for clarification in 1870. Judge Joseph Allison repeated the requirement that commitments specify the criminal act for which the prisoner was accused. He explicitly stated that drunk and disorderly meant nothing more than simple intoxication and that breach of the peace by itself "does not indicate anything for which any one can be committed or held."[19] Drunk and disorderly commitments decreased after this communication from the court, but the judge's advice seemed to have no effect on breach of the peace commitments, which reached 35 percent of the total by 1872. Although many of these minor offenses continued to be private prosecutions, the new police clearly provided aldermen with the opportunity to extend the old web of informal justice, to cement the practices developed during the first half of the century within the new world of preventative policing, and thus to make this new world not so unfamiliar after all.

Order after Consolidation

Although the operation of primary justice remained familiar, the practice of law enforcement on the street changed after 1854. During the first few years, the younger, stronger, and bolder policemen developed new practices and techniques of patrol and arrest, in response to both the instructions of their superiors and resistance from the objects of their attention. These new methods of state initiation of the criminal justice process were reinforced by the magistrates and contrasted sharply with the nonpoliced process of private prosecution. Resistance to arrests underscored the contrast. It was the popular mode of criticism of the police, a reflection of the fact that some portion of the population did not welcome the new form of law enforcement and that, despite the informality of primary justice, police prosecution threatened to upset the familiar world of private prosecution.

The number of drunkenness arrests after 1854 was so great that routine cases of drunkenness disappeared from the reports from the magistrates' offices. Only unusual cases or cases that led to more serious charges drew notice—the young mother from out of town, clutching her child and pleading with the magistrate to let her return home after being found drunk in the street (he refused), or the man dressed as a soldier who was able to prove his sobriety to Alderman Kerr by dancing about on his two artificial legs.[20]

Police violence became a regular feature of drunkenness arrests. In fact, the *Ledger*'s editors believed that, by 1872, excessively violent arrests of intoxicated people had become "typical of a class" of policemen, "the men who upon merest whim, or the slightest show of resistance, fly into a gust of passion, pull out their revolvers and make a serious affray out of what might have been passed off as an unimportant incident."[21]

Second in frequency to drunkenness arrests were arrests for disorderly conduct or disorderly houses. These cases directly reflected the mandate given the police to maintain public order. Sometimes as the result of a citizen complaint, sometimes without a stated reason, posses of police officers raided houses and saloons in which alleged disorderly persons were supposed to congregate. Usually they rounded up a substantial number of people in these raids—65 in a February 1855 raid, 52 in a March 1862 raid, 40 in a May 1869 raid. The police charged the proprietors or residents with operating a disorderly house and the others with disorderly conduct. Magistrates and judges usually held them all to bail to keep the peace, and those who could not afford the bail were sent to prison in lieu of payment.[22]

There were a number of important new variants on disorderly conduct after 1854. Isolated disorderly conduct arrests were now more common, the result of arguments, fights, and threatening public behavior. These arrests resulted, as before, in controversial prison commitments, often in lieu of bail to keep the peace, and occasionally in a return to the criminal court.[23] Corner-lounging by young men was another variant of disorderly conduct, which the police listed under a separate heading and usually accounted for no more than 2 percent of all arrests. The one exception to this occurred in 1866 when Mayor Morton McMichael, a veteran of battles with youth gangs, instructed the police to take special measures against corner loungers. Arrests that year numbered 715, up from 362 the year before. The end of the war probably aggravated the problem, and the mayor was hoping to nip it in the bud to set the tone for the postwar era. Corner-lounging arrests were generally the result of premeditated police swoops; as in disorderly house cases, magistrates held those arrested to bail for good behavior or simply discharged them with a reprimand.[24]

After 1854 vagrancy arrests still led to thirty-day prison commitments by magistrates or, in the case of children, to commitments to the house of refuge. Nevertheless, these cases were among the most varied and controversial. Most vagrants continued to be homeless drunkards, found sleeping outdoors, who were carted off to the magistrate and then prison, sometimes in large numbers and occasionally one at a time. However, the average time served by vagrants after 1854 fell to only fourteen days, suggesting either stepped-up aldermanic release practices, the intervention of the inspectors, or both.[25] During the initial administration of Mayor Conrad, this group also included prostitutes. Conrad urged the police to raid houses of prostitution and arrest streetwalkers. Large-scale arrests occurred several times during his administration. Magistrates discharged or held a number of prostitutes to bail, but they committed most to prison as vagrants.[26]

The two most controversial types of vagrancy cases involved "professional thieves"—usually pickpockets—and children. The demands of preventive policing required that policemen keep watch on the places in which thefts usually occurred—theaters, railroad depots, and hotels—and remember the faces of those previously arrested, but the police had no legal grounds on which to apprehend people before the commission of a crime. So, under instructions from their commanders, they arrested suspected thieves for vagrancy. This proved to be ineffective, however, because most thieves had enough money to bail themselves out or could obtain a release on a writ of habeas corpus by showing that they "did not come within the meaning of the law of vagrancy." As a result, the legislature passed a "professional thieves" law in March 1862, which allowed a magistrate to commit known pickpockets found in crowds to prison for ninety days.[27]

Arrests under the March 1862 professional thieves law were unique since magistrates could only make summary convictions without returning the prisoners to court. They amounted to about 2 percent of the cases heard by the committing magistrate at the central station, who had been chosen by the mayor to hear them all. The prisoner could appeal to the quarter sessions, but the judges upheld commitments unless the prisoner could offer proof that he had reformed. Alderman Beitler, who presided in the central station during the law's first years, often released persons arrested under this law because they were not apprehended in a crowd. He futilely appealed to the legislature to expand the law to allow arrests in "hotels, at private auctions, in uncrowded passenger cars. . . . I do not believe [thieves] are entitled to any privileges under the Constitution."[28]

Arrests of children were the most controversial of the vagrancy cases. Although clearly warranted by the police's orders, this was one area in which faulty police judgment prompted direct objections. The line between poverty and vagrancy was thin. When the police mistook poor children for beggars, the vulnerability of the poor to preventive policing was exposed. Parents protested the affront, and judges supported them by issuing strict guidelines to the police. Problems arose after Mayor Alexander Henry established a division of beggar detectives in October 1858 because of "the increase of vagrancy and street begging, mostly by children." In just a few months, these officers arrested 80 children and 70 adults; by the end of 1859, they had arrested 936 children. Of these, 205 were sent to institutions. Not all parents were pleased by this, however, and several times in 1859 they attempted to have their children released from the house of refuge on writs of habeas corpus. In most of these cases, the parents insisted that they could support their children and that the child was not begging but, because of unusual circumstances, going under instructions to ask a neighbor for some urgently needed item. When Judge James Ludlow released several such children in February 1859, he warned the police that they must be sure that there is "no doubt or difficulty as to the precise character of the child they arrest. . . . There should be evidence of a long continued habit of begging. . . . Officers should be extremely cautious."[29] Arrests by the beggar detectives fell off considerably after 1859, usually to two or three hundred a year. Nevertheless, objections to arrests by policemen and commitments by magistrates continued. The *Ledger's* police reporter remarked in March 1863 that "there seems to be a great lack of discretion among policemen, and this is nowhere made more apparent than in the arrest of children, charged with being vagrants," but in these cases, as in all the minor police cases, there was no way to prevent policemen and aldermen from exercising their powers. Several times during these years, the managers of the house of refuge lamented the fact that "many children are discharged in a short time after their admission, owing to illegality in the commitments."[30]

This obvious fact—"illegality in the commitments"—typified minor police cases, but there was also another, if secondary, aspect of police work: the investigation of indictable crime and the apprehension of serious criminals. This also, if with more difficulty, fit into the culture of informal justice and inspired criticism of the police and the aldermen.

After consolidation, the new police made arrests for indictable offenses in greater numbers than ever before. Although arrests for indictable crimes accounted for less than 30 percent of the total, they were the most controversial of all because they were a clear departure from past practices. These were the very cases that had formerly been rare and that demonstrated precisely what was different about a policed city.

Arrests for misdemeanors, suspicion, and assault and battery best illustrate this. Misdemeanors covered a wide range of unspecified acts below that of felony, and allowed magistrates to commit people to prison for an indictable offense without having to specify the act. The inspectors could not discharge prisoners in these cases, so the magistrates, according to Prison Agent Mullen, were easily able to "succeed in coercing the payment of costs, after which the case is never returned to court."[31] Suspicion arrests were important because officers were expressly urged by superiors to make such arrests. Prison Agent Mullen felt the need to interfere in suspicion commitments because many of the prisoners spent long periods awaiting trial, the prosecuting officers being unable to garner evidence easily on which to base a case. Indeed, Mullen thought these cases were a "monstrous thing" and was supported in his belief by the PSAMPP, which suggested "that the practice of arresting without special charge, is doing more harm than good." Most of these arrests involved people observed acting in a "suspicious manner," either loitering in places in which they could commit a theft or attempting to gain entry to a home, office, or store. Some were searched and found with items that suggested felonious intent, such as keys, burglar's tools, or inappropriate items of clothing. Aldermen committed the suspect to prison in nearly every instance.[32]

Charges of larceny resulting from suspicion arrests were also an object of criticism. Ranging between 4 and 5 percent of all arrests, larceny cases were the second largest category of arrests for indictable offenses.[33] Judge Joseph Allison warned policemen not to continue their "constant habit of arresting parties to search them," but this did not seem to have much effect. Sometimes policemen found stolen goods, sometimes they did not. Nevertheless policemen confiscated whatever they found.[34] As in years past, the majority of larceny arrests were for the theft of very small amounts of property. Usually a policeman caught the culprit in the act or in possession of the stolen property. The prison agent intervened in some of the most extreme instances—a woman held for six weeks for stealing 23 cents, a boy arrested for picking up a piece of rope in the street—but many more larceny suspects were committed and their cases returned to court for trial.[35]

Assault and battery arrests, extremely uncommon before 1854, were now the most frequent of those for indictable offenses, usually 5 to 6 percent of the total. Arrests occurred when officers happened upon fights or were called to public houses to stop disturbances or to remove unruly patrons. Assault and battery arrests also often resulted from hostile encounters between policemen and citizens. Mullen suggested that policemen frequently arrested the wrong person in fights and that on occasion the officers were actually the guilty parties.[36]

Foremost among the questionable assault and battery arrests were those that reporters called arrests for "angry words or impudent remarks." Judges told policemen, "It is a great mistake to suppose that such a circumstance justifies an arrest," and reporters repeated that advice whenever they noted such a case.[37] Arrests like these, and others as well, sometimes led to violence between the officer and prisoner and to private prosecutions against the arresting officer. People charged policemen with assault and battery when they believed that they were arrested either illegally or with the use of excessive force. In most of the reported cases, magistrates held the officer to bail for a trial, though such philanthropists as the Reverend Sewell claimed that aldermen who would hold a violent policeman were hard to find. Judge Allison, in a charge to the jury in a police violence case in 1868, stated that policemen encountering resistance to arrest must call for assistance before using violence and were justified in using personal violence only if the prisoner had a weapon. If an officer used unjustified violence, the prisoner could lawfully resist it.[38]

Also common were cases of assaults on policemen. Many of these began as charges leveled by the officers at citizens who resisted what they felt were unjust arrests. At trial, if the officer was found to have acted justly, the prisoner was convicted, but, as an 1855 grand jury noted, "The officers were, in many instances, shown to be the parties in the wrong." Judges in the trials of these cases also instructed jurors that officers should make arrests only if citizens were obviously breaking a law—drunks who were not disorderly should be taken home, not to jail—and repeated the point that only minimal necessary force was lawful.[39]

Policemen were also victims of the violence of those they were not attempting to arrest. These attacks were occasionally unprovoked; at other times they occurred at riots or lesser public disturbances. Most of them, however, were the result of an outsider's attempt to keep the prisoner from being conveyed to the stationhouse. Officers had to escort their prisoners to the station on foot, and this often gave friends and neighbors enough time to gather and attempt a rescue. These attempts often succeeded, and officers were sometimes seriously injured. All such violence, and there was a remarkably large amount of it at first, expressed the distrust of an essentially self-policing people of the new professional police. That the violence lasted, if on a somewhat diminished scale, reflected, in part, the inherent antagonism between the police and those they were charged to control and, in part, the persistence of the culture and values associated with private prosecution.[40]

The professionalization of the police had the impact on case initiation and primary justice which might have been predicted in 1854. Despite their imposing new presence, the authority of the police remained greatest on the streets, where their primary mandate was located. The magistracy supported this, and it was one of the two major new characteristics of the policed city. The other was the lucrative and equally imposing tie between magistrates and policemen, built on many of the traditional features of primary justice. These changes shifted the balance in criminal justice between state and private prosecution, though not in the way most reformers had hoped. As a result, the initial stages of criminal prosecution remained an arena of considerable uncertainty and controversy.

The Court's Continuing Woes

The courts of record did not fare much better in the aftermath of consolidation. Now laboring under an impossible case load, judges and grand jurors tried harder, but with little more success, to control the criminal justice process. The number of cases submitted to grand juries reached new heights in the years immediately following consolidation, as many as 1,532 in August 1857. Grand jurors duly noted the "appalling amount of misdemeanor and crime in our city." Some of it was caused by the depression beginning in 1857, and the number of cases abated with the coming of the Civil War, but after the war, the numbers increased to the high prewar levels. Jurors reacted with horror to an 1866 proposal that aldermen be required to return all misdemeanors to court, fearing that the consequence of such a law would be an intolerable number of criminal cases. Many observers believed that overwork had helped cause the death of Judge Oswald Thompson earlier that year at the age of fifty-seven. By the late 1860s and early 1870s, the number of bills per year routinely exceeded 5,000. According to a leading student of Philadelphia's courts, "by 1870, a crisis in the courts of Philadelphia had developed. . . . The Court . . . was hard pressed to keep abreast of its work."[41]

The reason for this was the increase in state-initiated cases and the persistence of widespread private prosecution. Between 1854 and 1874, the major weapon used by grand jurors to discourage petty prosecutions was still the power to place the court costs in ignored cases on the prosecutors. Judges told grand jurors that "by far the largest number of cases which will be submitted to you belong to a class originating in private spite. With those public justice has no concern. Criminal courts were not created to foment or to pander to either malice or extortion. We do not sit for the collection of bad debts or the accumulation of costs. All cases which fall within this category should be promptly ignored and the prosecutors ordered to pay the costs." Such an approach would "teach a few prosecutors not to repeat a costly experiment."[42]

However, despite the bench's unmixed resolve in favor of putting costs on prosecutors, "sometimes" the costs were paid "from the pockets of the prosecutor or defendant, but most generally from the county." Grand jurors, in practice, put costs on prosecutors in only 12 percent of ignored cases, down from 32 percent between 1838 and 1854. In assault and battery cases, the proportion fell from 52 to 16 percent, even though the percentage of assault and battery cases submitted and ignored was higher than since before the abolition of the mayor's court. Placing costs on prosecutors became virtually nonexistent in larceny cases.[43]

It is not clear why the practice diminished just when it was apparently most needed. With private prosecution still thriving and the police receiving something less than an enthusiastic welcome form the citizenry, the court was still faced with the delicate problem of encouraging reliance on the law while discouraging abuse of the law. There was also the problem of collecting costs from poor prosecutors, which made jurors feel it was futile to charge them with costs. The most likely reason was simply that so many cases were abandoned by prosecutors that the grand jurors were left with no place to put the costs. So, despite the judges' urgings, the use of costs to discourage prosecutions failed to free the courts from the burden of unsubstantiated cases.[44]

Judges also urged petit jurors in acquittals to discourage future cases by placing the costs on the prosecutors, occasionally announcing in advance that absent prosecutors would certainly be made liable for the costs. Judges, grand jurors, and reporters were especially excited by an 1859 law that empowered jurors to divide the costs between the defendant and prosecutor. The act was based on the notion that, in many trial cases, both parties were to blame for the case's coming to court, and that was why jurors could not charge the prosecutor with the costs. It would be a perfect way to acquit people of crime and punish them for going to law. As late as 1867, reporters called it "a favorite mode" of resolving cases.[45]

This power was, however, used less widely by petit juries than it was by grand juries. Overall, the county paid the costs in 91 percent of all acquittals; defendants, in 3 percent; and prosecutors, in 4 percent. Juries split the costs in but 1.4 percent of acquittals, all of them assault and battery cases. Here too there is no clear explanation of why jurors used their cost-placing power less at the very time that they were urged to use it more. One can only assume that it was often a futile exercise if the parties were absent or too poor to pay. Committing people in default would only increase the county's expenses and further crowd the prison. Once again, the conflicting pressures of criminal justice kept the court powerless to control the people who were using it.[46]

If jurors were unable to sustain a resolve to discourage private prosecution after 1854, perhaps they were influenced by continuing judicial ambivalence about the process. For example, in an effort to clear the court calendar of cases in which prosecutors had lost interest, Judge James Ludlow decided, in March 1859, to try assault and battery cases only when the prosecutor appeared, obtained a warrant, and brought the defendant into court. This experiment was short-lived, for just a few months later, the familiar complaints of nonattending parties reappeared. A September 1859 grand jury thought the problem rested at their stage of the process, and its members recommended that the court adopt a practice that they claimed had been used by Judge Edward King in years past and was similar to the one Ludlow had instituted only months before. King reportedly put all private prosecutions under his control and released them only when specifically requested to do so by the prosecutor. Otherwise, the case was never even presented to the grand jury.[47] King's solution, which received little attention during his time, spared the grand jury from having to consider cases it would otherwise have ignored, but it was wholly in keeping with the prepolice culture that emphasized citizen control over criminal justice. Discretion over whether to pursue a case remained with the private parties, and the public prosecutor remained insignificant.

Ludlow addressed only the trial and not the grand jury stage of the proceedings. His reluctance to allow private citizens to determine which cases would be presented to the grand jury was perhaps influenced by the increased authority of the district attorney. Nevertheless, Ludlow and other court officials still supported the traditional practice. The fee system and an 1866 law allowing private counsel to replace the public prosecutor were the most obvious expressions of the continuing strength of private prosecution. Even as late as 1872, a worried grand jury remarked that "unfortunately, we are too much accustomed to consider that laws will execute themselves, or that officers of the law should become public prosecutors."[48]

The quarter sessions was, as a result, permanently in arrears after the Civil War. An 1866 grand jury noted that, because of the unprecedented number of cases presented to them and the preceding grand jury, "many of the cases yet remain untried, and must necessarily go over to the next term of the Court." They thought that there was enough work to occupy five instead of the three judges who then comprised the court. During the early 1870s, judges regularly called special court sessions in order to deal with untried cases, both recently returned cases and those held over for longer periods. Nearly five hundred cases were heard in one special session at the beginning of 1871, many of them "a year or more old." These sessions were able to process cases faster than regular sessions, largely because of the absence or indifference of the parties involved.[49]

Even worse, the court's conviction rate fell precipitously. Judge F. Carroll Brewster lamented, "Only one person out of every ten whose cases will come before [the grand jury] is really guilty." Another judge preferred to make the point that only one out of every seventy-six persons arrested was guilty. However they illustrated the point, they all believed that a court that could not bring cases to final judgment was a court in trouble.[50]

The failure of magistrates to return cases was an especially vexing cause of this trouble because it effectively prevented the court from exercising any authority. Often the result of private settlements between aldermen and the parties, but sometimes simply the result of oversights, unreturned cases had the troubling effect of either allowing a defendant to go free or keeping a defendant incarcerated for an indefinite period. The court focused on them now because of the activities of the PSAMPP's new prison agent and a provision of the Consolidation Act which required magistrates to make their returns at least ten days in advance of each term. Both oversights and settlements had occurred repeatedly by early 1855, dashing the hopes of those who had put their faith in the new law.

Several times during the late 1850s, judges summoned delinquent magistrates to court and threatened them with prosecution, but the threats, and even periodic indictments, were not sufficient to keep magistrates abreast of the law. The same threats had to be issued from the bench during the 1860s. In 1869 Judge Brewster publicly examined at least seven aldermen who had failed to make returns, heard their largely lame excuses, warned them that "before the ink is dry on the commitment you ought to make a return of the case," and stated his intention to have them prosecuted in the future.[51]

Whatever success the judges had in forcing the aldermen to return cases only intensified other problems. Aldermen settled many cases after a commitment or return to court, and prosecutors then failed to appear before the grand jury. Why should an aldermen settle a case before a return when he could do so afterwards and thereby generate more income, especially when judges were threatening to punish aldermen who failed to make returns?[52] Frustrated by the dilemma in which it was placed, an 1859 grand jury requested that the district attorney refuse to submit cases likely to be dismissed to them, but the time for this solution had not yet arrived. The fee system and political connections of the district attorney still prevented him from exercising such discretion, and the court found itself in a hopeless bind.[53]

As a result, they continued to do only what they could, which was to proceed rapidly and dismiss many cases. By the late 1860s, because of the many defendants awaiting trial in prison and the continuing tide of cases, judges began urging grand jurors in unambivalent terms to process cases quickly and ignore as many as possible. Judge Brewster was among the clearest, in April 1869, when he told a grand jury that it was "imperative upon you to set your faces against all petty cases in which you find there is no foundation for an accusation" except malice or spite.[54] To speed the processing of cases, the court also instituted double sessions. Begun in early 1858, the practice became much more prevalent after the opening of the new courtroom and the addition of a fourth judge to the quarter sessions bench in 1867 even though regular sessions were held monthly instead of bimonthly starting that same year. Nonetheless, the burden of cases remained overwhelming.[55]

Finally, the judges tried to ensure the attendance of parties and witnesses at trials by issuing subpoenas, or "bench warrants," and having the tipstaves deliver them to the people whose attendance they desired. Sometimes this worked, and the court that had to adjourn early one day would be bustling with business the next. Other times it had no effect, and the court had to postpone cases or declare defendants not guilty. Even when the court succeeded in forcing people to attend, though, it was plagued by abuse. Tipstaves received 62 cents for each bench warrant they served on people who failed to answer a subpoena. Because of the crowded courtroom, many people who answered subpoenas were forced to wait outside until their case was called. This sometimes caused a few minutes delay before the person called actually entered the room. Tipstaves took this delay as evidence of nonresponse, rushed outside the room, served the warrant, and collected the fee. Occasionally they served a warrant without the prior issuance of a subpoena, and the ignorant individual who was served, supposing this was a legitimate process, paid the fee. One court reporter concluded that "no little suffering among the poor people who may be called to attend the court" was the consequence.[56]

So, in the wake of consolidation, the courts of record remained as plagued as ever by the practices associated with private prosecution and additionally burdened by the overwhelming volume of cases. Judges and grand jurors became increasingly frustrated, and as a result, they became sympathetic to reformers concerned about the excesses of the police, but especially preoccupied with the widening power of the aldermen. In part because of the priorities of judges and grand jurors, as the reformers developed their new critique of criminal prosecution, they focused increasingly on the link between aldermen and private prosecutors.

The Revival of Reform

If the court's exasperation with private prosecution prompted reformers to concentrate on that aspect of criminal justice after 1854, so did the enhanced power of politicians. Local authorities remained powerful in consolidated Philadelphia, but now some of their power stemmed from their connections to citywide institutions. A good example was the aldermen's increased reliance on the police. While, in the short run, this only intensified the informal culture of criminal justice characteristic of private prosecution, it also made this culture more anomalous by establishing an alternative mode of prosecution that was even more enriching for those aldermen who were most closely linked to the police. So, as the troubles of criminal justice prompted another campaign to reform primary justice, the politicians encouraged reformers to concentrate on private prosecution. Although it would not gain momentum until after the Civil War, this movement began to take shape during the first several years after consolidation. By 1860, court officials, especially the court's new prison agent, William J. Mullen, had developed a subtly new critique of primary justice, focusing primarily on private prosecutors and implicitly declaring a preference for an administrative state and a police-dominated process of prosecution. Postwar reformers would eagerly seize such arguments in future struggles against the politicians, but their origins presaged the influence politicians would have over the transformation of criminal justice.[57]

Consolidation quickly proved to be not so much reform as reorganization. Politics and patronage were not the movement's primary concern, and consolidationists did little to address it. As later generations of more properly political reformers who were committed to similar administrative ends understood, this seriously compromised their aims. The power of the politicians remained largely at the ward level for the first decade or so after consolidation, but with the emergence of a clear Republican majority in the consolidated city after the Civil War, the first citywide machine in Philadelphia's history was built on the foundation of the new charter.

Criminal justice, as it turned out, was the only area of government for which a viable structure of administrative control was created. The police department was completely under the control of the mayor, who had the ultimate authority to appoint, dismiss, and command officers and to promulgate rules and regulations for them. In all other areas of municipal administration, the mayor's executive authority was effectively negated by the councils' manipulation of the power of the purse.[58] In this sense, consolidation was an important step in the transformation of criminal justice, perhaps the first realm of urban government in which the administrative state emerged, but reform is probably too strong a term for what consolidation accomplished. Just as with the other aims of consolidation, supporters of the police paid scant attention to political considerations or political reform, and, as we have seen, this allowed politicians to retain control over the police and the process of primary justice.

The absence of any real attempt at political reform frustrated most of the ends of consolidation. Only the problem of public order was effectively solved, but even in criminal justice, its most conspicuous consequence was the strengthening of the aldermen. City councilmen, who seized control of most of the rest of the new powers of city government, were also ward politicians. In fact, if consolidation accomplished anything in the short run in Philadelphia politics, it was to solidify the power of professional politicians on the ward level. Consolidation actually had the immediate effect of encouraging decentralization, the specialization of space within the city, and the rapid growth of the remaining undeveloped areas near the central city. For the first time, population began to decline in the oldest, easternmost section of the old city. As a result, the new wards of the consolidated city became increasingly enticing fields of control and exploitation for local politicians who were still not yet beholden to any centralized political organization.[59]

A good example was the new Fourth Ward, an amalgamation of major sections of Moyamensing and Southwark, one of those areas near the central city which now became fully developed. Moyamensing had, before consolidation, been the home of the "Killers" gang, the violent Moyamensing Hose Company, and the Democratic Keystone Club. William McMullin, as we have seen, was a major figure in all three. Upon consolidation, McMullin, just thirty years old, opened a saloon in the heart of old Moyamensing, only two blocks from the Hose Company House. It quickly became the meeting place for the gang, company members, and local Democrats. After the new city government took shape, McMullin accepted an appointment to the board of prison inspectors, largely to be able to arrange the release of his friends and neighbors who got into trouble, which they frequently did. Thanks, in large part, to the favors he could bestow on Fourth Ward residents in his several roles, McMullin secured nomination for alderman in 1856 and, with the opposition in disarray, upset the incumbent. This made McMullin the most powerful man in the Fourth Ward, its Democratic boss, the "Squire" of Moyamensing. He remained an alderman until 1873, when he deserted the sinking ship and ran for the city council, where he remained until his death in 1901.[60]

The ward politicians were the major force in criminal justice, and their power would have to be reckoned with by any group of reformers seeking to change the system. By 1860, with the politicians help, Philadelphia's criminal justice reformers developed a reasoning that would allow them to condemn private prosecution without blaming the aldermen. With this, reformers could then transform criminal justice without overly antagonizing the politicians.

With people like McMullin serving as aldermen, it was not long before their role in the criminal justice process once again became a matter of controversy. Between consolidation and the Civil War, aldermen probably became more directly the focus of criticism than ever before. Largely because the immediate crisis of order had been solved, the court process stood out more clearly. To be sure, the police also received criticism, but this was primarily for the excessive use of force in making arrests or for being corrupted by magistrates, not for failing to do their primary job. To those reformers who supported an administratively accountable police force, primary justice increasingly became the central issue, and private prosecution appeared increasingly to be the central problem. By the outbreak of secession, the reformers had basically declared their preference for the alderman-police relationship.[61]

Things began to move quickly as the abolition of aldermen's fees immediately proved to be unenforceable. The prison inspectors, some of them ward politicians, understood that the magistrates' "ingenuity will soon discover a mode by which the provisions of the new law will be evaded." Salaries could not prevent aldermen from receiving fees because "magistrates have it in their power to demand their fees before issuing the process." The abolition of fees resulted in the removal of a means by which the court could exercise control over aldermen just at a time when their activities, thanks to the new police cases, became more extensive than ever.[62] So on 20 April 1855, the legislature restored the fee system for aldermen, with the proviso that, at the end of each month, magistrates would submit to the city treasurer all fees, costs, fines, and forfeitures received or face prosecution for misdemeanor in office. Each quarter they were also to submit a statement of all funds that they had paid to the treasurer.[63]

The revival of the fee system inspired grand jurors, PSAMPP reformers, and especially Prison Agent Mullen to resume their criticism of magisterial conduct. Mullen, though himself the object of some criticism, was given a boost in 1855 when the prison inspectors recognized his office, and the governor appointed him prison agent for the entire state. Emboldened by these developments, Mullen immediately intensified his attacks on the aldermen, accusing them of "outrages" that were designed "to gratify a spirit of revenge on the one part, and a love of gain on the other. . . . " Mullen bragged about having forced Alderman Dallas to stop committing people indiscriminately and instead to settle cases in his office without returning them to court, "which is no doubt more satisfactory to the aggrieved parties." Then, in early 1856, Alderman Freeman became the first in a long succession of postconsolidation aldermen to be charged with misdemeanor in office, for "corruptly and maliciously holding James Martin and others in excessive bail" in an assault and battery case. Partly in response to these revelations and accusations, the acting committee of the PSAMPP inaugurated the campaign for structural change, appointing a committee in February 1856 to petition the legislature "on the subject of the Committing Magistrates, to endeavor to procure a change in the system."[64]

The exclusive description of aldermen as corrupt and exploitative and as acting against the wishes of those who came before them was characteristic of Mullen but unprecedentedly one-dimensional. The new circumstances certainly afforded aldermen with frequent opportunities for corruption in office, and the convictions of aldermen for misdemeanor suggest that at least some took them. It is very difficult, however, to understand the continued vibrancy of private prosecution—or the power and popularity of a politician like McMullin—if aldermen did not also often meet the demands of their constituents. The complexity of these demands was what had critics running in circles before consolidation, repeatedly accusing magistrates of seemingly contradictory behavior.

The simpler criticism that Mullen now offered did not mean that the reality of criminal prosecution had become less complicated, but it did produce an unusual response. Aldermen defended themselves, not with claims of purity and honesty, but with a frank discussion of the complexity of their position, which clarified the difference between the particularistic assumptions of a system of private prosecution and those of an administrative state. This spoke clearly to the problems of criminal justice, but it also spoke to the larger problems of how the urban polity was to be structured.

Three days after the January 1857 grand jury made a presentment critical of aldermen, "Ferroz" wrote a lengthy letter that was published in the *Ledger*. Claiming only that he "had some experience in proceedings before Aldermen," he stressed the point that aldermen were required by law to return all cases except those assault and battery cases that the parties agreed to settle, but, according to "Ferroz," most parties who agreed to settle did so privately, in order to avoid paying the small cost involved. This, not the aldermen's greed, was the cause of the many returns to court for which no parties ever appeared. "Ferroz" recommended the establishment of a new alderman's court of summary jurisdiction which would relieve the quarter sessions of petty cases and "meet, what is really required, a place where a certain lawless set of individuals might have justice done them." "Ferroz" may not have been an alderman, but when "An Alderman" wrote to the *Ledger* several days later, he made it clear that "Ferroz" spoke for the magistrates. "An Alderman" stressed that magistrates were bound to return cases to court and added that "in such cases no costs accrue to the Aldermen. I can truly say that, in a practice of many years, I have never received one cent for any case which came before the Court, in the sense complained of by the Grand Juries." These correspondents challenged the notion that aldermen were corrupt and oppressive. Rather, the citizens found it too easy to resort to the law, and aldermen were virtually powerless to prevent them from clogging the courts. As a result, the aldermen were wrongly accused of venality and avarice. The private litigants were the ones to blame.[65]

The truth was more complex than this portrait indicated. A week later, "Ferroz" admitted as much in a strikingly insightful second letter. He conceded that the fee system was "a system of extortion, and in the hands of an unprincipled man, could be and had been an engine of oppression," especially on the "poor and unfortunate," but he then exonerated aldermen with the argument that a magistrate could not be impartial as long as he was "encouraged to give such judgment as will put money in his pocket." An alderman was "like any other tradesman, compelled to fashion his goods to suit his customers; and, in order to obtain a living, he must extort money from those whose want of it is often greater than his own, and, if he has any, smother his conscience and turn a deaf ear to many a piteous tale."

Or he might simply refuse to vend his wares. "Ferroz" illustrated this point with the story of a respectable hatter who wanted a noisy and quarrelsome neighbor held to keep the peace. The hatter was ready to swear to a warrant but could not pay the $1 fee, so the alderman declined to issue it. The alderman agreed that, in this instance, the law was not just, but he explained to the man that he sold law just as the hatter sold hats and could expect to starve if he began giving the law away. The hatter felt the inspiration of sudden wisdom: "I now see why Aldermen are sometimes accused of retailing the law to suit their friends." The system was wrong; "You should not be made to work for nothing, nor should I be turned away without redress." In the future, he would remember, when hearing of an alderman's abuse, that "he makes his Hats to suit his customers."[66]

Here was the most direct statement yet about the increasingly anachronistic nature of the alderman-litigant relationship. The fee system negated the magistrates' ability to properly dispense justice. Selling justice was their living, and their need to secure that living forced them to modify the product in order to suit those who could pay the most. One need not be dishonest at all. The problem sprang from the structure and tradition of particularistic justice in a time when paternalistic magistrates had disappeared and been replaced by professional politicians. What was obviously necessary was a new relationship that placed more distance between the alderman and his "customers." Only the elite magistrate of a bygone era or an independent salaried magistrate could afford to refuse cases, encourage settlement, and, in general, treat those cases that came before them in a consistently fair and just manner. "Ferroz" had made a case for a salaried magistracy without reference to examples of aldermanic abuse or oppression; he concentrated only on the citizens' typical, simple, and legitimate exercise of the law. It was as though the aldermen were ready to sacrifice private prosecution in order to quiet their critics and were proposing in return that they be paid salaries to go along with their lucrative new ties to the police. By 1857 this might have seemed like a pretty good deal to many magistrates.[67]

As the court became flooded with cases and the connections between the police and the aldermen became ever stronger, the magistrate's analysis of primary justice gradually became more persuasive. Critics, at first, maintained the position that trivial cases were caused by magisterial greed and should have been dismissed or settled. When four aldermen were convicted of corruption in office in the fall of 1857, Mullen blamed politics.[68] "The office is too much connected with politics, and, as it is a prize which is accessible to the lowest of ward politicians, there can be no wonder that it has become in a great measure degraded. . . . Too much respect has hitherto been paid to aldermen."[69]

For Mullen, the problem remained simple. Aldermen accepted too many private prosecutions and paid corrupt policemen to make arrests. Matters reached a head in August 1858 with a charge for misdemeanor in office against Alderman William Allen. Mullen took credit for having asked Judge Ludlow of the quarter sessions to sit as a committing magistrate to hear charges that Allen was an "habitual drunkard" who was "wholly unfit" for office and had been responsible for "numerous cases of oppression . . . while . . . he pretended to administer justice." Mullen believed that Allen was only one of many magistrates who made improper commitments and inadequate returns. At the hearing, District Attorney William B. Mann agreed, calling abuses the result of "the neglect of the Aldermen; not of one Alderman, but of many." Alderman Allen never attended these hearings, after which he was indicted and held in $600 bail.[70]

Once again aldermen defended themselves. One alderman wrote to the *Ledger* that charges of magistrates' failing to deposit their costs with the city were misleading. In terms similar to those of the alderman who wrote in 1857, this correspondent stated that most arrestees were too poor to pay fines or costs, so the aldermen collected much less than their critics supposed. The notion that aldermen returned so many trivial cases because the law required them to do so was finally included in a grand jury presentment in December 1858. All the jury could conclude, in the face of a year's worth of depressing disclosures, was that "a reform in our Court system is sadly needed."[71]

The most immediate reform on the horizon was not what they had in mind, however. In March 1859, in response to the growing number of police cases, the state legislature, beholden to the will of ward politicians, restored the fee system for private prosecutions. Aldermen no longer had to pay their costs received into the county treasury. That requirement now held only for police magistrates, and only for monies received "by them in virtue of their offices as such."[72]

The restoration of the fee system in full pushed critics further toward a more complex picture of the problems with primary justice. Building ironically on the aldermen's defense, they began to attack private prosecution and the alderman-litigant relationship directly. If aldermen were acting only according to the dictates of their office, then the real venality was to be found among the private prosecutors who demanded that aldermen give them the opportunity to use the law to take advantage of others. Prison Agent Mullen, in his annual report for 1859, for the first time concentrated on prosecutors. Excessive cases now resulted when "ignorant persons . . . hasten to a magistrate and prefer charges, which are wholly unfounded, but are yet quite sufficient to result in the imprisonment of the innocent." Mullen decried the "malignity and revenge," "intemperate habits," and "desire for pecuniary gain" of private prosecutors, even as he repeated his contempt for the "illegal and scandalous conduct of some of our magistrates."[73]

Though they had come to accept perfidy of private prosecutors as the key problem in criminal justice, reformers were never wholly comfortable with exonerating aldermen. Soon after Mullen's report, Alderman William Allen, who tried to defraud a man of $2,750, and at least four other aldermen faced charges of misdemeanor in office.[74] Reformers and judges resumed their attack on the fee system, so recently rehabilitated by the legislature, and on politics. In 1861 the prison inspectors proposed that magistrates be paid a fixed salary, hold their offices on good-behavior tenure, and receive their appointments "from some such appointing power as the Courts, instead of popular election."[75]

The explicit discussion of politics for the first time since 1840 completed the new picture of problem-ridden primary justice. Aldermen's ties to the people through electoral politics and political parties were, according to critics, as pernicious as their deeds in office. Politics in Philadelphia was especially heated and competitive during the early years of the consolidated city, and the balance between the Democrats and their various opponents was very close. Nativist Conrad was replaced by Democrat Richard Vaux in the second mayoral election in 1856. The Democrats were experiencing a brief revival at this time because of a widespread dislike among conservatives of Know-Nothing nativism and antislavery Republicanism. Yet, at the same time, some Democrats who still held to Jacksonian principles, such as William D. Kelley, were becoming Republicans.[76]

With the opposition in temporary disarray and control of the new city still uncertain, local Democrats employed their full bag of tricks. William McMullin, the most prominent political boss among the magistrates, repeatedly got into trouble at election time. In 1859 he was charged with riot when two men he was escorting to the polls were challenged by the election officials. In 1860 he intimidated a man into falsely swearing that he was brought to Philadelphia from Norristown in order to vote against McMullin's ticket. Behavior of this sort by ward politicians on election day was neither new nor uncommon. McMullin, after all, had cut his political teeth in antebellum Moyamensing where brawling and intimidation of voters was routine. Brute strength and large numbers of menacing supporters were often the determining factors in these days before secret ballots and voter registration. The unsettled and highly competitive character of politics during the late 1850s only intensified the use of roughhouse tactics.[77]

For the critics who were now coming to understand the fullness of the aldermen's power, this was most enlightening. They saw just how important ward politics was and how easily it could frustrate reform, even in the most administratively advanced part of city government. Political and judicial particularism were inextricably linked. The violence of politics was as unsavory as the corruption of primary justice and seemed to confirm the rectitude of damning both the officials and the residents of their wards. To many reformers, the power and initiative had to be removed from both groups and placed in quieter, more responsible, and more honest hands, but political realities would force reformers to disempower only one party to the relationship. The court officials' gradual acceptance of the magistrates' logic foretold which party this would be.

9. *The Transformation of Primary Justice*

The Civil War years were good ones for the prestige of Philadelphia's police. The absolute level of crime in the city diminished, but more importantly—while many other cities, notably nearby New York, were racked by civil disorder—Philadelphia remained quiet and orderly. Mayor Alexander Henry took physical command of the police and, using the mandate provided by consolidation, deployed them throughout the city so skillfully that every potential disturbance was cut short. In a border city that had considerable prosouthern sentiment at first and was later threatened by invasion, this was an impressive achievement.[1]

The rising stature of the police only made it easier for reformers to press on with their critique of private prosecution. PSAMPP members developed a plan for restructuring primary justice and assumed leadership of the campaign to destroy the traditional bases of private prosecution. Prison reformers were the natural leaders of a criminal justice reform movement; they had thought about the matter the longest, were least beholden to politicians, and were among the most frustrated of consolidation's supporters. Also, as long-time advocates of one of the first formal institutions within city government, they were among the clearest proponents of an administrative state. Their proposal was primarily the work of Prison Agent Mullen (who was eulogized in 1882 as the man "mainly instrumental" in replacing the aldermen with paid police magistrates). Following his lead, prison reformers made it plain that they were as concerned with undermining old centers of authority as they were with building new ones.[2]

They were not, however, able to effect change on their own. For this, they had to await the mobilization of a broader group of municipal reformers who would be directly concerned with breaking the power of the ward politicians. These reformers embraced the prison reformers' critique of aldermen and private prosecution and used it in their battle with the politicians. The result, embodied in the new state constitution of 1874, was like previous reforms a compromise, but one to which the prison reformers' critique of private prosecution was well suited. Like all compromises, it was based on what the disputants had in common, which in this case was a preference for the police over private prosecution. Under fire, the police magistrates and their political allies agreed to abandon private prosecution and the rest of the minor judiciary. Primary justice became far more centralized, much more directly tied to the police and the citywide political machine. Philadelphia got an imperfect police-centered administrative criminal justice system, and private prosecutors were disempowered.

The Prison Reformers' Solution

Although on a diminished scale, business went on as usual in criminal justice during the Civil War.[3] There was one difference about the war years, however, that contributed to the negative light in which reformers placed private prosecution. Because of wartime conditions, the participation of those left behind became more visible than ever before. Women and blacks were involved in criminal justice in unprecedented numbers now that so many white men were absent from the city. For example, white women had never exceeded 17 percent of those committed to prison before the war and comprised only 11 percent in 1860. But in 1861, they accounted for 18 percent of all persons committed; and by 1863 and 1864, over 25 percent. The percentage of black women committed to prison also increased slightly. Overall, white men, who had never made up less than 70 percent of prison commitments after 1854, fell below that level in 1861 and bottomed out at 63 percent in 1863.[4]

Grand jurors made the first proposals for change with these cases prominently in mind. Deploring the "avarice which seeks to convert litigation and contention into a source of gain," an 1863 inquest asked the legislature to pass a law "confining the number [of aldermen] to but one for each ward; requiring them to be persons of good moral character and learned in the law; abolishing, in criminal cases, the present system of fees, making them self-sustaining salaried officers . . . fixing the amount thereof at a sum that would . . . place them beyond temptation to oppress or extort." The "anomaly of an unlettered Dogberry" receiving triple the income of a judge would be no more. Overcrowded courts would disappear because aldermen would be "under the direction of the District Attorney, subject to the supervision of the Court," and their decisions would be final in "ordinary misdemeanors, surety of the peace, and such other cases as might be defined by statute."[5]

The next day "Fiat Justitia," claiming to be a former alderman, defended his brethren in the *Ledger*. He blamed prosecutors for initiating trivial cases and the district attorney for submitting them to grand juries. A few days later, the foreman of the grand jury responded with the colorful description of several typical cases involving Mrs. Fightall, Mrs. Fireup, Biddy McGab, and

Squire Niggerfip. He defended the inquest's proposals again, even as he implied that the system met the needs of the people using it. Grand jurors thus expressed their outrage not at the system's failure to work for the people using it but at the fact that it did not work for *them*.[6] The solution was to create a minor judiciary of lawyers, under court control, which would hopefully increase the sanctions given for trivial crimes and thereby dissuade use of the law. It would, in any event, inhibit the citizen's ability to manipulate the criminal justice system and decrease the number of petty cases returned to the higher courts.

Prison reformers had similar views but retained their characteristic emphasis on the unwarranted suffering of the victims of mean-spirited imprisonment. For them, the problem was not so much mundane trivial litigation as the willingness of aldermen to bend to the desires of malicious and extortionate prosecutors. Only the prison agent was a "peacemaker"; he was acting as an alderman—a justice of the peace—should.[7] The prison reformers denied the jurors' implication that the system had ever worked for anyone and suggested that it undermined law and order.[8] Crime and contempt for authority ran rampant because of "shameful trifling with the forms of law and the demands of justice." People believed that the administration of the law was not entrusted to "men of learning, purity and dignity of character." As a result, "the pernicious conviction is settling and extending every day, among a large class of the community, that a reliance upon [the law] for a redress of public or private wrongs is misplaced."[9]

Having once again ignored the possibility that people could have drawn the opposite conclusion, the PSAMPP detailed its proposal for change in the 1863 and 1864 volumes of the *Journal of Prison Discipline* and in it expanded upon this reasoning. Although the ideas were surely Mullen's, their publication by the society represented a consensus in favor of a change on the part of a broad segment of Philadelphia's older philanthropic, political, and business leaders. Many elite Philadelphia families were represented among the society's members. Its leadership included attorney James J. Barclay, a longtime philanthropist and for forty-six years president of the house of refuge; publisher and former congressman Joseph R. Chandler; and attorney Henry J. Williams, Benjamin Rush's son-in-law. Among the membership could be found financier Jay Cooke, Eli K. Price, industrialist Matthias Baldwin, publisher Joshua Lippincott, and such famous Philadelphia family names as Biddle, Duane, Binney, Cope, Ingersoll, Bache, Perot, and Shippen. Even prominent local politicians (some former aldermen) like George Erety, George Elkinton, and John Gilpin were members.

The society recognized the importance of both police cases and private prosecutions. Because they approached the subject from the vantage point of those victimized by imprisonment, they saw the similarity between the treatment of the accused in private and police cases and explicitly linked the two. But for this very reason their emphasis was on private prosecution and the alderman-litigant relationship, which they believed was the root of abuse in all criminal cases.

Before offering their proposal, the PSAMPP discussed the problems. Although the problems were very familiar by now, prison reformers rested their analysis of them on the assumption of a police-dominated system. After examining minor order cases, the society concluded that even those who needed it "received no good from their incarceration." Even worse, the system of justice had "fallen into disrepute . . . objects of its penalties" had come to "regard arrest and imprisonment as a misfortune which is as likely to fall upon one as another, if poor." The citizen's relationship to the law here was exclusively as "objects of its penalties." This was as it should be, the authors implied; the problem was that the behavior of the magistracy created injustice and thus disrespect for the law. Eliminate the foundation of these injustices and the system would operate properly—and the foundation of injustice was private prosecution.[10]

Private prosecutions accounted for "a considerable portion of the community that have acquaintance with the prison by commitment." These occurred among people "of a class that think all personal redress, and all protection from wrong, and all safety from the consequences of their own misconduct lie in an appeal to the magistrate." This "constant resort to litigation" was "one of the crying evils of the times," criminal justice as it should not be.[11] Citing the cases in which Mullen intervened, the PSAMPP concluded that rare was the honest private prosecutor. "Most of the complaints that come before our aldermen are brought by those who seek to gratify personal animosity and a sudden desire of vengeance rather than any wish to punish the wrong-doer for the sake of right." Unable to admit that the legitimate ends of the litigants and the criminal justice system could be contradictory, prison reformers assumed that what disturbed grand jurors and sometimes produced abuse was an unambiguous evil. The elimination of private prosecution would clear the courts, restore the dignity of the law, and save the poor from oppression.[12]

Aldermen, for their part, were just doing their jobs. "If people will 'sue and be sued'. . . it may seem to the functionary, rather a thankless exercise of his ability, to recommend such an adjustment of the case as will deprive him of the fees of office, by which he lives." Though "the cry against the magistracy is universal, the fault is really found in only a part of them," but even those in this group were not personally at fault. They were simply men of middling talents, capable of commanding votes, needing to maximize the modest rewards of their office. The analysis came down to a simple solution—shut out the private prosecutors. Electing better aldermen was not the answer. Few men could be expected to refuse cases under the fee system, but more importantly, because so much of the alderman's duties "are beyond the knowledge and sympathy of the respectable portion of the community, little interest is taken in his election by those who feel a sense of shame at the improprieties of a functionary connected with the administration of justice." Without their participation, no improvement could be hoped for through the ballot box. Instead, the solution was to eliminate elections and fees and to create a class of police magistrates who were salaried and had summary jurisdiction over all trivial and minor cases. "Placed by the tenor and fixed reward of their office above dependence upon those who shall demand justice in others, or receive it in themselves, they shall not shrink from their duty to condemn, more than from their sense of propriety to discharge."[13]

Eliminate aldermen, eliminate fees, create a minor judiciary directly tied to the police, allow magistrates to exercise final jurisdiction over minor cases, and private prosecutors will have been effectively shut out. They would no longer be able to strike a bargain with the magistrate or manipulate the law by avoiding final disposition of their cases. They would gain access to the magistrate primarily through the police. To secure this change, the PSAMPP suggested a revision of the state constitution that would transform the structure of Philadelphia's minor judiciary at its legal roots. There would be no significant variation in the reformers' argument until the constitution was actually changed and most of their proposals were implemented in 1874.

The power of the arguments made by grand juries and prison reformers during the Civil War years lay in their demonstration of the incompatibility of police and private prosecution and the ability to appeal ultimately to a variety of reformers without hopelessly alienating the politicians. The grand juries and prison reformers not only showed how the police made it possible to abandon private prosecution because they provided an alternative to it, but they also provided the logic that made it necessary to abolish private prosecution: it led to disrespect for the police and the legal system. Eliminate private prosecution, and the result would be a single agency for the enforcement of the law— the police—with neither the temptations to abuse nor a competing form to compromise its power and public respect. Such a system would be much more manageable and predictable than one that left so much power and discretion to the citizens themselves. Therefore, the same men who were aldermen might safely become the new system's police magistrates, for "it is not always the man—it is the circumstances in which he is placed."[14]

Prison reformers were correct in seeing private prosecution as a source of resistance to the police, but this was not simply because it established a pattern of oppression. Private prosecution was also preferred by many and, as the grand jury saw, bred respect for a certain kind of law. Judge Kelley also recognized this when he doubted whether a criminal law that had to rely on force could ever sustain the respect of the citizenry. By now, however, Judge Kelley was in Washington, and the grand jury's more jaundiced view of the kind of respect private prosecution bred had wider currency than in Kelley's day. The prison reformers made a powerful case that could appeal to the two groups who might do something about it—the benevolent reformers who were concerned about oppression and unwarranted suffering among the poor, and the municipal reformers who were concerned about the inefficient and corrupt practices of city government.

For the remainder of the decade, Prison Agent Mullen attempted to forge an alliance between the court and the prison reformers. Because he was, in practice, the liaison between the two, he was the logical person for this task. Not only would an alliance help advance the cause, but it served the agent's interest in increasing his effectiveness and credibility. Mullen threw himself into every issue that touched on the court's relationship with the aldermen. In 1864, for example, the quarter sessions clerk ordered the prison-keepers not to honor discharges submitted by magistrates within ten days of a term of the court. Mullen immediately rushed to the district attorney, claiming that aldermen had by law the right to discharge misdemeanors at any time before an indictment was found. To deny them this right would be to increase greatly the number of court cases and make the agent's work much more difficult. The clerk then issued a statement restricting the application of his order to felonies only.[15]

Mullen's admission to a seat "inside the bar" of the courtroom in 1867 further cemented his tie to the court. Mullen jumped at the opportunity to be accorded a physical position equal to that of the district attorney. From there, he could act as an officer of the court, and Mullen used this position to push the court to act on primary justice. In April 1868, Mullen gave a letter to Judge Brewster detailing various abuses by aldermen. Brewster forwarded the letter to the term's grand jury with instructions to examine the prison's records and to determine how many commitments were illegal. Meanwhile, Brewster called several aldermen into court. They admitted many of the abuses that Mullen had alleged; the judge rebuked them and threatened future prosecution.[16] Mullen's efforts also convinced the prison inspectors to adopt new rules for admitting and releasing prisoners in June 1870, the result of which was to reduce the number of commitments for "drunk and disorderly" and the undefined charge of "misdemeanor." Mullen took the credit for this reform and found his successes so exciting that he again alerted Judge Brewster to continued abuses in August, and the same scene of aldermen coming to court for rebuke was repeated.[17]

The prison agent was also largely successful in enlisting court support for the prison reformers' proposal for change. Mullen made sure to include many of the supportive comments of judges and grand jurors in his reports. Grand jury presentments and judges' charges now often spoke of private prosecutors in much harsher terms than before. Judge Brewster called the "returns of petty and malicious accusations" the main reason for the court's low conviction rate and called on the grand jury to act as a "barrier between the court and this flood of litigation." Grand jurors repeatedly endorsed the proposal for an abolition of the fee system and the establishment of a police court.[18]

Of course, the court's interest in reducing the number of cases and restoring respect for the law made it susceptible to the arguments of the prison reformers, but the court was never as sure as the reformers that private prosecution was an unambiguous evil. Judges, most of them reared in a legal culture that considered private prosecution the central, if problematic, support for the authority of the law, remained ambivalent. Judge Paxson, for example, urged grand jurors to dismiss cases rooted in petty spite, but in the same breath, he cautioned them not to disregard prosecutions that were "commenced in good faith against parties charged with misdemeanors. . . . You should discriminate between such cases and those that are wanton, malicious, or petty . . . or which have been brought to satisfy some private grudge, or accomplish some purely private end." He also told the jury not to treat any case superficially, no matter how large the volume of business. Judges never saw the problem as one of clear abuse, but the arguments of the defenders of aldermen during the late 1850s, the excessive use of private prosecution by the poor and disenfranchised during the Civil War, and the crisis faced by the courts made judges, despite their ambivalence, receptive to the proposal for a police magistracy.[19]

Support was no doubt increased by the continued publicity given to the failure of committing magistrates to pay their collected costs to the city and to charges of the official misconduct of aldermen. The most notable of these charges again involved Alderman William McMullin, who was accused in the summer of 1867 of being the leader of a riot between two fire companies. A grand jury dismissed charges against McMullin, but a special committee of the common council, appointed to investigate the matter, called him "the ringleader of a mob." The committee wanted to recommend his impeachment, but this action was thwarted by the city solicitor's opinion that councils had no power to impeach an alderman.[20]

So, by 1870, much had happened. For the first time, a full-time reformer committed to the abolition of the aldermanic system had become a permanent member of the criminal justice process, with much of his energy devoted to enlisting the support of other court officials in its behalf. Harassed as they were by the consequences of private prosecution, they were easy for the prison agent to convince. Reformers had many reasons to be optimistic, but they were not. Their plan for primary justice stalled by the end of the decade. The PSAMPP's Committee on a Salaried Magistracy reported in October 1869 that "it was hardly probable that anything could be done at present" and asked to be discharged. The society lamented that year that such an evil, "touching seriously and injuriously the citizen, so extensively as to be a public grievance, remains yet uncorrected, scarcely reached, indeed by any effort at improvement."

In fact, the proposal for a police magistracy faced several serious obstacles. The continued sentiment in favor of private prosecution, as reflected by Judge Paxson, was one but probably the least of them. The idea of a police court was also unpopular with some who otherwise supported the reformers' ideas. The *Ledger* strongly opposed an 1865 bill to give aldermen summary jurisdiction over assault and battery and other petty cases, although this proposal was made without a corresponding proposal to abolish fees or elections.[21] The greatest obstacles, however, were two political realities that the reformers themselves had recognized. One was the power and influence of the aldermen in the political parties that selected many of the state's legislators. It would not be easy to persuade a majority of legislators to abolish the economic and political base of many of their parties' local leaders. The second was the lack of interest of much of the city's younger elite with the activities of primary justice. These businessmen and lawyers had never entered an alderman's office, were personally untouched by the abuses of the criminal justice system, and were accused by reformers of ignoring elections for minor officials. Just as the noninvolvement of many of the city's elite in the struggle for consolidation had contributed to that movement's lack of success for many years, so their lack of participation hampered the movement to reform primary justice. Both of these obstacles would have to be overcome before the prison reformers' program could become a reality, and certain political developments in Philadelphia during the late sixties made the prospects brighter than the reformers had realized.

The Reformers Find Allies

Like consolidation, the creation of a police magistracy had supporters for many years before its enactment and was dependent for success on a similar combination of events. In both cases, an elite coalition broadly concerned with municipal administration needed to attain considerable influence in the city, and the right moment had to appear for them to navigate safely the turbulent waters of Philadelphia's local machine politics.

The most important political development preceding the abolition of the office of alderman was indirectly related to the conditions that had made consolidation possible. The balance in Philadelphia politics of the mid-fifties was, in part, a result of the dissolution of the second-party system, and it was short-lived. By the end of the Civil War, the Republican coalition, which had drawn adherents from all parties of the fifties and from all social and political types, established firm command of city government.

The first Republican party in Philadelphia was organized in 1855, "a minority of accomplished artisans, craftsmen, shopkeepers and men of professional stature having little connection with the local political machinery."[22] But some, like William D. Kelley, were young men with strong commitments to politics and parties, and as the national issues that came to dominate politics during the Civil War era brought ever more members into their ranks, the Republican party included many who had experience with the local political machinery. Among them were two young former Whigs, James McManes and William B. Mann, kingpins of the citywide Republican machine of the seventies.

The consolidated city remained decentralized at first, in part because of its unwieldy size and in part because the combination of city and county offices created so many elected officials. So, for example, in advance of the October 1871 elections, the Republicans held eighty-four separate conventions for ward and city offices. The local authority of ward politicians remained essential for the success of the party in the city.[23] Yet several factors now made a citywide machine possible, even though there was a marked devolution of authority to the local level. One was the very complexity of the structure of city government, which only full-time politicians could hope to understand, let alone control. More important were the opportunities for power and wealth the consolidated city offered. Particularly enticing was the Gas Trust, through which McManes made himself "King" James. Originally a private company, the Philadelphia Gas Works was acquired by the city in 1841 and administered by a board of trustees to which McManes was appointed in 1865. Within two years, through the manipulation of party connections in Harrisburg, McManes gained control of the Gas Trust, the over five thousand people directly or indirectly dependent on it for employment, and the banks, contractors, and street railways that relied on Gas Works funds. This also made him the effective boss of the city's Republican party.[24]

Other opportunities were provided by various city and county offices. The most rewarding was one centrally tied to criminal justice, the office of district attorney. William B. Mann won the office in 1862 and held it until 1874. He used the fees of office and his increasing control over criminal prosecution to become second to McManes among city Republicans and was a strong advocate of salaries (including an enormous one for himself) and the abolition of the aldermen, his main rivals for control over criminal justice. The machine also drew resources from those who held the fee-based "row" offices—recorder of deeds, receiver of taxes, and prothonotary of the district court—which were worth up to $200,000 annually, much of which went into party coffers.[25]

These were all the benefits of office. The Republicans' control of profitable office stemmed in large part from the Registry Act of 1869, passed by a Republican legislature, which gave the party's aldermen control of every election board and thus the power to approve every voter in the city. As a consequence, the party was able to send whatever number of repeaters and outsiders that might be necessary to the polls to secure victory. Often these "floaters" received police protection, the force being under the direct control of the mayor and comprised primarily of patronage recipients. Nothing would make municipal reformers more determined to do away with the aldermen than this law.

By 1869 the Republicans had a well-organized city executive committee that included many current or former aldermen, and they secured control of the councils and "row" offices in the elections of 1869 and 1870. Needing only to capture the mayoralty to cement its power, the machine's candidate, select councilman and former confectioner "Sweet" William Stokley, led a successful "reform" campaign to establish a paid fire department, one of the aims of consolidation. While this did, indeed, make a contribution to "law and order" and efficient fire protection, it was attractive to the emerging machine primarily because of image and because volunteer fire companies were either strongholds of the Democratic opposition or independent-minded ward-based Republicans whom the machine was still trying to control. The companies disappeared at the end of 1870, and wise aldermen should have taken notice.[26]

His "respectable" reputation established, Stokley captured the first of three consecutive three-year terms as mayor in the unusually violent (even for this age) election of 1871. The fix was now in, and the subsequent majorities that were thus ensured gave McManes, Mann, Stokley, and their cronies control of the city's election machinery, city councils, and major citywide offices. All that remained for the opposition were such ward offices as alderman and minority status on the city councils. The machine increased the city debt from twenty to over seventy million dollars in twenty years, but their ability to return majorities faithfully kept them protected by the state Republican stalwarts and business interests.[27]

Still there was opposition to the Philadelphia machine among Democrats, rival factions within the Republican party, and, eventually, Republican municipal reformers. Despite the machine's control of city government, there was always a struggle between the small group of "ring" leaders and jealous party rivals. For many others, the greatest consternation was caused by the Registry Law, which convened the city's aldermen as a board to appoint three citizens from each election district to serve as its election canvassers. Since the majority of aldermen were Republicans, this gave them control of the city's election machinery, including the power to appoint the Democratic canvassers.[28]

The Registry Law disturbed the Republican business and legal elite, who had withdrawn from city politics but who feared the consequences of the control of elections by aldermen. Elite Republicans were successful in getting the law declared unconstitutional in 1868, but its supporters secured virtually the same law from the next legislature. Then the local Democrats became disturbed because it was obvious that the Republican majority would not appoint regular Democrats to the minority positions among the ward election canvassers. Alderman McMullin, now the city Democratic leader, warned the board that he would not allow the canvassers chosen for his Fourth Ward to enter the area on election day. "We will crowd the place with men. . . . You will have club law there on election day." In the end, though, McMullin accepted the compromise that made two of the three canvassers in each district Republican. The Democratic canvasser would just have to work that much harder to register voters.[29]

Election days that year and in 1870 were relatively quiet but saw two ominous developments for the Democrats. One was the Republican's capturing of the councils and "row" offices, and the other was the admission of the almost entirely Republican black male population to the franchise. With Republican machine encouragement and the protection of federal troops, a relatively small number of blacks voted without major incident. Most of the black voters, however, were concentrated in McMullin's Fourth Ward, and he was concerned, especially as Republican canvassers continued to register blacks during 1871.[30]

No federal troops protected blacks in October 1871, and McMullin's Democrats, already on the offensive because of the crucial mayoral contest between Democratic incumbent Daniel Fox and Stokley, planned to make sure they would keep the Fourth Ward. Scattered violence marred the months before the election. Thugs attacked canvassers of both parties. Rock throwers broke up a meeting of blacks two days before the election, and a black man was murdered for no apparent reason in Moyamensing the day before. Election day began with a violent attempt to keep blacks from voting in Moyamensing and, with Mayor Fox turning his back, continued throughout the day, often initiated by the Democratic policemen whose jobs were on the line. Hundreds were injured, and three black men were killed. In retaliation, four blacks murdered a Democratic poll worker the next day. Among the dead was Octavius Catto, at thirty-one the principal of the Institute for Colored Youth, leader of the fight to achieve black suffrage in Philadelphia, and "the most magnetic and perhaps the most promising leader" yet of Philadelphia's black community. He was shot, possibly in the back, by a young Democratic tough, who was ushered from the scene and out of the city by a nearby policeman.[31]

Stokley won by nine thousand votes, and no one was ever brought to justice for any of the killings. This kept the score settled between rival political factions, but in the long run, it did McMullin and the ward politicians no good. A mass protest meeting took place on the Friday after the election, and Catto's funeral became a major demonstration of interracial outrage at racial violence. Stokley's victory, coupled with the abolition of the fire companies, severely weakened McMullin's Fourth Ward Democrats, and the ugliness of election day severely tarnished their image.[32] The response engendered by these events spelled trouble for ward politicians of both parties.

Republican businessmen in the Union League were grumbling about the McManes ring as early as 1868, fearing the dominance of "grasping politicians who sought office for personal interests." With the advent of the Registry Law, it seemed that these politicians would become entrenched, "just at the moment when [businessmen] most desired government aid for urban services."[33] Republican businessman reformers first organized in December 1869 in the Citizen's Association for the Improvement of Streets and Roads of Philadelphia. The association's intention was simply to investigate and present to city authorities the dangers of Philadelphia's deteriorating thoroughfares. Businessman reformers soon realized, however, that they could not hope to influence municipal affairs with a nonpolitical stance. Shut out of avenues of power within the local Republican party, and finding the Democrats anathema, many association members flocked into the Citizens Municipal Reform Association (CMRA), a nonpartisan group organized in June 1871 to select and support candidates sympathetic to the ideals of municipal reform.[34]

Members of the CMRA "were the city's most prominent bankers, lawyers, manufacturers and merchants," the majority Republicans. Most of the lawyers were directly involved with the business concerns of the bankers, manufacturers, and merchants. Their unifying idea was that business and government should form a partnership for the public good. They had few doubts that businessmen would act in the public interest but were not so sure about the politicians. Founder Henry Charles Lea, prominent publisher, historian, and the grandson of the great early nineteenth-century publisher and philanthropist Matthew Carey, believed that Philadelphia was misgoverned because businessmen, among others, had withdrawn from public affairs and allowed the city to be ruled by party bosses. CMRA members pledged themselves to a strict nonpartisanship and promised to vote only for candidates who placed honest government above personal ambition.[35]

In April 1871, the Law Association, an organization of attorneys which included several CMRA members, appointed John J. Ridgway as its counsel for the purpose of prosecuting corrupt "row" officials. When Prison Agent Mullen was informed of this development, he immediately became involved. Not only had Mullen and the other prison reformers been actively opposing the fee system for years, but the very issue of extortion on State House Row was one that Mullen had helped expose over twenty years earlier. Mullen immediately wrote Ridgway, assuring him that his labors could assist the work of the prison agent, and reminding him of the efforts of the Committee of Fifteen during the late 1840s. Ridgway responded by praising the efforts of Mullen and his committee and claiming that the lack of support by the bar had been the cause of their failure. He also suggested that the Law Association support the prison reformers' campaign against the aldermen. He knew that Mullen was "well acquainted with the corruption existing among Aldermen, and how can it well be otherwise when they are elected without any qualifications of education or standing, and entrusted with such large powers."[36]

Ridgway, the Law Association, and the CMRA achieved significant victories in late 1871 with the conviction of two deputy sheriffs and the city treasurer for extortion. Though their independent candidates were solidly beaten in the 1871 elections, the embarrassment the violence caused politicians left reformers optimistic. In early 1872, Lea, *Public Ledger* publisher George W. Childs, Ridgway, publisher Joshua Lippincott (a Prison Society member), industrialist Anthony J. Drexel, and several others formed the exclusive Reform Club to direct their efforts. The CMRA entered the year buoyed and ready to reach out into new arenas of municipal corruption. As a result, they came into direct conflict with the city's aldermen and developed an all-encompassing critique of aldermanic abuses.[37]

The year began with a February mass meeting at Horticultural Hall, where the reformers pledged to "break the power of the political rings that misgovern us, and correct the abuses that exist in the city departments." The meeting expanded the membership of the association's committee on abuses to thirty persons and authorized it to investigate all abuses within city government.[38] Aldermen soon became one of the committee's highest priorities. On February 7, a bill was introduced into the legislature extending the civil jurisdiction of Philadelphia aldermen to cases involving values up to $300. The timing of this proposal was perfectly suited to spur reformers to action. Not only were they itching to get at the aldermen because of their political power, but the proposed extension of aldermanic jurisdiction would increase the possibility that reformers would find themselves in the unthinkable position of having a civil case before an alderman. Chafing under the political power of aldermen, Philadelphia's elite was brought face to face with the possibility of suffering, like the poor, under their judicial power. As the prison reformers might have predicted, this combination made the elite much more concerned about primary justice.[39]

On February 24, the Bar Association held a meeting to take action against the proposal. Members called it "an iniquitous scheme on the part of the aldermen to increase their fees and emoluments of office, and to open a wider field for the practice of their extortions and oppressions upon the citizens of Philadelphia" and echoed Mullen in calling aldermen "a set of men whose interest it is not to compose, but to foment strife." Meanwhile, the *Ledger* editorialized against the bill and the political power of aldermen, calling them "worked by the ringmasters" and asked the CMRA to take action. Referring to the legislature, the association declared that "an element of the policy of gangs of conspirators against the public weal consisted in finding sources of profit for their tools and subordinates. Hence bills to enlarge the jurisdiction of ignorant aldermen to the perversion of the ends of justice were hatched in the hot-beds of corruption."[40] They dispatched John Ridgway to Harrisburg to lobby (successfully) against the measure, and he took the opportunity to also ask for the abolition of the board of aldermen. He called the aldermen, with only few exceptions, "quite incompetent and unfit" for office. They obstructed justice by almost always deciding for the plaintiff; their rule was "tyrannical and improper." A few weeks later, the committee on abuses issued its report on aldermen. Its focus was on criminal justice, especially the failure of committing magistrates to turn over their fees to the city treasurer, and it recommended that the treasurer take elaborate steps to examine aldermen's dockets and require payment.[41]

The CMRA was now beginning to sound a lot like the grand juries and prison reformers. Moved, perhaps, by Lea's inherited sympathy for the poor and certainly by the fact that after the 1871 elections aldermen had become an easy target, the CMRA grew even bolder as the elections of 1872 approached. At their May nominating convention, the association blamed the woes of city government on the "partisanship which has for many years plac[ed] the control of our city in the hands of a few adroit and unscrupulous political managers, whose cupidity and capacity for evil have been stimulated by the inordinate emoluments attached to many local offices."[42]

During the campaign, CMRA members focused on primary justice. Ridgway appealed to workingmen to support the reform candidates because "it is the poor not the rich that bear the burden of" aldermanic abuses. However, the results of the election only further enraged reformers by bringing them, as others had before, face to face with the bond between the aldermen and the electorate. Independent candidates received no more than thirteen thousand votes, and only a few of the reformer-supported Republicans were elected. CMRA spokesmen blamed their defeat on fraud and the inability of voters to separate the local election from national issues, which was their way of interpreting the strong partisan loyalties of Philadelphia's voters.[43]

Businessman reformers, after the fall 1872 elections, realized that their political initiatives would not be sufficient to achieve their ends, so they turned their energies to two other projects, both of which were already underway and would bring them even more in concert with prison reformers. The first was the prosecution of corrupt aldermen. Henry C. Lea reported to his organization at the end of 1872 that "the wrongs committed by many of the Aldermen of Philadelphia have engaged [the CMRA's] earnest attention." He noted the conviction of Alderman Devitt in a case brought by the association and claimed that the trial of another alderman was soon to occur.[44]

The second project was the convention to write a new constitution for Pennsylvania. This was, of course, precisely the mechanism that the PSAMPP had proposed for the reform of the minor judiciary in 1864. Now, a much wider reform movement sought the same mechanism to overcome the resistance of the legislature and the parties to a broad spectrum of reform measures. Support for a constitutional convention was first announced by the editors of the *Ledger* in April 1870, in protest against the private legislation that dominated the business of the legislature. Politicians in Harrisburg spent most of their time passing bills that favored the interests of their friends and that many reformers believed harmed Philadelphia. According to the reformers, the legislature was an arena of bribery and corruption, in large part a creature of the "rings," responsible for laws that limited the ability of reform-minded Philadelphians to govern themselves.[45]

The Union League Club, in October 1870, became the first local organization to support a constitutional convention. Many of the proposals of local reformers were championed in meetings supporting the convention throughout 1871 and 1872. The *Ledger* called for a new constitution to abolish fees, and the CMRA urged a convention to reduce the powers of aldermen. Support for a constitutional convention came from many prominent politicians, including Morton McMichael, former governor Andrew Curtin, and Governor John W. Geary, who sensed strong statewide support for the abolition of special legislation. During its 1871 session, the legislature agreed to a referendum on calling a convention, and it passed at the October elections. In April 1872, the legislature endorsed a plan to elect 133 delegates to a constitutional convention which would begin that fall. Prison reformers and their new allies would have their chance to get rid of the aldermen.[46]

Throughout 1871, reformers had actually been conducting a two-front battle, one electoral and the other, more quietly, in behalf of a constitutional convention. Aware that electoral success was highly unlikely and with the advice of old politicians like McMichael, Curtin, and others, reformers understood that securing a convention would be a much easier task. Not only did its statewide character make success more likely, but it might even be possible to secure the support of some local party leaders who were also interested in eliminating the power base of Democratic aldermen, the only serious political opposition left in Philadelphia, and taming some jealously recalcitrant Republican aldermen. Also, at least one "ring" leader, District Attorney Mann, had much to gain by further centralizing the criminal justice system.

In any event, aldermen provided their critics with ample evidence of continued wrongdoing, prompting the *Ledger* in 1873 to place criminal justice foremost among the "great many reasons why the present organization of our minor magistracy should be revised by the Constitutional Convention."[47] Once again the most notorious incident involving aldermen revolved around William McMullin.[48] In addition to his election thuggery, McMullin kept things lively in Moyamensing by refusing to disband his Moyamensing Hose Company even after the volunteer system was abolished in 1870. The company's continued attempts to respond to fire alarms caused confrontations on occasion with the police and kept the company alive as the political and social base of his power, which was probably McMullin's main objective. About a year before the company was outlawed, in September 1869, U.S. Revenue Detective James J. Brooks was shot by three of the hose company's members. At the trial, Aldermen McMullin, Collins, and Devitt testified to being with the defendants at Devitt's brother's tavern on the day of the shooting but offered no incriminating evidence. Nevertheless, the defendants were convicted. One of them died in prison, but McMullin was instrumental in obtaining a pardon for the other two in July 1872. Just a few weeks after the pardon, at a hose company banquet, one of the two, Hugh Marra, shot and seriously wounded McMullin. Nearly everyone, including the aldermen, was shocked. Marra disappeared and was not found for another month, during which time his fellow released convict, James Dougherty, was himself murdered. The entire affair received wide press coverage throughout the trial of Marra, at which he was sentenced to six years and eight months in prison. Only the Republican press suggested a plausible explanation, which was that Marra and his associates had shot Brooks under orders from McMullin because Brooks was investigating an illegal whiskey ring McMullin was operating. Because Marra failed to assassinate Brooks, McMullin failed to pay Marra for the job. Still bearing a grudge, Marra shot McMullin as soon as he was released from prison.[49]

This episode brought further infamy on aldermen and their influence on Philadelphia's politics and courts.[50] Grand juries repeated their support for a salaried magistracy so regularly in early 1872 that the aldermen held a special meeting to consider how to respond. They could develop no argument, however, other than the one they had been making for years—that the law required them to return all cases to court.[51]

As the constitutional convention drew nearer, the recommendations of grand juries became more specific. A November 1872 inquest, for example, proposed "such a change in the Constitution and laws of the Commonwealth as will abolish the offices of alderman and justices of the peace in the city of Philadelphia." Throughout 1873 grand juries repeated these recommendations.[52] The prison inspectors joined in, calling the aldermanic system "the great and foremost evil in the criminal department of Philadelphia." No im-·provement in prison conditions or the treatment of petty offenders would be possible unless the "traffic in the manipulation of petty crime" was ended by the removal of aldermen from "the sphere of politics," a change in their mode of selection, the establishment of good behavior tenure and fixed salaries, and the requirement of legal training for all magistrates.[53]

PSAMPP members repeated, with ever greater emphasis, their contention that the system of fees and wishes of private prosecutors were at fault. In so doing, they sounded much like the businessman reformers (which some of them were) who wanted the ethic of personal greed removed from the sphere of public administration.

> If people will come with silly complaints or frivolous charges, for swearing to which they are most ready and willing to pay, it can scarcely be supposed that their wishes will not be gratified. Perhaps there is nothing in all this, either in suitor or Magistrate, worse than is going forward in the business world elsewhere, where trade leaves its channel to dabble in the sweeping Maelstrom of speculation; and misery and want, disgrace and all but punishment follow the departure from the normal course.[54]

This point remained the foundation of the prison reformers' argument, and their solution was the one they had suggested in 1864. "[W]e do not think it necessary that there should be . . . any Aldermen. We want police magistrates."[55]

Only the quarter sessions judges remained ambivalent concerning aldermen and private prosecution. Their annoyance at petty litigation and official corruption was unmistakable. Judge Edward M. Paxson, for example, urged grand jurors, in December 1869, to ignore as many cases as possible and added that the fact that two-thirds of all persons committed were released without trial "is painfully suggestive of oppression and extortion in the name and under color of the law." On the eve of the constitutional convention, he was hopeful that "the time was not far distant when the Police Magistrates of the city would be limited in number and confined to men learned in the law, and be salaried officers." Paxson was a reliable member of the city's Republican party, the organization's candidate for the 1872 nomination for state supreme court. His comments were thus another suggestion that this was one change to which even the machine would consent.[56] Judge Thomas Finletter similarly tore into the aldermen in his decision to hold Alderman Hagar for trial in an 1872 illegal fee case.[57]

Yet the very same jurists championed the continuation of private prosecution and occasionally even defended the aldermen. Paxson told a grand jury in 1870 that it was the citizens' "duty when they know of the commission of an offense to make complaint before a magistrate in the usual and proper way, and bring the offender to justice." Two years later, he lamented the "indisposition on the part of individuals having knowledge of a crime to prosecute." This sounded much like the complaints about declining respect for the law which prefaced the prison reformer's proposals for change, but, instead, Paxson offered the novel suggestion that each ward organize "an association for the punishment of all crimes perpetrated within its boundaries" and pursue this work "with half the zeal displayed in many matters of far less importance."[58]

Judge Paxson's proposal for ward organizations for private prosecution might have represented the machine's idea of a compromise solution, but it also envisioned a very different form of community involvement in criminal justice than that which would develop in a city that was relying on the professional police. The bench also expressed ambivalence toward private prosecution and reliance on the police in comments critical of police arrest practices. These comments became far more frequent during the early 1870s. Judge Finletter was the major voice in the judicial effort to restrain the eagerness of police officers to make arrests for drunkenness. Several times Finletter issued lengthy statements instructing officers concerning the legal limits of their powers. People must be disorderly and presenting an evil example in order for their drunkenness to be a crime. The police had no right to arrest a person simply because they knew he had been drinking. People who were presenting no danger or annoyance to others were not proper objects of police action. No policemen could keep a person incarcerated in a stationhouse "without an oath or warrant against him." Echoing the antebellum Judge Kelley, Finletter suggested that policemen who did otherwise invaded, rather than protected, the rights of citizens.[59]

Statements like these made it clear that, despite their abhorrence of aldermanic misconduct, the judges remained uneasy about the transformation of criminal justice. Because they were in the unique position of having to judge police conduct from within legal traditions based on private prosecution, the quarter sessions bench implied that abolition of the fee system or even the office of alderman was not incompatible with continued private prosecution. However, in order for a structure that could accommodate the continued primacy of private prosecution to be implemented, criminal justice and businessman reformers—the architects of the new structure—would have had to relinquish two assumptions that they held much more unequivocally than did the judges and that were at the heart of the transformation of criminal justice.

One assumption was that virtually all private prosecution was exploitative or unnecessary; the second, that the preferred relationship of the citizenry to the state was the administrative one inherent in the police and the prison agency. To these ideas, reformers held steadfast, and in the end, the structure they created was most compatible with them.

The New Constitution

The election of delegates to the constitutional convention took place in October 1872. At its May convention, the CMRA recommended several candidates, and of those, George W. Biddle, Theodore Cuyler, and John P. Wetherill were elected. Other successful candidates associated with the reform movement included William Meredith, Lea's cousin Henry C. Carey, and William Littleton. Many of the Philadelphia delegates were prominent local businessmen—in coal, railroads, importing, hardware, flour, chemicals, and banking—but most of the delegates were lawyers. Of the 133 delegates, 95 were full-time lawyers, another 8 were lawyers engaged in business pursuits. Though only a few of the delegates had been especially active in the municipal reform movement, "the reformers were well represented in background and attitude."[60]

The convention opened on 12 November 1872 and continued until December of 1873. Two weeks into the proceedings John H. Campbell, an at-large delegate from Philadelphia, submitted a resolution to the convention to replace Philadelphia's aldermen with a justice's court, and debate on the subject began.[61] Both the CMRA and the PSAMPP made presentations to the convention early in 1873. The prison reformers needed only to advocate the plan that they had advanced years before, but the businessman reformers needed to formulate a comprehensive proposal. They did so in a document that directly tied together their major concerns. Aldermen ranked second in importance only to the matter of local self-government. After first locating the source of municipal corruption and "ring" control in the fact that "the people of our large cities really do not govern themselves" but are governed by a state legislature "without responsibility to those affected by it," the CMRA moved to those municipal officials with a real power to govern.

Aldermen were the same kinds of men as those who made laws for Philadelphia in Harrisburg, but the consequences of their actions seemed much worse. "No greater blot upon our civilization exists than the administration of justice as exercised in a great city such as Philadelphia. All the worst acts of the professional politician are exerted to secure the position of Alderman for those who are unfitted for it by training, by habits, and by character; and it is only because their victims are habitually the poor and friendless that their brutal and venal tyranny fails to attract general attention and to arouse the sternest popular indignation."[62]

Not even the prison agent had fashioned a more scathing denunciation of the minor judiciary. Their interest in doing as much damage to the "ring" as possible led the CMRA to propose an amendment that limited the magistrate's powers to a greater extent than any that the prison reformers or court officers had put forward. Aldermen would be replaced by magistrates, appointed by the governor for good behavior, paid a salary, and learned in the law. Their numbers would be strictly limited according to population, and their powers would be no greater than those currently held by justices of the peace. Magistrates could be removed from office by the court of common pleas "upon cause therefore being shown by any citizen." Adoption of this amendment would create "a system by which cheap and equal justice could be had by poor and rich alike" and would vastly reduce the number of cases returned to court. The CMRA completed their package of reform proposals by also urging the abolition of grand juries (a step that could only be taken after the prior abolition of aldermen), the adoption of more severe penalties for bribery, a limitation on municipal debt, a new registry law, and the end of the fee system in all public offices.[63]

In the judiciary committee of the convention, the reformers' cause was directed by Theodore Cuyler, an at-large delegate from Philadelphia. Though a Democrat, Cuyler was an active reformer and attorney, a member of the Reform Club and the Philadelphia Board of Trade. The section on Philadelphia aldermen reported by the committee called for the establishment of "one court [not of record] of police and small causes for each thirty thousand inhabitants in all cities of over 200,000 people," which included at the time only Philadelphia. Presiding over these courts would be "judges learned in the law" with five years' experience. They would be elected for seven-year terms on a citywide general ticket, have the same civil and criminal jurisdiction as the aldermen, and be paid only by salaries, with all costs and fees going directly to the city treasury.[64]

The debate over this section was long and heated. Supporters of the committee's recommendation argued directly from the statements of prison inspectors and the CMRA. Cuyler pointedly stated that "individual instances of pure and upright and honest men . . . are comparatively few." The office of alderman had to be abolished because it had "become so odious in the city of

Philadelphia that you cannot get decent men to accept the position. . . . If we are to elevate it, if we are to dignify it, we must provide another name for it."[65]

Though there was never any doubt that some change along the lines Cuyler proposed would be approved, defenders of the aldermen made several alterations in the original section. Opponents had objections to many aspects of the proposal. Non-Philadelphians protested because they believed that the convention was not supposed to pass special legislation for only one place within the state; indeed, this was a prime reason for calling the convention in the first place. Many rural delegates felt that the entire discussion unfairly besmirched the reputations of justices of the peace throughout Pennsylvania. The rural delegates also insisted that one of the objects of the convention was to create a uniform system of justice for the state, which this proposal would obviously prevent, and delegates from Pittsburgh were especially worried that their aldermen would be abolished once that city reached the requisite population.[66]

Several Philadelphia delegates raised the most telling objections. The main defenders of aldermen were leading city Democrat Benjamin L. Temple and Republican W. B. Hanna, with lesser roles played by Edward C. Knight, J. Alexander Simpson, and the elder traditionalist Democratic statesmen George M. Dallas and George W. Biddle. They first made an unsuccessful attempt to retain the office of aldermen as it had been, with the exception of salaries instead of the fee system. Their arguments were remarkable for the way in which they captured the central themes that had surrounded primary justice for decades. Temple began by implicitly accusing reformers of cynical opportunism. "The office of alderman in the city of Philadelphia was not considered so great a nuisance" until the registry law was passed, which, of course, was true in the case of the businessman reformers. Once the board of aldermen was organized, "the office of alderman became a stench in the nostrils of all honest people." Just eliminate this political power, and the same aldermen will again be honorable and acceptable. Hanna was more assertive. He first delivered a brief but laudatory history of the Anglo-American tradition of the minor judiciary. Many of these officials in Philadelphia had been "honorable, upright men." Nevertheless, some abused the fee system (sometimes out of necessity), and the time had, therefore, come to make the aldermen salaried. But that was all. Abolition of the office was not only unnecessary, it was unwanted. "The people have sent us no remonstrances, no memorials to abolish the body." He then made one of the rare public statements that acknowledged the way in which the aldermanic system was supposed to work and, perhaps, represented the sentiments of those who had failed to besiege the convention with remonstrances: "I say that we as a community require a body of men to whom the mass of the people can go with freedom. We want a magistracy known to the people. . . . We have a class of population who, instead of appealing to members of the bar, would rather go to their neighbor, and ask his advice." Police courts scattered randomly about the city, presided over by lawyers elected on citywide tickets, would rob people of their neighborhood justice and give them, instead, courts that would soon become as odious as the already notorious police courts of New York. Temple contended that "if the courts contemplated by this section are established, in less than five years . . . a far greater cry will come up from the people . . . to have these courts abolished."[67]

This moved a non-Philadelphia delegate to agree. "I have not heard whether the people are opposed to it or not. The lawyers who represent them here say they are. But, sir, these are eminently courts of the people, and I am not so certain that they wish any change." To abolish an office "without any cause or complaint from the people" was highly improper. What did it matter if some aldermen spell the word spoon "spune," or wife "y-"? "Is it not just exactly the true way to spell it among some people?" The point was that it was good to have magistrates that close to the people. Temple added that all of the corruption and venality of which aldermen had been accused had also been "said and applied to members of the Legislature." Yet, did anyone propose abolishing the legislature and establishing an English-style parliament? Were the delegates willing to "abolish the office of alderman and take away an indefensible right belonging only to the people, and which we should leave with them? The office of alderman is indispensable, and is brought directly home to the people for the transaction of a class of business that aldermen, whether learned in law or not, can perform."[68]

Despite the very clear message provided by the aldermen's defenders that the office's abolition would constitute a transformation of criminal law and criminal justice that was not altogether salutary, the amendments offered by Temple and others to retain the office of alderman were rejected by voice vote. The people may have sent no remonstrances against the aldermen, but neither did they send the convention any petitions in their support. This was, of course, because so many of the people who relied on aldermen were disenfranchised, politically disorganized, and hardly in a position to mobilize in the defense of aldermanic justice with anything resembling the effectiveness of the reformers who were attacking it. The poor were hardly in a position to mobilize politically on their own at all, and while this is unsurprising, it was one of the important political realities of the centralized city which made the abolition of aldermanic justice possible. So, rebuked in their efforts to keep the people close to their magistrates, the defenders of aldermen moved on to what was probably the realistic politicians' main object all along, keeping the current aldermen eligible for the new office of police magistrate.[69]

The debate over whether to require that police magistrates be learned in the law was the most heated of all the debates about the magistracy. Temple and Hanna had greater support here, and they did not hesitate to pull out all the stops. The first objection to the requirement was raised by J. Alexander Simpson, who stated simply that the election provision would not weed out bad men and that good men who were not lawyers should be eligible for the office. Much of Temple's contention that the new system would be even worse than the old was based on the fact that only the worst lawyers would seek the office and that it was precisely these lawyers who were responsible for many of the abuses of the current aldermen.[70]

When the convention met in July 1873 to put final approval on the article on the judiciary, George M. Dallas offered an amendment to dispose of the requirement that the new magistrates be learned in the law. He argued that only very young or old, failed lawyers would become magistrates. Better to allow "gentlemen in the city of Philadelphia, retired merchants and men of that character" to serve in that office. Simpson, Knight, and Temple all spoke in support of the change, with Temple adding that, if the convention would decide to dispense with the whole section on magistrates, "I think the people of Philadelphia would be just as well satisfied." Dallas's amendment was opposed by Cuyler, Littleton, and J. R. Reed, who stated outright that, without the requirement that magistrates be lawyers, "it will be almost as easy" for the current incumbents to be elected as it had been. Advocates of the amendment "ignore with contempt the appeals of the Municipal Reform Association."[71]

Temple responded that, if the convention was to heed all the admonitions of the CMRA, "We would abolish almost every department of the city government." Hanna repeated his opposition to any reform of the aldermanic system and echoed Dallas's claim that gentlemen and merchants would be better than lawyers. "Reduce the number and give them fixed salaries; but we do not want . . . a sort of trivial court to be presided over by some members of the bar. . . . We need men known to their neighbors, known to the people of the localities in which they have their offices, and in their wards and districts." He meant, of course, ward politicians and suggested again that opposition to aldermen commenced only with the registry law.[72]

The clincher in the debate was provided by George W. Biddle. Though claiming to support the change, he argued that the requirement that magistrates be learned in the law "would be most unacceptable to the people." More specifically, "you would certainly array [against the constitution] every man who has aspiration to this office who has not the qualifications which the section now requires." The political power of aldermen may have been objectionable, but it was still a factor with which to reckon. Other delegates immediately picked up on this point. One thought that it was not worth provoking "hostility from sources which the Constitution ought not to encounter" just to have lawyers for a magistracy that was "more analogous to voluntary arbitration." Knight thought that to exclude the current aldermen from the magistracy would "produce a prejudice against the actions of the Convention that will tell very materially when we want the votes of the people to confirm our work." The Republican machine in Philadelphia, after all, was not above fixing the ratification election for the constitution, and they had already taken some lumps. The ward leaders had been badly hurt by the changes already made in the minor judiciary; it might be too much to try to harm the central machine even further. Literally minutes after this argument was raised, Dallas's amendment passed the convention by voice vote.[73]

Several other changes directly met the political and personal complaints of the reformers. Throughout the debate, critics placed great emphasis on the civil responsibilities and political duties of aldermen. Delegates made these concerns clear by putting explicit language in the constitution prohibiting the legislature from increasing the civil jurisdiction of, or conferring any political duties upon, the new magistrates. Both clauses passed by voice vote immediately after the provision making all magistrates learned in the law was defeated. The final section read as follows:

> In Philadelphia there shall be established for each thirty thousand inhabitants, one court, not of record, of police and civil causes, with jurisdiction not exceeding one hundred dollars; such courts shall be held by magistrates whose term of office shall be five years, and they shall be elected on general ticket by the qualified voters at large; and in the election of the said magistrates no voter shall vote for more than two-thirds of the number of persons to be elected when more than one are chosen; they shall be compensated only by fixed salaries, to be paid by said county; and shall exercise such jurisdiction, civil and criminal, except as herein provided, as is now exercised by aldermen, subject to such changes, not involving an increase of civil jurisdiction or conferring political duties, as may be made by law. In Philadelphia the office of alderman is abolished.[74]

This compromise did not please the most ardent municipal reformers. The *Ledger* thought it "impossible to believe" that the new magistrates would not have to be learned in the law. Lea was so disturbed that he wrote and published a letter to Cuyler lamenting the fact that "the new plan contains two of the features that have principally contributed to the shocking abuses that exist. These are the election of the presiding magistrates and the absence of the requirement of any legal training for men who are to expound and administer the law." Lea quoted liberally from a report by New York lawyer Dorman B. Eaton on that city's police justices, warning, as several convention delegates had, that Philadelphia's magistrates would ultimately be no better. Elections would make the magistrate's offices "political prizes to be struggled for by the worst class of politicians, and to be used primarily for political purposes." Allowing nonlawyers to compete for these places virtually assured that the selection of the minor judiciary would remain in the hands of the political bosses and that the magistrates themselves would be "sharpers, bullies, ignorant party hacks, brutal, uneducated tools of the great party demagogues."[75]

The reformers achieved many of the other changes they sought, however.[76] The reform association and its allies were satisfied enough to campaign strenuously for passage of the constitution at the ratification election on 16 December 1873, but Philadelphia's political bosses were most unhappy, and they tried hard to defeat it. The victory of the "ring" in retaining control of the magistrate's offices did not make up for the fact that the new constitution reduced the number of those offices from 78 to 24, and that it abolished the fee system and registry law. The party managers arranged to have Philadelphia reject the constitution by 50,000 votes, believing that this would assure its statewide defeat, but the constitution passed outside the city by 120,000 votes. Though newspapers had already published the first fraudulent city returns, Mayor Stokley decided that, under the circumstances, the better strategy would be not to fix the election so blatantly and to try to make do with the situation. The "ring," after all, got off fairly lightly and was even left with a structure that might be more susceptible to machine control. Stokley and his allies never were entirely comfortable with the ward leaders, even those who were Republican, and decided that they had done enough for them. Stokley let the constitution's 26,000-vote majority in the city stand, and reformers rejoiced.[77]

With this final acquiescence of the "ring," it seemed for the moment that, as the *Ledger* put it, "their time has come." The provisions implementing the new office of magistrate called for the first election to be held in 1875, and the new officials were to assume office in April of that year. Legislation passed in 1875 set their annual salaries at $3,000 and divided the city into districts to which the magistrates would be assigned by lot.[78]

Reformer T. Morris Perot commented that the new constitution marked "a new epoch in the history of our city."[79] Whether this would truly be a new epoch was for the future to tell; still, as the aldermen's defenders implied, the alliance between businessman and criminal justice reformers had produced a major step in the transformation of criminal justice in Philadelphia. As with the creation of the police in 1854, the change could be attributed at least as much to political interest and municipal vision as to dissatisfaction with the process of criminal justice. The municipal reformers, who had been able to effect the abolition of the aldermen, adopted the prison reformers arguments but were more concerned with the civil jurisdiction and political responsibilities of the minor judiciary than they were with criminal justice. Yet, private prosecutors were those most likely to be the losers as a result of the abolition of the fee system, the nearly 70 percent reduction in the number of magistrates, and the elimination of the physical offices (and officers) to whom they had been bringing their cases for generations. The politicians who had filled the office of aldermen were still eligible to become magistrates, and even without fees or private litigants, they could be expected to maintain their close and lucrative ties to the police. The failure of the constitutional convention's lawyers to professionalize the magistracy was in this sense a victory for the politicians. If the people who had brought cases to the aldermen in the past began now to use the police instead, fewer inappropriate cases would be returned to court, and the new constitution would be a victory for the judges and officials of the court of quarter sessions. Prison commitments would likewise be reduced, and the prison reformers' aims, already bolstered by the opening of a house of correction for drunks and vagrants early in 1874, would be further advanced.

The structural elements that would force the formerly litigious citizenry into a new relationship with the criminal justice apparatus of the state were now in place. The house of correction had opened, and the vagrants and minor offenders who had often been subject to only token punishment could now be confined for much longer periods. Prison Agent Mullen continued to offer state-sanctioned relief. Most significantly, the oldest and most accessible officers to whom complaints of criminal misconduct could be brought would now be the police, whose traditional relationship with the citizenry was much more punitive and coercive than the relationship with aldermen had been.

Private prosecution and the legal culture that it created were in a position to truly become a thing of the past. The now dominant features of the criminal justice system represented a new passive relationship of the citizenry to the state, born out of the idea that there was a special, "dangerous" class of citizens who were the proper objects of the system's punitive and benevolent activity. The relatively few new police magistrates would likely be so burdened with civil litigation and police cases that they would hardly have time for private criminal cases. In any case, the ethos of the new institutions no longer required popular use of the criminal law to ensure its authority.

Yet, the changes were not absolute. The constitutional convention did not alter the magistracy as fully as it might have done. Primary justice still would not be controlled by members of the legal profession but, rather, by politicians. Judges were still occasionally encouraging private use of the law right up to the point of new constitution's approval, and private prosecution still had statutory sanction. The partial victory of the "ring" meant that the old relationship would not be entirely moribund, even though it would now be dwarfed by the newer relationship between politicians and the police. A new era was about to begin, but not without the mark of the old.

Epilogue

Philadelphia's notoriously corrupt late nineteenth-century system of criminal justice, controlled by the machine and dominated by the police, was built on the structure of primary justice that had been created by the new constitution. No one really had just such a criminal justice system in mind when the constitution was ratified, but then no one involved in shaping the new structure got just what they wanted. So, as the politicians gained control of the centralized structure of prosecution, they drew from their experience with the decentralized one. The corruption of the police and the magistrates after 1874 rested largely on the now extinct relationship between aldermen and private litigants.

Nonetheless, when the first twenty-four police magistrates were elected in February 1875, the criminal justice system in Philadelphia was markedly different from what it had been just a generation earlier. Before 1850 the gates of criminal justice were kept by fee-dependent aldermen who, along with the grand jury, courts of record, and the prison, comprised virtually the entire system. The city's paltry assemblage of night watchmen and day police had little impact on the criminal courts. At the dawn of the magistrates' courts era, the city's criminal justice apparatus was dominated by a large, professional police department. The new magistrates, like all other criminal justice officials, were now salaried officers of the state. The prosecution of cases in the courts of record was more frequently overseen by the district attorney, and the consequences of these prosecutions were ameliorated when necessary by the prison agent. Not only was there now a county prison and a state penitentiary, but there was also a house of correction for minor offenders.

However impressive these structural changes were, their practical effects were to bring an end to endemic street disorder and to delegitimize private prosecution. All of the major new components of the process of criminal justice—the police, the district attorney, the prison agent, and the police magistrates—were designed to place control over the process in the hands of salaried officials of city administration and to remove it from ordinary citizens and neighborhood politicians. Together these changed signalled a new epoch in criminal justice.

With the fee system and the old alderman's offices abolished, the traditional mode of access of private prosecutors to the law was gone. Direct payment by the citizen to the official dispensing justice was now illegal. The traditional way of exercising the criminal law had been redefined; now, it was simple corruption. Certainly the fee system had deteriorated since its colonial origins and had been subject to much abuse, but now, even its honest use was outlawed. Before the constitutional reforms, aldermen, the initial dispensers of justice, were dependent for their living on the citizenry's voluntary use of the law. Now, the magistrates and the police, who would in practice fill the place of the former aldermen, would depend on the public treasury and each other for their livelihood. On the one hand, this made criminal prosecution free for all citizens, but, on the other, it delegitimated the relationship through which the citizenry had exercised considerable control over the process of prosecution and through which there had been widespread and ready access to the criminal law. The interdependence of citizen and alderman created by the fee system had been the practical foundation of a culture that made the authority of the criminal law dependent on its voluntary popular use, in much the same way that the civil law functioned. The fee system expressed the era's ideal of the proper exercise of the law, equally accessible to all through a direct, personal relationship of magistrate and citizen. Now, the bureaucratic and coercive relationship between the police and the people would be the foundation of a culture of criminal justice in which the authority of the criminal law was dependent upon the intervention of state-employed officials in the lives of citizens.

The new structure of 1875 brought into sharp relief the contrast between these two epochs of criminal justice. While private prosecution had prevailed, the dominant relationship in criminal justice had been the alderman-litigant relationship. Though allegedly rife with abuse and corruption, this relationship was also characterized by a legitimate form of voluntarism on the part of the litigants and a reliance on popular participation to ensure the authority of the law and the equality of all citizens before the law. Anyone could, and everyone should, have ready access to an alderman and thus the ability to use the criminal law against another. No legitimate differences among citizens were admitted, and when such differences in treatment became obvious, both journalists and court officials protested.

The era dominated by the police would change all that. The ideal of this era was expressed in the rules of conduct instructing the police to arrest persons based on their appearance and wealth (or lack of it). The police were expected to ensure order and, in so doing, to treat the poor differently than they did other people. Because policemen, not private citizens, were to initiate most cases, a fundamental alteration would result in the relationship of the lower classes to the criminal justice system. Whereas judges had, in years past, spoken of "respect for" and "reliance upon" the criminal law, police officials spoke of the "dread of the law." Now, the special access of the poor would be only to punishment in an involuntary and punitive way—as suspect or defendant—as the ideal as well as in practice.[1]

The changes in the fundamental relationship of the citizenry to the criminal justice system and the ideal of the proper exercise of the criminal law constituted the transformation of criminal justice in Philadelphia. But the old system had never worked exactly as the ideal would have had it, and neither would the new. Centralized political control of primary justice was no less corrupt or informal than the decentralized form had been, but it proved immediately to be less receptive to typical private prosecution. Intoxication and breach of the peace dominated the prison commitments as never before, accounting for 64 percent of all commitments between 1876 and 1880. There were no longer any commitments for nonpayment of court costs or vagrancy, the latter because the house of correction was used for that purpose. Assault and battery commitments remained at about the same level, but they were now less evenly distributed among the magistrates than before. A significantly greater proportion, 17 percent, of these cases were now heard at the central police station. The same was true for larceny cases, which were, predictably enough, proportionally greater after 1875. Now accounting for 13 percent of all commitments, one-third of the larceny cases were heard at the central station.

Because prison overcrowding had been relieved by the house of correction and the abolition of the aldermen had removed local politics from prison administration, far fewer prisoners were now released by the prison inspectors. Only 7 percent were so released, compared to nearly 30 percent between 1854 and 1874. Now 42 percent of the prisoners served out a full term, up from 19 percent. Discharges by the committing magistrates also fell, from 38 percent of all prisoners before 1875 to 30 percent afterwards. Such discharges for assault and battery occurred 80 percent of the time between 1854 and 1874, but only 48 percent of the time between 1876 and 1880. Only the number of breach of the peace charges that were released remained the same, suggesting that this troublesome category of police cases continued to be an arena of police and magisterial abuse. Finally, the proportion of women committed to prison fell to 18 percent of the total, down from 26 percent between 1854 and 1874 and over 30 percent before consolidation. Apparently, the "mere quarrels of busy women" which had accounted for so much of the court's exasperation with private prosecution were having a more difficult time entering the system.

Figures from the court of quarter sessions are even more revealing. The number of cases returned to court did not diminish, but the kinds of cases and their disposition changed markedly. Women were also less involved at this level of criminal justice, comprising 13 percent of all defendants in 1876 and 1878, down from 19 percent during the previous twenty years. More significantly, the proportion of assault and battery cases fell to 29 percent, lower than during any other period under study. In contrast, larceny cases rose to over 36 percent of the total, higher than for any previous period. The crisis in the court eased considerably. The conviction rate rose to nearly 25 percent, and the guilty plea rate more than doubled to 10 percent. Both were higher than at any time since consolidation. Similarly, the imprisonment rate rose to 21 percent, higher than in any previous period, and the ignored rate fell to 29 percent, lower than any time since 1819. The no disposition rate nearly vanished, falling to a mere 1 percent of all cases. Costs were placed on prosecutors now in less than 3 percent of all cases, lower than any other period under study. This was done only in cases ignored by the grand jury and occurred in only 9 percent of these cases, lower than in any other period. Costs were placed on prosecutors in only 8 percent of the ignored assault and battery cases, down from 16 percent between 1854 and 1874. The ignored rate for assault and battery fell under 50 percent for the first time since 1838; the ignored rate for larceny fell to 25 percent, down from 39 percent during the previous twenty years. As might be expected from the increased ability of the courts to convict and imprison defendants, the average prison term fell to 5 months. Larceny terms were halved, from 10 months to 5, and assault and battery terms rose from 2 to 5 months.[2]

These statistics suggest that at least the short-run effect of the new system was to reduce the relative number of private prosecutions and increase the ability of the criminal courts to punish offenders; apparently the desires of the court and prison reformers had been met. There was a certain ironic symbolism in the fact that the prison inspectors and the prison agent stopped issuing annual reports around this time, and the police department reports expanded to the point where they became the largest section of the mayor's annual message.

The desires of the businessman municipal reformers were not met, however. Within a year, it had become apparent that the strategy of the "ring" in accepting the constitution and making the best of it was working. Reformers tried to get their own candidates nominated by the Republicans in February

1874 but failed. Despite a new elections bill passed shortly before the election, its enforcement was left in the hands of officials appointed under the Registry Law. Mayor Stokley was reelected over a renegade Republican of dubious reputation, Alexander McClure, whom even reformers like Lea opposed. The legislature failed until 1876 to pass a constitutionally mandated law enacting a salary structure for municipal offices other than police magistrate, so the fee system remained in effect by default until then. When the salary law was finally passed, the reason for the delay became clear. Republicans insisted on laws that gave officeholders salaries well in excess of any then in existence, and they could defeat any bill that provided otherwise. The law they finally got gave the district attorney and sheriff $15,000 a year, the recorder of deeds $12,000, court clerks and the prothonotary $10,000. The only real setback for the machine was the defeat of William B. Mann in the election for district attorney, which unfortunately for Mann still took place in the fall along with the general election and was influenced by a mid-term Democratic revival in Pennsylvania. Even *The Nation* commented on Mann's defeat, hoping it was auguring yet another reform era, but two years later, Mann was appointed prothonotary of the district court by the still entrenched Republican "ring."[3]

Similarly, the first election for police magistrates went just as Henry C. Lea had predicted. Each party nominated sixteen candidates for the twenty-four offices, since no voter could vote for more than sixteen. This meant that all of the Republicans were assured of victory and that the contest for the remaining eight places would be among the Democrats. Eight reform candidates trailed badly behind the regular party candidates, so the party managers were the ones who chose the new magistrates. At least eight of the new magistrates had previously been aldermen, but so had several of the defeated Democrats.[4]

By no later than 1878, the new magistrates were already held in opprobrium by reformers. Together they returned only $14,695 in fees and fines for 1877; not one returned as much as his salary. For decades afterwards, Philadelphia's magistrates remained men "who have risen through the ranks of their political parties after years of service which ordinarily culminates with being a ward leader." One investigator commented in 1931 that for the preceding fifty years, public opinion in Philadelphia had believed that "the magisterial system as set up and administered strikes at the good repute of the criminal administration in its entirety." The system remained an object of intense criticism and reform activity until well after World War II.[5]

In the long run, the reformers' intentions were unrealized in this sphere as well as in others. Salaries and the decline of private prosecution ended neither political control of the minor judiciary nor the abuses of the magistrates. Much of this was, of course, predicted by the businessman reformers and evident in the relationship that the aldermen had established with the police. However, the continued corruption and political control of the minor judiciary did not necessarily mean that the relationship between the criminal justice system and the citizenry remained the same. According to the reformers, a position on the minor judiciary was now a reward for a successful ward leader which put him on a citywide stage, not a ward-based stepping-stone to a different citywide office.

So by 1875, the attempts by benevolent and municipal reformers to grapple with the particularistic, decentralized, and highly informal methods of law and city government had resulted in a much more centralized city government that was much more firmly and profitably under the control of corrupt politicians. The politicians' ability to take control of a municipal reform originally directed against them was, in part, a consequence of the transformation of criminal justice: the creation of centrally controllable policemen and police magistrates, and the reduction of the place in criminal justice of proactive citizen participation and the process of litigation. The new political machine was not just bigger than the old ward-based machines, it was fundamentally different insofar as it rested on the disempowerment of private citizen prosecutors and informal relations among state officials. The people of Philadelphia, and subsequent generations of reformers, would have to negotiate a very different structure of officialdom in order to gain either intercession with the law or honest city government.

Conclusion

Historians have been known to speculate about the course of history "if all the world was Philadelphia" or, at least, if all of the United States or some significant part of it was. This study of Philadelphia, no less than previous studies, is conducive to such speculation. Criminal justice does not generally receive much attention in discussions of municipal reform and the political machine, yet its story was intimately involved with both in nineteenth-century Philadelphia. Each had a profound effect on the other, and not without some irony. One of the main complaints of early nineteenth-century reformers was that, because of politics, the city was unable to govern itself. Yet reformers were thwarted by the fact that the very politicians they were seeking to disempower took command of the city once a structure for centralized self-government was created. Part of the reformers' problem was that their contention that the city could not govern itself was true only for their class and from their perspective. In trying to create opportunity for themselves, however, one of their first real achievements was the destruction of a system of criminal justice that was, in its way, a vibrant and effective means of neighborhood-based self-government. The attempt to achieve metropolitan self-government may actually have undermined local community self-government, at least as far as criminal justice was concerned.

In the end, of course, subsequent generations of municipal reformers succeeded in breaking the backs of the machines if not in eliminating corruption. They did this, in part, by continuing to expand the administrative state, elaborating the bureaucracy, and putting even more administrative discretion in the hands of professionals, all proceeding along lines implicit in the transformation of criminal justice. The resulting "institutional state" has been primarily concerned since the late nineteenth century with providing services to, and controlling the behavior of, people much like those who filled Philadelphia's criminal courts with private litigation before 1875. "Deliberate agencies of social policy . . . formal organizations with specialized clienteles and a reformist or character-building purpose," they included schools, prisons, hospitals, and asylums that were designed for the poor, criminal, sick, disturbed, and ignorant. They rapidly became custodial, consumed by a struggle to control the "casualties of the new society," including underemployed, landless wage laborers; people who were injured or made ill by the harsh conditions of work; people who were denied a fair competitive chance to sell their labor because of their age, sex, race, or ethnicity; and people who were unable to face the pressures of the competitive, insecure world of the free labor market.[6]

The troubles of the institutional state are also related to the transformation of criminal justice. Something was gained by the rise of the police, the prison agency, and the rest of the administrative state, but something was lost as well. The world of private prosecution which was eclipsed by this was relatively democratic, flexible, expandable, and familiar. It was also corrupt, easily manipulated, harsh, and sometimes even cruel. It was not at all compatible with an administrative institutional state, largely because of its particularism and location of discretion. Not surprisingly, then, the new ethic of state initiation and control of criminal prosecution guided changes in the structure and culture of criminal justice after the era of private prosecution. Now having assumed the discretion that formerly allowed private parties to settle cases, the court needed new methods for rapidly processing the many cases within the criminal courts. One method, plea bargaining, explicitly recognized the control of the district attorney over prosecutions. It gave him the power to decide how and when to dispense justice in much the same way that it had been dispensed most of the time under the control of private litigants, that is without a jury trial. The second method relied on the massive proliferation of specialized courts and the decriminalization of formerly criminal acts (for example, wifebeating); both of these further separated the citizenry according to age and sex and met the court and prison reformers' demands that what they considered petty private matters would not be involved in criminal justice.

The drive toward centralized institutional power was a conscious activity among those who stood, in different ways, to benefit from it by gaining power and prestige—lawyers, reformers, businessmen and even politicians with a municipal vision (or grasp). Those who had the most to lose, those who would move from litigants to clients and suspects, resisted in various ways and have remained the institutional state's most recalcitrant problem.[7]

In their resistance to the institutional state lies a hint that the world of private prosecution, though long gone, is neither lost nor entirely forgotten. If this system of law and justice developed out of anything in early republican Philadelphia, it was out of the same logic of self-government that inspired the creation of the United States, a logic that contended that, as long as the people controlled it, the law and state power could be beneficial and benevolent. As renowned visitors to early national America pointed out, two major components of this were popular participation in local government and the centrality of law in daily life and national culture. In their own way, the private citizen litigants of Philadelphia were also elaborating that logic, asserting, in a way that seems somewhat strange to us today, that the United States was a place in which "the law is king" and the people could control it.

Private prosecution was, for them, a democratic form of law enforcement and criminal justice, involving in great numbers citizens of all social and economic groups with state officials who responded directly and personally (if not always satisfactorily) to their requests. It was a practical aspect of the democratic spirit that captured Americans of all classes in the early nineteenth century. Through private prosecution, even the poor, many of them disenfranchised, had a stake in the legal and political system, received something palpable from it, and asserted that democracy in America was something special. This might explain their persistence in this practice—even in the face of the abuses of aldermen—and their violent resistance to police methods of law enforcement. The police were not imposed on an amorphously democratic-spirited people but on a community with a firmly established tradition of democratic law enforcement. An expectation of continued informal, personal, and accessible law enforcement made sense in this context, as did popular resistance to the police and their methods.[8]

Local self-government and proactive political participation are certainly not cure-alls for the problems of justice and equality plaguing the institutional state and the modern city, but neither are they unimportant to a political culture that insists that its legitimacy rests on the twin pillars of law and democracy. The experience of a more vibrant and participatory—if less efficient or reformist—system of criminal law, obliterated by the rise of the institutional and administrative state, speaks to the crisis of law and citizenship that has marked American life in the twentieth century. The relationship of the citizenry to the state, even in a large city, can take different forms. While no one form ensures either, perhaps the recovery of the American tradition of private prosecution can help in fashioning a way to revive an American commitment to law and democracy. As a beginning, we might ask whether we must less frequently be clients and suspects in order more often to be citizens.

Appendix

The following tables illustrate many of the points made in the text concerning the number and disposition of cases in Philadelphia's courts. Several also provide information on the number and types of prison commitments and inmates and other details of criminal justice activity.

Unless otherwise noted, the data came from four manuscript sources. Data on pretrial commitments to, and discharges from, prison are from the Philadelphia County Prison Daily Occurrence Docket. The information in this docket consists of the name of the person committed (from which I derived the prisoner's gender), the date of commitment, the charge, the person authorizing the commitment, the date of discharge, the sentence (when applicable), and the name of the person authorizing, or the reason for, the discharge. I took a 1 percent sample of the entries in this docket for every even numbered year between 1800 and 1880 and a 10 percent sample for the simple process of calculating percentages of charges.

Data on the courts of record are from the Docket Books of the Philadelphia County Court of Quarter Sessions and the Philadelphia City Mayor's Court. The information in these dockets consists of the defendant's name, the charge, the grand jury disposition, plea, verdict, sentence, and the name of the presiding judge. For the quarter sessions, I took a 5 percent sample for 1800, 1810, 1815, 1820, 1825, and every even numbered year from 1830 to 1880. For the mayor's court, I took a 20 percent sample for the same years through 1836, the final year of this court's operation.

Many of the entries in the court dockets are incomplete, but they sometimes included additional information that I could make use of, such as information on the placing of costs on prosecutors. When there was no mention of the costs, I assumed that they were absorbed by the county. Infrequent charges could not be meaningfully analyzed by themselves, so I combined them to the general categories of morals, order, serious personal and property crime, and minor property crime.

Data on the characteristics of convicts in the county prison are from the Philadelphia County Prison Convict Description Docket. Information in this docket consists of the convict's name, race, sex, age, place of birth, occupation, crime, sentence, and number of times sentenced to prison. I took a 20 percent sample of first-time convicts and a 33 percent sample of recidivists. All of the dockets are located in the Philadelphia City Archives. I am very grateful for the assistance that Ward Childs and his staff gave me in the collection of this information.

The tables below are organized according to topic and time. The first several tables provide overall information on the criminal justice system for the entire period under study. Next are tables examining use of the courts, first for the entire period, then for the periods 1800–38, 1844–54, and 1856–74. The first period covers the years in which the criminal courts were divided; the second, the time after court unification but before the establishment of the police; and the third, the time between consolidation and the abolition of the aldermen. The gap in the data from 1838 to 1844 results from the fact that the court dockets for the two criminal courts that served the county during these years are too incomplete to be usefully analyzed. The last several tables concern commitments to, and discharges from, prison and prison inmates.

Table A.1 Arrests by Year, 1855–1874

Year	Number	Year	Number	Year	Number
1855	38,651	1861	27,283	1869	38,749
1856	25,385	1862	27,576	1870	31,171
1857	21,537	1863	34,050	1872	40,007
1858	22,367	1864	34,221	1873	30,400
1859	32,225	1866	43,226	1874	32,114
1860	32,051	1867	42,963		

SOURCE: *Annual Reports* of the chief of police.

Table A.2 Total Prison Commitments, 1815–1871

Year	Number	Year	Number	Year	Number
1815	1,403	1848	4,578	1860	21,257
1820	3,037	1849	5,799	1861	16,549
1825	3,787	1850	7,687	1862	14,894
1830	4,193	1851	10,862	1863	17,434
1832	4,513	1852	11,158	1864	14,282
1834	4,748	1853	11,905	1865	16,888
1836	1,477[a]	1854	10,858	1866	19,468
1840	4,917	1855	14,170	1867	18,575
1842	5,182	1856	14,430	1868	17,620
1844	3,278	1857	15,809	1869	18,305
1846	5,897	1858	15,252	1870	15,288
1847	5,185	1859	20,236	1871	13,171

SOURCE: County Prison Daily Occurrence Dockets to 1846; *Annual Reports* thereafter.

[a] Figures for January to May only.

Table A.3 Criminal Court Cases, 1800–1876

Year	Number	Year	Number	Year	Number
1800	582[a]	1844	1,297	1862	3,028
1810	844[b]	1846	1,668	1864	4,054
1815	1,234	1848	1,735	1866	4,641
1820	1,127	1850	2,009	1868	5,108
1825	1,169	1852	2,771	1870	5,057
1830	1,107	1854	3,050	1872	3,048[e]
1832	870	1856	3,474	1874	3,073[e]
1834	1,459	1858	2,999[d]	1876	3,985[e]
1836	1,199[c]	1860	4,155[d]		

SOURCE: Mayor's Court and Quarter Sessions Dockets.

NOTE: Data for 1800–1836 combined mayor's court and quarter sessions. Data for 1838–42 missing or fragmentary. Data collected for even numbered years only from 1830 to 1876.

[a] Data for 5 of 6 mayor's court sessions.

[b] Data for 3 of 4 mayor's court sessions.

[c] Data for 2 of 4 mayor's court sessions.

[d] Data for 4 of 6 court sessions.

[e] Data for 6 of 12 court sessions.

Table A.4 Percentage of Arrests for Minor Offenses by Charge, 1855–1874

Year	Intoxication	Disorderly	Vagrancy	Total
1855	29.1	47.5	3.4	80.0
1856	26.8	44.9	4.4	76.1
1857	19.6	48.9	6.0	74.5
1858	19.9	49.8	6.0	75.7
1859	22.3	48.4	6.7	77.4
1860	26.9	45.2	6.9	79.0
1861	22.9	49.6	6.6	79.1
1862	23.1	51.1	4.6	78.8
1863	25.8	49.4	3.1	78.3
1864	26.2	46.8	1.8	74.8
1866[a]	22.5	51.7	3.1	77.3
1867	24.1	49.1	3.5	76.7
1869[a]	35.3	39.5	2.5	77.3
1870	38.2	36.7	2.8	77.7
1872[a]	39.4	36.1	1.9	77.4
1873	33.1	39.2	4.6	82.2
1874	32.1	43.3	6.7	82.1

SOURCE: *Annual Reports* of the chief of police.

[a] Data missing for 1865, 1868, and 1871.

Table A.5 Percentage of Prison Commitments
for Nonindictable Offenses, 1815–1874

Year	Percentage	Year	Percentage	Year	Percentage
1815	28.5	1849	48.8	1862	65.9
1820	26.7	1850	54.8	1863	60.0
1825	43.2	1851	58.7	1864	56.7
1830	31.7	1852	58.7	1865	61.4
1832	42.2	1853	61.0	1866	65.0
1834	38.3	1854	58.2	1867	68.3
1838[a]	50.9	1855	61.4	1868	63.9
1840	57.1	1856	58.3	1869	66.4
1842	65.3	1857	58.7	1870	59.9
1844	53.4	1858	62.5	1871	53.6
1846	59.4	1859	70.6	1872	68.0
1847	53.3	1860	70.7	1874[a]	65.1
1848	50.0	1861	69.3		

SOURCE: Daily Occurrence Dockets, 1815–46, County Prison *Annual Reports*, 1847–74.

[a] Data for 1836 and 1873 missing or insufficient.

Table A.6 Quarter Sessions Cases, 1800–1878

	Percentage
Assault and assault/battery	39.0
Serious personal crime	3.2
Larceny and minor property crime	34.8
Serious property crime	7.2
Liquor offenses	8.4
Morals offenses	2.4
Order offenses	3.6

SOURCE: Quarter Sessions Dockets.

Table A.7 Mayor's Court Cases, 1800–1836

	Percentage
Assault/battery	34.2
Serious personal crime	0.9
Larceny and minor property crime	37.3
Serious property crime	2.7
Liquor offenses	16.5
Morals offenses	3.3
Order offenses	4.0

SOURCE: Mayor's Court Dockets.

Table A.8 Quarter Sessions Cases, 1800–1838

	Percentage
Assault and assault/battery	44.4
Serious personal crime	0.1
Larceny and minor property crime	27.2
Serious property crime	0.2
Liquor offenses	16.3
Morals offenses	3.5
Order offenses	4.8

SOURCE: Quarter Sessions Dockets.

Table A.9 Quarter Sessions Cases, 1844–1855

	Percentage
Assault and assault/battery	32.9
Serious personal crime	2.4
Larceny and minor property crime	35.4
Serious property crime	6.6
Liquor offenses	12.3
Morals offenses	3.5
Order offenses	6.0

SOURCE: Quarter Sessions Dockets.

Table A.10 Quarter Sessions Cases, 1856–1874

	Percentage
Assault and assault/battery	42.0
Serious personal crime	2.9
Larceny and minor property crime	34.9
Serious property crime	7.9
Liquor offenses	6.0
Morals offenses	2.0
Order offenses	2.3

SOURCE: Quarter Sessions Dockets.

Table A.11 Quarter Sessions Case Disposition by Charge, 1820–1874

	Guilty plea	Guilty verdict	Acquitted	Ignored	No disposition
Assault and assault/ battery	3.1	15.0	18.0	53.0	14.0
Larceny and minor property crime	9.5	19.5	18.9	34.8	13.0
Serious personal crime	2.2	29.0	43.0	17.2	9.7
Serious property crime	8.1	17.1	32.0	21.8	19.4
All cases	6.4	15.1	22.5	37.4	16.6

SOURCE: Quarter Sessions Dockets.

Table A.12 Quarter Sessions Conviction Rate, Cases Tried

	All cases	Larceny and minor property crime	Assault and assault/battery
1819–74	40.2	48.6	40.3
1819–38	57.9	58.6	65.4
1844–54	46.2	48.2	54.8
1856–74	37.7	47.0	33.0

SOURCE: Quarter Sessions Dockets.

Table A.13 Criminal Court Case Disposition, 1800–1836

	Mayor's court	Quarter sessions
Guilty plea	17.9	10.2
Guilty verdict	25.3	22.0
Acquitted	13.7	14.1
Ignored	18.2	25.2
No disposition	12.0	10.2
Other disposition	12.1	18.3

SOURCE: Mayor's Court and Quarter Sessions Dockets.

Table A.14 Case Disposition by Charge, 1800–1836

Mayor's Court			
	Assault and assault/ battery	Larceny	Liquor
Guilty plea	10.9	19.1	34.8
Guilty verdict	22.4	37.7	5.8
Acquitted	12.5	13.7	9.0
Ignored	30.2	14.3	13.5
No disposition	10.9	5.8	23.2
Other disposition	9.0	7.9	12.9

Quarter Sessions			
	Assault and assault/ battery	Larceny	Liquor
Guilty plea	2.8	10.1	33.3
Guilty verdict	19.0	40.5	3.9
Acquitted	9.9	19.0	9.8
Ignored	31.0	17.7	23.5
No disposition	19.0	2.5	21.6
Other disposition	18.3	10.1	7.8

SOURCE: Mayor's Court and Quarter Sessions Dockets.

Table A.15 Case Disposition by Year, 1800–1836

	Mayor's Court								
	1800	1810	1815	1820	1825	1830	1832	1834	1836
Guilty	53.5	48.1	41.4	42.2	47.9	48.1	29.8	41.3	36.0
Imprisoned	22.4	27.8	19.8	25.7	34.0	34.3	19.4	26.8	16.3
Ignored	13.8	20.3	16.6	15.6	22.2	11.8	14.9	21.0	24.0
No disposition	3.4	6.3	6.4	9.2	4.2	12.7	28.4	21.7	20.9
	Quarter Sessions								
	1800	1810	1815	1820	1825	1830	1832	1834	1836
Guilty	24.2	44.1	30.0	28.6	43.5	62.6	37.0	30.8	15.8
Imprisoned	13.6	20.6	16.7	5.7	26.1	31.2	11.1	7.7	11.5
Ignored	16.7	23.5	6.7	31.4	26.1	18.8	40.7	38.5	28.9
No disposition	10.6	2.9	26.7	11.4	0	0	0	10.3	21.1

SOURCE: Mayor's Court and Quarter Sessions Dockets.

Table A.16 Combined Criminal Court Case Disposition, 1820–1838

	All cases	Larceny and minor property crime	Assault and assault/battery
Guilty plea	11.5	11.8	3.9
Guilty verdict	25.8	40.7	21.8
Acquitted	15.5	19.8	11.3
Ignored	25.6	17.3	37.8
No disposition	11.6	10.1	17.5

SOURCE: Mayor's Court and Quarter Sessions Dockets.

Table A.17 Costs on Prosecutors, Assault and Battery, 1800–1836

| | Ignored | | Acquitted | |
	1800–15	1820–36	1800–15	1820–36
Mayor's Court	33.3	61.6	40.0	16.0
Quarter Sessions	18.2	48.5	40.0	11.1

SOURCE: Mayor's Court and Quarter Sessions Dockets.

Table A.18 Quarter Sessions Case Disposition, 1844–1854

	Percentage
Guilty verdict	18.2
Guilty plea	7.1
Acquitted	20.5
Ignored	34.9
No disposition	18.2

SOURCE: Quarter Sessions Dockets.

Table A.19 Quarter Sessions Conviction Rates, 1844–1854

	Guilty plea	Guilty verdict	Conviction rate
Property cases	9.4	22.2	31.6
Personal cases	5.8	17.5	23.3
All cases	7.1	18.2	25.3

SOURCE: Quarter Sessions Dockets.

Table A.20 Quarter Sessions Conviction Rates, Personal Cases, 1844–1854

	Assault and assault/ battery	Serious offenses
Guilty plea	5.8	6.6
Guilty verdict	15.9	40.0

SOURCE: Quarter Sessions Dockets.

Table A.21 Quarter Sessions Conviction Rates, Property Cases, 1844–1854

	Guilty plea	Guilty verdict	Conviction rate
Larceny	11.4	24.1	35.6
Serious offenses	7.1	23.8	30.9
Minor offenses	5.2	15.5	20.7
All property cases	9.4	22.2	31.6
All cases	7.1	18.2	25.3

SOURCE: Quarter Sessions Dockets.

Table A.22 Quarter Sessions Ignored and
No Disposition Rates, 1844–1854

	Ignored	No disposition	Total
Property cases	27.8	12.0	39.8
Larceny	31.9	6.6	37.5
Minor property crime	25.9	27.6	53.5
Serious property crime	16.7	11.9	28.6
Personal cases	51.6	11.2	62.8
Assault and assault/battery	54.3	10.1	64.4
Serious personal crime	13.3	26.7	40.0
All cases	34.9	18.2	53.1

SOURCE: Quarter Sessions Dockets.

Table A.23 Imprisonment Rates and Sentence Lengths,
Property Cases, 1844–1854

	Imprisonment rate	Average term (months)
Larceny	34.3	10.2
Serious offenses	23.8	24.9
Minor offenses	13.8	8.1
All property crime	28.2	11.9
All cases	16.6	13.0

SOURCE: Quarter Sessions Dockets.

Table A.24 Costs on Prosecutors, Personal Cases, 1844–1854

	Dismissed	Acquitted
Assault and assault/battery	52.2	44.8
Serious offenses	50.0	0.0
All personal crime	52.2	41.9

SOURCE: Quarter Sessions Dockets.

Table A.25 Quarter Sessions Case Disposition, 1856–1874

	Percentage
Guilty verdict	12.7
Guilty plea	4.7
Acquitted	20.8
Ignored	42.0
No disposition	20.0

SOURCE: Quarter Sessions Dockets.

Table A.26 Quarter Sessions Conviction Rates, 1856–1874

	Guilty plea	Guilty verdict	Conviction rate
Property cases	7.1	14.8	21.9
Personal cases	2.2	10.8	13.0
All cases	4.7	12.7	17.4

SOURCE: Quarter Sessions Dockets.

Table A.27 Quarter Sessions Conviction Rates, Personal Cases, 1856–1874

	Guilty plea	Guilty verdict	Conviction rate
Assault and assault/battery	2.3	9.9	12.2
Serious offenses	2.0	24.5	26.0

SOURCE: Quarter Sessions Dockets.

Table A.28 Quarter Sessions Conviction Rates, Property Cases, 1856–1874

	Guilty plea	Guilty verdict	Conviction rate
Larceny	9.4	18.9	28.3
Minor offenses	0.6	4.1	4.7
Serious offenses	8.2	15.7	23.9

SOURCE: Quarter Sessions Dockets.

Table A.29 Quarter Sessions Ignored and No Disposition Rates, 1856–1874

	Ignored	No disposition	Total
Property cases	37.9	20.0	57.9
Larceny	38.6	11.8	50.4
Minor property crime	44.8	34.9	79.7
Serious property crime	26.9	26.9	50.5
Personal cases	51.8	14.0	65.8
Assault and assault/battery	53.8	13.5	67.3
Serious personal crime	22.4	10.2	32.6
All cases	42.0	20.0	62.0

SOURCE: Quarter Sessions Dockets.

Table A.30 Costs on Prosecutors, Personal Cases, 1856–1874

	Ignored	Acquitted
Assault and assault/battery	16.0	8.5
Serious personal crime	0	0
All personal	15.5	7.4

SOURCE: Quarter Sessions Dockets.

Table A.31 Ratio of Arrests to Commitments, Minor Offenses, 1855–1870

Year	Disorderly	Drunkenness	Vagrancy
1855	3.23	4.58	0.51
1856	1.91	3.12	0.48
1857	2.11	2.41	0.54
1858	2.51	2.00	0.50
1859	2.41	1.91	0.56
1860	1.34	2.26	0.60
1861	1.58	2.15	0.67
1862	1.82	3.66	0.66
1863	1.70	9.50	0.58
1864	2.00	7.06	0.57
1866[a]	2.09	4.76	0.68
1867	1.89	5.31	0.98
1869[a]	2.08	3.85	0.79
1870	3.07	3.04	0.65

SOURCE: County Prison *Annual Reports*; *Annual Reports* of chief of police.

[a] Data missing for 1865 and 1868.

Table A.32 Pattern of Releases from Prison,
Minor Offenses, 1815–1874 (in percentages)

	Disorderly	Drunkenness	Vagrancy
1815–1854			
By alderman	38.5	2.2	7.5
By inspectors	37.2	0	30.1
By others	24.3	3.3	4.3
Full term	0	94.4	58.1
1855–1874			
By alderman	33.2	4.4	3.8
By inspectors	55.4	2.4	70.1
By others	1.6	0	2.5
Full term	0	93.2	23.6

SOURCE: County Prison Daily Occurrence Dockets.

Table A.33 Occupational Classification of Larceny Convicts,
1843–1851 (in percentages)

	First offenders	Recidivists	Total
Low white-collar, proprietary	9.4	6.6	8.6
Skilled craftsmen	38.7	38.5	38.6
Unskilled workers	27.8	22.0	26.1
Laborers	13.2	11.0	12.5
No occupation	7.1	9.9	7.9
Blank	3.8	13.2	6.6

SOURCE: County Prison Daily Description Dockets.

Notes

Abbreviations

CMRA   Citizens Municipal Reform Association
JPD   *Journal of Prison Discipline*
PL   Philadelphia *Public Ledger*
PSAMPP Philadelphia Society for Alleviating the Miseries of Public Prisons

Introduction

1. *The Mysteries and Miseries of Philadelphia*, pp. 12–14, 17–18.
2. *PL*, 27 June 1836.
3. The use of the law was a common thing among nineteenth-century Americans and a matter of frequent note, especially by European travelers like Tocqueville. Yet its role as an aspect of political participation has been strangely neglected by both legal and political historians. This is in part due to the artificial separation between the two fields and the unfortunate tendency of the literature to equate political participation with voting. The latter is one of those historical contingencies that may well characterize the United States of the 1980s but should not therefore be assumed to be the case for the nineteenth century. One interesting exception to this tendency is Paludan, "The American Civil War Considered as a Crisis in Law and Order," pp. 1013–34. More recently some political scientists have begun to reconsider the subject. See Zemans, "Legal Mobilization," pp. 690–703; and from the perspective not of the law but of political parties, Bridges, *A City in the Republic*.
4. The literature on this subject is vast and growing. Many of the important relevant books and articles are cited and discussed below. Among the clearest statements about the transformation of the national government is Skowronek's study of the expansion of the early American "state of courts and parties" in *Building a New American State*. The transformation of local government is still treated best in Frisch, *Town into City*. See McGerr, *The Decline of Popular Politics*, for a discussion of the depopularization of electoral politics.
5. Some of the better discussions of the early nineteenth-century state can be found in Hartog, *Public Property and Private Power*, especially Part II, and Bridges, *A City in the Republic*. The reactive and particularistic state is also a key part of the notion of a "state of courts and parties" developed by Skowronek for the federal government in *Building a New American State*. Shefter skillfully uses this characterization of city government in building his typology of the stages of the political machine in "The Emergence of the Political Machine: An Alternative View."
6. The question of the relationship between the "public" and "private" spheres lurks prominently behind the surface of this study and will be highlighted from time to time.

It is a matter of increasing concern to historians in recent years, especially to historians concerned with the law and the state in the nineteenth century. Although the matter is far from well understood, the process of change in its most general terms seems to have included, early in the nineteenth century, a sharpening of the difference between public and private in the law, and then, after the Civil War, the expansion in size and power of distinctly public institutions. This study is concerned mostly with the earlier part of the process; it emphasizes the transformation of the legal and political relationships among citizens and between citizens and the state, a major part of this process. Among the important books treating the subject are Horwitz, *The Transformation of American Law, 1780–1860*; Hartog, *Public Property and Private Power*; Keller, *Affairs of State*; and Hammack, *Power and Society*.

For a provocative discussion of the consequences of this process for the development of American public culture as a whole, and a reminder that the "public" sphere is a historically contingent thing, "made and remade in time," see Bender, "Wholes and Parts," pp. 120–36.

7. See Thompson, *Whigs and Hunters*, esp. pp. 258–69, and Hay, "Property, Authority, and the Criminal Law," in Hay et al., *Albion's Fatal Tree*, esp. pp. 52–56.

8. Hay, "Crime and Justice in Eighteenth- and Nineteenth-Century England," pp. 67–68.

Another similar point, from a quantitative perspective, has been made by Eric Monkkonen, who praised studies that conceived of "data" generated by criminal justice institutions not as a sample of "real" crime but as a universe of "formal interactions between the criminal justice system and the larger society." This approach, he argues, "tells more about social structure" than speculations about the actual number of crimes and characteristics of criminals. See Monkkonen, "Systematic Criminal Justice History," pp. 458–59. See also related comments by Ignatieff, in "State, Civil Society, and Total Institutions," p. 153; and Hindus, in "The History of Crime," p. 235.

9. Indeed, some legal scholars, responding to the crisis of legal institutions provoked by the upheavals of the 1960s, have argued that the process of litigation itself, especially the active initiation of complaints by aggrieved citizens, is one important way of relieving the widespread public alienation from the bureaucratic state. Thus, Philippe Nonet, for example, found that the workmen's compensation administration was more successful when enforcement took the form of dispute settlement of privately initiated claims rather than working through administrative initiative. Nonet found this to be a more democratic, even liberating, process, because the injured person was an active party rather than a passive object of a state agency. What made this process liberating was the virtual transformation of the workmen's compensation commission into a court. See Nonet, *Administrative Justice*. See also Selznick, *Law, Society, and Industrial Justice*, and, from a theoretical standpoint, Nonet and Selznick, *Law and Society in Transition*.

10. See, for example, Lane, *Policing the City*; Richardson, *The New York Police*; Johnson, *Policing the Urban Underworld*; Miller, *Cops and Bobbies*, and "Police Authority in London and New York City"; Schneider, "Public Order and the Geography of the City"; Fogelson, *Big-City Police*; and Liebman and Polen, "Perspectives on Policing in Nineteenth-Century America."

Another perspective, that the police were designed especially to suppress the organized activity of workers, is presented in Harring, "The Development of the Police Institution in the United States"; and Harring and McMullin, "The Buffalo Police."

Virtually all police historians assume that the functions of the police were either located in the woefully inadequate institutional precursors of the police—the night watch, constabulary, and militia—or did not involve the state in any continuous fashion. Samuel Walker, in *Popular Justice*, the only comprehensive text on criminal justice history in the United States, makes virtually no mention of either private prosecution or the minor judiciary. Eric Monkkonen insists that criminal justice "was not a system of informal community sanctions," and he describes the formal sanctions only as "a diverse set of civil institutions" that acted "as a crisis-oriented public service." Monkkonen, "Toward a Dynamic Theory of Crime and the Police," p. 337.

Prison studies, concerned with the origins of modern concepts of corrections and reformation, have been directly concerned with the relationship between these concepts and larger social, economic, and ideological issues. Deviance, reform, punishment, social control—the ideas central to the establishment of the relationships dominant within prisons and other incarcerative institutions—have been often brilliantly connected to nineteenth-century concern over disorder, social class, capitalism, and industrial discipline. Justice and law enforcement, though certainly related, have correctly been of secondary importance in these studies. See especially Rothman, *The Discovery of the Asylum*; Foucault, *Discipline and Punish*; and Ignatieff, *A Just Measure of Pain*.

The relatively few studies of the criminal courts almost always assume that the people whose cases are being scrutinized are passive captives of the criminal justice system. They generally disregard the matter of case initiation. Too often, these studies are dominated by disembodied concepts like "the legal system . . . turned its attention from morality to property." See Hindus, "The History of Crime," p. 235. Quantitative studies, basing their inquiries on data generated by criminal justice institutions and usually eschewing questions concerning the social relationships that produced the data, are the works obviously most prone to these fallacies. See the otherwise fine and important Monkkonen, *The Dangerous Class*.

Studies of nineteenth-century courts and the law using traditional methods also usually avoid questions of case initiation or the objectives of the people using the courts, but they are interested in changes from "traditional" to "bureaucratic" administration of the law. See Hindus, *Prison and Plantation*, and "The Contours of Crime and Justice in Massachusetts and South Carolina." See also Nelson, *The Americanization of the Common Law*, and "Emerging Notions of Modern Criminal Law in the Revolutionary Era"; and Salkin, "Crime in Pennsylvania." Salkin recognizes that "the state enacted penal statutes but the individual . . . played a significant role in the production of crime rates," p. xii. An important recent contribution is Ayres, *Vengeance and Justice*.

These scholars do suggest that the criminal courts were the most important sources of authority and law enforcement during the eighteenth century. Several other works reinforce this impression, especially Greenberg, *Crime and Law Enforcement in the Colony of New York*; an analysis of the symbolic significance of court proceedings in Virginia by Roeber, "Authority, Law, and Custom"; and Hindus and Jones, "Quantitative and Theoretical Approaches in the History of Crime and Law," pp. 25–33.

Police magistrates figure prominently in two studies of late nineteenth- and twenti-eth-century criminal justice. Private citizen initiative is not an issue in these studies, but the "rough" quality of justice and the interaction of citizens and magistrates which characterize the courts are. These works also have the advantage of being detailed investigations of one locality. See Friedman and Percival, *The Roots of Justice*, and Katz, Doucet, and Stern, *The Social Organization of Early Industrial Capitalism*, ch. 6, esp. pp. 228–35.

11. Although a much understudied subject, private prosecution in England is treated in Philips, "Good Men 'to Associate and Bad Men to Conspire," and in Little and Sheffield, "Frontiers and Criminal Justice." Philips especially treats English private prosecution as an important means of establishing the authority of the law in a manner much like it seems to have functioned in Philadelphia, with, of course, the great difference that the authority being reinforced in America was democratic.

The subject is also touched on in Philips, *Crime and Authority in Victorian England*; Brewer and Styles, *An Ungovernable People*; Langbein, "Albion's Fatal Flaws," and "The Criminal Trial before the Lawyers"; Thompson, *Whigs and Hunters*; and Hay, *Albion's Fatal Tree*.

12. This is all succinctly stated in Warren, *A History of the American Bar*, pp. 1–18. Quotations are from pp. 5, 13. Tilghman's remarks were made in *Poor v. Greene* (5 Binney 554), quoted in Warren, *A History of the American Bar*, p. 15. See also Friedman, *A History of American Law*, pp. 29–32.

13. See Hurst, *The Growth of American Law*, pp. 92–94, 147–49; and Ellis, *The Jeffersonian Crisis*, pp. 5–6. Ellis notes that courts decided cases, punished criminals, assessed local taxes, administered the building and maintenance of roads, bridges, jails, workhouses, courthouses, and ferries; decided where these things would be located; set and paid bounties on game; settled quarrels and issued licenses. See also Friedman, *A History of American Law*, pp. 32–49, and Gilmore, *The Ages of American Law*, p. 15.

14. Hurst, *The Growth of American Law*, p. 147.

15. Friedman, *A History of American Law*, p. 29. Crevecoeur's remark is from *Letters of an American Farmer* quoted in Warren, *A History of the American Bar*, p. 217.

16. See Friedman, *A History of American Law*, pp. 81–83; Hurst, *The Growth of American Law*, pp. 250–251; and Warren, *A History of the American Bar*, pp. 4–11.

17. Spindel, "The Administration of Justice in North Carolina," p. 148; Ellis, *The Jeffersonian Crisis*, ch. 15; Greenberg, "The Effectiveness of Law Enforcement in Eighteenth-Century New York," pp. 184–85, 197; Goebel and Naughton, *Law Enforcement in Colonial New York*, pp. 341, 347–50, 366–67, 379–82; Nelson, "Emerging Notions of Modern Criminal Law in the Revolutionary Era," p. 468; Gaskins, "Changes in the Criminal Law in Eighteenth Century Connecticut," p. 316; and Chitwood, *Justice in Colonial Virginia*, pp. 518–19.

18. Thayer, "Town into City," p. 99; Foner, *Tom Paine and Revolutionary America*, pp. 24–25.

19. Thayer, "Town into City," pp. 98–99; Foner, *Tom Paine and Revolutionary America*, p. 26.

20. Thayer, "Town into City," pp. 98–99; Foner, *Tom Paine and Revolutionary America*, pp. 28–39. Estimates of the artisan population vary depending on the definition one uses and the approach one adopts. So Foner sees artisans as half of the male population, and Thayer as "the largest part of the middle class."

21. Thayer, "Town into City," p. 99; Foner, *Tom Paine and Revolutionary America*, pp. 45–47; Alexander, *Render Them Submissive*, pp. 26–29, 89–90, ch. 5.

22. Alexander, *Render Them Submissive*, pp. 61–64; Thayer, "Town into City," pp. 76–78. The court structure is detailed in Surrency, "The Evolution of an Urban Judicial System," pp. 98–101.

Chapter 1

1. See *PL*, 13 May 1839, 3 September 1839, 10 September 1839, 8 November 1839, 2 February 1841, 22 July 1842.

2. *PL*, 21 June 1865, 19 July 1866.

3. The social transformation of nineteenth-century Philadelphia is treated in a number of important recent monographs and articles. Two of the best places to start for an overview are Weigley, *Philadelphia;* and the more technical collection of essays produced by the Philadelphia Social History Project, Hershberg, *Philadelphia*.

4. Warner, *The Private City*, p. 50; Geffen, "Industrial Development and Social Crisis," p. 361.

5. Thayer, "Town into City," pp. 74–76; Foner, *Tom Paine and Revolutionary America*, pp. 21–23.

6. Richardson, "The Athens of America," p. 218.

Of course, the Revolution did spur "a great extension and development of capitalist institutions and market orientation in the city's life." While this helped some to accumulate great fortunes and led a segment of the artisan community to become merchant-entrepreneurs, it also left the city vulnerable to the vagaries of the modern economic ills of inflation and depression, accelerated the decline of meaningful apprenticeship and of unfree labor in general, and increased the percentage of people who were simply wage laborers. Poverty and unemployment took on unprecedented dimensions. Depression set in as the city tried to adjust economically to war's end in 1783. New organizations sought to relieve the poor and ameliorate conditions in prisons and hospitals. Journeymen, recognizing that the progress of wage-labor reflected a new condition for themselves, organized and conducted the first strikes in Philadelphia's history. See Foner, *Tom Paine and Revolutionary America*, pp. 26–27, 40–43; Miller, "The Federal City," pp. 156–57; Alexander, *Render Them Submissive*, pp. 70–78, 84–85, chs. 6–7; and Laurie, *Working People of Philadelphia*, pp. 1–10.

7. Laurie, *Working People of Philadelphia*, p. 6.

8. Ibid., pp. 7–8; Richardson, "The Athens of America," pp. 234–39.

9. Laurie, *Working People of Philadelphia*, p. 8; Wainwright, "The Age of Nicholas Biddle," pp. 266, 272–74.

10. Laurie, *Working People of Philadelphia*, pp. 9–10; Wainwright, "The Age of Nicholas Biddle," pp. 274–77, 280–81.

11. Laurie, *Working People of Philadelphia*, p. 29. Of the adult male work force of

100,404 in 1850, 27,152 were Irish born and 11,427 were German, the two largest immigrant groups. See Laurie, Hershberg, and Alter, "Immigrants and Industry," p. 106.

12. By 1850, Philadelphia, with 1.75 percent of the nation's population, accounted for roughly 6 percent of American manufacturing output and employment, second only to New York. See Whitney, "The Uses of Urban Space in Nineteenth-Century Philadelphia"; Laurie, Hershberg, and Alter, "Immigrants and Industry," p. 99; Warner, *The Private City*, pp. 56–59; Laurie, *Working People of Philadelphia*, ch. 1; Hershberg, *Philadelphia*, pp. 37–120; and McLeod, "The Philadelphia Artisan."

13. Observers have estimated the minimum annual family cost of living for the 1850s at between $520 and $580. Even the best-paid of journeymen could earn no more than $400 a year. Most workers fell far short of this sum. Hand-loom weavers were fortunate to earn $200. The average annual income of male workers in fourteen major industries in 1851 was only $288. Women, of course, fared far worse than men, often earning no more than $100 annually. As a result, to make ends meet, the families of working people had to restrict consumption, rely on the additional income of wives and children who could find work, and adopt various strategies for survival. Those might include scavenging for wood, shopping in second-hand and pawn shops or from street peddlers, participating in the thriving illegal market for small purloined goods, sending children into the street to beg, taking in boarders, or even prostitution. Laurie, *Working People of Philadelphia*, pp. 12–13; Geffen, "Industrial Development and Social Crisis," pp. 335–37; Glassberg, "Work, Wages, and the Cost of Living"; and Carey, *A Plea for the Poor*.

A spate of recent monographs have traced the history of the early American working class and the transformation from artisanal to capitalist work relations. See Dawley, *Class and Community*; Wilentz, *Chants Democratic*; and Laurie, *Working People of Philadelphia*. Wilentz and Laurie provide especially useful analyses of economic change in New York and Philadelphia. See Wilentz, chs. 1 and 3, and Laurie, ch. 1. Quote is from Laurie, p. 9. See also pp. 5, 14–17, and McLeod, "The Philadelphia Artisan," p. 56. A good discussion of the beginnings of this transformation in Philadelphia can be found in Foner, *Tom Paine and Revolutionary America*, ch. 2.

14. Beers, "The Centennial City," pp. 419–21.

15. Warner, *The Private City*, p. 52; Geffen, "Industrial Development and Social Crisis," pp. 310–12, 315. See also Hershberg, *Philadelphia*, pp. 121–204.

16. Poverty was especially pronounced in the "infected" district—so-called for its propensity for disease—of south Philadelphia, Southwark, and Moyamensing. Not surprisingly, this was the area most heavily populated by blacks, about 5 percent of the city's population. The poorest and most despised of Philadelphia's people, blacks experienced a "remarkable deterioration in socioeconomic condition(s) . . . from 1830 to the Civil War." But in even this poorest of areas, blacks were not the majority of residents.

Especially in the poorest areas, the line between legality and illegality was easily crossed and vital social relationships could be quite exploitative. Reporter Sounder believed that between 4,000 and 5,000 people lived by begging and stealing. Building owners rented small rooms to tenants who then rented floor space to others for a night at a time, fitting as many people as possible into a room. One such landlord paid $100 for a building that returned $600 annually, another $1,300 for a house which realized $1,600 a year. Petty thieves of small and miscellaneous articles found a market among pawnbrokers and junk dealers who then sold them to poor customers who could afford only the low prices that were attached to stolen goods. Poverty produced a cycle that encouraged, even necessitated, petty theft.

See Hershberg, "Free Blacks in Antebellum Philadelphia," p. 369; Geffen, "Industrial Development and Social Crisis," pp. 335, 352–53; Weigley, "The Border City in Civil War," pp. 385–86; *Mysteries and Miseries of Philadelphia*, pp. 12–15; *Second Annual Report of the Young Christian's Missionary Association*; *A Statistical Inquiry into the Condition of the People of Colour*, p. 38; *Life of Charles A. Chester*, pp. 29–30; Lapsansky, "South Street Philadelphia," p. 138; Johnson, "The Search for an Urban Discipline," p. 111; and Clark, *The Irish in Philadelphia*, pp. 41–43.

17. Very little research has been conducted on aldermen and other local political figures in antebellum Philadelphia, or anywhere else for that matter. One of the few studies of Philadelphia to look at them at all is Lapsansky, "South Street Philadelphia."

18. *PL*, 9 April 1838, 15 June 1848.

19. *PL*, 16 February 1847. Reports of proceedings regularly opened with an introduction like this one. See also *PL*, 3 October 1837, 21 May 1839, 31 July 1849. The absence of a crowd, usually because there were few cases that day, was also at times a matter of note to court reporters. See *PL*, 15 November 1836, 6 December 1837, 16 May 1839, 4 October 1841.

20. *PL*, 31 May 1841, 21 October 1841, 26 October 1841.

21. *PL*, 22 July 1836, 29–31 May 1836, 31 May 1841, 14 October 1841, 27 December 1841, 16 September 1852, 6 July 1854, 1 August 1854.

22. See Grimsted, *Melodrama Unveiled*, ch. 3; Levine, "William Shakespeare and the American People," pp. 42–46; and Johnson, "The Guilty Third Tier." The transformation of the theater about which Levine writes strongly parallels the transformation of criminal justice discussed here, and is all the more striking when one considers the dramatic and participatory quality of court proceedings.

23. See Davis, "Theatre of the Streets," esp. chs. 4, 5. The transformation of the street demonstration she discusses is very much like the transformation of the theater and another aspect of the larger transformation of especially *public* popular culture.

24. *PL*, 4 August 1838, 31 May 1841, 16 September 1852. Examples of crowded prisoners' docks abound; very busy days occurred nearly every week. See also Lane, *The Roots of Violence in Black Philadelphia*, pp. 82–87.

25. *PL*, 3 March 1842, 18 April 1842.

26. *PL*, 16 September 1852, 29–31 May 1837, 3 April 1844, 16 February 1847. This last case was brought under a 1705 law against "drinking and tippling" on Sundays. Since "tippling" meant drinking to excess, the alderman concluded that the prosecutors had to prove that customers were intoxicated in order to warrant a conviction, and this they had failed to do.

27. *PL*, 3 September 1839, 10 September 1839, 8 November 1839, 2 February 1841, 22 July 1842.

28. *PL*, 26 June 1837, 4 October 1837, 4 December 1839, 26 November 1841.

29. *PL*, 1 February 1859, 7 November 1860, 21 June 1865, 19 July 1866.

30. Kneass Scrapbook, newspaper clipping.

31. *PL*, 21 March 1839. Certainly too many trials of blacks occurred for the mayor's claim to be literally true, yet the very frequency with which blacks were arrested and taken to court may well have been enough reason to mobilize many in the black community to protect themselves in the courts. There is considerable evidence of blacks being private prosecutors, and it is possible that their practice of attending trials bred a familiarity with the halls of justice that encouraged them to initiate criminal cases. An interesting examination of this entire subject is in Lane, *The Roots of Violence in Black Philadelphia*, esp. ch. 3.

32. *PL*, 23 October 1839, 12 December 1839, 19 February 1840.

33. *PL*, 21 November 1843, 13 July 1846, 10 January 1848, 15 February 1850, 4 May 1850, 31 March 1852.

34. *PL*, 8 December 1836, 30 October 1839; Eastman, *Courts and Lawyers of Pennsylvania*, pp. 557–58; and Greco, "William Darrah Kelley," p. 146. Judge Conrad's penchant for order was more fully displayed in 1855 when, as the consolidated city's first mayor, he directed the new police force to adopt an unprecedented policy of widespread arrest.

35. *PL*, 11 August 1858, 7 November 1860, 11 March 1861, 15 March 1861, 19 July 1866. Parties to cases also rushed the bench to address the judge, and lawyers would do so at times in an effort to persuade a litigant to engage his services. Exchanges between lawyers sometimes stirred the spectators. One day in 1861 a lawyer referred to his adversary as a "Greek," meaning Irishman, eliciting the response, "Would to God we had now as brave men as the Greeks of old, for then we should not this day occupy the humiliating position of surrendering Fort Sumter to traitors!" The spectators broke into sustained applause.

36. *PL*, 11 July 1839, 21 June 1865; Westcott, *The Official Guide Book to Philadelphia*, pp. 104, 106; Kelley to Catherine Bonsall, 31 August 1854, Kelley Collection.

37. *PL*, 29 January 1866; Philadelphia *American and Gazette*, in Kneass Scrapbook.

38. *PL*, 13 May 1839, 30 August 1839, 2 February 1841, 28 July 1847.

39. *PL*, 7 March 1843, 11 January 1848, 17 January 1848, 5 March 1867.

40. Throughout this book, and to be fair to the social importance of criminal litigation, a case will be understood to be any matter that anyone brought to an alderman or justice for criminal action, even if absolutely no other action was taken on it. This is one major reason why the estimation of numbers is so difficult, but as should become very clear, from the citizen-litigant's perspective, even this kind of act might have an important impact on the private matter that inspired it.

41. *PL*, 30 October 1862, 19 August 1839, 26 November 1847, 28 April 1848.

42. *PL*, 12 February 1840, 14 May 1840.

43. Milnor Docket Book; Gregg Docket Book; and Alderman's Court Criminal Docket. There is no telling whether these were the only docket books kept by these aldermen for those years. The first two books are at the Historical Society of Pennsylvania, the third at the Philadelphia City Archives.

44. Milnor Docket Book; Gregg Docket Book; Alderman's Court Criminal Docket; and *PL*, 12 February 1840.

45. Gregg Docket Book; Milnor Docket Book; and Alderman's Court Criminal Docket.

46. Comparable 1830 figures for prison commitments are between 12,579 and

16,772 cases for an unpoliced population of about 200,000. For 1870, prison commitments yield estimates of from 45,864 to 61,152 cases among a population of 674,000; arrests 69,339 cases, and court returns anywhere from 8,542 to 41,113 indictable offenses. The estimates for 1870 suggest that the rates for private prosecutions might have stayed relatively stable after the introduction of the police, but the rate of police prosecutions fell after the force's first few years.

47. Milnor Docket Book; Gregg Docket Book; and Alderman's Court Criminal Docket.

48. Throughout the period under study, the pattern of commitments for different crimes remained relatively stable. For example, Gregg committed 25 percent of those brought before him charged with a nonindictable offense, 21 percent of those charged with assault and battery, 38 percent of those charged with larceny, and 57 percent of those charged with serious personal or property crime. Milnor committed only one of the seven minor offenders brought before him and 10 percent of those charged with assault and battery, but 85 percent of those charged with larceny. See docket books.

49. *PL*, 19 March 1849, 7 October 1851.

50. Milnor Docket Book; Gregg Docket Book; and Alderman's Court Criminal Docket.

51. Ibid.

52. Percentages derived form the Philadelphia County Prison Daily Occurrence Dockets.

53. Milnor Docket Book; Gregg Docket Book; and Alderman's Court Criminal Docket.

54. Ibid. County Prison Daily Occurrence Dockets. Both of Kenney's commitments for indictable offenses were for larceny.

55. Milnor Docket Book; Gregg Docket Book; Alderman's Court Criminal Docket; and Philadelphia County Prison Daily Occurrence Dockets. The kinds of acts that fall into the category of serious crime are discussed below.

56. Philadelphia County Prison Daily Occurrence Dockets.

Chapter 2

1. *PL*, 30 September 1863.

2. *PL*, 7 April 1869. Or, as one reporter put it, "People . . . will go to law about matters of no moment whatever." *PL*, 25 August 1860.

3. Alexander, *Render Them Submissive*, p. 72; Miller, "The Federal City," p. 166. The office of justice of the peace was reestablished in Philadelphia city in 1810 after the abolition of the alderman's court. The latter court consisted of three aldermen who had the responsibility, since 1789, of hearing civil cases dealing with sums between 40 shillings and £10. When the civil jurisdiction of individual justices was raised to $100, this court became unnecessary, and the city became reacquainted with justices who were not aldermen. See Surrency, "The Evolution of an Urban Judicial System," pp. 100–101.

In 1796, following the stipulations of the 1790 Pennsylvania Constitution, aldermen became officers who were appointed by the governor for good behavior. The mayor would not be popularly elected until 1826, and the aldermen not again until 1841.

4. John Binns, *Binns' Justice*, p. 63.

5. Fee bills were revised from time to time. Aldermen and justices also had civil jurisdiction. In cases in which the amount disputed did not exceed $5.33, the justice's decision was final. The sum of $5.33 represented the American equivalent of the English 40 shillings, which traditionally was the maximum amount over which English justices of the peace held exclusive civil jurisdiction and which was recognized in Pennsylvania in 1715. See Binns, *Binns' Daily Companion*, p. 228. This restriction effectively gave justices total power over civil cases among the poor. See Surrency, "The Evolution of an Urban Judicial System," pp. 98–101.

6. Lapsansky, "South Street Philadelphia," pp. 138–39.

7. Occupation and property data are from a sample of aldermen located in The City of Philadelphia Directories and the Philadelphia Social History Project 1850 manuscript census of Philadelphia.

8. *Justice of the Peace* 3 (1902); Binns, *Recollections of the Life of John Binns*, pp. 297–300.

9. Montgomery, "Gutman's Nineteenth-Century America," p. 427.

10. In misdemeanor and most felony cases, the magistrate could admit a defendant to bail after having committed that person to prison in lieu of bail. However, a magistrate could not admit to bail, under any circumstances, in cases of homicide, robbery, burglary, rape, arson, and horse stealing. Magistrates could also bind a person (or commit a person in lieu of bond) to keep the peace until the next session of the criminal court and, after 1846, for breach of the peace, even though this was not an indictable offense and was usually tried summarily by the criminal court judge. See *Commonwealth ex relatione Chauncey* and *Nixon* v. *Keeper of the Prison*, 2 Ashmead 227 (1838), *Moore* v. *Commonwealth*, 6 Watts and Sergeant 314 (1843); *Aldermen and Justices of the Peace Cases*, 2 Parsons Equity Cases 458 (1847).

11. Milnor Docket Book and Alderman's Court Criminal Docket.

12. Binns, *Binns' Justice*, p. 64.

13. *Reports of Some Criminal Cases on Primary Hearing Before Richard Vaux*, p. 28.

14. *PL*, 11 October 1847.

15. *PL*, 24 April 1840.

16. Philadelphia County Prison Daily Occurrence Docket; PSAMPP Minute Book, 8 January 1821; *Report of the Commissioners on the Penal Code*; Mease, *Observations on the Penitentiary System and Penal Code*, pp. 34–35. Mease recorded 2,117 white and 1,070 black prison commitments in 1818; 176 of 407 convicts were black in July 1816; 165 of 474 in August 1819; and 263 of 687 during 1829.

17. See the Philadelphia County Prison Convict Description Docket. The makeup of the convict population remained basically the same after 1851. The occupational classification used here is the ten category vertical (Vert) hierarchy developed by the Philadelphia Social History Project in their analysis of the 1850, 1860 and 1870 federal manuscript census. No classification scheme is flawless; this one's major defect for our purposes is the inclusion of farmers among low white-collar and proprietary workers. While this decision made sense for the general population, it places in an inappropriately high ranking the unskilled farm laborers who called themselves "farmers" in the

prison dockets. This group comprised over half of all the low white-collar and proprietary workers in the prison sample and should have been included among unskilled workers. Thus the ranking system overstates the percentage of high-ranked occupations among prisoners. For a full discussion of the Vert ranking system, see *Historical Methods Newsletter* 9 (1976) pp. 66–68.

18. *PL*, 27 June 1836.

19. See *PL*, 19 October 1837, 7 June 1838, 18 June 1838, 27 August 1839, 4 November 1839, 11 June 1840, 3 August 1840, 6 October 1840, 7 September 1841, 17 January 1849, 7 July 1853.

20. See *PL*, 7 November 1837, 10 July 1843, 10 April 1846, 7 August 1847, 7 October 1853.

21. See *PL*, 4 August 1836, 8 May 1838, 18 September 1848. See also 21 May 1839, 2 March 1841, 3 October 1843, 13 January 1846, 3 April 1849.

22. See Alderman's Court Criminal Docket. Not all cases of wifebeating were brought directly by private prosecutors. Sometimes, in fear of serious injury, a woman or neighbor would first call a watchman to subdue the batterer, and the officer would arrest the man and bring the charge. Occasionally the watchman heard the woman's screams and interceded on his own. See *PL*, 9 November 1836, 21 April 1838, 18 June 1842, 17 August 1853.

23. *PL*, 25 July 1836, 30 September 1837, 21 April 1838, 27 August 1839, 16 October 1839, 26 October 1841, 20 May 1841, 28 May 1841, 13 August 1841, 15 June 1843, 25 January 1854; Alderman's Court Criminal Docket.

24. *PL*, 23 September 1837, 7 August 1838, 18 June 1842, 10 July 1843, 7 December 1847.

25. *PL*, 4 August 1836, 8 May 1838, 21 May 1839, 2 March 1841, 10 September 1841, 3 October 1843, 13 January 1846, 18 September 1848, 3 April 1849.

26. *PL*, 21 May 1839, 2 July 1840, 20 August 1852, 7 July 1853. See also 2 August 1839.

27. *PL*, 9 February 1841, 3 February 1842, 17 February 1842.

28. *PL*, 30 September 1837, 27 August 1841, 23 May 1843, 15 June 1843. Alderman's Court Criminal Docket. Cases resulted from a wide variety of events. A man hit by falling debris from a burned-out building prosecuted the superintendent of the demolition crew for "negligence and carelessness." Francis Tiers prosecuted Henry Paul Beck for bumping into him on the street opposite the Franklin Library. *PL*, 10 May 1836, 19 October 1839. See also 4 February 1839, 4 June 1839, 21 January 1842, 9 February 1854.

29. *PL*, 30 September 1837, 15 August 1840, 28 January 1841, 30 July 1851, 19 October 1853, 27 April 1842.

30. *PL*, 9 November 1846, 9 February 1853. Alderman's Court Criminal Docket.

31. *PL*, 14 June 1838, 7 August 1838, 28 July 1840, 22 November 1841. Alderman's Court Criminal Docket. See also *PL*, 17 November 1837, 27 March 1839. Critics claimed that landlords brought disorderly conduct or disorderly house charges against tenants as a pretext, with the intention of having the tenant committed and then repossessing the premises.

32. *PL*, 21 October 1840, 29 September 1843, 28 April 1851, 1 December 1851.

33. *PL*, 23 September 1837, 3 April 1844, 6 July 1854, 18 August 1854.

34. *PL*, 11 May 1836, 29 May 1837, 27 August 1839, 2 July 1840, 6 October 1840, 3 October 1843, 7 March 1848, 22 July 1852.

35. *PL*, 5 June 1839, 4 February 1840, 20 May 1841, 3 March 1842.

36. *PL*, 14 May 1838, 17 June 1840, 3 August 1840.

37. *PL*, 28 August 1840, 13 August 1841.

38. This is partly reflected by the erratic relationship of arrests to commitments for assault and battery and larceny after 1854. Some years arrests exceeded commitments, some years the reverse. See the *Annual Report of the Chief of Police* and *Annual Reports of the Philadelphia County Prison*. For both charges, arrests were relatively the greatest in 1855 because of the new police force's zealous behavior. Things calmed down thereafter. For assault and battery, arrests were greater in 1856, 1863–64, 1866–67, and 1869. For larceny arrests exceeded commitments in 1859, 1861–64, and 1867. Data were missing for 1865, 1868, and after 1870. The point is that, because these crimes were so frequently privately prosecuted and because commitment was so dependent on the relationship of the alderman and the citizens involved, arrests for these crimes are a very poor guide to the frequency of either their actual incidence or their prosecution, even after 1854.

39. *PL*, 25 August 1860, 7 April 1869. *JPD* [n.s.] 3 (1864): 72–73, 77.

40. Philadelphia County Prison Daily Occurrence Docket. For minor personal crimes, aldermen released 84.2 percent of those they committed, and for minor property crimes, 86.2 percent. The percentage of those committed to prison for larceny and released by the committing magistrate also rose after 1854 to 38.8 percent.

41. *PL*, 26 February 1855, 7 March 1855, 12 November 1855, 26 October 1857, 8 November 1862, 11 August 1869, 27 October 1870, 29 May 1871. See also 28 November 1855, 30 January 1856, 25 March 1858, 27 March 1858, and *Annual Report of William J. Mullen* (1870), pp. 46–50.

42. *JPD* [n.s.] 3 (1864): 72. Charges of assault and battery made by women against their husbands remained probably the most common of privately prosecuted cases. A reporter, in 1860, noted "It is no uncommon thing, we are sorry to say, to find men in the dock on a charge of beating their wives." Examples of these cases abound and demonstrate the continuing seriousness with which the women brought them. Sometimes they asked for leniency, sometimes for only a bond to keep the peace. Often they blamed liquor and asked only that the man be scared into staying sober and providing for his family. But in serious assaults, or if the couple had already separated, the prosecutrix was usually willing to let the law take its course and have the man sentenced to prison.

Examples of the various types of wifebeating cases can be found in *PL*, 22 June 1860, 16 July 1857, 14 September 1858, 11 December 1858, 4 August 1859, 22 May 1860, 7 August 1860, 24 July 1867, 2 June 1869, 3 September 1869, 25 March 1870, 20 July 1870, 27 October 1870, 4 March 1871, 6 April 1871, 17 November 1871, 19 November 1871, 26 February 1872, 9 August 1872, 8 October 1872, 16 October 1872, 8 January 1873, 14 February 1873, 25 November 1873. Family problems of other sorts also resulted in private criminal cases. Wives assaulted husbands, though much less often than the reverse. See, for example, *PL*, 23 July 1856, 7 June 1873. Jealous lovers assaulted their rivals, siblings fought among themselves, parents fought with their children. Examples of all of these continued to fill the court dockets. See, for example, *PL*, 17 November 1854, 8 September 1858, 15 September 1860, 22 September 1869, 24 September 1869, 2 July 1873. The prosecutors' power in intrafamily assaults sometimes even interfered with cases brought by the police. When a mother refused to testify against her son who had stabbed her, the alderman was forced to let the young man go despite the policeman's insistence that she take the stand. *PL*, 23 June 1871.

43. See, for example, *PL*, 30 October 1862, 27 August 1857, 20 July 1859, 11 August 1859, 3 July 1860, 15 September 1860, 29 June 1863, 8 September 1864, 1 November 1864, 14 April 1865, 15 June 1870, 2 August 1870, 17 January 1871, 19 April 1873, *JPD* [n.s.] 11 (1872): 39-40.

44. See *PL*, 15 January 1858, 4 August 1859, 11 August 1859, 3 July 1860, 10 August 1861, 17 November 1861, 24 December 1861, 25 December 1863, 24 August 1864, 7 January 1871, 12 July 1872, 16 April 1873. See also, for example, 15 March 1861, 19 September 1863, 3 May 1867, 7 January 1870, 9 February 1871, 5 January 1872, 25 February 1872, 7 April 1873, 8 September 1873, 25 November 1873.

45. For example, a woman charged another with malicious mischief for cutting down a clothesline which the two shared; a washerwoman was charged with larceny because a lock of hair left inadvertently in a vest pocket by its owner was lost in the wash; a man was accused of larceny for picking up a newspaper he thought had been abandoned in a hotel lobby. One tavernkeeper instituted eight different larceny cases against his wife, as well as nine other cases, within an eight-year period. *PL*, 29 January 1856, 22 November 1860, 29 November 1860, 17 January 1871; *JPD* [n.s.] 10 (1871): 32-33; 5 (1866): 39; PSAMPP Minute Book, 16 February 1865, 19 October 1865, 16 November 1865; *Annual Report of William J. Mullen* (1870), pp. 48-49.

Property private prosecutions were reported as frequently in the press as were assault and battery cases. See, for example, *PL*, 10 July 1856, 3 July 1857, 16 July 1857, 8 September 1858, 15 February 1859, 24 October 1862, 7 October 1869, 22 December 1869, 3 March 1870, 9 February 1871, 11 February 1871, 27 July 1871, 13 October 1871, 19 December 1871, 17 January 1872, 6 January 1873, 8 January 1873.

46. See *PL*, 17 July 1855, 24 October 1855, 8 February 1860, 22 November 1860, 6 February 1873.

47. See *PL*, 8 July 1854, 27 November 1856, 7 December 1857, 8 September 1858, 16 November 1868, 17 January 1871, 16 April 1873, 7 June 1873.

48. *PL*, 25 December 1865, 3 May 1867, 26 March 1872. See also 23 April 1872.

Other notable private prosecutions included those arising between landlords and tenants. These cases were generally for disorderly house, and they were usually attempts by the landlord to force the tenant out in order to raise the rent. According to one critic, "hundreds of these charges are well founded, that is to say, disorder exists," but even so, "the disorder only becomes intolerable when something can be gained by bringing an accusation." Few of these cases reached trial, since the object was to imprison the tenant to force compliance with the landlord's wishes. When a case did reach trial, the defendant was almost always acquitted. *JPD* [n.s.] 5 (1866): 36-37; 3 (1864): 73-74; *Annual Report of William J. Mullen* (1856), p. 12; Sewell, *Sorrows Circuit*, pp. 324-28; *PL*, 22 June 1861, 3 September 1869, 7 June 1873.

Master-servant cases were similar to landlord-tenant cases, but they established the principle that masters could use force to remove discharged servants from their homes. When, in an 1862 case, the jury nevertheless found the accused master guilty, Judge Allison's sentence was only a one-cent fine. He noted that servants were bound to "respectful obedience" to their employers, who could use "all the force necessary to enforce an order to leave." See *PL*, 19 January 1859, 3 September 1861, 13 February 1862.

49. Salkin, "Crime in Pennsylvania," pp. 292–95.

Chapter 3

1. *PL*, 25 August 1860, 7 April 1869; *JPD* [n.s] 3 (1864): 72–73, 77.

2. *PL*, 22 June 1860, 29 October 1862.

3. *PL*, 11 July 1856, 7 December 1857, 24 November 1858, 25 August 1860, *Annual Report of William J. Mullen* (1866), p. 13. See also, for example, *PL*, 26 October 1850, 27 November 1856, 7 October 1858, 12 March 1859, 27 September 1859, 3 November 1859, 22 September 1864, 4 April 1870, 2 September 1872; *Annual Report of William J. Mullen* (1870), p. 65.

4. *Annual Report of William J. Mullen* (1859), p. 5; *PL*, 11 July 1856. For examples, see *PL*, 12 March 1859, 27 September 1859, 26 October 1859, 3 November 1859, 20 March 1862, 16 May 1863, 24 August 1867, 4 February 1870, 12 July 1870, 17 June 1871, 17 September 1872.

5. *PL*, 26 July 1859. See also 7 December 1857, 24 November 1858, 12 March 1859, 27 September 1859, 3 November 1859, 27 November 1859, 25 August 1860, 24 August 1867.

6. Descriptions of criminal procedure can be found scattered throughout the various legal handbooks and pamphlets published during this era. There were also occasions on which judges detailed it from the bench, especially if a case departed from the ordinary mode of procedure. One such circumstance, particularly relevant to the present discussion, took place in February 1863 during a controversy over whether a grand jury could originate a prosecution on its own. Judge Joseph Allison detailed the "ordinary" mode of procedure, and any mention of the police or of arrest was conspicuously absent until after a complaint to a magistrate and the subsequent issuance of a warrant. See Kneass Scrapbook, p. 14.

7. See Act of Incorporation, 11 March 1789; Daly, *Descriptive Inventory of the Archives of the City*, p. 189; Eastman, *Courts and Lawyers of Pennsylvania*, p. 215; Martin, *Martin's Bench and Bar of Philadelphia*, pp. 75–76. The mayor's court was originally established under the 1701 city charter and disbanded in 1777 when the old corporation of the city ended. See Surrency, "The Evolution of an Urban Judicial System," p. 99.

8. The county had yet another criminal court, the Recorder's Court of Northern Liberties, which heard criminal cases from the northern districts of the county. No records remain from this court, and thus it will not be treated here. See Pennsylvania Constitution of 1790, Art. V; Eastman, *Courts and Lawyers of Pennsylvania*, pp. 295–96, 301–2; Martin, *Martin's Bench and Bar of Philadelphia*, p. 40.

9. Because the criminal sessions dockets cover only two sessions each in 1839 and

1840, and the general sessions dockets only four sessions in 1841, statistics from those courts and those years are not considered here.

Property cases were 57 percent of the criminal sessions and 46 percent of the general sessions sample. The dismissed rate for the criminal sessions was 18.9 percent; the no disposition rate, 14.9 percent. For the general sessions, the rates were 27.6 and 16.8 percent, respectively.

10. Even if a grand jury returned an indictment, as the century progressed, chances were that the defendant would be acquitted. Of those who entered a plea between 1820 and 1838, 23 percent pleaded guilty, 25.5 percent were tried and acquitted, and 47.3 were tried and convicted. But conviction rates began to fall markedly after 1830, and once the quarter sessions reassumed jurisdiction in 1844, the statistics reflected this. Between 1844 and 1854, only 15.3 percent of those indicted pleaded guilty, 44.2 percent were tried and acquitted, and 39.1 percent were tried and convicted. From 1854 to 1874, 12.3 percent pleaded guilty, 54.2 percent were tried and acquitted, and 33.1 percent were tried and convicted.

Imprisonment rates naturally were even lower: 14.2 percent between 1820 and 1838, 16.6 percent from 1844 to 1854, and 11.1 percent afterwards. Sentences averaged 8.8, 13, and 12.2 months, respectively.

11. This pattern was the result of a real increase in the relative number of minor property prosecutions during the 1840s rather than of a decline in personal cases. When the proportion of liquor, order, and morals cases fell by over 50 percent after 1854, the compensatory increase was almost entirely among personal cases, while the proportion of property cases remained stable. Liquor law violations were the third most common type of case, 16.5 percent before 1838 and steadily decreasing thereafter.

12. From 1820 to 1836, almost all imprisonment came after a conviction for larceny. Virtually all those convicted of larceny (186 of 187 in the sample) were sentenced to prison terms in the mayor's court for an average of 17.7 months. In contrast, only 17.8 percent of the assault and battery convicts and 9.5 percent of the liquor law violators were sent to prison for the much shorter average terms of 3.4 and 9.2 months, respectively. Similarly, in the quarter sessions virtually all larceny convicts (39 of 40 in the sample) were sentenced to prison, here for an average of 10.7 months, while only 15.4 percent of the assault and battery convicts and 5.3 percent of the liquor law violators were imprisoned for average terms of 2.5 and 3 months, respectively.

Despite lower conviction rates, convicts were treated more harshly between 1844 and 1854 than before. The imprisonment rate rose to 16.6 percent from 14.2 percent between 1820 and 1838. The average prison term also increased during this period, up to 13 months from only 8.8 during the earlier period. This was due in part to the opening of the county prison in 1835, and in part to the increased percentage of property cases—in which imprisonment and lengthy sentences were far more likely to occur than in other cases. The imprisonment rate increased slightly for personal crimes during this period. For property crime, this rate, though much higher than for personal crime, actually decreased slightly from the earlier period.

Sentencing patterns did not change much after 1854. The overall imprisonment rate fell, along with the conviction rate, to 11.1 percent. The average sentence fell only slightly, from 13 to 12.2 months. The average sentence for larceny, the charge for which the overwhelming majority of convicts were imprisoned, remained the same—

10.2 months. Assault and battery prison sentences fell to 2.2 months, and terms for major property crime rose from 24.9 to 29.3 months.

The average sentence for first-time convicts was 12.5 months, for recidivists 16.8 months. The only descriptive characteristic of convicts that made a significant difference in sentence length was gender. First-time men averaged 13 months, first-time women 10.1 months; recidivist men averaged 18.1 months, recidivist women only 8.5 months.

When these categories are further refined, however, important patterns emerge regarding sex differences. In the occupational category in which 72 percent of the women were clustered—unskilled workers—the difference in sentence length between the sexes almost disappears. This category was only 56 percent male, and the average sentence among first-timers was 12.1 months for men and 11.2 for women. The somewhat lower sentences for the unskilled and those with no mention of occupation were accounted for largely by the high percentage of women in these two groups. Similarly, black women, 45 percent of all women first-time convicts, received virtually no advantage in sentencing over black men, 14.1 months for women to 14.8 for men. Their sentences were much higher than those for first-time white (8.5 months) and mulatto women (2.2 months) and even higher than those for first-time white (12.4 months) and mulatto men (10.3 months). See the Philadelphia County Prison Convict Description Dockets.

Among recidivists, black women, 61.5 percent of all women recidivists, did receive a clear sentencing advantage relative to black men. However, while their sentences averaged just under half the length of those for black men, white women recidivist sentences averaged one-fifth the length of those for white men. Sentences for black women recidivists (9.5 months) were nearly three times as long as those for white women recidivists (3.3 months). Though women larceny convicts received significantly lower sentences than men overall, this advantage did not exist at all for black women and was virtually nullified for unskilled women relative to unskilled men. Unskilled and black larceny convicts were punished as a group by the criminal court judges regardless of gender. Perhaps this helps explain Mayor Roach's claim that blacks, when they did use the courts, mobilized their entire community to ensure that justice was done. They may have used the courts, but, with good reason, they did not trust them. See the Philadelphia County Prison Convict Description Docket. For a fuller discussion, see Steinberg, "The Criminal Courts and the Transformation of Criminal Justice in Philadelphia," pp. 180–82, 193–96.

13. This point is convincingly made for Philadelphia and elsewhere in Johnson, *Policing the Urban Underworld*, ch. 2.

14. *Report on the Philadelphia County Prison to the County Board*, p. 20.

15. The average sentences for each category of these factors was taken from a sample of convicts sentenced to the Philadelphia County Prison between 1843 and 1851. The ranges were for three race categories: 3.3 months; sex, 6.8 months; five ethnicity categories, 7.8 months; six occupational categories, 6.7 months. Among ten age categories, the oldest age group received very low sentences, and though there were too few cases in this category for the findings to be significant, it may be the only exception to the rule.

16. Examples of this are similar to those before 1854. They were included in

newspaper court reports virtually every day although, as time went on, with somewhat less detail. See, for example, *PL*, 27 April 1857, 8 August 1857, 16 August 1860, 17 August 1860, 7 February 1861, 9 April 1861, 11 June 1863, 22 November 1871.

17. The other quarter sessions judges during this period, Parsons and Finletter, are not included because the sample included too few cases of theirs before 1876.

18. *PL*, 5 March 1841, 2 March 1847, 5 March 1847. See also 12 July 1843.

19. *PL*, 4 August 1868. Not only grand jurors but also aldermen and the parties involved in assault and battery cases were blamed for the court's difficulties. See, for example, *PL*, 10 April 1858, 26 July 1859, 6 December 1860, 29 June 1863, 11 December 1869.

20. *PL*, 21 January 1846. See also 27 September 1844.

21. *PL*, 24 February 1858, 20 March 1862. See also 31 May 1859, 26 October 1859, 3 November 1859, 25 August 1860, 25 October 1860, 13 June 1861, 26 June 1861, 25 August 1864, 5 September 1864, 8 September 1864.

22. *PL*, 26 October 1859, 26 June 1861, 25 August 1864, 5 September 1864, 6 January 1871, 19 January 1871, 3 February 1871, 17 September 1872. See also, for example, 12 July 1870, 13 July 1870, 5 January 1871, 7 January 1871, 4 February 1871, 28 March 1871, 31 March 1871, 17 June 1871, 17 October 1871, 19 September 1872.

This problem was not limited to assault and battery cases, but it also plagued liquor prosecutions. Defendants failed to appear in these cases, most either having moved away or relocated their businesses. An effort to prosecute license offenders in May 1860 was totally thwarted because of this; over a decade later the court had scarcely any greater success—only 5 of 41 defendants appeared. See *PL*, 16 May 1860, 22 July 1870.

23. *PL*, 28 September 1838, 20 January 1842, 14 July 1847. Sometimes defendants were simply discharged by the court. See *PL*, 13 August 1839.

24. *PL*, 14 July 1838, 6 December 1839, 28 May 1841, 11 May 1842, 27 July 1842. See also 4 June 1840, 13 January 1847, 24 August 1848, 5 September 1848, 14 September 1848.

25. *PL*, 19 March 1844, 2 March 1847, 8 February 1849, 11 September 1852, 26 February 1853.

26. Between 1844 and 1854, for example, prison terms for guilty pleaders averaged 2 months, for convicts 3.6; fines for those pleading guilty averaged $1.70, for convicts $2.80. The rate of guilty pleading fell from 16 percent of those entering a plea from 1844 to 1854 to 7 percent after 1854. If plea bargaining had been common, more serious personal offenders would surely have taken advantage of it; many of them were convicted when tried, and those tried and convicted were sentenced to average terms of 69 months, but those who confessed were sentenced to an average of just 15 months. Yet the practice was probably no more frequent here than in other personal cases. See Quarter Sessions Court Dockets.

27. *PL*, 16 June 1859, 7 February 1861, 17 July 1861, 29 October 1862.

28. *PL*, 13 November 1839.

29. *PL*, 29 September 1837, 19 August 1839. See also for example 8 March 1838, 20 May 1839, 13 August 1839, 4 June 1840, 9 November 1843, 5 September 1848, 8 February 1849, 4 September 1849, 18 April 1854.

30. *PL*, 26 June 1837, 7 February 1839, 7 January 1847, 14 April 1848, 14 June 1848, 24 August 1848, 7 December 1848, 5 January 1853, 26 February 1853, 23 April 1853, 23 January 1854.

31. *PL*, 13 January 1847, 14 June 1848, 18 August 1852, 23 April 1853.

32. *PL*, 27 September 1838, 11 March 1839, 14 June 1848, 5 January 1853, 23 January 1854.

33. *PL*, 11 March 1839, 13 January 1842, 24 August 1848, 14 September 1848, 18 August 1852, 26 February 1853.

34. *PL*, 10 April 1839, 17 April 1839.

35. *PL*, 24 August 1858, 10 February 1860, 17 August 1860, 20 March 1862, 16 May 1863. See also 16 June 1859, 7 June 1860, 25 August 1860, 9 April 1861, 7 February 1871.

36. *PL*, 17 April 1839, 13 August 1839, 27 March 1846, 20 December 1847, 6 January 1849.

37. *PL*, 31 June 1866; *JPD* [n.s.] 5 (1866): 33. See also, for example, *PL*, 2 July 1867, 2 August 1869, 7 December 1869, 5 September 1870, 27 October 1870.

As though this were not enough, the court was also plagued by lost and stolen bills of indictment, 700 of which were discovered in March 1858, and accusations that cases against prominent persons or political figures were conveniently overlooked by the district attorney. See *PL*, 24 March 1858, 21 September 1858, 4 October 1859.

38. This is true only in a relative sense. Roger Lane suggests that fornication and bastardy prosecutions, numbering about 20 per year during the 1840s, often constituted "the substitution of official processes for private justice," an attempt by the unwed mother to use the threat of court action to gain a private settlement. Remember, still roughly half of these cases never reached a verdict. See Lane, *Violent Death in the City*, pp. 94–95. See also *PL*, 9 November 1943, 12 November 1844, 1 December 1848.

39. *PL*, 10 September 1839, 2 December 1839, 4 December 1839, 6 December 1839, 13 January 1842, 12 January 1843, 5 November 1846, 11 January 1848, 7 April 1848, 11 September 1852, 12 November 1852, 23 May 1853, 25 February 1854.

40. See *PL*, 11 July 1854, for example.

41. Occasionally reports included a case in which a defendant was convicted of stealing the property of a "person unknown," but this was unusual. See, for example, *PL*, 13 January 1842, 6 February 1852. In the latter instance, a man was arrested for stealing handkerchiefs after he tried to sell them at a reduced price. No evidence was presented to show that the goods had been stolen, and the defendant claimed he was given the handkerchiefs by a man in the street. The accused was convicted of receiving stolen goods.

42. *PL*, 19 February 1840, 11 July 1854. "The cases were rattled off with utmost rapidity," noted the reporter on that day, but this was not exceptional. On most of the dates cited in this section, many petty larceny cases were disposed of.

43. Hundreds of cases were reported each year in the daily reports of the courts of record in the *Public Ledger*. They simply stated the name of the defendant and sometimes the prosecutor, described the property stolen, and recorded the sentence. These made up the bulk of the larceny case reports included in the newspaper. Coats and outerwear were taken from the front halls of residences, stores, schools, hotels, and

theaters. These were the most easily and commonly stolen articles of clothing, but all kinds of garments were taken; in one case, James Body, a frequent offender, was convicted of the theft of ladies' underwear. The stealing of foodstuffs was common—flour, chickens, butter, potatoes, and occasionally meat that was packed in bags or barrels. Quantities were small; one of the most unusual was David Denny's theft in 1849 of forty pounds of beef, for which he received an uncommonly long eighteen-month sentence. Thefts of tools included saws, harnesses, rope, wheelbarrows, and iron. Each of these thefts consisted of only one or two items. See, *PL*, 8 March 1838, 4 June 1840, 5 May 1842, 3 July 1844, 11 January 1848, 5 September 1848, 17 October 1848, 8 February 1849, 4 September 1849, 5 January 1853, 25 February 1854.

44. *PL*, 2 May 1840, 13 January 1842, 12 March 1842, 7 April 1848.

45. *PL*, 6 December 1839, 12 May 1840, 5 May 1842, 6 February 1852. In the first instance, a servant girl was acquitted because of the position of women in marriage. The property stolen was described in the indictment as belonging to a woman, but because her husband was alive, she technically owned no property and thus the indictment was defective.

46. *PL*, 19 March 1844, 5 November 1846, 26 June 1854.

47. See, for example, *PL*, 5 November 1846, 11 January 1848. Cases like these were also dismissed by grand juries. See *PL*, 5 May 1842.

48. *PL*, 12 May 1840, 9 November 1843, 11 March 1844, 14 September 1848.

49. *PL*, 3 July 1844, 5 November 1846, 14 September 1848.

Leniency was sometimes granted by the court through the defendant's efforts. John Baker was convicted in 1843 of stealing a sledge hammer. He had come from New Jersey to seek work but could find none. After sleeping outdoors without food for a few days, he was driven to steal in order to raise money with which to return home to his wife and children. Because he had neither friends nor bail, he had already spent 37 days in prison without contact with his family. The judge sentenced him to just one day, and the jury raised the court costs from among themselves to prevent Baker from having to spend an additional 30 days in jail. John Robbins and Henry Conner were also sentenced to one day for stealing some butter, because the prison keeper testified that they were of great assistance in caring for cholera victims during their pretrial confinement. See *PL*, 11 November 1843, 4 September 1849.

Judges often held hearings before sentencing if a defendant was unknown to them and would impose light sentences if the defendant could demonstrate good character. See, for example, *PL*, 11 March 1839, 5 September 1848, 29 September 1849. This practice may have accounted for some of the disparity in sentencing for minor thefts of similarly valued property, but it hardly amounted to a significant protection for defendants.

50. Those confessing to larceny after 1854 received on the average a sentence of 9.7 months, less than a month shorter than those choosing a trial. The difference had been six months during the previous period.

After 1854, because of overcrowding, judges sent only those with the shortest sentences to the county prison. Sentences for larceny convicts in the county prison fell to 7.8 months for first-timers and 9.5 months for recidivists. The rest went to the Eastern State Penitentiary. Other prisoner patterns remained the same. While sentences for blacks committed to the county prison were now lower than those of whites (7.3

months for blacks, 7.8 for whites), black women continued to be punished much more severely than black men and more severely than were the women of any other ethnic group relative to the men of that group. Overall, sentences for black first-timers in the county prison were exactly half of what they had been before 1854. This especially marked decline in black sentences occurred as the proportion of blacks imprisoned also declined sharply. Before 1850 blacks averaged over 40 percent and, in some years, were over half of the prisoners committed to hard labor. That figure fell to 29 percent in 1850, and exceeded 30 percent again only in 1855 and twice during the Civil War. The proportion of blacks fell as low as 13.2 percent of the convicts in 1865. This paralleled a decrease in the percentage of blacks committed to prison to await trial and for minor offenses, which also began during the early 1850s. Both changes were the result of the impact of the police on the rest of the criminal justice system. The percentage of blacks arrested by the police was always lower than the percentage of blacks in prison; thus, the police exerted a downward pressure on the latter figure after 1850. Blacks accounted for between 3.1 and 8.5 percent of all arrests. Of course, even this percentage was higher than the percentage of blacks in Philadelphia's population. See Lane, *The Roots of Violence in Black Philadelphia*, ch. 3.

Falling larceny sentences remained a pattern through the 1870s. See Naylor, "Crime, Criminals, and Punishment in Philadelphia," pp. 150–58, 167–68. Naylor believes that this period established a trend that saw more people imprisoned for less time than earlier, but court records suggest that relatively fewer larceny defendants were imprisoned now than before. Naylor also found that toward the end of the nineteenth century, when sentences for whites increased, the percentage of white prisoners declined; but sentences for blacks remained lower and their proportion of the prison population increased. This would be a distinct reversal of the trend of the immediate postpolice era when the percentage of black prisoners fell.

51. *PL*, 13 January 1842, 11 January 1848.

52. *PL*, 12 May 1840, 14 April 1848.

Chapter 4

1. *PL*, 23 May 1853. See also *PL*, 12 January 1843. See also *PL*, 11 January 1848, 12 December 1853.

2. Kneass Scrapbook, p. 14. See also Vaux, *Some Remarks on the Writ of Habeas Corpus*, pp. 4–5, 15, 20–21; Hilliard, *The Elements of Law*, pp. 414–19; and Edwards, *The Grand Jury*, pp. 106–10.

3. Act of 29 March 1819; Ingersoll, *Report Made by J. Ingersoll, Esquire, Attorney General of Pennsylvania*; *Report of the Commissioners on the Penal Code*, p. 144; and *Notes on the Penal Laws of Pennsylvania*, pp. 6–7. For a fuller discussion of the practical role and legal responsibilities of the public prosecutor in Pennsylvania and elsewhere, see Steinberg, "From Private Prosecution to Plea Bargaining."

4. Vaux, *Reports of Some of the Criminal Cases on Primary Hearing*, p. 223; Chambers, *Speech on the Judicial Tenure*, p. 11.

5. See Henderson, "The Attack on the Judiciary in Pennsylvania," pp. 115–24; Bushey, "William Duane," p. 143; Salkin, "Crime in Pennsylvania," pp. 51, 64–68, 272, 276. Brown, *The Forum*, pp. 34–37, 40–41; Brown, *Speech of David Paul Brown*

(1825); D. Webster to John M. Read, 1846, Read Letter Book; and Brown, *First Speech of David Paul Brown* (1858), p. 6.

6. This position was reinforced five years later when the prosecuting attorneys adopted the practice of forbidding counsel to appear for the commonwealth under the auspices of the private prosecutor in *felony* cases only. *PL*, 9 February 1841, 2 December 1841, 15 July 1846.

7. Act of 29 March 1819; Act of 9 June 1832; *PL*, 20 November 1841, 15 July 1846.

8. Continued ambivalence about the power of the public prosecutor was also reflected in an 1866 law that entitled a prosecutor's private counsel, with the court's consent, to conduct a case if the district attorney refused to do so or failed to do so in a manner that conformed to the private prosecutor's wishes. The district attorney still did not conduct all criminal cases but was rather a sort of buffer between the court and the private prosecutor, and a limited one at that. For example, when children were involved, the district attorney took the case from private counsel in order to explain to the jury the special legal circumstances surrounding their prosecution; when the prison agent sought to obtain a discharge in a case, he often went to the district attorney. But overall, until 1874, he remained, in practice, the public prosecutor primarily in serious crimes. Law of 12 March 1866; *PL*, 15 February 1859, 25 October 1860, 25 October 1862, 7 February 1863; 29 May 1866, 25 July 1867, 11 April 1871, 8 January 1873, 16 April 1873. *JPD* [n.s.] 5 (1866): 33; [n.s.] 2 (1863): 21.

9. Law of 3 May 1850, Public Law 634; *PL*, 27 September 1844.

10. "Report on the Criminal Code," p. 149.

11. Salkin, "Crime in Pennsylvania," p. 269.

12. Ibid., pp. 276–81.

13. During the pre-1838 period, there were no instances of costs being placed on prosecutors in any property case in the sample.

14. *PL*, 27 June 1836, 19 September 1837.

15. *PL*, 27 June 1836.

16. *PL*, 14 March 1843, 4 July 1843, 10 July 1843, 21 November 1843, 6 February 1844, 5 September 1845. General sessions judge Barton made a similar comment during that court's waning days, praising the criminal law as a protector of society, its authority vindicated in the course of its use by the public. *PL*, 24 September 1842.

17. See *Aldermen and Justices of the Peace Cases*, 2 Parsons Equity Cases 458 (1847). *PL*, 30 July 1846. See also 4 July 1836, 7 July 1846, 9 July 1846.

18. This is, of course, not to say that the court's policy had no effect on the disposition of these cases or the fate of prisoners. Although its major importance was as a significant early attempt to diminish the power of aldermen, the policy may indeed have had some short-term salutary effect upon prison crowding; it also may have had other effects that do not appear in the dockets because of the rapid changes in arrest practices after 1850, which no doubt nullified whatever the court policy had accomplished.

19. The aldermen could not yet have begun to comply with the court's order, so the procedure for this term was simply to send to court every person in prison. Aldermen, as might have been expected, were nervous about the new court order. Some even closed up shop for a while, fearing that they had lost their major source of revenue. See *PL*, 9 July 1846, 13 July 1846, 27 July 1846.

20. *PL*, 10 July 1847, 10 January 1848, 30 October 1848. See also 1 February 1847.
21. *PL*, 10 July 1847, 10 January 1848, 30 October 1848, 14 July 1851.
22. *PL*, 9 November 1846. See also 17 January 1848.
23. *PL*, 21 August 1848, 31 March 1851, 9 February 1853.
24. *PL*, 4 May 1850, 31 March 1852.
25. The policy of keeping cases like these hidden from public view was also, in a sense, a departure from the formerly dominant principle that public exposure of criminal cases would be an example to other individuals, both to prosecutors to bring cases and to offenders to obey the law. The key here was the concept of individual responsibility to invoke the law. In both wanting to make the law a terror and to keep cases hidden from publicity, the judges were rejecting this concept in favor of one that considered criminal justice to be the province of groups, both groups of designated prosecutors and especially crime-prone citizens. Such thinking would become a key element in the thinking of criminal justice officials and reformers in the police era.

Chapter 5

1. *PL*, 6 July 1836, 13 July 1836, 15 July 1836.
2. Paine, *Common Sense*, p. 98.
3. Given what rapidly developed within criminal justice in nineteenth-century Philadelphia, fears of corruption among American legal thinkers seem justified. See Ferguson, *Law and Letters in American Culture*, esp. ch. 2.
4. The popularization of politics began in the 1760's, motivated by the deep and bitter factional divisions within the ruling elites of Pennsylvania. Mobilization of the people for a variety of purposes, notably militia service, continued the process during the prerevolutionary crisis. It culminated with the 1776 Pennsylvania Constitution, which included a broadly extended franchise, unicameral legislature, frequent rotation in office, and other uncommonly democratic features. Foner, *Tom Paine and Revolutionary America*, pp. 62–67, ch. 4; Miller, "The Federal City," pp. 158–59. See also Rosswurm, " 'As a Lyen Out of His Den,' " and Nash, *The Urban Crucible*, chs. 11, 13.
5. The episode of the trading justices is treated most completely in Alexander, *Render Them Submissive*, pp. 71–72.
6. Thomas Paine stated flatly in his last political pamphlet that "all government has consistently to do . . . is to establish the process by which the parties concerned shall proceed and bring the matter to decision themselves, by referring it to impartial and judicious men of the neighborhood, of their own choosing." Paine here was thinking of the civil law, but as he recognized earlier, magistrates were acting in similar ways in criminal cases at a time when the line between civil and criminal litigation was quite indistinct. See *To the Citizens of Pennsylvania on the Proposals for Calling a Convention* (1805) in Foner, *The Complete Writings of Thomas Paine*, 2:996.
Revolutionary leaders, especially the most democratically inclined of them, had no doubts about the importance of the judiciary. Paine asserted that "so far as regards the execution of the laws, that which is called the judicial power, is strictly and properly the executive power of every country." Thomas Jefferson claimed that "the dignity and stability of government in all its branches, the morals of the people, and every blessing of society, depends so much upon an upright and skillful administration of justice."

Both believed that such important results could be assured only by the people's participation. Paine thought that the choice of justices of the peace, precisely because they were officers of "arbitration or compromise between neighbors differing with each other," was one for which "the judgement of the public, as a public, is supposed to be the most complete." Jefferson thought that if he had to choose "whether the people had best be omitted in the Legislative or Judiciary department, I would say it is better to leave them out of the Legislative. The execution of the laws is more important than the making of them."

Paine's remarks are from *The Rights of Man* and the *Address to the People of Pennsylvania*. See Foner, *The Complete Writings of Thomas Paine* 1:388 and 2:300. Jefferson's comments were made in a 1776 letter to George Wythe and a 1789 letter to the Abbe Arnoux. See Boyd, *The Papers of Thomas Jefferson*, 1:410 and 15:283.

7. Ellis, *The Jeffersonian Crisis*, pp. 111–15, 157–62.

8. See ibid, pp. 162–70. The legislation was then passed over the governor's veto.

Duane's personal interest was provoked as the result of a hostile prosecution of a sympathetic judge which reminded him of his own persecution under the Alien and Sedition Laws by the Adams administration. He had been earlier persecuted by the British before independence as well, so episodes of this sort generally spurred him to action. See ibid., pp. 164–67, and Bushey, "William Duane."

It was in the midst of this controversy that Pennsylvania legislators gave juries the power to place the court costs on the private prosecutor in misdemeanor cases that resulted in a dismissal or acquittal. The concern of the law's framers with disorder within the legal process itself was underscored by an 1808 court decision that allowed the prosecutor to be saddled with the costs even if the charge was substantial but the indictment technically defective. See Salkin, "Crime in Pennsylvania," pp. 276–81.

9. The law allowing court costs to be placed on prosecutors was a precedent for future attempts to limit and ultimately undermine the system of private prosecution, but at this point, it may well have been directed more at lawyers than at ordinary private litigants. See Henderson, "The Attack on the Judiciary in Pennsylvania," pp. 115–24; Bushey, "William Duane" p. 143; and Salkin, "Crime in Pennsylvania," pp. 51, 64–68, 272, 276.

Most of the revered leaders of the Revolution were lawyers, as were most of the young republic's great men of letters. A brilliant analysis of the centrality of law in American national consciousness and culture during the revolutionary and early national eras is Ferguson, *Law and Letters in American Culture*, esp. chs. 1–3. Ferguson notes that this connection has been forgotten by Americans of the twentieth century, just as the particularly law-centered form of criminal justice with which the present study is concerned has been.

10. See Salkin, "Crime in Pennsylvania," pp. 64–74, 269.

11. Ellis interprets the battle over the judiciary as being between commercially oriented urban moderates and agrarian radicals. This, no doubt, was an important line of division among Republicans after 1800, but it is also true that the radical persuasion had considerable support among nonrural people who were adamantly opposed, not to commerce, but to what they would have termed "speculation." See Ellis, *The Jeffersonian Crisis*, pp. 256–61, and Banning, *The Jeffersonian Persuasion*, pp. 203–5. See also Foner, *Tom Paine and Revolutionary America*, p. 260.

Ellis is aware of urban radicalism, of course, but understates the extent to which their ideals dovetailed with the rural agrarians' vision of "the kind of country (they) wanted to see America become." Ellis, *The Jeffersonian Crisis*, p. 338. The point here is that the support of urban radicals for justices of the peace and the simple, accessible court system championed by rural reformers, given the evidence of an urban tradition of popular private criminal prosecution, suggests that Ellis's argument about social visions reflected not simply urban-rural differences but also intra-urban differences closely attached to the different ideals various urban groups had about the kind of society America was and was to become.

12. Alexander, *Render Them Submissive*, pp. 68–72; Remick, "The House of Refuge of Philadelphia," pp. 107–9; and Teeters, *The Cradle of the Penitentiary*, pp. 51–52. See also Teeters, *They Were in Prison*, the standard work on the PSAMPP, later known as the Pennsylvania Prison Society, especially pp. 5, 90–92, 94–97, 118–19, 122, 152.

13. This point is established for the early national period in Rothman, *The Discovery of the Asylum*, ch. 2. Research in the history of incarceration in Pennsylvania indicates that this idea was already prominent among revolutionary-era prison reformers, especially the leading light among them in Philadelphia, the PSAMPP's founder, Benjamin Rush. See Meranze, "The Penitential Ideal in Late Eighteenth-Century Philadelphia."

14. For a fuller discussion of the process of prison construction in Philadelphia before 1836, see Steinberg, "The Criminal Courts and the Transformation of Criminal Justice in Philadelphia," pp. 20–25, 67–70. See also Tyson, *Essay on the Penal Law of Pennsylvania*, pp. 51–52, 55–56; Vaux, *Notices of the Original and Successive Efforts to Improve the Discipline of the Prison at Philadelphia*, pp. 37–38; Mease, *Observations on the Penitentiary System*, p. 34; *A Statistical View of the Operation of the Penal Code of Pennsylvania*, pp. 5–6; *Annual Report of the Philadelphia Society for Alleviating the Miseries of Public Prisons*, p. 4; PSAMPP Minute Book, 9 October 1806, 10 January 1820, 8 January 1821, 13 January 1834, 12 August 1836; Teeters, *The Cradle of the Penitentiary*, pp. 55–56, 92–93, 107, 110–15, 121.

15. PSAMPP Visiting Committee Reports, 21 October 1809; Report of Bartholomew Wistar of Visiting Committee to Acting Committee of PSAMPP, 27 March 1822; PSAMPP Minute Book, 13 June 1823; *Report of the Committee Appointed to Investigate the Causes of Cholera in the Arch Street Prison*, pp. 13–15. See also PSAMPP Minute Book, 10 January 1820, 9 October 1820, 13 March 1822, 17 March 1824, 11 November 1829, 8 June 1830, 13 July 1831.

16. PSAMPP Minutes, 10 June 1833, 12 September 1833. Not only were lawyers hesitant to prosecute other legal officers, but the legislature was prepared to extend the aldermanic system despite the criticism. By the Law of 4 May 1832, aldermen were to be appointed by the governor on 1 January 1833 in the suburbs of Northern Liberties, Southwark, Moyamensing, Passyunk, Spring Garden, and Kensington. With the Law of 16 June 1836 all the justices in these districts appointed before 4 May 1832 were declared to be aldermen. Thus the office of alderman became the dominant form of the minor judiciary throughout Philadelphia County.

17. Before 1814, an eighteenth-century court decision ruled that justices could take illegal fees if that was the usual practice. Law of 28 March 1814; *Respublica* v.

Hannum, 1 Yeates 71; *Collins* v. *Hunter,* 1 Ashmead 60; *Coates* v. *Wallace,* 13 Sergeant and Rawle 74.

18. Supporters of the house of refuge swiftly obtained a legislative charter, and elected as the corporation's first president the prominent attorney and congressman John Sergeant. Like the leaders of the PSAMPP, Sergeant's enthusiasm for incarceration derived from an elitist, organic sense of order and hierarchy that allowed him to support innovation here while remaining committed to traditional legal processes. On the house of refuge, see Steinberg, "The Criminal Courts and the Transformation of Criminal Justice in Philadelphia," pp. 63–67, and Remick, "The House of Refuge of Philadelphia," pp. 134, 140–44. Philadelphia was, of course, not alone in the movement to establish refuges and training schools for delinquent and vagrant children. In fact, the New York Refuge opened nine years earlier. See Mennel, *Thorns and Thistles,* and Hawes, *Children in Urban Society.* On Sergeant, Vaux, and the relationship between their Whig beliefs in an organic hierarchical society and their support for prison reform, see Zachary, "Social Disorder and the Philadelphia Elite before Jackson," pp. 290–93, 296–97, and Hartz, *Economic Policy and Democratic Thought,* pp. 138–42. See also *An Address from the Managers of the House of Refuge to Their Fellow Citizens; Act of Incorporation of the House of Refuge; The Design and Advantages of the House of Refuge;* and the *Annual Reports of the House of Refuge,* 1829–35.

On the county prison and the prison society, see Teeters, *The Cradle of the Penitentiary,* pp. 105, 108–12; and the Laws of 30 March 1831 and 14 April 1835.

19. *Legislative Journal of Pennsylvania,* pp. 130–31.

20. On the press, and especially the one-cent-per-copy daily newspapers, or the "penny press," which popularized criminal justice and advocated reform, see Robinson, "The *Public Ledger,*" and "The Dynamics of American Journalism from 1787 to 1865." The *Ledger* is generally regarded as "the first prominent example of an American newspaper published at one cent a copy." See Oberholtzer, *Philadelphia,* pp. 221–22. Throughout the period under consideration here, the *Ledger* remained an independent, nonpartisan newspaper devoted to public improvement and the largest possible circulation, following the design of its principal editor, William H. Swain, a journeyman printer who became rich as a newspaperman. Thus the *Ledger* immediately began publishing the names of defendants in court in order to deter crime and complaining bitterly whenever the courts seemed to be treating the "better sort" preferentially, which among other things kept the paper from printing their names. See *PL,* 11 April 1836, 22 September 1836, 15 November 1836, 3 January 1837, 17 January 1837, 12 August 1837, 23 September 1837.

21. See Klein, *Pennsylvania Politics,* pp. 50, 53, 69–71, 111–12.

22. *PL,* 6 July 1836, 13 July 1836, 15 July 1836, 22 September 1836, 29 April 1837. The normal procedure for taking bail was not to actually accept money but rather the assurance that an individual of known means would be responsible for the sum should the defendant abscond. It was therefore necessary for a defendant only to have the alderman accept the person he or she presented as bail.

23. *PL,* 27 September 1837, 28 September 1837, 2 November 1837. On McMichael, see Bloom, "Morton McMichael's North American." Political patronage, of course, benefited many people in Jacksonian American and boosted many a political career,

including very distinguished ones. Among them, for example, was William D. Kelley, whose extraordinary talents gained him an appointment as a judge in 1845. See Laurie, *Working People of Philadelphia*, chs. 5–6; Greco, "William Darrah Kelley."

24. PSAMPP Minute Book, 19 January 1838; *PL*, 12 January 1838.

25. *PL*, 8 February 1838, 9 February 1838, 10 February 1838, 14 February 1838.

26. *PL*, 20 February 1838, 8 March 1838; *Pennsylvania House of Representatives Journal*, pp. 766–67. The vote in favor was 49 to 38.

27. *PL*, 21 March 1838. See also Eastman, *Courts and Lawyers of Pennsylvania*, and Martin, *Martin's Bench and Bar of Philadelphia*. The quarter sessions retained jurisdiction over tavern licensing and roads. Its judges were freed to attend to civil business as judges of the court of common pleas, but they lost criminal jurisdiction. Three new judges were appointed by the governor to the criminal sessions bench, including John Bouvier, former recorder of the city.

28. *PL*, 28 September 1837.

29. The debate is summarized in the *Proceedings and Debates*, 3:567–644. The quote is from Representative Brown of Philadelphia, p. 588.

30. Sergeant's reference to the extension of the justices' jurisdiction meant the extension of their civil jurisdiction to $100. He ignored the repeated refusal of the legislature to extend the criminal jurisdiction of justices. See ibid., 3:579–80.

Sergeant was, in this instance, curiously ready to adapt to changing conditions. Though he believed magistrates and all officials of the state should be respected, he recognized the declining status of aldermen and justices. His support of a salaried magistracy at this early date, like his support of the Bank of the United States and public improvements, reflected Sergeant's sense that the spirit of private enterprise was becoming dominant and that the state should act to prevent this spirit from dominating in areas in which private ends would conflict with the public welfare. If canals and roads were one such area, so was criminal justice. See Hartz, *Economic Policy and Democratic Thought*, pp. 29–31, 139–42.

31. The votes were 80 to 24 and 70 to 35. See *Proceedings and Debates*, 3:608–9, 612.

The mayor of Philadelphia also became an elected official with the new document. The constitution is most famous, though, for removing the franchise from black men even as it was extending it for whites. *Proceedings and Debates*, 9:38–53; 1838 Constitution of Pennsylvania, Art. VI, Sec. 7; and Law of 21 June 1839.

32. *PL*, 2 May 1838, 21 August 1838, 19 December 1838. In the latter case, the editors of the *Ledger* used examples of disorderly persons who were actually taken from their homes and committed as vagrants to defend the prison inspectors from charges that they too often released vagrants before the expiration of their terms. Though they obliquely criticized aldermen in the course of this argument, the editors were incorrect when they asserted that these were examples of persons who "are sometimes sentenced as vagrants, who, in legal contemplation, are not such." We have seen that the law clearly allowed aldermen to commit disorderly persons to prison as vagrants and that the magistrate had great latitude in interpreting behavior as disorderly.

33. *PL*, 21 August 1839.

34. *PL*, 13 July 1838, 19 July 1839, 28 August 1839, 16 October 1839.

35. The politicians were right about the 1840 presidential contest. Harrison carried Pennsylvania by 343 votes.

See Act of 21 June 1839; *PL*, 11 January 1840, 1 February 1840. The best suggestion of the strength of ward politics in Philadelphia is provided by Laurie in *Working People of Philadelphia*, esp. pp. 110–15 and "Fire Companies and Gangs in Southwark," esp. pp. 72–74, 82–83. See also Snyder, *The Jacksonian Heritage*, pp. 50–67, 75–95. For ward politics in antebellum New York, see Shefter, "The Emergence of the Political Machine"; Hammack, "Problems in the Historical Study of Power"; and Bridges, *A City in the Republic*, chs. 4, 6. A recent provocative discussion of urban politics in American history by Terrence J. McDonald reinforces the point that urban machines remained highly decentralized well into the nineteenth century and that one of the dominant ideas in the recent historiographical rehabilitation of machine politics was that they provided services to urban residents without idealism or attempts to reform them. See McDonald, "The Problem of the Political in Recent American Urban History." This is an abstraction that applies well to the story of criminal prosecution presented here, and it may be helpful in understanding the continuity between these activities of early ward politicians and some of the values and policies of traditional Whig jurists and leaders like Sergeant, especially those regarding the legal process itself, which allowed Sergeant to continue to defend aldermen and justices even as they were obviously becoming, at least in urban areas, the creatures of ward politics.

36. *PL*, 17 March 1840. See also 4 February 1840, 14 February 1840, 12 March 1840.

37. *PL*, 14 February 1840.

38. The idea that litigation can be a form of political participation, especially important when the franchise is restricted, has recently been raised by historians and students of the court system. See, for example, Grossman and Sarat, "Litigation in the Federal Courts," and Laura L. Becker, "The People and the System."

39. *PL*, 24 February 1840; Bloom, "Morton McMichael's North American," p. 165.

40. *PL*, 6 March 1840. Kelley, his talent already in evidence, had recently returned to Philadelphia from Boston at the invitation of Democratic party leaders in order to establish a political career. McMullin, although still a teenager, was already a stalwart of the rabidly Democratic Moyamensing Hose Company. See Greco, "William Darrah Kelley," pp. 168–89, and Silcox, "William McMullen," pp. 389–91.

41. *PL*, 11 February 1840.

42. *PL*, 19 March 1840, 20 March 1840.

43. On the extreme population mobility in nineteenth-century America, see Thernstrom, *Poverty and Progress: Social Mobility in a Nineteenth-Century City*, and Katz, Doucet, and Stern, *The Social Organization of Early Industrial Capitalism*, ch. 3.

On the working class and politicians in the nineteenth century, see Montgomery, "Gutman's Nineteenth-Century America," pp. 427–28.

44. Walker, *Popular Justice*, p. 115. See also McKitrick, "The Study of Corruption," especially his comment about the importance of "intercession with the law" as a service of the political machine.

45. A typical comment insisted that "very many cases . . . could and should . . . be

disposed of by the Aldermen and Justices of the Peace, before the complaints are instituted. They are made for the most part when the parties are in a state of excitement, laboring under a sense of imaginary rather than real injuries. A conciliatory and firm course on the part of the magistrate . . . might allay angry feelings among neighbors in many instances, and smother dissensions in the bud." *PL*, 16 January 1840, 14 May 1840, 24 June 1840, 12 August 1840, 12 December 1840, 8 February 1841, 11 February 1841, 12 February 1841.

46. Act of 12 July 1842; Act of 30 July 1842; *PL*, 30 November 1842.

47. *PL*, 1 November 1842, 12 January 1843, 25 February 1843, 4 March 1843.

48. *PL*, 20 December 1839.

49. *PL*, 24 December 1839. Bouvier made his not inconsiderable nineteenth-century reputation on his efforts to be an early American Blackstone. The results of his quest, which remained major legal texts for decades, were *A Law Dictionary Adapted to the Constitution and Laws of the United States and the Several States of the American Union* (1839) and *Institutes of American Law* (1851).

50. *PL*, 20 May 1841, 27 August 1841. See also 20 November 1841, 22 September 1843. Throughout the early 1840s, sensitivity to the issue remained high. In January 1842, the police reporter tied the "pillaging" of honest labor to widespread cheating and crime. People simply were not encouraged to be honest and fell upon fraud in self-defense. He suggested that criminals brought before the court tell the judge that they were driven to crime by "the institutions of my country." Most of the time, the reporter insisted, "that plea would deserve serious attention." *PL*, 27 January 1842. The *Ledger*'s editors compared American justice unfavorably with the socially ranked and biased criminal justice system of Japan. See *PL*, 23 March 1841. Judge Conrad, in an 1842 charge to a grand jury, asked for the moderation of the "inordinate love of gain which unfortunately characterizes our people." See *PL*, 24 September 1842. See also 14 February 1841, 2 May 1843. Judge Kelley's similar remarks in public speeches are discussed below.

51. Alderman Mitchell, for instance, was fined $50 for overcharging parties in a case in June 1846. Popular writers also explicitly suggested that justice was biased. Defenders of the city's small black population accused aldermen of "gross prejudice and injustice" because only 18 percent of the blacks committed to prison before trial in January 1846 were ever convicted. The reason for this was that magistrates looked "less to the satisfaction of justice, than to the justice's pocket," and blacks were singularly incapable of buying their way out of jail. Some critics went further to accuse the higher courts (probably incorrectly) of convicting blacks of crimes for which whites were acquitted and giving blacks more severe punishment than whites for similar crimes. *PL*, 25 June 1846. Needles, *A Review of a Pamphlet Entitled "An Appeal to the Public on Behalf of a House of Refuge for Colored Juvenile Delinquents,"* pp. 6–9. *PL*, 28 January 1847.

52. This account of the origins of *The Letters of Junius* was taken from a lengthy unidentified newspaper account of Dickerson's life which was published at the time of his death on 12 May 1892. By this time, the *Letters* were a distant footnote to the life of Dickerson, who was best known as "the scapegoat of the famous Whitaker will forgery case," for which he spent the last several years of his life in prison.

53. Ibid., pp. 5–19.

54. Ibid., pp. 17, 42–43.

55. *The Almighty Dollar*, p. 26. Lippard, *The Quaker City*, pp. 74–76, 294, 474.

56. *PL*, 28 January 1847, 2 March 1847, 5 April 1847, 4 May 1847, 7 October 1847. See also 2 February 1848.

57. *PL*, 4 June 1847, 16 October 1848, 27 April 1850.

58. *JPD* 2 (July 1847): 65.

59. *PL*, 18 January 1847, Teeters, *They Were in Prison*, pp. 303, 306–7.

60. The county commissioners, for example, denied them access to information on the amounts of money paid to public and court officers. *PL*, 29 August 1848.

Grand jurors regularly repeated the simple demand that citizens prosecute aldermen who tried to extort illegal fees. Obviously, the alliance between aldermen and litigants kept this from often happening; when it did, the result dissuaded further prosecutions. Aldermen Isaac Boileau was accused of conspiracy by citizens several times but was regularly acquitted. *PL*, 9 February 1848, 12 April 1848, 29 June 1848, 27–28 January 1848, 5 October 1849. In 1849, Boileau and Alderman Weygandt were charged by fourteen persons for extorting money from unlicensed liquor dealers, to no avail.

61. *Report of the Committee of 15 Citizens*, pp. 11–14.

62. Ibid., pp. 18–19, 27. The influence of Mullen is especially clear here, where the report voiced the same concerns and showed the same biases that would appear in Mullen's prison agent reports after 1854.

63. *PL*, 4 July 1849, 4 October 1849, 27 February 1850. See also 22 August 1848, 10 January 1849, 5 March 1849.

64. Law of 24 January 1849; *PL*, 6 October 1849.

65. *PL*, 11 October 1849. Dickerson's cbituary claimed that his showing was "regarded as an exceptionally large vote" but conceded that his prominence subsided after the election.

66. *PL*, 14 September 1850, 11 October 1850.

Chapter 6

1. This sketch is taken from Warner, *The Private City*, pp. 133–36; and *Report of the Committee on Police*.

2. Sprogle, *The Philadelphia Police*, pp. 73–75; Johnson, "The Search for an Urban Discipline"; and Allinson and Penrose, *Philadelphia, 1681–1884*, pp. 99–100. No statistics on police activity are available for this period. However, we can infer from reports after 1833, when the police force was somewhat improved, that most arrests were for vagrancy and drunkenness.

3. Johnson, "The Search for an Urban Discipline," ch. 1; Sprogle, *The Philadelphia Police*, pp. 75–76; *A Digest of Laws in Force Relating to the Police*, p. 9.

4. For example "a whole lot" in August 1838 and twenty-seven on one day in 1840. *PL*, 14 August 1838, 30 June 1840, 6 July 1854. See also *PL*, 13 March 1838, 15 June 1841, 15 November 1852.

5. See, for example, *PL*, 17 February 1842.

6. *PL*, 3 January 1837; 23 January 1838, 31 March 1838, 3 April 1839, 15 June 1841, 18 August 1854. Of course, sometimes liquor simply made people violent or reckless. Some people attacked companions or others against whom they felt a certain

enmity, such as whites attacking blacks. See *PL*, 23 March 1841. Others might simply wander into someone's home. See *PL*, 12 December 1853.

Drinking was more widespread and frequent during the first half of the nineteenth century than at any other time in American history, so much so that it has been estimated that the per capita annual consumption of pure alcohol at this time was as much as five gallons. See Rorabaugh, *The Alcoholic Republic*, pp. 5–11.

7. Laws of 21 February 1767, 5 April 1790, 22 April 1794.

8. See *PL*, 25–26 May 1836, 18 March 1838, 24 October 1838, 3 April 1839, 4 September 1839, 15 June 1841, 5 October 1841, 7 January 1842, 17 February 1842, 21 June 1842.

9. See among many others *PL*, 19 March 1836, 21 March 1836, 6–7 April 1836, 18 April 1836, 20 April 1836, 1 October 1836, 25 October 1836, 28 June 1837, 20 September 1837, 13 March 1838, 4 September 1839.

10. *PL*, 16 February 1847. See also *PL*, 11 October 1836, 20 June 1837, 13 March 1838, 24 October 1838, 3 April 1839, 5 June 1839.

11. Gregg Docket Book.

12. Philadelphia County Prison Daily Occurrence Docket.

13. *PL*, 11 January 1841. See also *PL*, 21 March 1836, 5 November 1838, 21 May 1839, 5 June 1839, 21 June 1842, 29 May 1854. Katz, Doucet, and Stern emphasized the especially harsh treatment drunks received from both the court and the press. See Katz, Doucet, and Stern, *The Social Organization of Early Industrial Capitalism*, ch. 6. Except for cases that involved additional charges or vagrancy commitments, this does not seem to have been the case in Philadelphia's mid-century aldermanic courts. However, court reporters did regularly criticize drinking and seek to make examples of drunks:

> The process by which a number of the human race satisfy their craven appetites for rum, may be compared to an iron foundry: they produce their dollars and half dollars, and melt them down to liquid . . . they gulp down the heated draught of intoxication with avidity, which, when all their means are spent, leaves them beggars and outcasts. . . . The devil himself is not a greater enemy to mankind, than is the cup of intoxication. (*PL*, 5 June 1839)

Sometimes the reporter spiced his moral tales with a measure of irony and cynicism about the entire process of punishing drunkenness:

> George Mintsinger was brought up by watchman Butcher. "You do swear," etc., repeated the clerk, rising and qualifying the watchman.
> "What's his offence?" said the Mayor. "Your honor, I caught him in the street, with this demijohn," replied the watchman, giving the vessel a shake and making its contents rattle against the sides. Another demijohn! The Mayor was petrified with astonishment. The clerk, with a convulsive shudder, dropped his pen and sank back powerless in his chair.
> The officers who were sitting cross-legged on the settee, reading the newspapers, sprang up and thrust their horrified faces over the top of the railing.
> Some of the audience laughed—not at the officers' faces.
> The only man who retained his self possession was little Gibbs, who stood, calm as a philosopher, with no other evidence of emotion than a slight twinkle which was perceptible in the left corner of his right eye, that said, as plainly as

twinkles can speak, that Mr. Gibbs was uttering the following mental apostrophe to the demijohn: "Ah! you long-necked sinner, I see you, in fancy's eye, labelled *Cogniac*, and standing in the halls below, by the side of that reprobate round-bellied bottle which was taken up, a month or two since, for disorderly conduct in the street. O! the wickedness of demijohns is awful to think of."

The same awful sense of their depravity probably by this time struck the Mayor; for so soon as he had recovered from his state of petrification, traces of perplexing thought were visible upon his countenance, occasioned, it is supposed, by doubt as to the kind of punishment that should be measured out to the culprit. He first directed that Mintsinger should pay a fine for having been intoxicated—then slowly, deliberately and impressively, in a manner befitting the solemn sentence he was about to utter, decreed that the demijohn should be sent to solitary confinement, never to be visited by anybody but its keeper, or to have any communication with any other during the whole term of its weary incarceration. The cogniac gave three distinct sobs of anguish at the sentence, and was hurried off from the face of man forever. (*PL*, 26 March 1839)

See also *PL* 13 March 1838, 12 November 1838, 2 March 1841, 25 November 1850.

14. *PL*, 25 January 1842, 20 December 1847.

15. *PL*, 23 March 1841, 15 June 1841, 28 October 1841, 7 January 1842.

16. *Annual Report of the Philadelphia County Prison* (1850), p. 4; ibid. (1851), pp. 5–7. As the century progressed, the treatment of this ever larger segment of Philadelphia's population fell into two categories, both more or less decriminalized. One was the large number of people who spent nights as lodgers in police station houses; the other, a smaller group of the most dissolute, targeted for rehabilitation in the house of correction. The prison inspectors wondered, "Why put a man in a cell because he has no home?" when they made their first proposal for a house of correction in 1851.

17. *PL*, 19 December 1837. See also *PL*, 25 March 1836, 4 October 1836.

18. Philadelphia County Prison Daily Occurrence Docket.

19. PSAMPP Minute Book, 13 June 1823. See also the minutes for 17 March 1824, 11 November 1829, 8 June 1830, 13 July 1831.

20. *Report of Bartholomew Wistar*; PSAMPP Minute Book, 13 June 1823.

As early as 1809 the Prison Society worried about magistrates who, more concerned "to enrich themselves than to serve the purposes of publick justice," were in the habit of committing people to prison and, for an "emolument," releasing them within several hours. See Vaux, *Visiting Committee Reports*.

21. *Report of the Committee on Cholera*, pp. 13–14.

22. PSAMPP Minute Book, 10 January 1820. See also *PL*, 21 August 1839.

23. See Acts of 22 March 1836 and 13 June 1836. The latter specifies five categories of vagrants, which include persons found begging, refusing to work, and persons from outside Pennsylvania found loitering or living with no visible means of subsistence within Pennsylvania. In an 1846 decision, quarter sessions judge Anson V. Parsons affirmed the powers of magistrates to commit disorderly persons as vagrants, but he also emphasized that the quarter sessions judges could at any time take jurisdiction over persons committed for, or accused of, vagrancy, disorderly conduct, or breach of the peace. The court did just this in July 1846. See *Aldermen and Justices of the Peace Cases*, 2 Parsons Equity Cases 458 (1847).

24. Hoffner and McGarry together made 31.7 percent of all the breach of the peace commitments sampled, while the remainder were widely distributed among all of the other aldermen. By contrast the mayor was responsible for just over one quarter of the disorderly conduct commitments, Alderman Hoffner 12 percent, with the others also widely distributed. See the Philadelphia County Prison Daily Occurrence Docket.

25. *PL*, 30 June 1836, 14 May 1838, 4 August 1838, 3 April 1839, 7 February 1842, 6 July 1854. See also *PL*, 26 August 1836, 21 March 1839, 2 March 1841, 28 May 1841, 31 May 1841, 15 June 1841, 5 October 1841, 30 January 1849.

26. *PL*, 4 December 1838, 15 January 1839.

27. *PL*, 22 October 1836, 3 January 1837, 27 June 1839.

28. *PL*, 21 March 1836, 7 September 1837, 14 August 1838, 31 July 1849, 23 November 1849, 25 February 1852, 21 February 1854. See also 16 January 1849.

Katz, Doucet, and Stern similarly found that most larcenies in Hamilton police court were petty and did not involve "professional" thieves. See their *The Social Organization of Early Industrial Capitalism*, ch. 6. This fact does not necessarily conflict with David Johnson's claim that property crime in Philadelphia was clustered in the downtown area and followed the expansion of commercial and wealthier residential neighborhoods to other parts of the city as the century progressed. Though most thefts were of personal property coveted for its usefulness as well as its exchange value, even this kind of property was most accessible in the more well-to-do and commercial areas. Johnson's notion that most larcenies depended on "opportunity and inclination" is consistent with the findings here, both of which emphasize the relatively small values involved in most cases. See Johnson, *Policing the Urban Underworld*, ch. 2.

29. *PL*, 21 February 1854. See also 25 February 1852, 3 January 1853, 18 August 1854.

30. *PL*, 17 June 1840, 17 January 1849, 2 September 1851, 25 February 1852, 16 August 1852, 15 November 1852, 9 February 1853, 4 April 1853, 23 August 1853, 12 December 1853.

31. *PL*, 11 April 1836, 23 November 1836, 19 May 1838. Recent immigrants might also be subject to arrest for suspicion of larceny when seen with unusual parcels by a watchman. See *PL*, 14 November 1839.

There were, of course, instances of serious and substantial larcenies. Sometimes they were as random and seemingly unplanned as lesser crimes, such as when Jane Nicholas took $200 in gold and bank notes from the home of a man in Camden. Most were more complex, however. William Crissy was arrested at his home in possession of clothing and dry goods he had collected in a series of crimes. John Williams stole clothing and jewelry from residents of three different boarding houses within a two-week period in 1852. *PL*, 30 January 1849, 2 September 1851, 16 August 1852.

Other serious property crimes were variations on larceny. Robbery and burglary charges resulted from actions not very different from larceny. These crimes usually had a more specific character, such as taking money directly from a person or entering a store or residence surreptitiously in order to commit a theft. Frequently these were the cases that involved groups, sometimes even formal gangs, who together planned and executed their crimes. Jane Mullin and Elizabeth Teal, each fourteen years old, regularly represented themselves to dry goods dealers as agents of well-known persons in order to be entrusted with some valuable item that they then kept for themselves. *PL*,

18 October 1852, 12 December 1853. See also 16 October 1839, 13 December 1852, 4 April 1853, 23 August 1853. Pickpockets were not yet very common during this period. See *PL*, 17 June 1840, 15 November 1852.

32. *PL*, 25 May 1837.

33. *PL*, 20 September 1837, 3 April 1839, 21 April 1851, 17 August 1853, 7 December 1853, 18 August 1854. In 1839 the mayor severely reprimanded the father of a black boy arrested for larceny because he gathered together a mob of neighbors to prevent the arrest. The officer complained that whenever anyone attempted to make an arrest in the black areas of Moyamensing they were similarly mobbed. *PL*, 21 March 1839.

34. *PL*, 4 May 1836, 25 January 1837, 15 March 1837, 24 October 1837; *Impositions and Frauds in Philadelphia*, pp. 4–5. The anonymous author of this pamphlet specifically commended the *Ledger* as the only paper not tied to party interest and therefore the only one dedicated to exposing "vice, dishonest and illegal proceedings." See also Johnson, *Policing the Urban Underworld*, on the vast popularity of gambling in the nineteenth century and the consequent impossibility of enforcing antigambling laws.

35. *PL*, 22 December 1837, 29 April 1837.

36. Such was the case, for example, in the January term of 1848, the December term of 1850, and the December term of 1852.

37. *PL*, 23 March 1841, 15 June 1841. The court of criminal sessions, created in 1838, won considerable praise during its first year. See, for example, *PL*, 22 March 1839. But by early 1840, the problem of pretrial delays began to recur. Governor David R. Porter blamed the still somewhat divided jurisdiction of the county's criminal courts. More serious felonies could still be tried in the court of oyer and terminer, but because this court met only twice a year, defendants could be forced to wait up to six months for a trial. Thus, most serious felony trials were actually conducted in the criminal sessions, and although a defendant could object to this, none ever did. *Message of Governor David R. Porter to Both Houses of the Legislature*, p. 39; *PL*, 6 May 1840. In response to the governor's recommendation that a court with complete criminal jurisdiction be established, the legislature abolished the criminal sessions and created a new court of general sessions in March 1840, which was given all the powers of the criminal sessions plus concurrent jurisdiction with that of the court of oyer and terminer. In addition, two of the three criminal sessions judges were replaced. The new jurists were appointed by Governor Porter, a privilege he would not have enjoyed had his recommendation for a new court not been approved.

38. The abolition of the court of general sessions was provoked by resistance to the appointment of the non-Philadelphian conservative Anson V. Parsons to its bench. Ironically, Parsons was soon appointed as a new fourth judge of the quarter sessions and became the leading force behind the court's activism and the dominant figure on the bench during the 1840s. *PL*, 4 August 1842, 28 December 1842, 4 January 1843, 30 January 1843, 1 February 1843, 16 February 1843; Steinberg, "The Criminal Courts and the Transformation of Criminal Justice in Philadelphia," pp. 280–81; Surrency, "The Evolution of an Urban Judicial System," p. 104.

39. *PL*, 14 March 1843, 26 June 1843, 4 July 1843, 16 November 1843, 21–22 November 1843. The judges listened to excuses presented by constables for their laxity.

One constable complained that he was once almost made subject to the costs by a jury when he was sure he had enough evidence to convict. Parsons assured him that in the future he would refuse to allow any constables to be saddled with costs unless he was convinced that the prosecution was malicious.

40. *PL*, 4 December 1837, 27 November 1844, 3 January 1853, 19 January 1853. According to the dockets, 1844 had the highest percentage of ignored tippling-house cases and costs placed on prosecutors of any year through 1880.

41. *PL*, 4 July 1843, 8 June 1847.

42. See Neilly, "The Violent Volunteers," p. 61; *Full and Accurate Report of the Trial for Riot*; Warner, *The Private City*, pp. 126–29. *PL*, 10 May 1836, 3 December 1836, 15 February 1837, 17 April 1837, 5 June 1837.

43. *PL*, 20 May 1838. See also *PL*, 20 October 1838, 17 May 1852.

44. *PL*, 16 March 1837, 18 June 1842, 16 September 1852, 9 February 1853. When an alderman held a defendant in a knife attack only to bail to keep the peace, he was specifically referred to in the press as a "merciful magistrate." *PL*, 7 July 1853. The use of handguns in violent encounters was infrequent until the mid-1850s if Roger Lane's conclusions about homicide can be extended to include assault. See his *Violent Death in the City*, pp. 61–63.

45. *PL*, 15 June 1841. See also 12 December 1853, 6 July 1854, 10 August 1854.

46. *PL*, 11 August 1836, 23 March 1841, 5 October 1841, 12 January 1854.

47. Laurie, *Working People of Philadelphia*, pp. 154–60. See also his "Fire Companies and Gangs in Southwark." Laurie examined the membership of several Southwark companies during the early 1840s and found that 78 percent were journeymen and laborers and that only three nonofficers among the 71 members owned property.

48. Fire companies, gangs, and Philadelphia's violent decades have been the subject of considerable scholarly inquiry. General discussions can be found in Barker, "Philadelphia in the Late Forties"; Geffen, "Violence in Philadelphia in the 1840s and 1850s"; and Feldberg, "The Crowd in Philadelphia History," and "Urbanization as a Cause of Violence." The 1844 riots were the subject of a dissertation by Feldberg, later published as *The Philadelphia Riots of 1844*. The first important riot study was by Montgomery, "The Shuttle and the Cross," an analysis of the Kensington weaver riots precipitated by a Protestant attack on Catholics in May 1844. The first specific study of fire companies was Neilly's "The Violent Volunteers." Since then, Laurie has been most responsible for establishing the central role of fire companies and gangs in working-class community life and culture, first in two articles, "Nothing on Impulse" and "Fire Companies and Gangs in Southwark," and then in *Working People of Philadelphia*. The activities of youth gangs have not been so extensively studied. The closest look appears in parts of Johnson, "The Search for an Urban Discipline," which agrees with Laurie's assessment that members of those organizations were "admired" in their communities and which also establishes the important ties gangs had to machine politicians—and, most importantly for our purposes, to some aldermen. A recent assessment of this link with regard to one alderman, William McMullin, can be found in Silcox, "William McMullen." This kind of political tie is elaborated on in great detail for New York in the classic by Asbury, *The Gangs of New York*.

49. Laurie, *Working People of Philadelphia*, pp. 161–63. See also Johnson, "The Search for an Urban Discipline," pp. 93–98.

50. *PL*, 18 June 1839, 9 October 1853, 6 July 1854. See also 21 April 1851, 17 May 1852, 22 July 1852, 15 November 1852, 23 May 1853. Members of fire companies did try to defend themselves from legal action. One method they used was cross-prosecution. Another was to use their influence with aldermen, some of whom were closely connected to, or even members of, fire companies, to get cases brought by the police dropped. Though no evidence of this was found in the published reports of preliminary hearings, the marshal of police complained in 1852 that his officers' ability to preserve the peace was impaired by aldermen who settled fire riot cases without returning them to court.

51. *PL*, 8 October 1838, 9 December 1839.

52. *Report of the Committee on Police*, pp. 18, 23.

53. The continuing depression hit Pennsylvania particularly hard after the collapse of the Philadelphia-based Bank of the United States in 1842. By the summer of that year, the *Ledger* called the state of every trade and branch of commerce in the city "completely desolate." "The majority of skilled and unskilled workers . . . probably saw their incomes decline" during the decade following 1837. A good discussion of the sources of the depression and Philadelphia's particular vulnerability to it is in Wainwright, "The Age of Nicholas Biddle," pp. 301–6. See also Laurie, *Working People of Philadelphia*, pp. 12–13, 108.

54. Warner, *The Private City*, p. 138.

55. *PL*, 26 February 1840, 3 August 1840. When apprehended, these rowdies were still generally bound over by the mayor to keep the peace. See *PL*, 27 December 1841.

56. See Laurie, *Working People of Philadelphia*, p. 165, and "Nothing on Impulse," p. 349. Quotation by Charles Leland is cited in Neilly, "The Violent Volunteers, p. 73.

57. *PL*, 22 September 1843, 25 November 1843.

58. See Laurie, "Nothing on Impulse," pp. 345–48; McLeod, "The Philadelphia Artisans," p. 56; and Johnson, "Search for Urban Discipline," pp. 101–4. Philadelphia's workers even had their own temperance organizations, formed along craft and ethnic lines, during the moral revivals following the panic of 1837. Many involved leaders of trade unions that found labor organizing difficult in the wake of the panic. See Laurie, *Working People of Philadelphia*, pp. 105–8. At least half of the male population drank regularly; the drinking cult among men included adolescents, and this was widely approved of by adults. See especially Rorabaugh, *The Alcoholic Republic*, pp. 11–15. One saloon-keeper alderman was McMullin. See Silcox, "William McMullen," p. 394.

59. The *Ledger* called the policy a "source of gratification" and went to some length to disassociate itself from the opposition to outsider Judge Anson V. Parsons, which earlier that year had led to the abolition of the court of general sessions. Being the newcomer, Parsons reaped most of the credit for the changes. He was also a most assertive judge, given to lengthy opinions, elaborate charges to the grand jury, and lectures to constables, attorneys, and witnesses. When a group of women asked the judges to explain their efforts to wipe out tippling houses, for example, Parsons drafted the court's reply. He regularly lectured grand jurors on the law, upholding the legitimacy of private prosecution as he lashed out at those he believed abused it. However, once it became clear to Parsons that private use of the law was not sufficient to maintain public order, he became a leading advocate of the preventative police. *PL*, 14 March

1843, 4 July 1843, 10 July 1843, 5 September 1843, 21 November 1843, 6 February 1844.

60. *Proceedings of the Eastern Pennsylvania Temperance Convention of 26 December 1843*, p. 4; Taylor, " 'Philadelphia in Slices' by George G. Foster," p. 38; *PL*, 10 January 1844, 17 June 1844, 6 November 1844, 12 November 1844.

61. *PL*, 27 August 1841.

62. *PL*, 30 May 1839, 1 July 1843, 3 July 1844, 25 November 1843, 24 October 1844. See also 13 July 1838, 21 August 1838, 12 August 1840.

63. Laurie, *Working People of Philadelphia*, p. 164.

64. *PL*, 18 July 1843, 29 January 1844.

65. Feldberg, *The Philadelphia Riots of 1844*, p. 51; Laurie, *Working People of Philadelphia*, pp. 132–34, 146–48, and "Nothing on Impulse," pp. 356–63.

66. Bloomfield, *American Lawyers in a Changing Society*, pp. 199–200; Warner, *The Private City*, pp. 140–43; Clark, *The Irish in Philadelphia*, p. 20; Laurie, *Working People of Philadelphia*, pp. 116–17; *PL*, 10 November 1842, 14 December 1842.

67. Accounts of the riots are derived from Warner, *The Private City*, pp. 144–51; and Bloomfield, *American Lawyers in a Changing Society*, pp. 202–13, 217–26.

68. See *PL*, 9–10 May 1844. The "peace police" was organized on the suggestion of attorney Horace Binney. See Bloomfield, *American Lawyers in a Changing Society*, p. 212.

69. *PL*, 10 May 1844, 16 May 1844.

70. *PL*, 17 June 1844; Nolan, *The Most Reverend Francis Patrick Kenrick*, pp. 324–25; Bloomfield, *American Lawyers in a Changing Society*, p. 216.

71. Feldberg, *The Philadelphia Riots of 1844*, pp. 180–81; Bloomfield, *American Lawyers in a Changing Society*, pp. 227–28. Some of the names at the top of the petition were Binney (who was the author), Ingersol, Sergeant, Norris, Wharton, Biddle, and Tilghman.

72. *Street Talk About an Ordinance of Councils*.

73. *PL*, 5 August 1844.

74. Bloomfield, *American Lawyers in a Changing Society*, pp. 228–29; *PL*, 28 December 1844.

75. Bloomfield, *American Lawyers in a Changing Society*, p. 230; *Street Talk About an Ordinance of Councils*, p. 17.

76. *PL*, 25 July 1844; Feldberg, *The Philadelphia Riots of 1844*, p. 187–88; Warner, *The Private City*, p. 152; Bloomfield, *American Lawyers in a Changing Society*, pp. 230, 232; Act of 12 April 1845.

77. Act of 12 April 1845. The number of officers, according the plan, were 146 for the city, 50 for Northern Liberties, 54 for Spring Garden, 45 for Southwark, 40 for Kensington, and 23 for Moyamensing. The city already had 177. Bloomfield, *American Lawyers in a Changing Society*, p. 231.

78. *PL*, 12 January 1847; Lapsansky, "South Street Philadelphia," pp. 138–39, 209–11; Johnson, "The Search for Urban Discipline," pp. 96–97, 101–4; Geffen, "Violence in Philadelphia in the 1840s and 1850s," p. 407; Silcox, "William McMullen," pp. 391–94.

79. *PL*, 7 October 1847; Taylor, " 'Philadelphia in Slices' by George G. Foster," pp. 34–35. By gaining control of the politics of Moyamensing the Killers could, under

the banner of "LIBERTY, EQUALITY and WASHINGTON," usher in a "GOLDEN AGE . . . OF PEACE AND HAPPINESS." The anonymous author of *The Almighty Dollar* described the pitiful existence of a young unwed mother who was forced into poverty. She had earlier been employed, but the "miserable pittance" was inadequate, and the hard work nearly killed her. "Employers are cold extortionists; they seem to give employment as a gracious favor, while they suck drop by drop the blood and devour the vitals of their laborers!" *The Almighty Dollar*, pp. 7–8, 15–16.

80. *PL*, 13 June 1846, 4 May 1847, 8 July 1847, 7 October 1847, 27 January 1848, 2 February 1848. There were occasional successes for the courts. In December 1846 fourteen members of the Killers were arrested for an attack on the Moyamensing police which grew out of a police search for fugitive members of the gang. Henry Bartholomew, a leader of the Good Will Engine Company, received an eighteen-month term from Judge Kelley in 1847, despite his having an ill wife and two small children. Two boys convicted with Bartholomew for riot were sentenced to four months each. Nevertheless, through 1847, despite the courts' announced "determination to suppress all the disorderly gangs," their record was one of overwhelming failure. *PL*, 28 December 1846, 22 April 1847, 13 December 1847.

81. This change amounted to an increase of 19 day and 23 night officers. *PL*, 26 July 1847, 7 October 1847, 2 February 1848; *A Digest of Laws in Force Relating to the Police*, pp. 11–14. Other related complaints were made in grand jury presentments about masters who committed apprentices to prison for disobedience, and in judges' charges, which held the "relaxed discipline observed in the domestic environment" of apprentices and children to be the cause of the minor disturbances that plagued Philadelphia during the 1840s. In 1845 Judge Jones thought the practice of allowing apprentices to live with their parents enough of an evil to ask a grand jury to suggest remedies. *PL*, 7 January 1845, 7 October 1847. Companies found to be guilty of riot could be disbanded by the court for six months for the first offense, permanently for the second. No minors could be members, and malicious destruction of fire company apparatus was made a felony punishable by up to a year's imprisonment. Act of 7 March 1848. The law withstood a constitutional challenge in 1850, based on the fact that it required no trial by jury. See *In re The Northern Liberty Hose Company*, 1 Harris 193. See also Geffen, "Violence in Philadelphia in the 1840s and 1850s," p. 407.

82. *PL*, 11 December 1848, 6 February 1849, 5 March 1849; Johnson, *Policing the Urban Underworld*, p. 82; *Street Talk About an Ordinance of Councils*, p. 14. The managers of the house of refuge were especially articulate in contending that the replacement of apprenticeship with "the system of hiring children out to work for wages" was a leading cause of "immorality and crime," precisely because "the intellectual culture of the child . . . is entirely neglected." *Annual Report of the House of Refuge* (1848), p. 9. See also ibid. (1852), p. 9; (1855), p. 7.

83. *PL*, 19 June 1849, 6 July 1849, 18 July 1849.

84. *Paid Fire Departments*, p. 8; Wainwright, *A Philadelphia Perspective*, p. 226; *PL*, 19 June 1849, 23 June 1849, 28 August 1849, 1 October 1849, 2 October 1849; and Kelley, *Address Delivered at the Coloured Department of the House of Refuge*, pp. 13–14. See also Barker, "Philadelphia in the Late Forties," p. 263.

85. The author characterized the riot as a diversion that allowed gang members to foil the designs of some of its enemies. *The Life and Adventures of Charles A. Chester*,

pp. 29–33; Warner, *The Private City*, p. 155; Neilly, "The Violent Volunteers," pp. 82–83; Schell MSS, p. 7.

86. *PL*, 13 October 1849, 10 November 1849, 12 November 1849, 17 November 1849, 26 April 1850; Warner, *The Private City*, p. 155; Feldberg, *The Philadelphia Riots of 1844*, p. 188; Johnson, "The Search for an Urban Discipline," pp. 140–43; Leffman, *The Consolidation of Philadelphia*, p. 30.

87. *PL*, 13 October 1849, 10 November 1849, 1 May 1850; Act of 3 May 1850; Feldberg, *The Philadelphia Riots of 1844*, p. 188–89; *A Digest of Laws in Force Relating to the Police*, pp. 26–35; Smith, *Philadelphia As It Is in 1852*, pp. 369–73; *Act of the Legislature Establishing the Uniform System of Police*; Johnson "The Search for an Urban Discipline," pp. 140–45; Sprogle, *The Philadelphia Police*, pp. 93–95; and *Rules and Regulations of the Police Department*. The force was distributed in the following proportions: City 55, Spring Garden 26, Kensington 24, Northern Liberties 21, Southwark 18, Moyamensing 12, Penn Township 4, Richmond 4, and West Philadelphia 12. This was similar to the policies adopted at about the same time in New York City, where the power of officers to arrest on suspicion led to an arrest rate of 1 per 109 people in 1851. See Miller, "Police Authority in London and New York City," pp. 87–88.

Chapter 7

1. *PL*, 4 June 1850, 28 June 1850, 24 August 1850, 17 September 1850.

2. Laurie, *Working People of Philadelphia*, pp. 177–78; Johnson, "The Search for an Urban Discipline," p. 102; and *The Firemen's Songster*, pp. 55, 35.

3. *PL*, 2 July 1851, 8 November 1851.

4. *PL*, 4 September 1851, 11 May 1853; *Report of the Rosine Association* (October 1852), pp. 10–11.

5. Johnson, "The Search for an Urban Discipline," pp. 144–45; Feldberg, *The Philadelphia Riots of 1844*, p. 180. Fears of exactly this outcome were expressed in the *Ledger* when the new police law was passed. See *PL*, 1 May 1850.

6. *PL*, 27 April 1850.

7. *Act of the Legislature Establishing the Uniform System of Police*, pp. 34, 36; *JPD* 6 (1851) p. 103.

8. *PL*, 31 March 1851, 2 July 1851, 15 November 1851.

9. *PL*, 14 September 1852, 21 September 1852, 6 December 1852.

10. *PL*, 7–8 November 1853. To be sure, the familiar complaints about the informal relations of private prosecution also continued during these years. See for example *PL*, 3 January 1851, 3 February 1851, 4 February 1851, 3 July 1851, 15 November 1851, 11 November 1852, 22 January 1853, 9 February 1853, 27 September 1853, 24 October 1853, 26 October 1853, 13 January 1854. They are discussed in some detail in Steinberg, "The Criminal Courts and the Transformation of Criminal Justice in Philadelphia," pp. 344–47.

11. Quaker abolitionists also complained from time to time about discrimination against blacks in the courts, but they remained relatively marginal. See *Report of a Committee Appointed by the Pennsylvania Society for Discouraging the Use of Ardent*

Spirits, pp. 4–6, 11–12; *Report of the Committee on Vice and Immorality, Relative to Intemperance*, p. 2; *Proceedings of the Eastern Pennsylvania Temperance Convention*, p. 4; *Present State and Condition of the Free People of Color of Philadelphia*, p. 16; *Ten Years Progress*; Needles, *A Review of a Pamphlet Entitled "An Appeal to the Public,"* pp. 6–9.

12. *PL*, 9 February 1846, 10 December 1846, 8 July 1847, 8 November 1847. For other references to this subject, see, for example, *PL*, 26 July 1847, 7 September 1847, 7 October 1847, 26 November 1847, 2 February 1848, 27 September 1848, 10 January 1849, 6 February 1849, 5 June 1849. See also Hartz, *Economic Policy and Democratic Thought*, pp. 209–11.

13. Barker, "Philadelphia in the Late Forties," p. 259; *The Liquor Law of the State of Pennsylvania*, p. 12; *PL*, 17 April 1849; Law of 16 April 1849.

14. *PL*, 25 February 1849, 4 June 1850; *Proceedings of Pennsylvania State Temperance Convention*, pp. 18–19. See, for example, the presentment in *PL*, 15 March 1854. This inquest reported 2,125 licensed taverns, 1,241 beer houses, and estimated "one half this number" of unlicensed houses, bringing the total number of drinking houses in Philadelphia to 5,050.

15. *PL*, 4 June 1850, 4 February 1851, 27 September 1850, 7 May 1851, 2 July 1853, 13 January 1854; Mullen, *An Appeal to Taxpayers*, p. 21.

16. *PL*, 24–25 January 1851, 4 February 1851, 10 March 1851. See also 7 February 1854. Mullen, *An Appeal to Taxpayers*, p. 25.

17. See Art, V, Sec. 2 of the Amended Pennsylvania Constitution of 1838.

18. On Kelley, see Greco, "William Darrah Kelley," pp. 168–89. On the Boston radicals, see Schlesinger, *Orestes A. Brownson*, pp. 50–88; Schlesinger, *Age of Jackson*, pp. 144–76; Handlin, *George Bancroft*, pp. 154–73. Kelley's commitment to temperance, although not prohibition, is one example of how he fits Bruce Laurie's typology of the radical political workingmen who supported temperance, not on moral grounds, but as a way to heighten the political influence and dignity of workers. See Laurie, *Working People of Philadelphia*, ch. 4.

19. Laurie, *Working People of Philadelphia*, pp. 195–96; *PL*, 14 September 1851, 18 September 1851, 8 October 1851; Eastman, *Courts and Lawyers of Philadelphia*, p. 559; and Martin, *Martin's Bench and Bar of Philadelphia*, p. 87.

20. *PL*, 20 July 1852, 31 December 1852, 19 January 1853, 22 January 1853, 7 June 1853.

21. See *PL*, 9 February 1852, 11 March 1852, 14 March 1852, 10 May 1853.

22. *PL*, 15 March 1854; *Proceedings of the Pennsylvania State Temperance Convention and Report of the Central Committee*, pp. 18–23, 47–48.

23. An antisaloon law that prohibited the sale of liquor in quantities under one quart was passed by the legislature just after consolidation but was repealed less than a year later. Eli K. Price had prohibitionist support for consolidation, but he disappointed his supporters by opposing it in the legislature. See Act of 13 April 1855; Brown, *Pennsylvania Reformers*, p. 44; McCarthy, "The Philadelphia Consolidation of 1854," p. 538.

24. PSAMPP Minute Book, 2 November 1850, 8 July 1851.

25. Ibid., 7 October 1853, 4 November 1853.

26. Ibid., 6 January 1854, 4 August 1854; *PL*, 16 January 1854; Teeters, *They Were in Prison*, pp. 292–98.

27. *First Report of the Philadelphia Society for the Employment and Instruction of the Poor*, p. 6; Glassberg, "Philadelphians in Need," pp. 269–70.

28. Report of the Rosine Association (May 1848), p. 8; (May 1849), p. 3.

29. See Glassberg, "Philadelphians in Need," pp. 169–73; *The Parish Gleaner*; and *Annual Report of the American Emigrant's Friend Society* (1852), p. 4. Mullen's name appeared repeatedly in the *Ledger* in connection with his many activities. A few of these activities were mentioned on 2 April 1850, 5 December 1850, 2 January 1851, 12 April 1851, 19 April 1851, 6 May 1851, 4 June 1851, 20 June 1851, 2 August 1851, 4 August 1851, 23 August 1851, 16 September 1851, 20 December 1851, 14 February 1852, 1 May 1852, 9 April 1853, 6 July 1853, 25 July 1853, 13 October 1853.

30. In this Mullen differed from his fellow reformer and former radical, William Kelley. Kelley, remaining a partisan, took sides, identified less with even those reformers with whom he sympathized, and, as a result, remained more troubled by such new state institutions as the police. Mullen believed crime was caused by deprivation and objected to abusive policemen; Kelley believed that crime was caused by "the culture of the age" and worried that the majesty of the law could never rest on coercion. Kelley, *Characteristics of the Age*, pp. 8–9.

31. *PL*, 4 February 1851, 11 March 1852; *Evening Bulletin*, 2 February 1854, quoted in McCarthy, "The Philadelphia Consolidation of 1854," p. 535.

32. See for example, *PL*, 25 November 1850, 21 April 1851, 30 July 1851.

33. Geffen, "Violence in Philadelphia in the 1840s and 1850s," p. 407; *Paid Fire Departments*, pp. 8–9. *PL*, 20 July 1852, 28 September 1852, 5 October 1852.

34. *PL*, 22 March 1852, 11 September 1852, 2 August 1852, 25 August 1852, 20 September 1852, 6 December 1852, 13 December 1852.

35. *PL*, 28 June 1852, 11 September 1852, 14 September 1852, 5 October 1852, 6 December 1852, 13 December 1852.

36. *PL*, 5 April 1853, 2 August 1853, 7 August 1853, 12 September 1853, 27 September 1853, 12 November 1853, 21 November 1853, 6 December 1853, 13 January 1854.

37. *Paid Fire Departments*, p. 5. See also *Report of a Committee . . . To Consider the Propriety of Organizing a Paid Fire Department*.

38. For the argument that metropolitan modernization was the real impulse behind consolidation and not law and order, see McCarthy, "The Philadelphia Consolidation of 1854," pp. 540–41, and Gillette, "The Emergence of the Modern Metropolis," pp. 9–14. The quote from Price is on p. 10. A more balanced account is in Geffen, "Industrial Development and Social Crisis," pp. 359–60. At least one historian has suggested that consolidation made Philadelphia the fourth largest city in the Western world. See Weigley, "The Border City in Civil War," p. 363.

39. Gillette, "The Emergence of the Modern Metropolis," pp. 12–13; McCarthy, "The Philadelphia Consolidation of 1854," pp. 540–41; Warner, *The Private City*, pp. 153–54.

40. Leffman, *The Consolidation of Philadelphia*, p. 32; Feldberg, *The Philadelphia Riots of 1844*, p. 190; *PL*, 7 December 1853: Warner, *The Private City*, p. 155; McCarthy, "The Philadelphia Consolidation of 1854," pp. 542–45; *Sunday Dispatch*, 16 October 1853. See also Price, *The History of Consolidation in the City of Philadelphia*, esp. pp. 41–43.

41. Sprogle, *The Philadelphia Police*, pp. 98–99; Act of 2 February 1854, *PL*, 1 February 1854, 7 February 1854, 8 July 1854, 13 July 1854, 19 July 1854.

42. Leffman, *The Consolidation of Philadelphia*, p. 34; Johnson, *Policing the Urban Underworld*, pp. 129–30; "The Search for an Urban Discipline," pp. 186–89; Feldberg, *The Philadelphia Riots of 1844*, p. 189; Sprogle, *The Philadelphia Police*, p. 101.

The concept of this shift is Michael Frisch's. See *Town into City*, pp. 249–50. The quotation is a paraphrase by Howard Gillette. See "The Emergence of the Modern Metropolis," p. 11.

43. See Shefter, "The Emergence of the Political Machine," pp. 15–17, for the typology of political machine development in New York to which the development of the consolidated city in Philadelphia (which took place much earlier than in New York) roughly corresponds.

The conflict between machine politics and the supporters of the police was also present in New York. The lower classes were the "constituency" of elected police justices in New York, while the propertied were the supporters of the police. The justices' ties to the poor and machine politics undermined many of the aims of the supporters of the police. State control of the New York Metropolitan Police made the conflict especially stark in the Empire City. See Miller, "Police Authority in London and New York City," pp. 90–93, and Richardson, The New York Police, pp. 74–80.

Chapter 8

1. Many scholarly efforts have been, and are being, made to describe and characterize the process of the reform of urban government, politics, and law during the nineteenth century. Especially relevant to the concerns raised here is the work of Skowronek, *Building the New American State*. Although concerned with national and not local government, the notion of "the state of courts and parties" that Skowronek employs is at least as applicable to Philadelphia as it was to the United States. Martin Shefter's typology of political change in nineteenth century New York is also helpful in understanding the movement from local to city-wide machine politics, which was the most prominent consequence of consolidation in Philadelphia. See Shefter, "The Emergence of the Political Machine." He emphasizes the "rapacious individualism" of ward politicians and the extreme decentralization of city politics in New York, which also was clearly characteristic of Philadelphia before 1854. Also helpful in this regard is Bridges, *A City in the Republic*, and Hammack, "Problems in the Historical Study of Power," pp. 335–38, 342–43.

Very useful for conceptualizing the emergence of reformers and metropolitanists is Frisch, *Town into City*, esp. pp. 173–75. Frisch's emphasis in these pages on the new way city government "conceived of and conducted" its affairs applies to Springfield after the Civil War, but it appears that, among leading consolidationists, this new consciousness was already present in Philadelphia during the previous decade.

2. *Manual of the Consolidated Police*, pp. 21, 25, 32–33, 34–36.

3. Through June 1858 the recorder of the city sat as committing magistrate at the central police station adjacent to the mayor's office. That month the mayor suspended this practice, but it was resumed in March 1860 when the mayor was empowered either

to sit as a committing magistrate or to appoint an alderman to do so at his pleasure. *PL*, 23 June 1858, 26 January 1859; Ordinance of 20 October 1859; Act of 28 March 1860, Public Law 318; Act of 9 April 1873, Public Law 575. Allinson and Penrose, *Philadelphia, 1681–1887*, p. 157. In 1873 the reform-spirited legislature required that the magistrate be learned in the law, eliminating most aldermen from consideration.

4. Ordinance of March 1867, Public Law 102; Ordinance of 15 June 1866, Public Law 207; Ordinance of 12 November 1860. Allison and Penrose, *Philadelphia, 1681–1887*, pp. 209–10.

5. Sprogle, *The Philadelphia Police*, pp. 144–46. An effort to create a state-controlled police board, like New York's metropolitan police, was defeated by gubernatorial veto. See *PL*, 19 January 1860, 12 March 1860, 28 March 1860. The mayor's power to appoint all police officers led to the regular scene of hundreds of Philadelphians besieging each new mayor with applications for appointments. A semblance of stability was reached only during the administration of Mayor Alexander Henry (1858–65), who engineered a law giving policemen tenure dependent on good behavior. Johnson, "The Search for an Urban Discipline," pp. 152–53, 168; *Second Annual Message of Alexander Henry*, pp. 187–96; *First Annual Message of Alexander Henry*, p. 13.

6. *PL*, 23 October 1854, 11 November 1854, 9 February 1855, 18 May 1855; Sprogle, *The Philadelphia Police*, pp. 99–101.

7. On 31 October 1854, the police made 108 arrests, 85 for a new (but traditionally nonstatutory) charge of drunk and disorderly. A "quiet day," 8 December, listed only 65 arrests, mostly for drunkenness and vagrancy. A reporter, who spent a day in July 1855 touring the police stations, found 234 arrestees, most of them victims of "King Alcohol." *PL*, 19 July 1855, 1 November 1854, 9 December 1854.

8. *PL*, 7 September 1854, 23 October 1854, 30 July 1855, 2 August 1855.

9. Minutes of the Acting Committee on the County Prison for the PSAMPP, 23 February 1858; *Annual Report of William J. Mullen* (1870), p. 8; (1857), p. 7; (1871), p. 80; PSAMPP Minute Book, 2 April 1858, 7 October 1859; *JPD* [n.s.] 16 (1861): 153; *PL*, 11 January 1862, 14 January 1862.

10. *PL*, 28 June 1855, 28 November 1855. See also *Reports and Realities from the Sketch-Book*, pp. 196–98; *The Homeless Heir*, pp. 19–20; Sewell, *Sorrow's Circuit*, pp. 332–35; *Annual Report of William J. Mullen* (1856), p. 5; (1857), pp. 6–7.

11. *PL*, 3 August 1858; *Reports and Realities from the Sketch-Book*, pp. 197–98.

12. *PL*, 10 August 1855.

13. PSAMPP Minute Book, 5 October 1855; *PL*, 17 February 1858, 10 April 1858, 6 January 1859, 11 January 1862, 22 July 1862, 5 February 1863, 23 June 1863, 16 July 1864, 12 August 1864. For other comments on this matter, see *PL*, 8 January 1862, 19 February 1862, 12 August 1862, 11 November 1862, 9 December 1862, 7 January 1863, 12 May 1863, 13 August 1863, 18 January 1864, 4 March 1864, 11 May 1865.

14. *PL*, 15–16 December 1854; 28 June 1855, 16 December 1855.

15. *Annual Report of William J. Mullen* (1870), p. 45.

16. See *Annual Report of the Philadelphia County Prison* (1870), pp. 6–7; *JPD* [n.s.] 3 (1864): 68–71; 16 (1861): 31–32.

17. *Annual Report of the Philadelphia County Prison* (1870), pp. 6, 13–14; *Annual Report of William J. Mullen* (1870), pp. 56–57.

18. *Annual Report of the Philadelphia County Prison* (1871), p. 12.

19. Ibid., pp. 12–14; *Annual Report of William .J. Mullen* (1870), pp. 74–75.

20. *PL*, 27 September 1854, 9 November 1869.

21. *PL*, 15 February 1859, 5 September 1872, 14 October 1873. See also 23 July 1856, 20 August 1856, 20 July 1859. Excessive violence was often used in making arrests by policemen in other American cities. See Miller, "Police Authority in London and New York City," p. 86.

22. *PL*, 25–26 February 1855, 27 April 1857, 5 February 1862, 6 March 1862, 22 March 1862, 31 July 1862, 24 February 1863, 15 January 1868, 25 May 1869, 16 April 1873.

23. *PL*, 19 December 1871, 27 December 1862; *Reports and Realities from the Sketch-Book*, p. 197; *JPD* [n.s.] 3 (1864): 37. Returns to court for more serious charges sometimes resulted from arrest for drunkenness. See, for example, *PL*, 3 July 1857, for a disorderly arrest that led to a commitment for passing counterfeit notes. Sometimes, though, it was a result of the disorderly act itself, but the specific charge was not given by the police reporter. See, for example, *PL*, 11 November 1873.
Akin to disorderly conduct arrests were those for breach of the peace. PSAMPP Minute Book, 16 April 1860. As with some disorderly arrests, breach of the peace arrests might involve the commitment of a robbery or assault victim whose assailant had escaped, leaving the officers with no one but the victim to hold responsible for the resulting minor tumult. See, for example, *JPD* [n.s.] 12 (1873): 31, 3 (1864): 37.

24. *First Annual Message of Morton McMichael*, p. 13; Sprogle, *The Philadelphia Police*, p. 128; *PL*, 23 June 1856, 25 July 1856, 8 October 1872.

25. See, for example, *PL*, 23 June 1856, 10 July 1856, 2 July 1861, 26 July 1861, 25 May 1869, 17 January 1872.

26. See *PL*, 4 September 1854, 18 September 1854, 6 June 1855. Raids continued to occur, but infrequently. See *PL*, 14 September 1865.

27. See *PL*, 21 January 1862, 28 January 1862, 25 February 1862; Act of 11 March 1862.

28. *PL*, 8 August 1862, 29 March 1863, 13 October 1863; *Fifth Annual Message of Alexander Henry*, p. 231. Arrests are reported, for example, in *PL*, 27 March 1862, 3 April 1862, 10 June 1862. The judges did require that the magistrate return the case to court if the prisoner was actually observed committing a crime and that a ninety-day commitment could not be made at the same time.

29. *First Annual Message of Alexander Henry*, p. 18; *Second Annual Message of Alexander Henry*, p. 26; *PL*, 21 February 1859, 28 February 1859.

30. *PL*, 30 March 1863; *Annual Report of the House of Refuge* (1861), p. 8. See also ibid. (1862), p. 4.

31. *Annual Report of William J. Mullen* (1870), p. 45; *JPD* [n.s.] 3 (1871): 69.

32. *Annual Report of William J. Mullen* (1864), p. 8; *JPD* [n.s.] 10 (1871): 83–84. Examples of such arrests can be found in *PL*, 11 July 1856, 22 October 1857, 11 August 1858, 9 November 1869, 9 August 1870, 17–18 January 1872, 11 March 1873, 8 December 1873; PSAMPP Minute Book, 19 April 1866, 21 June 1866.

33. Examples of petty larceny cases can be found in the court and police reports virtually every day. Some examples are in *PL*, 9 June 1857, 8 August 1857, 15 February 1859, 3 August 1869, 7 June 1870, 11 February 1871, 20 January 1872, 20 August 1872, 6 January 1873, 8 January 1873, 14 February 1873, 21 August 1873, 8 September 1873, 30 December 1873.

34. Examples of the former can be found in *PL*, 11 July 1856, 21 January 1861, 7 January 1870, 29 March 1872, 21 August 1873; of the latter, in *PL*, 14 June 1848, 18 October 1860; PSAMPP Minute Book, 21 June 1866.

35. PSAMPP Minute Book, 17 September 1863; *JPD* [n.s.] 11 (1872): 43.

36. PSAMPP Minute Book, 20 February 1862; *PL*, 16 November 1858, 9 August 1870, 11 April 1871, 18 June 1872.

37. *PL*, 6 January 1859, 11 January 1861, 14 January 1862, 19 January 1863. Miller found the same activity among the New York police. See his "Police Authority in London and New York," p. 87. There were other instances in which officers made arrests for what they considered disrespect of their authority, usually when officers encountered resistance to their attempts to enforce city ordinances. See *PL*, 18 February 1868, 17 June 1873.

38. *PL*, 14 September 1857, 6 April 1863, 26 January 1869, 2 August 1870, 19 January 1872.

39. See *PL*, 28 November 1855, 15 February 1858, 8 September 1858, 16 December 1858, 9 January 1859, 13 July 1860, 13 January 1871, 12 October 1872, 19 September 1873. See also 4 May 1858.

40. See, for example, *PL*, 27 August 1856, 27 April 1857, 11 August 1858, 11 June 1859, 7 August 1860, 25 August 1863, 21 June 1869, 17 August 1869, 25 March 1870, 8 September 1870, 11 April 1871, 20 June 1871, 19 January 1872, 18 June 1872, 8 October 1872, 21 August 1873.

41. *PL*, 5 October 1857, 24 September 1863, 30 September 1863, 9 January 1866, 31 January 1866. See also 22 December 1857, 30 January 1858, 8 December 1858. *Annual Report of William J. Mullen* (1867), p. 8; (1868), p. 8; (1870), p. 7; (1871), p. 7; Surrency, "The Evolution of an Urban Judicial System," pp. 110–12.

42. *PL*, 24 November 1858, 3 August 1860, 8 June 1869. See also 11 July 1856, 4 August 1868, 7 April 1869.

43. No cases in which this was done appeared among the 161 ignored larceny bills in the sample.

44. *PL*, 6 December 1860. Another possible factor for the reluctance of grand jurors to place costs on prosecutors was the lingering ambivalence of the law, reflected in the insistence of judges that there be "good and sufficient" reasons to do so. If the judge thought the reasons insufficient, he could reverse the ruling. See *PL*, 13 February 1863.

45. *PL*, 21 June 1850, 7 October 1858, 26 July 1859, 25 October 1860, 24 August 1867.

46. Costs usually amounted to something in excess of $10, a substantial amount for most people. Judges sometimes released people who could not pay with a warning not to return to court. See *PL*, 29 June 1863.

47. *PL*, 12 March 1859, 27 September 1859, 20 March 1862. This recommendation was made again by a grand jury in March 1862.

48. Other examples included a rule prohibiting police officers from discharging persons arrested on the complaint of a citizen. Note Francis Wharton's 1857 statement that grand juries were still important as "restraints upon the violence of popular excitement and the malice of private prosecutors," and Judge Edward Paxson's 1870 remark, "It is a [citizen's] duty when they know of the commission of an offense to make complaint before a magistrate in the usual and proper way." *Police Manual of the Consolidated Police*, p. 20; Younger, *The People's Panel*, p. 64; *PL*, 8 December 1870, 10 November 1871, 5 January 1872. This last statement referred specifically to liquor prosecutions, which the state had great difficulty sustaining. See also 4 August 1868, for a judge's remark on the importance of grand juries.

49. *PL*, 31 June 1866, 12 July 1870, 5–6 January 1871, 3–4 February 1871, 28 March 1871, 17 October 1871, 22 November 1871, 17 September 1872, 19 September 1872.

50. *PL*, 27 September 1859, 4 August 1868, 6 April 1869, 7 April 1869. *JPD* 16 (1861): 31. *Annual Report of William J. Mullen* (1867), p. 7; (1868), p. 8; (1870), p. 7; (1871), p. 7. See also Surrency, "The Evolution of an Urban Judicial System," p. 112.

51. *PL*, 19 November 1855, 25 October 1857, 27 March 1858, 8 November 1862, 11 August 1869; *Annual Report of William J. Mullen* (1870), pp. 46–49.

52. *PL*, 28 November 1855, 30 January 1856, 11 July 1856, 27 November 1856, 22 December 1857, 30 January 1858, 18 May 1858, 24 November 1858, 8 December 1858, 27 September 1859.

53. *PL*, 27 September 1859. See also 11 July 1856, 22 December 1857, 30 January 1858, 18 May 1858, 8 December 1858. The inquest was supported in its request by the editors of the *Ledger*. A report of one case, noteworthy because of the refusal of the officer to settle, showed how cases got settled after a return. A man arrested for robbing his employer was released on bail and a return was sent to the district attorney. Soon afterward he approached the policeman who made the arrest and said, "I don't want that case of mine to go to Court." The officer said that the return was made and only the district attorney could now keep it out of court. The startled defendant replied, "I supposed that it might be settled as other cases are." Perhaps his misfortune was that he had gone through the police officer rather than the alderman or prosecutor. In any event, the court reporter regarded this case as evidence of "how universal the belief is in the efficacy of money" to prevent a criminal trial. *PL*, 6 August 1859.

54. *PL*, 6 April 1869. Similar comments can be found, for example, on 4 August 1868, 7 April 1869, 8 June 1869, 3 August 1869. Grand jurors' continuing complaints can be found, for example, on 4 October 1862, 22 September 1864, 4 April 1870, 7 August 1871, 10 November 1871, 1 September 1873. See also *Annual Report of the Philadelphia County Prison* (1872), p. 18; *PL*, 19 January 1866.

55. *PL*, 12 February 1858, 5 December 1866, 5 March 1867, 13 July 1870, 10 December 1870, 7 June 1874: Act of 13 March 1867, Public Law 420; Surrency, "The Evolution of an Urban Judicial System," p. 111.

56. *PL*, 26 October 1854, 3 November 1859, 9 November 1859, 5–6 September 1864, 5 December 1861, 25 June 1862.

57. The first several decades after consolidation were marked by a struggle between the informal and locally oriented Philadelphia of recent tradition and the emerging metropolitan and bureaucratic Philadelphia of the future. This is not to be confused

with the struggle between corruption and honest government although that language often shaped the debates. Both elements stood on each side of the divide, but they took different forms. Indeed, the consolidated city government of late nineteenth-century Philadelphia was renowned for its combination of corruption and elite satisfaction. See Price, *The History of Consolidation in the City of Philadelphia*, and Gillette, "Corrupt and Contented."

58. See Weigley, "The Border City in Civil War," p. 368, 372.

59. "If anything the disparate parts of the expanded metropolis became even further divided from one another than they had been before consolidation," says Gillette in "Emergence of the Modern Metropolis," p. 14. See also Weigley, "The Border City in Civil War," pp. 368, 372–75.

60. In general, on McMullin, see Silcox, "William McMullen," pp. 394–95. See also Weigley, "The Border City in the Civil War," p. 373.

61. The only significant group of criminal justice officials that remained ambivalent about a police-centered criminal justice process and the associated diminishing stature of the process of litigation was made up of a number of criminal court judges. This ambivalence endured into the 1870s. See below and Kelley, *Characteristics of the Age*, for example.

62. *Annual Report of the Philadelphia County Prison* (1854), p. 10.

63. *PL*, 23 August 1855; Law of 21 April 1855, Public Law 264; Law of 26 April 1855, Public Law 315. The statement was made a monthly requirement by the Law of 13 May 1856, Public Law 572.

64. *PL*, 16 September 1854, 23 October 1854, 17 April 1856, 18 April 1856; *Philanthropist*, pp. 1–2, 23; and PSAMPP Minute Book, 5 October 1855, 1 February 1856.

65. *PL*, 27 January 1857, 30 January 1857, 3 February 1857.

66. *PL*, 11 February 1857.

67. *PL*, 9 April 1857.

68. Aldermen McGarry and Haines were convicted of receiving illegal fees, Alderman Collins was charged with keeping a portion of some recovered stolen money, and Alderman Williams was convicted of committing a man to prison without holding a hearing. *PL*, 20 July 1857, 5 October 1857, 8 October 1857, 16–17 November 1857, 19 November 1857, 7 December 1857, 10 December 1857, 22 December 1857, 6 January 1858. One reporter commented, regarding costs payments, that "there is either a disregard of the law by some of the aldermen, or they are without business." See also *PL*, 3 February 1858, 25–26 March 1858.

69. *Annual Report of William J. Mullen* (1857), pp. 6–7.

70. PSAMPP Minute Book, 21 September 1858; *PL*, 12 August 1858, 14 August 1858, 23 August 1858.

71. *PL*, 12 April 1858, 8 December 1858.

72. Law of 1 March 1859, Pamphlet Laws 89.

73. *Annual Report of William J. Mullen* (1859), p. 5; PSAMPP Minute Book, 7 January 1859, 16 April 1860, 17 January 1861. Defenders of the aldermen tried to strike back at Mullen in 1859. Former Alderman Henry Manderfield submitted a motion to the city councils which would reduce the agent's modest salary from $200 to $150. Various members accused Mullen of receiving payoffs and of being a tool of

others and the author of mischief, but the motion was eventually withdrawn. See *PL*, 12 January 1859, 17 January 1859.

74. Alderman J. B. Freeman was twice charged with misconduct, once for attempting to settle a forgery case and once for issuing fraudulent tax receipts. Alderman Hellfricht was convicted of assault and battery and false imprisonment; Alderman Curry, of conspiracy. Alderman George Williams was again before the court, this time on a charge of being intoxicated and refusing to take legitimate bail in a breach of the peace case. See *PL*, 19 March 1859, 3 May 1859, 23 May 1859, 6 June 1859, 5 September 1859, 7 October 1859, 6 December 1859, 7 January 1860, 12 April 1860, 24 April 1860, 28 April 1860, 8 September 1860, 7 November 1860, 16 January 1861, 14 March 1861, 29 March 1861, 29 April 1861. The *Ledger*'s editors could conceive of "no greater tyranny" than the kind of abuse practiced by Alderman Allen. When Judge Thompson reluctantly sentenced the alderman to nine months imprisonment (and his coconspirator to one year), the newspaper complained that Allen should have been given the greater sentence because of his violation of a "public trust."

75. *PL*, 29 November 1859; *Annual Report of the Philadelphia County Prison* (1861), p. 7. The Philadelphia Prison Society revived its committee to persuade the legislature to change the aldermanic system. PSAMPP Minute Book, 10 January 1860. Though calling the magistracy "an engine of petty oppression and extortion," the prison inspectors claimed that this was only because of the fee system. *Annual Report of the Philadelphia County Prison* (1860), p. 7.

76. Weigley, "The Border City in Civil War," pp. 369–72.

77. *PL*, 21 April 1860, 25 April 1860; Silcox, "William McMullen," pp. 391, 394.

Similar disapproval was expressed about the influence of popular politics in the selection of policemen. A police board was established in 1860 to prevent the mayor from controlling all officer appointments, but the *Ledger* was dubious, asking how the board would be kept immune from control by one or another political party. See *PL*, 19 January 1860, 12 March 1860; *Second Annual Message of Alexander Henry*, pp. 187–89. See also Sewell, *Sorrow's Circuit*, for a discussion of the close ties in poor communities among aldermen, policemen, barkeepers, politicians, and landlords. Lane, *The Roots of Violence in Black Philadelphia*, pp. 56–59, makes this same point and also discusses how politics remained violent and raucous into the 1870s.

Chapter 9

1. See Weigley, " 'A Peaceful City,' " pp. 163–69; Gallman, "Disorder and the Pursuit of Order in Civil War Philadelphia."

2. Teeters, *They Were in Prison*, p. 316.

3. According to reformers, aldermen committed misdemeanors in office and other misdeeds, policemen made improper arrests and used excessive force, and ordinary citizens kept bringing their everyday disputes into court. Alderman McMullin was again accused of procuring criminals to vote illegally, Alderman Curry was charged with extortion, Alderman Mascher was convicted of taking illegal fees, Alderman Hagar was convicted of extortion from a girl he caught stealing, Alderman Riley was convicted of failing to return a case against a friend, and Alderman McPeak was tried for conspiracy to rob a man who had been arrested for assault and battery. See *PL*,

25 December 1861, 8 February 1862, 13 November 1862, 1 December 1862, 24 March 1863, 6 April 1863, 15 October 1863, 17 March 1864, 29 May 1865.

Policemen were called political hacks, incompetent, neglectful of their duties, excessively violent, and "no better than those who come out of the penitentiary." See *PL*, 14 January 1862, 4 December 1863, 22 December 1863.

4. These percentages are taken from the statistics included in the *Annual Report of the Philadelphia County Prison*. A somewhat less striking decline in the percentage of white men among persons arrested by the police also occurred during the Civil War.

5. *PL*, 24 September 1863.

6. Their time was being spent on such things as "the larceny of a hoe, valued at six and a quarter cents," or two sausages "valued at 4 cents"; the trial of a man for stealing his own goat; and assault and battery cases that "turn out to consist in pushing or throwing water and some such paltry annoyance." *PL*, 25 November 1854, 5 October 1857, 26 July 1859, 4 August 1868.

7. PSAMPP Minute Book, 15 January 1863; *JPD* [n.s.] 3 (1864): 59.

8. The prison agent interfered almost exclusively in cases of unjust imprisonment. His reports emphasized cases in which thieves levied charges of larceny at their victims; abusers prosecuted battered women; landlords prosecuted tenants; aldermen committed defendants and returned cases against the expressed wishes of the prosecutors; and the desperately poor stole to meet basic survival needs. By 1864 he asserted simply that "the Aldermanic system, with very few exceptions, is a failure, and should be changed." See PSAMPP Minute Book, 19 January 1862, 14 May 1862, 9 October 1862, 18 December 1862, 19 February 1863, 16 April 1863, 17 September 1863, 17 December 1863, 6 January 1864, 17 August 1864, 16 February 1865. See also the cases included in the *Annual Reports of William J. Mullen* during this period. *JPD* [n.s.] 3 (1864): 68–69, 71–72.

9. *JPD* 16 (1861): 150–55.

10. *JPD* [n.s.] 3 (1864): 68–69, 71–72.

11. Ibid., pp. 72–73, 77.

12. The six "typical" cases appended to the 1863 article on magistrates were a mistaken commitment of a soldier for homicide; a conspiracy among a sergeant and two others to have an innocent marine arrested as a deserter; a revenge-inspired charge of enticing soldiers to leave a regiment which was made against an Army captain by a former colleague; a kidnapping charge leveled at a woman for taking possession of her own child; an extreme example of extortion by an alderman and his constable upon a poor single mother of three; and a landlord's attempt to remove a tenant through a misdemeanor prosecution. *JPD* [n.s.] 2 (1863): 37–40; ibid., 3 (1864): 77.

13. *JPD* [n.s.] 3 (1864): 75–76, 78–81; 2 (1863): 35–37.

14. *JPD* [n.s.] 3 (1864): 79.

15. A similar issue arose in 1867 when the legislature increased the number of court terms from six to twelve. The original version of the bill would have required aldermen to return all cases within two days of a binding over instead of within ten days of the beginning of the court term. This would also have made the settling of cases and the agent's interference much more difficult. Mullen went to the judges and told them that the court calendar would increase, not decrease, if this law was passed. He went to the magistrates and asked them to lobby their friends in Harrisburg. He went to the *Ledger*

and got them to publicize his objections. The bill was changed to meet Mullen's requirements. *Annual Report of William J. Mullen* (1865), pp. 23–32; *JPD* [n.s.] 8 (1869): 79.

16. PSAMPP Minute Book, 18 April 1867; *Annual Report of William J. Mullen* (1868), pp. 11–12.

17. Mullen proudly asserted that aldermen "now fully understand that it is the Agent's influence which has been brought to bear against them through the Court who is determined to make them act in accordance with law." *Annual Report of William J. Mullen* (1870), pp. 44–64; *PL*, 22 April 1869, 11 August 1869.

18. Jurors accused prosecutors of malice, spite, extortion, irresponsibility, and being "equally, if not more, guilty" than those they accused. *PL*, 22 September 1864, 31 June 1866, 4 August 1868, 17 August 1868, 7 June 1869, 3 August 1869; *Annual Report of William J. Mullen* (1870), p. 64; (1867), p. 9; (1869), p. 13.

19. Ibid., (1870), p. 67.

20. See, for example, *PL*, 29 May 1865, 26 September 1865, 12 April 1866, 15 September 1866, 6 November 1866, 10 July 1867. Thanks to the increased pressure of the city councils, more magistrates began observing the costs payment law in 1867.

On McMullin see *PL*, 7 August 1867, 10 August 1867, 13 September 1867, and Silcox, "William McMullen," p. 396. Councilman William H. P. Barnes was accused along with McMullin of leadership of the riot.

21. PSAMPP Minute Book, 21 October 1869; *JPD* [n.s.] 8 (1869): 78–79; *PL*, 15 February 1865.

22. Whiteman, *Gentlemen in Crisis*, p. 1. Among the names mentioned in this celebratory account was William Rotch Wister, historian of the game of cricket.

23. Lane, *The Roots of Violence in Black Philadelphia*, pp. 58–59. Lane compares the city machine to a coalition of Italian condottieri or Chinese warlords.

24. Beers, "The Centennial City," pp. 438–39; Evans, *Pennsylvania Politics*, pp. 13–15. The Gas Trust built its power on the provision that prevented it from paying any profits to the city until all its loans were paid off but did not prevent the trust from accepting additional loans with the same provision. So the trustees continually negotiated loans in order to award favors and create the dependence of various local business interests, with no public oversight or accountability. The trustees were officially unpaid, but they were amply rewarded by these arrangements.

25. Evans, *Pennsylvania Politics*, p. 15.

26. *PL*, 16 June 1869; Beers, "The Centennial City," pp. 437–40; Evans, *Pennsylvania Politics*, pp. 15–16. Beers noted that the minority members of election boards were actually appointed by the majority, usually for "their stupidity or corruptibility."

27. Evans, *Pennsylvania Politics*, p. 16.

28. For more on the Registry Act in Philadelphia and the role of William B. Mann in engineering its enactment, see Gillette, "Corrupt and Contented," pp. 61–62, 93.

29. See Act of 17 April 1869, Pamphlet Laws 49; *PL*, 1 June 1868, 4–5 June 1868, 3 July 1868, 7 May 1869, 17 June 1869, 10 September 1869, 14 September 1869, 30 September 1869, 1 October 1869; Silcox, "William McMullen," p. 399. The first version of the law was invalidated by the state supreme court because of technical provisions covering the process by which the canvassers were to judge voters' qualifications. The political considerations in the selection of canvassers and the board of

aldermen were not susceptible to legal challenge. During the session following the law's invalidation, legislators passed a Registry Law that met the court's objections. The chief advocate for the opposition was prominent Republican municipal reformer George W. Biddle. William B. Mann argued in defense of the law's constitutionality.

30. Silcox, "William McMullen," p. 401; Beers, "The Centennial City," p. 438. McMullin was actually accused of rioting at a meeting of the return judges on the days following the 1870 election, but no charge against him could be sustained. See *PL*, 21 October 1870.

31. Silcox, "William McMullen," pp. 402–3; Lane, *The Roots of Violence in Black Philadelphia*, pp. 45–46; Beers, "The Centennial City," p. 438.

32. Beers, "Centennial City," p. 440; Silcox, "William McMullen," p. 404; Lane, *The Roots of Violence in Black Philadelphia*, p. 46.

33. Gillette, "Corrupt and Contented," pp. 46–48, 61. Gillette described the politicians about whom Union League members complained as "local jobbers and contractors." Their list of occupations—builder, cutter, salt merchant, plumber, gas fiter, coal dealer, carpenter, and lumber dealer—were not unlike those of the aldermen.

34. *PL*, 19 January 1870; Gillette, "Corrupt and Contented," pp. 50–51; Scott, "The Businessman," pp. 170–74.

35. Lists of members and their occupations can be found in Gillette, "Corrupt and Contented," pp. 52–54, and Scott, "The Businessman," pp. 174–75. Lea was descended from two great old Philadelphia families, one Quaker and one Catholic, and was very well connected to Philadelphia's upper-class Friends. One historian called him "the original mugwump." Benjamin, "Gentlemen Reformers in the Quaker City," p. 65.

Gillette argues that the members of the CMRA were mostly men who had formed businesses individually or in partnership rather than by incorporation. They were, therefore, part of a tradition of private enterprise and commerce receiving government support. Their life courses established during the antebellum period, these men believed in the tradition of public administration exemplified by men like John Sergeant. Roads, rivers, canals, and postal service, all should be maintained by the state as aids to business and commerce, not run on a strictly private profit-motivated basis. For essential services that should be the responsibility of the state, private profit did not necessarily conform to public good. The businessman's critique of city government was implicit in this ideology. See Gillette, "Corrupt and Contented," pp. 57–59. Lea's articulation of these ideals, as well as his sympathy to the benevolent reform ideals of a William J. Mullen, also demonstrated the enduring influence of his grandfather Matthew Carey. See Lea, *Address*.

36. *Annual Report of William J. Mullen* (1871), pp. 81–85, 95–96. Ridgway conducted a study of the fees collected by public officers and estimated that some of the amounts were outrageous, such as the $60,000 annually amassed by the sheriff. Gillette, "Corrupt and Contented," p. 61. In response to the law association's new campaign, William R. Dickerson revised his *Letters of Junius* and sent a copy to Mullen, with a letter that praised Mullen's commitment to the cause "heart and soul."

37. Scott, "The Businessman," pp. 176–83; *PL*, 23 October 1871; Gillette, "Corrupt and Contented," pp. 59–64; Beers, "The Centennial City," p. 442. Only reform

candidates who were also regular Republican nominees were elected in 1871. Independent reformers received "only a few thousand votes of the 90,000 cast." This was almost inevitable given the "slip ticket" method of voting that required independent candidates to furnish, at their own expense, printed ballots for each of the city's more than seven hundred election districts—twice that number if they wanted to garner votes from both parties.

38. *PL*, 8 February 1872, 12 February 1872; Scott, "The Businessman," pp. 185–86.

39. *PL*, 14 February 1872.

40. *PL*, 27 February 1872, 1 March 1872.

41. *PL*, 3 March 1872, 27 March 1872. See Scott, "The Businessman," pp. 187–88, for a discussion of some of the other reports on official abuses made by the CMRA's Committee on Abuses.

42. The CMRA moved even closer to direct confrontation with the political managers when the board of aldermen rejected their request that one of the canvassers for each district be chosen from a list drawn by the association. They appealed to the U.S. District Court to appoint election supervisors under the Federal Enforcement Acts, which gave the federal bench the authority to supervise congressional elections. However, their frustration was heightened when the court allowed supervisors to be appointed by the Republican and Democratic party organizations.

PL, 22 May 1872, 30 July 1872, 19 August 1872, 21 August 1872; Gillette, "Corrupt and Contented," p. 64: Scott, "The Businessman," p. 168; *Citizens, Be Vigilant*, p. 1.

43. *PL*, 18 September 1872; Gillette, "Corrupt and Contented," p. 65; Scott, "The Businessman," pp. 191–92; Evans, *Pennsylvania Politics*, p. 71.

44. Lea, *Report for 1872 Made to the Central Council of the CMRA*, p. 3. CMRA involvement in cases of aldermanic abuse continued well into the following year. See, for example, *PL*, 13 September 1873.

45. Hellerich, "Origin of Pennsylvania's Constitutional Convention," p. 159; Gillette, "Corrupt and Contented," p. 68–72. Gillette reports that only 9 of 1,113 acts passed by the legislature in 1872 "were of a general or public nature." The rest pertained to special or private interests. Specific complaints surrounded the state's role in the granting of street railway licenses, bridge and highway construction, real estate taxation, and the creation of needless public officers who abused the fee system. Scott, "The Businessman," pp. 111–12.

46. Hellerich, "Origin of Pennsylvania's Constitutional Convention," pp. 164–69, 175; Gillette, "Corrupt and Contented," pp. 69–71; Scott, "The Businessman," pp. 112–13; *PL*, 8 February 1872, 27 February 1872.

47. *PL*, 3 January 1873. See also 17 February 1872, 18 January 1873.

48. Among the misdemeanor in office cases were charges against Alderman Mc-Closkey for binding over a man who let the alderman's dog escape from the office; Alderman Charles Burns for refusing to issue a transcript of a case so that he could demand illegal payments; Alderman Devitt for taking bail without recording it in his records and for keeping the money won by a plaintiff in a suit before him; Alderman Mackin for improperly deputizing a citizen to act as his constable; Alderman Gallagher

for conspiring with a landlord to dispossess a tenant; and Alderman Belshaw for refusing to pay a debt. *PL*, 30 August 1870, 6 May 1871, 21 August 1871, 27 April 1872, 19 August 1872, 20 August 1872, 26 August 1872, 18 February 1873.

Extortion and illegal fee cases were more numerous. Alderman Gallagher was charged with extortion at least twice. Charges were also made against Aldermen Guyger, Crawford, McColgan, Mackin, Hagar, and Nichols. *PL*, 27 November 1871, 6 January 1872, 9 May 1872, 11 May 1872, 20 August 1872, 2 September 1872, 28 May 1873, 11 June 1873, 5 September 1873, 8 September 1873.

Alderman Hagar's case prompted a lengthy opinion on magisterial conduct by Judge Thomas Finletter. Alderman Nichols's case resulted in a sentence to nine months imprisonment, which came over two months after the trial because the alderman disappeared after his conviction. *PL*, 9 September 1872, 11 June 1873, 19 August 1873, 28 August 1873.

49. *PL*, 25 October 1870, 23–24 July 1872, 30–31 August 1872; *Forney's Press*, 25 November 1872.

50. A November 1870 inquest concentrated on cases that demonstrated the "disregard of the liberty of the citizens . . . by certain aldermen." They criticized aldermen for setting bail much higher than the gravity of the offenses charged warranted, and concluded that, though in theory no one could be deprived of liberty in Philadelphia, "practically the circumstances of friendlessness, poverty, ignorance, and degraded social condition, prevent the full enjoyment of these rights and advantages which ardent friends and ready means and intelligence command." *PL*, 7 November 1870. The jurors cited the cases of a ten-year-old boy incarcerated for five weeks with no return ever being made, and a couple committed for larceny on the oath of a policemen who told the jury that he never made the charge.

51. *PL*, 5 June 1871, 3 July 1871, 7 August 1871, 5 February 1872, 5 August 1872, 20 August 1872.

52. *PL*, 2 September 1872, 4 November 1872, 6 January 1873, 1 September 1873, 6 October 1873. They called for the appointment by the mayor of two inferior justices for each ward, who would be paid a salary and hold office as long as they maintained good behavior.

53. *Annual Report of the Philadelphia County Prison* (1870), pp. 7, 12; (1871), pp. 11–12; (1872), pp. 18–19.

54. *JPD* [n.s.] 9 (1870): 65. Although businessmen who were reformers might have agreed about the results of the actions of aldermen, they were unlikely to have been as pessimistic about the consequences of the activities of the business world in general.

55. *JPD* [n.s.] 12 (1873): 44–45.

56. *PL*, 7 December 1869, 6 April 1870, 23 October 1871, 5 August 1872.

57. "Complaints of the rapacity of the local magistrates have come down to us, continuously, from the earliest periods." Many aldermen regarded the "sacred trust" of their office only as "the means by which they can plunder the poor and defenceless with impunity." Finletter repeated these remarks a year later when another magistrate ignored his instructions and overcharged a citizen. *Commonwealth* v. *Alderman Hagar,* 574 Philadelphia Reports (1872); *PL*, 28 August 1873.

58. Later, Judge Finletter criticized overzealous grand juries for ignoring too many cases and blaming aldermen for having returned them. If any testimony supported

the charge in the bill of indictment, the grand jury must return the bill as true. *PL*, 8 December 1870, 4 May 1871, 6 November 1871, 10 December 1872.

59. *PL*, 13 January 1871, 19 September 1873. Police violence also remained a matter of public concern during these years. The *Ledger* criticized policemen for using excessive force when making arrests and was especially outraged when a police sergeant beat a man to death in the Filbert Street stationhouse in early 1873. *PL*, 5 September 1872, 27 January 1873.

60. Gillette, "Corrupt and Contented," pp. 72–74; Scott, "The Businessman," p. 115; Hellerich, "Origin of Pennsylvania's Constitutional Convention," pp. 181–82; *PL*, 9 October 1872, 8 January 1873.

61. Justices would be required to be at least thirty years of age and practicing attorneys with at least five years' experience. There would be three justices for every 45,000 citizens, elected annually. They would be paid a salary, have civil jurisdiction over all matters of up to $250, and have criminal jurisdiction over misdemeanors for which the penalty did not exceed one month imprisonment or a $100 fine. Defendants could demand a jury trial before a seven-man panel that could reach a verdict by simple majority. *Debates of the Convention*, 1:130; *PL*, 27 November 1872.

62. *Memorial to the Constitutional Convention*, pp. 2, 4; *Debates of the Convention*, 1:214; PSAMPP Minute Book, 21 November 1872, 20 March 1873.

63. *Memorial to the Constitutional Convention*, pp. 4–8; *Debates of the Convention*, 1:214–16; Gillette, "Corrupt and Contented," pp. 74–75.

64. Gillette, "Corrupt and Contented," p. 53; *Debates of the Convention*, 4:257.

65. *Debates of the Convention*, 4:273–74, 279.

66. Rural delegates failed in their attempt to raise the civil jurisdiction of Philadelphia magistrates to the $300 limit of justices in the rest of the state, but Pittsburgh's representatives succeeded in restricting the section specifically to Philadelphia. *Debates of the Convention*, 4:262–65, 275, 278–79, 281–82, 302, 308–10; *PL*, 13 May 1873. Other objections surrounded the fact that the establishment of a special court was simply too specific a matter for inclusion in the constitution; it was the stuff of regular legislation, not "organic law."

67. *Debates of the Convention*, 4:287, 297–99.

68. Ibid., pp. 300–301, 312.

69. Ibid., pp. 303, 315.

70. Ibid., pp. 283, 288. For another discussion of this debate, see Ervin, *The Magistrates' Courts of Philadelphia*, pp. 172–74.

71. *Debates of the Convention*, 6:319–21.

72. Ibid., pp. 323, 325, 327.

73. Ibid., pp. 326, 328–29. See also ibid., 4:291–92.

74. Ibid., 6:334–35; *PL*, 2 July 1873; Fertig and Hunter, *Constitutions of Pennsylvania*, p. 40.

75. *PL*, 14 July 1873; Lea, *Justices' Courts in Philadelphia*, pp. 1–3.

76. The constitution increased the number of judges available to the court of quarter sessions to twelve, abolished the fee system for all county officers, gave the court of common pleas the power to appoint election judges and inspectors, and separated local and national elections. It carefully defined bribery, abolished much special legislation, set a debt limit for cities, and tightened legislative procedures. Gillette, "Corrupt and

Contented," pp. 75–76; Surrency, "The Evolution of an Urban Judicial System," pp. 113–14; Beers, "The Centennial City," p. 442; *PL*, 6 February 1874.

77. *PL*, 13 November 1873, 13 December 1873, 17 December 1873, 19 December 1873; Gillette, "Corrupt and Contented," pp. 80–81; Beers, "The Centennial City," p. 442.

78. *PL*, 17 December 1873, *Debates of the Convention*, 8:432–36; Ervin, *The Magistrates' Courts of Philadelphia*, pp. 9–10.

79. Scott, "The Businessman," p. 115.

Epilogue

1. *PL*, 9 February 1846; *Annual Report of the House of Refuge* (1847), p. 11.

2. Another index of change was the frequency with which the costs in criminal cases were assumed by the county instead of either of the parties. Between 1876 and 1880, this happened in 75 percent of all cases in which a plea of not guilty was entered and in 94 percent of all acquittals. During the 1854–74 period, the corresponding proportions were 57 and 91 percent; before consolidation, 43 and 82 percent. This practice stands as a reflection of the increasing recognition that the state was the proper and legitimate conductor of criminal prosecutions.

3. Beers, "The Centennial City," p. 443; Evans, *Pennsylvania Politics*, pp. 95–98, 245; Speakman, *The People vs. the Politicians*, pp. 2–3.

4. *PL*, 16 February 1874, 1 March 1874.

5. Speakman, *The People vs. the Politicians*, p. 6; Commonwealth of Pennsylvania, *Report of the Attorney General*, pp. 2–3; Ervin, *The Magistrates' Courts of Philadelphia*, p. 12; Bureau of Municipal Research, *Magistrates' Courts of Philadelphia* (an update of Ervin); Pennsylvania Bar Association, *Minor Courts in Pennsylvania*; and Law Association of Philadelphia, *Report of the Crimes Survey Committee*.

6. Katz, "The Origins of the Institutional State."

7. This point does not mean that supporters of the transformation of criminal justice consciously intended and succeeded at creating an institutional structure that furthered their interests at the expense of others. If this story shows anything, it is that the supporters of reform had many different and conflicting interests and that none of the results of their efforts was precisely what any one group of reformers desired. Conflicts among reformers and between reformers and their objects persisted, and one can imagine consequences that would have better suited the interests of any of them. Still, people from the groups that gained the most from the institutional state built it, even if they created neither the criminal justice system nor the society they envisioned.

8. This may apply as well to national and regional variations in Anglo-American criminal justice. The English practice of private prosecution, in the more ambiguous common-law tradition of "rights" but not democracy, may have been less vital to the authority of the law in prepolice English cities and less of a contradictory precedent for the kind of authority wielded by the police. Extralegal forms of conflict resolution and nongovernmental sources of authority were more often relied upon by ordinary people in England, where liberty was something that had to be wrested from the state rather than being the sacred condition of a people which government was created to protect.

This helps explain the less violent response given the police in nineteenth-century England. There, although the police may have been an equally impositional innovation, it was oddly also a democratic one, making the law more, not less, accessible to ordinary people. A similar pattern might have something to do with the long persistence of extralegal forms of dispute resolution in the American South, where the democratic state was least well-developed. This might mean that the South's history of access to the criminal law was, like England's, marked by restriction and less like Pennsylvania's. Four studies of obvious relevance here are Miller, *Cops and Bobbies*; Hindus, *Prison and Plantation*; Ayers, *Vengeance and Justice*; and Phillips, *Crime and Authority in Victorian England*.

Bibliography

Published Primary Sources

Act of Incorporation of the House of Refuge. Philadelphia, 1829.
Act of the Legislature Establishing the Uniform System of Police for the Philadel- phia Police District (3 May 1850) and Rules and Regulations of the Police Department. Philadelphia, 1852.
An Address from the Managers of the House of Refuge to Their Fellow Citizens. Philadelphia, 1826.
Address of the Pennsylvania State Temperance Society. Philadelphia, 1834.
The Almighty Dollar; or, the Brilliant Exploits of a Killer. Philadelphia, 1847.
Annual Message of the Honorable Richard Vaux. Philadelphia, 1857.
Annual Report of the American Emigrant's Friend Society. 1852.
Annual Report of the Chief of Police. Philadelphia, 1856.
Annual Reports of the Eastern State Penitentiary. Philadelphia, 1833–64.
Annual Reports of the House of Refuge. Philadelphia, 1829–62.
Annual Reports of the Managers of the Magdalen Society. Philadelphia, 1838–65.
Annual Reports of the Managers of the Rosine Association. Philadelphia, 1848–63.
Annual Reports of the Philadelphia County Prison. Philadelphia, 1848–72.
Annual Reports of the Philadelphia Society for Alleviating the Miseries of Public Prisons. Philadelphia, 1831, 1833.
Annual Reports of William J. Mullen, Prison Agent. Philadelphia, 1856–72.
Binns, John. *Binns' Daily Companion*, Philadelphia, 1843.
_____. *Binns' Justice.* Philadelphia, 1840.
_____. *Recollections of the Life of John Binns.* Philadelphia: Parry and McMillan, 1854.
Boyd, Julian P., ed. *The Papers of Thomas Jefferson.* Princeton: Princeton Univer- sity Press, 1950.
Brown, David Paul. *First Speech of David Paul Brown Delivered in 1818 in the Case of Commonwealth of Pennsylvania v. John Binns.* Philadelphia: Robb, Pile, & McElroy, 1858.
_____. *The Forum, or Forty Years Full Practice at the Philadelphia Bar.* Vol. 2. Philadelphia: R. H. Small, 1856.
_____. *Speech of David Paul Brown Before the Mayor's Court of Philadelphia, September 17, 1825, on the Subject of a Riot and Assault and Battery in Philadelphia.* Philadelphia, 1825.
Carey, Matthew. *A Plea for the Poor.* Philadelphia, 1836.
Chambers, George. *Speech on the Judicial Tenure.* Chambersburg, Pa., 1838.
Citizens, Be Vigilant. Philadelphia, 1872.

City of Philadelphia Directories, 1820–1875.

Debates of the Convention to Amend the Constitution of Pennsylvania. Vols. 1, 4, and 6. Harrisburg, 1873.

The Design and Advantages of the House of Refuge. Philadelphia, 1835.

A Digest of Laws in Force Relating to the Police of the City of Philadelphia with Some Account of the History of the Police Forces of the Same, from the Year 1682 to the Present Time. Philadelphia, 1851.

Fifth Annual Message of Alexander Henry. Philadelphia, 1863.

The Firemen's Songster. Philadelphia, n.d.

First Annual Message of Alexander Henry. Philadelphia, 1859.

First Annual Message of Morton McMichael. Philadelphia, 1867.

First Report of the Philadelphia Society for the Employment and Instruction of the Poor. Philadelphia, 1848.

Foner, Philip, ed. *The Complete Writings of Thomas Paine.* 2 vols. New York: Citadel Press, 1945.

Full and Accurate Report of the Trial for Riot Before the Mayor's Court of Philadelphia, on the 13th of October, 1831, Arising Out of a Protestant Procession of the 12th of July and in Which the Contending Parties Were Protestants and Roman Catholics. Philadelphia, 1831.

Hilliard, Francis. *The Elements of Law: Being a Comprehensive Summary of American Jurisprudence.* New York: J. S. Voorhies, 1848.

The Homeless Heir; or, Life in Bedford Street, A Mystery of Philadelphia by John, the Outcast. Philadelphia, 1856.

Impositions and Frauds in Philadelphia. Philadelphia, 1837.

Ingersoll, Jared. *Report Made by J. Ingersoll, Esquire, Attorney General of Pennsylvania, In Compliance With a Resolution of the Legislature, Passed the Third Week of March 1812, Relative to the Penal Code.* Harrisburg, 1813.

Institutes of American Law. Philadelphia: R. E. Peterson, 1851.

Journal of Prison Discipline, 1864–72.

Kelley, William D. *Address Delivered at the Colored Department of the House of Refuge.* Philadelphia: T. K. & P. G. Collins, 1850.

————. *Characteristics of the Age: An Address Delivered Before the Linnaean Association of Pennsylvania College.* Gettysburg: H. C. Neinstedt, 1850.

A Law Dictionary Adapted to the Constitution and Laws of the United States and the Several States of the American Union. Philadelphia: T. and J. W. Johnson, 1839.

Lea, Henry C. *Address: Citizens' Municipal Reform Association.* Philadelphia, 1873.

————. *Justices' Courts in Philadelphia.* Philadelphia, 1873.

————. *Report for 1872 Made to the Central Council of the CMRA.* Philadelphia, 1872.

Legislative Journal of Pennsylvania. Vol. 2. Harrisburg, 1833.

The Letters of Junius. . . . Philadelphia, 1848.

The Life and Adventures of Charles A. Chester, the Notorious Leader of the Philadelphia "Killers." Philadelphia, 1850.

Lippard, George. *The Quaker City.* Philadelphia, 1847.

The Liquor Law of the State of Pennsylvania. Philadelphia, 1856.

Manual of the Consolidated Police. Philadelphia, 1855.

Martin, John Hill. *Martin's Bench and Bar of Philadelphia.* Philadelphia: Rees Welch & Co., 1883.

Mease, James. *Observations on the Penitentiary System and Penal Code of Pennsylvania with Suggestions for Their Improvement.* Philadelphia, 1828.

Memorial to the Constitutional Convention of Pennsylvania from the Citizen's Municipal Reform Association. Philadelphia, 1873.

Message of Governor David R. Porter to Both Houses of the Legislature, January 1840. Harrisburg, 1840.

Mullen, William J. *An Appeal to Taxpayers in Opposition to the Existing Law for the Sale of Intoxicating Liquors.* Philadelphia, 1852.

The Mysteries and Miseries of Philadelphia, As Exhibited by a Late Presentment of the Grand Jury, and by A Sketch of the Condition of the Most Degraded Classes in the City. Philadelphia, 1853.

Needles, Edwin. *A Review of a Pamphlet Entitled "An Appeal to the Public on Behalf of a House of Refuge for Colored Juvenile Delinquents."* Philadelphia, 1846.

Notes on the Penal Laws of Pennsylvania. Harrisburg, 1822.

The Olive Branch. Philadelphia, 1844.

Ordinances and Joint Resolutions of the Select and Common Council of the Consolidated City of Philadelphia. Philadelphia, 1855.

Ordinances of the City of Philadelphia and the Several Supplements to the Act of Incorporation. Philadelphia: Zachariah Paulson, Jr., 1800.

Ordinances of the Corporation of the City of Philadelphia and Acts of the General Assembly of the Commonwealth of Pennsylvania Relating to the City. Philadelphia: Richard Beresford, 1847.

Paid Fire Departments: Letters of the Judges of the Court of Quarter Sessions and the Marshal of Police, and Report of the Board of Trade. Philadelphia, 1853.

Paine, Thomas. *Common Sense.* New York: Penguin, 1976.

Pamphlet Laws of the Commonwealth of Pennsylvania. Harrisburg, 1789–1874.

The Parish Gleaner: With Supplement in Reference to the Benevolent Labors of William J. Mullen 1 (1872).

Pennsylvania Constitution of 1790.

Pennsylvania House of Representatives Journal 1 (1838).

The Pennsylvania Journal of Prison Discipline. Philadelphia, 1847–75.

Philadelphia Society for Alleviating the Miseries of Public Prisons. *Report of the Committee on Comparative Health, Mortality and Length of Sentence, etc. of White and Coloured Convicts.* Philadelphia, 1849.

The Philanthropist. Philadelphia, 1856.

Police Manual of the Consolidated Police. Philadelphia, 1856.

Present State and Condition of the Free People of Color of Philadelphia. Philadelphia, 1838.

Price, Eli K. *The History of Consolidation in the City of Philadelphia.* Philadelphia, 1873.

Prize Essays on Juvenile Delinquency. Philadelphia, 1855.

Proceedings and Debates of the Convention of the Commonwealth of Pennsylvania to Propose Amendments to the Constitutions. Vols. 3, 9, and 10. Harrisburg, 1837.

Proceedings of the Eastern Pennsylvania Temperance Convention of 26 December 1843. Philadelphia, 1844.

Proceedings of the Pennsylvania State Temperance Convention. Harrisburg, 1854.

Proceedings of the Pennsylvania State Temperance Convention and Report of the Central Committee. Harrisburg, 1854.

Report of a Committee Appointed at a Meeting Held Friday Evening, December 3rd 1852, To Consider the Propriety of Organizing a Paid Fire Department. Philadelphia, 1853.

Report of a Committee Appointed by the Pennsylvania Society for Discouraging the Use of Ardent Spirits. Philadelphia, 1828.

Report of Bartholomew Wistar of the Visiting Committee the Acting Committee of the Philadelphia Society for Alleviating the Miseries of Public Prisons. Philadelphia, 1822.

Report of Some Criminal Cases on Primary Hearing Before Richard Vaux. Philadelphia, 1846.

Report of the Commissioners on the Penal Code. Harrisburg, 1828.

Report of the Committee Appointed to Visit and Inquire into the Condition and Circumstances of the Eastern Penitentiary and the House of Refuge in the County of Philadelphia and the Moyamensing Prison. Harrisburg, 1837.

Report of the Committee of 15 Citizens Appointed at a Mass Meeting of the City and County of Philadelphia, Held at Franklin Hall to Investigate and Report Upon the Corruption in the Administration of the Law, the Taking of Illegal Fees, and Extortion Practiced by Public Officers, etc. Philadelphia, 1849.

Report of the Committee on Cholera Appointed to Investigate the Local Causes of Cholera in the Arch Street Prison in the City of Philadelphia. Philadelphia, 1833.

Report of the Committee on Police on the Circumstances Attending and Connected with the Destruction of the Pennsylvania Hall, and Other Consequent Disturbances of the Peace. Philadelphia, 1838.

Report of the Committee on Vice and Immorality, Relative to Intemperance. Philadelphia, 1829.

Report of the Rosine Association. May 1948, May 1949, October 1952.

"Report on the Criminal Code." *Hazard's Register of Pennsylvania* 1 (1828).

Report on the Establishment of One or More Union Schools in Philadelphia or its Suburbs, Similar in Their Design to the "Ragged Schools" of London. Philadelphia, 1847.

Report on the Philadelphia County Prison to the County Board. Philadelphia, 1851.

Reports and Realities from the Sketch-Book of a Manager of the Rosine Association. Philadelphia, 1855.

Second Annual Message of Alexander Henry. Philadelphia, 1860.

Second Annual Message of Richard Vaux. Philadelphia, 1858.

Second Annual Report of the Young Christian's Missionary Association. Philadelphia, 1854.

Sewell, Benjamin T. *Sorrow's Circuit, or Five Year's Experience in the Bedford Street Mission*. Philadelphia, 1859.

Smith, R. A. *Philadelphia As It Is in 1852*. Philadelphia: Lindsay & Blakiston, 1852.

Speakman, Thomas H. *The People vs. the Politicians*. Philadelphia, 1878.

Sprogle, Howard O. *The Philadelphia Police: Past and Present*. Philadelphia, 1887.

A Statistical Inquiry Into the Condition of the People of Colour, of the City and Districts of Philadelphia. Philadelphia: Kite & Walton, 1849.

A Statistical View of the Operation of the Penal Code of Pennsylvania. Philadelphia, 1817.

Street Talk About an Ordinance of Councils Passed the Eleventh of July 1844 Organizing A Military Force for the Government of Philadelphia. Philadelphia, 1844.

Ten Years Progress; or, A Comparison of the State and Condition of the Coloured People in the City and County of Philadelphia, 1837–1847. Philadelphia, 1849.

Tocqueville, Alexis de. *Democracy in America*. Garden City, N.Y.: Doubleday & Co., 1969.

Tyson, Job R. *Essay on the Penal Law of Pennsylvania*. Philadelphia: Law Academy, 1827.

Vaux, Richard. *Reports of Some of the Criminal Cases on Primary Hearing Before Richard Vaux*. Philadelphia, 1846.

Vaux, Roberts. *Notices of the Original and Successive Efforts to Improve the Discipline of the Prison at Philadelphia, and to Reform the Criminal Code of Pennsylvania*. Philadelphia: Kimber & Sharpless, 1826.

————. *Some Remarks on the Writ of Habeus Corpus*. Philadelphia, n.d.

————. *Visiting Committee Reports*. Philadelphia, 1809.

Wainwright, Nicholas B. *A Philadelphia Perspective: The Diary of Sidney George Fisher, 1837–1841*. Philadelphia: Historical Society of Pennsylvania, 1967.

Westcott, Thompson. *The Official Guide Book to Philadelphia*. Philadelphia: Porter & Coates, 1876.

Wines, E. C., and Dwight, Theodore W. *Report on the Prisons and Reformatories of the United States and Canada*. Albany, N.Y.: Van Benthuysen and Sons' Steam Printing House, 1867.

Unpublished Primary Sources

Alderman's Court Criminal Docket, April 1845 to February 1847. Philadelphia City Archives.

Gregg, Alderman Amos. Docket Book, October 1854 to January 1878. Historical Society of Pennsylvania.

Kelley, William D. Collection. Historical Society of Pennsylvania.

Kneass, Joseph A. Scrapbook. Historical Society of Pennsylvania.

Milnor, Alderman William. Docket Book, April 1823 to December 1829. Historical Society of Pennsylvania.

Minute Books of the Acting Committee of the Philadelphia Society for Alleviating the Miseries of Public Prisons. 1806–75.

Philadelphia City Mayor's Court Docket Book. Philadelphia City Archives. 1800–1838.

Philadelphia County Court of Criminal Sessions Docket Book. Philadelphia City Archives. 1839–40.

Philadelphia County Court of General Sessions Docket Book. Philadelphia City Archives. 1841.

Philadelphia County Court of Quarter Sessions Docket Book. Philadelphia City Archives. 1800–1880.

Philadelphia County Prison Convict Description Docket. Philadelphia City Archives. 1841–64.

Philadelphia County Prison Daily Occurrence Docket. Philadelphia City Archives. 1800–1880.

Philadelphia Social History Project 1850 Manuscript Census of Philadelphia.

Philadelphia Society for Alleviating the Miseries of Public Prisons Minute Book. 1821, 1860, 1865, 1866.

Read, John M., Letter Book, Historical Society of Pennsylvania.

Schell, Frank H. MSS. Historical Society of Pennsylvania.

Newspapers

Forney's Press. 1872.
Public Ledger. 1836–75.
Public Record. 1874.
Sunday Dispatch. 1853.

Legal Documents

Aldermen and Justices of the Peace Cases, 2 Parsons Equity Cases 458 (1847).
Coates v. *Wallace*, 13 Sergeant and Rawle 74 (1927).
Collins v. *Hunter*, 1 Ashmead 60 (1824).
Commonwealth ex relatione Chauncey, 2 Ashmead 227 (1838).
Commonwealth v. *Alderman Hagar*, Philadelphia Reports 574 (1872).
Commonwealth v. *McKeagy*, 1 Ashmead 248 (1831).
Ex parte Crouse, 4 Wharton 9 (1838).
In re The Northern Liberty Hose Company, 1 Harris 193.
Justice of the Peace 1 (1900); 3 (1902).
Moore v. *Commonwealth*, 6 Watts and Sergeant 314 (1843).
Nixon v. *Keeper of the Prison*, 2 Ashmead 227 (1838).
Pamphlet Laws of Pennsylvania, Harrisburg, 1787–1875.
Poor v. *Greene*, 5 Binney 554.
Respublica v. *Hannum*, 1 Yeates 71 (1791).

Published Secondary Sources

Alexander, John K. *Render Them Submissive: Responses to Poverty in Philadelphia, 1760–1800.* Amherst: University of Massachusetts Press, 1980.

Allinson, Edward P., and Penrose, Boies. *Philadelphia, 1681–1887: A History of Municipal Development.* Philadelphia: Allen Lane & Scott, 1887.

Asbury, Herbert. *The Gangs of New York.* New York, 1929.

Ayres, Edward L. *Vengeance and Justice.* New York: Oxford University Press, 1984.

Banning, Lance. *The Jeffersonian Persuasion: Evolution of a Party Ideology.* Ithaca: Cornell University Press, 1978.

Barker, Charles R. "Philadelphia in the Late Forties." *Philadelphia History* 2 (1931).

Becker, Laura L. "The People and the System: Legal Activities in a Colonial Pennsylvania Town." *Pennsylvania Magazine of History and Biography* 105 (1981).

Beers, Dorothy Gondos. "The Centennial City, 1865–1876." In *Philadelphia: A 300-Year History*, edited by Russell F. Weigley. New York: W. W. Norton, 1982.

Bender, Thomas. "Wholes and Parts: The Need for Synthesis in American History." *Journal of American History* 73, no. 1 (June 1986).

Benjamin, Philip S. "Gentlemen Reformers in the Quaker City, 1870–1912." *Political Science Quarterly* 85 (1970).

Bloom, Robert L. "Morton McMichael's North American." *Pennsylvania Magazine of History and Biography* 77 (1953).

Bloomfield, Maxwell. *American Lawyers in a Changing Society, 1776–1876.* Cambridge: Harvard University Press, 1976.

Brace, Charles Loring. *The Dangerous Classes of New York and 20 Years Work Among Them.* New York: Wynkoop & Hallenbeck, 1880.

Brewer, John, and Styles, John, eds. *An Ungovernable People: The English and Their Law in the Seventeenth and Eighteenth Centuries.* New Brunswick, N.J.: Rutgers University Press, 1980.

Bridges, Amy. *A City in the Republic.* New York: Cambridge University Press, 1984.

Brown, Ira V. *Pennsylvania Reformers: From Penn to Pinchot.* University Park: Pennsylvania State University Press, 1966.

Bureau of Municipal Research and the Pennsylvania Economy League. *Magistrates' Court of Philadelphia.* Philadelphia: Bureau of Municipal Research, 1958.

Bushey, Glenn Leroy. "William Duane, Crusader for Judicial Reform." *Pennsylvania History* 3 (1938).

Cale, Edgar B. *The Organization of Labor in Philadelphia, 1850–1870.* Philadelphia: University of Pennsylvania Press, 1940.

Chitwood, Oliver P. *Justice in Colonial Virginia.* Baltimore: Johns Hopkins University Press, 1905.

Clark, Dennis. *The Irish in Philadelphia*. Philadelphia: Temple University Press, 1973.

Commonwealth of Pennsylvania, Department of Justice. *Report of the Attorney General on the Investigation of the Magisterial System*. Harrisburg: Department of Records, 1965.

Daly, John. *Descriptive Inventory of the Archives of the City and County of Philadelphia*. Philadelphia: Department of Records of the City of Philadelphia, 1970.

Dawley, Alan. *Class and Community: The Industrial Revolution in Lynn*. Cambridge: Harvard University Press, 1976.

Du Bois, W. E. B. *The Philadelphia Negro*. New York: Schocken Books, 1967.

Eastman, Frank M. *Courts and Lawyers of Pennsylvania: A History, 1623–1923*. New York: American Historical Society, 1923.

Edwards, G. J., Jr. *The Grand Jury*. Philadelphia: G. T. Bisel Co., 1906.

Ellis, Richard E. *The Jeffersonian Crisis: Courts and Politics in the Young Republic*. New York: Oxford University Press, 1971.

Ervin, Spencer. *The Magistrates' Courts of Philadelphia*. Philadelphia: Thomas Skelton Harrison Foundation, 1931.

Evans, Frank B. *Pennsylvania Politics, 1872–1877: A Study in Political Leadership*. Harrisburg: Pennsylvania Historical and Museum Commission, 1966.

Feldberg, Michael. "The Crowd in Philadelphia History." *Labor History* 15 (1974).

―――. *The Philadelphia Riots of 1844: A Study of Ethnic Conflict*. Westport, Conn.: Greenwood Press, 1975.

―――. "Urbanization as a Cause of Violence." In *The People of Philadelphia*, edited by Allen F. Davis and Mark M. Haller. Philadelphia: Temple University Press, 1975.

Ferguson, Robert A. *Law and Letters in American Culture*. Cambridge: Harvard University Press, 1984.

Fertig, John H., and Hunter, Frank M. *Constitutions of Pennsylvania. Constitution of the United States*. Harrisburg: Legislative Reference Bureau, 1916.

Fitzroy, Herbert William Keith. "The Punishment of Crime in Provincial Pennsylvania." *Pennsylvania Magazine of History and Biography* 60 (1936).

Fogelson, Robert M. *Big-City Police*. Cambridge: Harvard University Press, 1977.

Foner, Eric. *Tom Paine and Revolutionary America*. New York: Oxford University Press, 1976.

Foucault, Michel. *Discipline and Punish*. New York: Vintage Books, 1978.

Friedman, Lawrence M. *A History of American Law*. New York: Simon and Schuster, 1973.

Friedman, Lawrence M., and Percival, Robert V. *The Roots of Justice: Crime and Punishment in Alameda County, California, 1870–1910*. Chapel Hill: University of North Carolina Press, 1981.

Frisch, Michael H. *Town into City: Springfield, Massachusetts and the Meaning of Community, 1840–1880*. Cambridge: Harvard University Press, 1972.

Gaskins, R. "Changes in the Criminal Law in Eighteenth-Century Connecticut." *American Journal of Legal History* 25 (1981).

Geffen, Elizabeth M. "Industrial Development and Social Crisis, 1841–1854." In *Philadelphia: A 300-Year History*, edited by Russell F. Weigley. New York: W. W. Norton, 1982.

_____. "Violence in Philadelphia in the 1840s and 1850s." *Pennsylvania History* 36 (1969).

Gillette, Howard F., Jr. "The Emergence of the Modern Metropolis: Philadelphia in the Age of Its Consolidation." In *The Divided Metropolis: Social and Spatial Dimensions of Philadelphia, 1800–1975*, edited by Howard F. Gillette and William W. Cutler III. Westport, Conn.: Greenwood Press, 1980.

Gilmore, Grant. *The Ages of American Law*. New Haven: Yale University Press, 1977.

Gipson, Lawrence H. "Crime and Its Punishment in Provincial Pennsylvania." *Lehigh University Publications* 9 (1935).

Glassberg, Eudice. "Work, Wages, and the Cost of Living: Ethnic Differences and the Poverty Line, Philadelphia, 1880." *Pennsylvania History* 66 (1979).

Goebel, Julius T., and Naughton, Thomas R. *Law Enforcement in Colonial New York*. New York: Commonwealth Fund, 1944.

Greenberg, Douglas. *Crime and Law Enforcement in the Colony of New York, 1691–1775*. Ithaca: Cornell University Press, 1976.

_____. "The Effectiveness of Law Enforcement in Eighteenth-Century New York." *American Journal of Legal History* 19 (1975).

Grimsted, David. *Melodrama Unveiled: American Theatre and Culture, 1800–1850*. Chicago: University of Chicago Press, 1968.

Grossman, Joel, and Sarat, Austin. "Litigation in the Federal Courts: A Comparative Perspective." In *American Court Systems*, edited by Sheldon Goldman and Austin Sarat. San Francisco: W. H. Freeman, 1978.

Hammack, David. *Power and Society*. New York: Russell Sage Foundation, 1982.

_____. "Problems in the Historical Study of Power in the Cities and Towns of the United States, 1800–1960." *American Historical Review* 83 (1978).

Handlin, Lilian. *George Bancroft: The Intellectual as Democrat*. New York: Harper & Row, 1984.

Harring, Sidney. "The Development of the Police Institution in the United States." *Crime and Social Justice* 5 (1976).

Harring, Sidney, and McMullin, Lorraine M. "The Buffalo Police, 1872–1900: Labor Unrest, Political Power and the Creation of the Police Institution." *Crime and Social Justice* 4 (1975).

Hartog, Hendrik. *Public Property and Private Power: The Corporation of the City of New York in American Law, 1730–1870*. Chapel Hill: University of North Carolina Press, 1983.

Hartz, Louis. *Economic Policy and Democratic Thought: Pennsylvania, 1776–1860*. Cambridge: Harvard University Press, 1948.

Hawes, Joseph M. *Children in Urban Society*. New York: Oxford University Press, 1971.

Hay, Douglas. "Crime and Justice in Eighteenth- and Nineteenth-Century England." In *Crime and Justice: An Annual Review of Research* 2 (1980), edited by Michael Tonry and Norval Morris.

Hay, Douglas, et al. *Albion's Fatal Tree: Crime and Society in Eighteenth-Century England*. New York: Pantheon Books, 1975.

Hellerich, Mahlon H. "The Origin of Pennsylvania's Constitutional Convention of 1873." *Pennsylvania History* 34 (1967).

Henderson, Elizabeth K. "The Attack on the Judiciary in Pennsylvania, 1800–1810." *Pennsylvania Magazine of History and Biography* 61 (1937).

Hershberg, Theodore. "Free Blacks in Antebellum Philadelphia: A Study of Ex-Slaves, Freeborn and Socioeconomic Decline." *Journal of Social History* 5 (1972).

————, ed. *Philadelphia: Work, Space, Family, and Group Experience in the Nineteenth-Century City*. New York: Oxford University Press, 1981.

Hindus, Michael S. "The Contours of Crime and Justice in Massachusetts and South Carolina, 1767–1878." *American Journal of Legal History* 21 (1977).

————. "The History of Crime: Not Robbed of Its Potential, But Still on Probation." In *Criminology Review Yearbook* 1 (1979), edited by Sheldon L. Messinger and Egon Bittner.

————. *Prison and Plantation: Crime, Justice, and Authority in Massachusetts and South Carolina, 1767–1878*. Chapel Hill: University of North Carolina Press, 1980.

Hindus, Michael S., and Jones, Douglas L. "Quantitative and Theoretical Approaches to the History of Crime and Law." *Newberry Papers in Family and Community History* (1977).

Historical Methods Newsletter [Special Issue on the Philadelphia Social History Project] 9 (1976).

Horwitz, Morton J. *The Transformation of American Law, 1780–1860*. Cambridge: Harvard University Press, 1977.

Hurst, James Willard. *The Growth of American Law: The Lawmakers*. Boston: Little, Brown, 1950.

Ignatieff, Michael. *A Just Measure of Pain: The Penitentiary in the Industrial Revolution, 1750–1850*. New York: Pantheon Books, 1978.

————. "State, Civil Society, and Total Institutions: A Critique of Recent Social Histories of Punishment." In *Crime and Justice: An Annual Review of Research* 3 (1981), edited by Michael Tonry and Norval Morris.

Johnson, Claudia D. "That Guilty Third Tier: Prostitution In Nineteenth-Century American Theatres." *American Quarterly* 27 (1975).

Johnson, David R. *Policing the Urban Underworld: The Impact of Crime on the Development of the American Police, 1800–1887*. Philadelphia: Temple University Press, 1979.

Katz, Michael B. "The Origins of the Institutional State." *Marxist Perspectives* 4 (1978).

Katz, Michael B.; Doucet, Michael J.; and Stern, Mark J. *The Social Organization of Early Industrial Capitalism*. Cambridge: Harvard University Press, 1982.

Katznelson, Ira. *City Trenches: Urban Politics and the Patterning of Class in America*. New York: Pantheon Books, 1981.

Keller, Morton. *Affairs of State*. Cambridge: Belknap Press of Harvard University Press, 1977.

Klein, Philip S. *Pennsylvania Politics, 1817–1832: A Game Without Rules*. Philadelphia: Historical Society of Pennsylvania, 1940.

Konig, David Thomas. *Law and Society in Puritan Massachusetts: Essex County, 1629–1692*. Chapel Hill: University of North Carolina Press, 1979.

Lane, Roger. *Policing the City: Boston, 1822–1885*. Cambridge: Harvard University Press, 1967.

―――――. *The Roots of Violence in Black Philadelphia, 1860–1900*. Cambridge: Harvard University Press, 1986.

―――――. "Urban Police and Crime in Nineteenth-Century America." In *Crime and Justice: An Annual Review of Research* 2 (1980), edited by Michael Tonry and Norval Morris.

―――――. *Violent Death in the City: Suicide, Accident and Murder in 19th-Century Philadelphia*. Cambridge: Harvard University Press, 1979.

Langbein, John H. "Albion's Fatal Flaws." *Past and Present* 98 (1983).

―――――. "The Criminal Trial before the Lawyers." *University of Chicago Law Review* 45 (1977–78).

Laurie, Bruce. "Fire Companies and Gangs in Southwark: The 1840s." In *The People of Philadelphia*, edited by Allen F. Davis and Mark M. Haller. Philadelphia: Temple University Press, 1975.

―――――. "Nothing on Impulse: Life Styles of Philadelphia's Artisans, 1820–1850." *Labor History* 15 (1974).

―――――. *Working People of Philadelphia, 1800–1850*. Philadelphia: Temple University Press, 1981.

Laurie, Bruce; Hershberg, Theodore; and Alter, George. "Immigrants and Industry: The Philadelphia Experience, 1850–1880." In *Philadelphia: Work, Space, Family and Group Experience in the 19th Century*, edited by Theodore Hershberg. New York: Oxford University Press, 1981.

Law Association of Philadelphia. *Report of the Crimes Survey Committee*. Philadelphia: George H. Buchanan Co., 1926.

Leffman, Henry. *The Consolidation of Philadelphia*. Philadelphia: City Historical Society of Philadelphia, 1908.

Lermack, Paul. "Peace Bonds and Criminal Justice in Colonial Philadelphia." *Pennsylvania Magazine of History and Biography* 100 (1976).

Levine, Lawrence W. "William Shakespeare and the American People: A Study in Cultural Transformation." *American Historical Review* 89 (1984).

Liebman, Robert, and Polen, Michael. "Perspectives on Policing in Nineteenth-Century America." *Social Science History* 2 (1978).

Little, Craig B., and Sheffield, Christopher P. "Frontiers and Criminal Justice: English Private Prosecution Societies and American Vigilantism in the Eighteenth and Nineteenth Centuries." *American Sociological Review* 48, no. 6 (December 1983).

Lloyd, William M., Jr. "The Courts of Pennsylvania in the Eighteenth Century

Prior to the Revolution." *University of Pennsylvania Law Review* 56 (1908).

McCarthy, Michael P. "The Philadelphia Consolidation of 1854: A Reappraisal." *Pennsylvania Magazine of History and Biography* 110 (1986).

McDonald, Terrence J. "The Problem of the Political in Recent American Urban History: Liberal Pluralism and the Rise of Functionalism." *Social History* 10 (1985).

McGerr, Michael. *The Decline of Popular Politics.* New York: Oxford University Press, 1986.

McKitrick, Eric L. "The Study of Corruption." *Political Science Quarterly* 72 (1957).

Magistrates' Courts of Philadelphia. Philadelphia: Bureau of Municipal Research and the Pennsylvania Economy League, 1958 (an update of Ervin).

Mennel, Robert M. *Thorns and Thistles: Juvenile Delinquents in the U.S., 1825–1940.* Hanover, N.H.: University Press of New England, 1973.

Meranze, Michael. "The Penitential Ideal in Late Eighteenth-Century Philadelphia." *Pennsylvania Magazine of History and Biography* 100 (October 1984).

Miller, Richard G. "The Federal City, 1783–1800." In *Philadelphia: A 300-Year History*, edited by Russell F. Weigley. New York: W. W. Norton, 1982.

———. *Philadelphia, the Federalist City: A Study of Urban Politics, 1789–1801.* Port Washington, N.Y.: Kennikat Press, 1976.

Miller, Wilbur R. *Cops and Bobbies: Police Authority in New York and London, 1830–1870.* Chicago: University of Chicago Press, 1977.

———. "Police Authority in London and New York City, 1830–1870." *Journal of Social History* 8 (Winter 1975).

Minor Courts in Pennsylvania. University Park: Pennsylvania Bar Association and the Institute of Public Administration, Pennsylvania State University, 1962.

Monkkonen, Eric. *The Dangerous Class: Crime and Poverty in Columbus, Ohio, 1860–1885.* Cambridge: Harvard University Press, 1975.

———. "Systematic Criminal Justice History: Some Suggestions." *Journal of Interdisciplinary History* 9 (1979).

———. "Toward a Dynamic Theory of Crime and the Police: A Criminal Justice System Perspective." In *Criminology Review Yearbook* 1 (1979), edited by Sheldon L. Messinger and Egon Bittner.

Montgomery, David. "Gutman's Nineteenth-Century America." *Labor History* 19 (1978).

———. "The Shuttle and the Cross." *Journal of Social History* 5 (1972).

Nash, Gary B. *The Urban Crucible: Social Change, Political Consciousness, and the Origins of the American Revolution.* Cambridge: Harvard University Press, 1979.

Nelson, William E. *The Americanization of the Common Law.* Cambridge: Harvard University Press, 1975.

———. "Emerging Notions of Modern Criminal Law in the Revolutionary Era: An Historical Perspective." *New York University Law Review* 42 (1967).

Nolan, Hugh J. *The Most Reverend Francis Patrick Kenrick, Third Bishop of Philadelphia.* Washington, D.C.: Catholic University of America, 1949.

Nonet, Philippe. *Administrative Justice.* New York: Russell Sage Foundation, 1969.

Nonet, Philippe, and Selznick, Philip. *Law and Society in Transition: Toward Responsive Law.* New York: Octagon Books, 1978.

Oberholtzer, Ellis P. *Philadelphia: A History of the City and Its People, a Record of 225 Years.* Philadelphia, 1911.

Paludan, Phillip S. "The American Civil War Considered as a Crisis in Law and Order." *American Historical Review* 77 (1972).

Parks, Evelyn L. "From Constabulary to Police Society." *Catalyst* 5 (1970).

Pennsylvania Bar Association. *Minor Courts in Pennsylvania.* University Park: Pennsylvania State University Press, 1962.

———. *Survey of the Minor Judiciary in Pennsylvania.* State College: Pennsylvania Municipal Publications Service, 1942.

Philips, David. *Crime and Authority in Victorian England: The Black Country, 1835–1860.* Totowa, N.J.: Rowman & Littlefield, 1977.

Report of the Attorney General on the Investigation of the Magisterial System. Harrisburg: Department of Justice, Commonwealth of Pennsylvania, 1965.

Report of the Crimes Survey Committee. Philadelphia: Law Association of Philadelphia and George H. Buchanan, 1926.

Richards, Leonard. *Gentlemen of Property and Standing: Anti-Abolition Mobs in Jacksonian America.* New York: Oxford University Press, 1970.

Richardson, Edgar P. "The Athens of America, 1800–1825." In *Philadelphia: A 300-Year History*, edited by Russell F. Weigley. New York: W. W. Norton, 1982.

Richardson, James F. *The New York Police: Colonial Times to 1901.* New York: Oxford University Press, 1970.

Robinson, Elwyn B. "The Dynamics of American Journalism from 1787 to 1865." *Pennsylvania Magazine of History and Biography* 61 (1937).

———. "The *Public Ledger*: An Independent Newspaper." *Pennsylvania Magazine of History and Biography* 64 (1940).

Roeber, A. G. "Authority, Law, and Custom: The Rituals of Court Day in Tidewater, Virginia, 1720–1750." *William and Mary Quarterly* 3d ser., 37 (1980).

Rorabaugh, W. J. *The Alcoholic Republic.* New York: Oxford University Press, 1979.

Rosswurm, Steven J. " 'As a Lyen Out of His Den': Philadelphia's Popular Movement, 1776–80." In *The Origins of Anglo-American Radicalism*, edited by James and Margaret Jacob. Boston: George Allen & Unwin, 1984.

Rothman, David J. *The Discovery of the Asylum; Social Order and Disorder in the New Republic.* Boston: Little, Brown & Co., 1971.

Scharf, J. Thomas, and Westcott, Thompson. *History of Philadelphia, 1609–1884.* Philadelphia: L. H. Everts & Co., 1884.

Schlesinger, Arthur M., Jr. *Age of Jackson.* Boston: Little, Brown, and Co., 1945.

———. *Orestes A. Brownson: A Pilgrim's Progress.* Boston: Little, Brown & Co., 1939.

Schneider, John. "Public Order and the Geography of the City: Crime, Violence and the Police in Detroit, 1845–1875." *Journal of Urban History* 4 (1978).

Selznick, Philip. *Law, Society, and Industrial Justice*. New York: Russell Sage Foundation, 1969.

Shefter, Martin. "The Emergence of the Political Machine: An Alternative View." In *Theoretical Perspectives on Urban Politics*, edited by Michael Lipsky et al. Englewood Cliffs, N.J., 1976.

Silcox, Harry. "William McMullen, Nineteenth-Century Political Boss." *Pennsylvania Magazine of History and Biography* 110 (1986).

Silver, Allan. "The Demand for Order in Civil Society: A Review of Some Themes in the History of Urban Crime, Police and Riot." In *The Police: Six Sociological Essays*, edited by David J. Bordua. New York: John Wiley & Sons, 1967.

Skowronek, Stephen. *Building a New American State: The Expansion of National Administrative Capacities, 1877–1920*. New York: Cambridge University Press, 1982.

Snyder, Charles M. *The Jacksonian Heritage: Pennsylvania Politics, 1833–1848*. Harrisburg: Pennsylvania Historical and Museum Commission, 1958.

Spindel, Donna J. "The Administration of Justice in North Carolina, 1720–1740." *American Journal of Legal History* 25 (1981).

Steinberg, Allen. "From Private Prosecution to Plea Bargaining." *Crime and Delinquency* 30 (1984).

Surrency, Edwin C. "The Evolution of an Urban Judicial System: The Philadelphia Story, 1683 to 1968." *American Journal of Legal History* 18 (1974).

Taylor, George R. " 'Philadelphia in Slices' by George G. Foster." *Pennsylvania Magazine of History and Biography* 93 (1969).

Teeters, Negley K. *The Cradle of the Penitentiary: The Walnut Street Jail at Philadelphia, 1773–1835*. Philadelphia: Pennsylvania Prison Society, 1955.

――――. *They Were in Prison*. Philadelphia: Pennsylvania Prison Society, 1937.

Thayer, Theodore. "Town into City, 1746–1765." In *Philadelphia: A 300-Year History*, edited by Russell F. Weigley. New York: W. W. Norton, 1982.

Thernstrom, Stephen. *Poverty and Progress: Social Mobility in a Nineteenth-Century City*. Cambridge: Harvard University Press, 1964.

Thompson, E. P. *Whigs and Hunters: The Origin of the Black Act*. New York: Pantheon Books, 1975.

Wainwright, Nicholas B. "The Age of Nicholas Biddle, 1825–1841." In *Philadelphia: A 300-Year History*, edited by Russell F. Weigley. New York: W. W. Norton, 1982.

Walker, Samuel. *A Critical History of Police Reform: The Emergence of Professionalism*. Lexington, Mass.: Lexington Books, 1977.

――――. *Popular Justice: A History of American Criminal Justice*. New York: Oxford University Press, 1980.

――――. "The Urban Police in American History: A Review of the Literature." *Journal of Police Sciences and Administration* 4 (1976).

Warner, Sam Bass, Jr. *The Private City: Philadelphia in Three Periods of Its Growth*. Philadelphia: University of Pennsylvania Press, 1968.

Warren, Charles. *A History of the American Bar*. Boston: Little, Brown & Co., 1911; Buffalo: W. S. Hein, 1980.

Weigley, Russell F. "The Border City in Civil War, 1854–1865." In *Philadelphia: A 300-Year History*, edited by Russell F. Weigley. New York: W. W. Norton, 1982.

————. "'A Peaceful City': Public Order in Philadelphia from Consolidation Through the Civil War." In *The Peoples of Philadelphia*, edited by Allen F. Davis and Mark M. Haller. Philadelphia: Temple University Press, 1975.

Whiteman, Maxwell. *Gentlemen in Crisis: The First Century of the Union League in Philadelphia, 1862–1962*. Philadelphia: The League, 1975.

Wilentz, Sean. *Chants Democratic: New York City and the Rise of the American Working Class*. New York: Oxford University Press, 1984.

Younger, Richard D. *The People's Panel: The Grand Jury in the United States, 1634–1941*. Providence, R.I.: Brown University Press, 1963.

Zachary, Alan M. "Social Disorder and the Philadelphia Elite before Jackson." *Pennsylvania Magazine of History and Biography* 99 (1975).

Zemans, Frances Kahn. "Legal Mobilization: The Neglected Role of the Law in the Political System." *American Political Science Review* 77 (1983).

Unpublished Secondary Sources

Davis, Susan Gray. "Theatre of the Streets: Parades and Ceremonies in Philadelphia, 1800–1850." Ph.D. dissertation, University of Pennsylvania, 1983.

Diamondstone, Judith. "The Philadelphia Corporation." Ph.D. dissertation, University of Pennsylvania, 1969.

Gallman, James Matthew. "Disorder and the Pursuit of Order in Civil War Philadelphia." Paper presented at the Annual Meeting of the Social Science History Association, New Orleans, 1987.

Gillette, Howard F., Jr. "Corrupt and Contented: Philadelphia's Political Machine, 1865–1887." Ph.D. dissertation, Yale University, 1970.

Glassberg, Eudice. "Philadelphians in Need: Client Experiences with Two Philadelphia Benevolent Societies, 1830–1880." Ph.D. dissertation, University of Pennsylvania, 1979.

Greco, Michael Robert. "William Darrah Kelley: The Antebellum Years." Ph.D. dissertation, Johns Hopkins University, 1974.

Hindus, Michael S. "Prison and Plantation: Criminal Justice in Nineteenth-Century Massachusetts and South Carolina." Ph.D. dissertation, University of California at Berkeley, 1975.

Johnson, David R. "The Search for an Urban Discipline." Ph.D. dissertation, University of Chicago, 1972.

Lapsansky, Emma S. "South Street Philadelphia: A Haven for Those Low in the World." Ph.D. dissertation, University of Pennsylvania, 1975.

Laurie, Bruce. "The Working People of Philadelphia, 1827–1853." Ph.D. dissertation, University of Pittsburgh, 1971.

McLeod, Richard A. "The Philadelphia Artisan, 1828–1850." Ph.D. dissertation, University of Missouri, 1971.

Naylor, Timothy J. "Crime, Criminals, and Punishment in Philadelphia, 1866–1916." Ph.D. dissertation, University of Chicago, 1979.

Neilly, Andrew H. "The Violent Volunteers: A History of the Volunteer Fire Department of Philadelphia, 1736–1871." Ph.D. dissertation, University of Pennsylvania, 1959.

Parris, Cecile M. "The House of Refuge of Philadelphia." Ed.D. dissertation, University of Pennsylvania, 1975.

Philips, David. "Good Men to Associate and Bad Men to Conspire: Associations for the Prosecution of Felons in England, 1760–1860." Unpublished manuscript in author's possession.

Remick, Cecile P. "The House of Refuge of Philadelphia, 1786–1859." Ph.D. dissertation, University of Pennsylvania, 1975.

Salkin, Barry L. "Crime in Pennsylvania: A Legal and Sociological Study." Ph.D. dissertation, Harvard University, 1975.

Scott, James Allen. "The Businessman, Capitalism and the City: Businessmen and Municipal Reform in Philadelphia from the Act of Consolidation (1854) to the Bullitt Bill (1887)." Ph.D. dissertation, University of Delaware, 1974.

Steinberg, Allen. "The Criminal Courts and the Transformation of Criminal Justice in Philadelphia, 1815–1874." Ph.D. dissertation, Columbia University, 1983.

Whitney, William G. "The Uses of Urban Space in Nineteenth-Century Philadelphia: Manufacturing at Mid-Century." Paper presented at the Annual Meeting of the Social Science History Association, Philadelphia, 1976.

Index